The Great Transformation:
Scottish Freemasonry 1725–1810

THE
GREAT
TRANSFORMATION

SCOTTISH FREEMASONRY 1725-1810

Dr. MARK C. WALLACE

Westphalia Press
An Imprint of the Policy Studies Organization
Washington, DC
2018

THE GREAT TRANSFORMATION:
SCOTTISH FREEMASONRY 1725–1810

All Rights Reserved © 2018 by Policy Studies Organization

Westphalia Press
An imprint of Policy Studies Organization
1527 New Hampshire Ave., NW
Washington, D.C. 20036
info@ipsonet.org

ISBN-10: 1-63391-698-7
ISBN-13: 978-1-63391-698-2

Cover and interior design by Jeffrey Barnes
jbarnesbook.design

Cover art by Veronica L. Kessenich

Daniel Gutierrez-Sandoval, Executive Director
PSO and Westphalia Press

Updated material and comments on this edition
can be found at the Westphalia Press website:
www.westphaliapress.org

TABLE OF CONTENTS

FOREWORD

In the late sixteenth and seventeenth centuries, Scotland played a fundamental role in the development of Freemasonry as a social institution. David Stevenson in his classic study, *The Origins of Freemasonry: Scotland's Century 1590–1710*, enumerated the Scottish innovations which helped pave the way for the emergence of Freemasonry as one of the most popular and widespread social phenomena in the world. These Scottish contributions included:[1]

- Earliest use of the word "lodge" in the modern masonic sense, and evidence that such permanent institutions exist

- Earliest official minute books and other records of such lodges

- Earliest examples of men other than working stonemasons joining lodges

- Earliest evidence connecting lodge masonry with specific ethical ideas expounded by the use of symbols

- Earliest references to the mason word

- Earliest evidence of the use of two degrees or grades within Freemasonry

By the time a Grand Lodge was established in London and John Duke of Montagu installed as its Grand Master with great public fanfares in 1721, Scottish Freemasonry already had a strong and active network of 49 lodges spread across the country.

As a result of the antiquity of Scottish Freemasonry, the process by which a Grand Lodge was established and the social and cultural dynamics influencing the development of Freemasonry in Scotland were very different to those in England. In this book, Mark Wallace provides an authoritative and thoroughly documented account of the fascinating social history of Scottish Freemasonry in the eighteenth century. Dr. Wallace's account not only clearly and entertainingly traces the institutional history of Freemasonry in Scotland but also shows how Freemasonry played a key part in one of the most exciting and dynamic periods in Scottish history.

---

1   D. Stevenson, *The Origins of Freemasonry: Scotland's Century 1590–1710* (Cambridge: Cambridge University Press, 1988), 7.

The records and artefacts held by masonic lodges in Scotland are one of the most important elements of the country's cultural heritage. It is sad that these records are too often in the custody of lodge secretaries who are suspicious of requests for access. Dr. Wallace has done a remarkable job in locating and securing access to many eighteenth-century masonic minute books and records. His book is packed with fascinating vignettes from these records illustrating the convivial sociability, charitable assistance and social dynamics of local lodges. These records memorably evoke the social high spots and frequent hardships of life in many small Scottish towns and villages in the eighteenth century.

Perhaps the most striking theme to emerge from Dr. Wallace's research are the social tensions evident in the development of Scottish Freemasonry in the eighteenth century. The lodges, which had been established in the seventeenth century, were dominated by working stonemasons who were wary of being overrun by outsiders. Trade regulation and charitable support for itinerant workers were a significant concern. The creation of a Grand Lodge by a group of Edinburgh lodges was viewed with suspicion. Some lodges refused to have anything to do with this innovation, and throughout the century Grand Lodge struggled to exert its authority.

The creation of the Grand Lodge in Scotland in 1736 was part of a drive for civic improvement, which pervaded Scottish society in the 1720s and 1730s.[2] The Grand Lodge was integral to the civic development which gave Edinburgh a Medical School in 1726, an infirmary in 1738, and a theatre in 1737. As Dr. Wallace illustrates, a major feature of this movement was the creation of clubs and societies, ranging from Honourable the Improvers in the Knowledge of Agriculture in Scotland established in 1723, to the Musical Society in Edinburgh formally constituted in 1728, and the Philosophical Society of Edinburgh established in 1737 which in turn became the Royal Society of Edinburgh. The cross-connections between these groups are fascinating and suggestive and are carefully traced by Dr. Wallace.

The Grand Lodge of Scotland was created in emulation of the Grand Lodge in London, and Dr. Wallace shows how its creation was driven by

---

2   Roger Emerson, "The Contexts of the Scottish Enlightenment," in *The Cambridge Companion to the Scottish Enlightenment*, ed. Alexander Broadie (Cambridge: Cambridge University Press, 2003), 9–30.

concerns that Scottish Freemasonry had suffered because of the lack of a coordinating body comparable to that south of the border. The difficulty of trying to impose a genteel Grand Lodge on a network of largely operative lodges created social tensions that continued right through the eighteenth century. Dr. Wallace provides an exemplary case study of the sort of difficulties experienced in Scotland by such attempts to import English administrative methods. Roger Emerson has noted how "[t]he melding of English administrative procedures in the collection of taxes and the management of affairs with Scottish ways, institutions and laws was never easy" and not fully achieved until the time of Henry Dundas.[3] The parallels and links between Dundas's management of Scottish politics and the Grand Lodge's attempts to enhance its authority by prosecuting lodges accused of radical sympathies, memorably described by Dr. Wallace, are both striking and instructive.

The significant role of Freemasonry in the Enlightenment has been explored by many distinguished scholars in recent years, including Margaret Jacob, Charles Porset, Cécile Révauger, Pierre-Yves Beaurepaire and Steven Bullock. The distinctive character of the Scottish Enlightenment has also been the subject of great scholarly interest. By providing a nuanced and carefully researched overview of Scottish Freemasonry in the eighteenth century, Dr. Wallace makes an important contribution both to our understanding of the sociability of the Scottish Enlightenment and to the various roles performed by Freemasonry in the Enlightenment.

Dr. Wallace makes it clear that the chief role of Freemasonry in the Scottish Enlightenment was one of the most important means by which a wide-ranging form of sociality, embracing different classes and covering both town and country, was generated. Masonic lodges in Scotland did not show any immediate enthusiasm for Newtonian ideas and were slow to adopt the idea of "the Great Architect of the Universe" as a Newtonian paradigm. However, masonic lodges provided venues where university professors, lawyers, authors, musicians might meet with merchants, customs officials, and craftsman over a "chearful glass and song." Their processions and theatrical outings enhanced the growing public sphere. In this way, Dr. Wallace reminds us how Scotland was a society based on strong social networks and Freemasonry by feeding these networks helped nourish the Scottish Enlightenment.

---

3   Ibid., 14.

The complex power dynamic between Scottish and English Freemasonry, expressed in a sometimes uneasy dialogue between the two Grand Lodges, reached a troubling and difficult apotheosis for both Grand Lodges in the passage of legislation under Pitt's government to curtail the activities of radical groups. As Dr. Wallace describes, this legislation had a profound impact on the structure of Freemasonry despite the best attempts of both Grand Lodges to ameliorate its effects. The way in which the Grand Lodges in Scotland and England sought to work together to counter these threats reflect the wider shifts taking place in the structure of the British state in the course of the French wars.

It is easy to forget how important Scotsmen were in the development of English Freemasonry. James Anderson, the author of the first *Book of Constitutions* of the Grand Lodge in London, was a Presbyterian minister from Aberdeen. A number of distinguished Scottish noblemen, including the 2nd Duke of Buccleuch, the 7th Earl of Abercorn and the 7th Earl of Strathmore, served as Grand Masters of the Grand Lodge in London during its earlier years. William Preston, who compiled the influential handbook, *Illustrations of Masonry* and had a titanic dispute with the Grand Lodge over the rights of lodges, was a Scottish printer whose advice on matters of style was said to have been valued by authors such as Adam Smith and David Hume.[4]

Dr. Wallace describes how, notwithstanding the prominence of Scottish writers on Freemasonry south of the border, Scottish Freemasonry was less concerned with recording its own story. Murray Pittock has pointed out how writers of the Scottish Enlightenment such as Adam Smith and David Hume sought to escape Scottish particularism by keeping quiet about their debt to earlier Scottish writers.[5] He suggests a similar tendency is evident among the history of Scottish clubs and societies in the eighteenth century, which stressed their modernity rather than their links to older Scottish organisations. Pittock sees in this historiographical tendencies the origins of what came to be known as Whig history, with its stress on human progress.

---

4   H. Tedder, "Preston, William (1742–1818), Printer and Writer." *Oxford Dictionary of National Biography*. Retrieved 22 Apr. 2018

5   M. Pittock, "History and the Teleology of Civility in the Scottish Enlightenment," in *Enlightenment and Emancipation*, eds. S. Manning and P. France (Lewisburg: Bucknell University Press, 2006), 81–96.

It seems that the story of Scottish Freemasonry has also fallen victim to the teleologies of this historiography of progress. The early Scottish contribution to the development of Freemasonry came to be forgotten and the distinctive character of Scottish Freemasonry in the eighteenth century overlooked. We must all be grateful to Dr. Wallace and his fellow historians for their excellent work in retrieving and helping to preserve this fascinating history, locked away in precious minute books and records in masonic halls and lodges across Scotland.

Andrew Prescott
University of Glasgow

ABSTRACT

Modern Freemasonry emerged in Britain during the eighteenth century, combining earlier stonemason customs and methods of organization with the popular passion for clubs and societies. Although by no means unique in its ideology and constitution, Freemasonry established itself after 1700 as a prominent fixture in both British communal and social life.

Some mocked Masonic lodges and their rituals, but they were an accepted feature on the social scene and, given that they avoided political and religious discussion and swore loyalty to the existing regime, their position was largely uncontroversial. The French Revolution, however, caused a severe backlash against the masons in Britain and Europe. During the 1790s, Masonic lodges, which were once viewed simply as charitable and convivial organizations, were now seen as convenient vehicles for allowing radical groups to pursue covert revolutionary activities. As a result, legislation was passed which attempted to regulate these societies and eradicate any traces of secrecy. Despite its commitment to the establishment, Freemasonry came under suspicion.

This book examines the structure, nature, and characteristics of Scottish Freemasonry in its wider British and European contexts between the years 1725 and 1810. As we shall see, Masonic lodges and their members changed and adapted as these contexts evolved. The Enlightenment effectively crafted the modern mason and propelled Freemasonry into a new era marked by increasing membership and the creation of the Grand Lodge of Scotland, with the institution becoming part of the contemporary fashion for associated activity.

ACKNOWLEDGMENTS

This study would not have been possible without the involvement of many people. I would like to thank my parents, Wiley and Carole Wallace, for their constant encouragement. I would also like to thank my grandmother, Marion Fetterolf, for giving me the opportunity to complete my Ph.D. at the University of St. Andrews, and my wife Melinda for her support and patience.

In writing a history of eighteenth-century Freemasonry, I am especially indebted to the insights of Andrew Prescott, Rick Sher, Susan Sommers, and David Stevenson, who read parts of my thesis and helped me to improve the overall structure and content of my work.

My research has taken me to numerous Masonic lodges in Scotland and England. I am grateful to Robert Cooper and the members of the Grand Lodge of Scotland, Martin Cherry and the United Grand Lodge of England, No. 1 Mary's Chapel, No. 1(3) Aberdeen, No. 3 Scoon & Perth, No. 3bis Glasgow St. John, No. 6 Old Inverness Kilwinning St John's, No. 11 St. John's Maybole, No. 25 St. Andrew, No. 27 The Lodge of Glasgow St. Mungo's, No. 30 Ancient Stirling, No. 49 Ancient Dundee, No. 160 Roman Eagle, and No. 198 Royal Arch Maybole for permitting me to examine their minutes and records.

I also would like to express my appreciation to the Department of Special Collections at the University of St. Andrews, the Edinburgh University Library for allowing me to reprint several manuscripts, the National Library of Scotland, and the staff at the National Archives in Edinburgh for their assistance. Also, a special thanks is owed to several people at Lyon College, including Andrew English, Brian Hardin, and Kathy Whittenton for their help and insights.

A final debt is owed to David Allan. I am immensely grateful for his guidance, counsel, and friendship.

CHAPTER ONE: INTRODUCTION

THE "HAPPY HUNTING GROUND": TRACING THE ORIGINS AND DEVELOPMENT OF SCOTTISH FREEMASONRY[1]*

T he study of modern Masonic scholarship has gained significant traction over the course of the last few decades, due, largely in part, to the recognition of its historical significance—more especially during the Enlightenment. The structure, organization, and ritualistic aspects of Freemasonry all exhibited a preponderant influence on both the associational movement during the Enlightenment, and the myriad individual clubs and societies that flourished during the eighteenth century.[2] Its acceptance into the academic canon—though still somewhat reluctantly—is further legitimized through contributions by respected and notable historians and academics such as Margaret Jacob, Andrew Prescott, David Stevenson, Ric Berman, and John Robertson. More recently, journals devoted to the study of Freemasonry, dedicated research centers, and international conferences have all lent an air of respectability

---

1   * Author's Note: the research for this study was carried out while I was a doctoral student at the University of St. Andrews, from 2001 to 2006. Portions of this work have been published elsewhere in various forms.

2   The scope of this present study takes into account the social, cultural, intellectual, and political impact of Freemasonry, though not the ritualistic aspect and—as an extension—the exclusion of women from the society. Though, more information on ritual and exclusivity, see A. Piatigorsky, *Who's Afraid of Freemasons? The Phenomenon of Freemasonry* (London, 1997); J. A. M. Snoek, "Retracing the Lost Secret of a Master Mason," *Acta Macionica* 4 (1994): 5–53; J. A. M. Snoek, "On the Creation of Masonic Degrees: A Method and its Fruits," in *Western Esotericism and the Science of Religions, Selected Papers Presented at the 17th Congress of the International Association for the History of Religions*, eds. A. Faivre and W. J. Hanegraaff (Leuven, 1998); J. A. M. Snoek, "The Evolution of the Hiramic Legend in England and France," *Heredom* 11 (2003): 11–53; *Women's Agency and Rituals in Mixed and Female Masonic Orders*, eds. A. Heidle and J. A. M. Snoek (Leiden, 2008); J. A. M. Snoek, *Initiating Women in Freemasonry. The Adoption Rite* (Leiden, 2012); D. Goodman, *The Republic of Letters: A Cultural History of the French Enlightenment* (Ithaca, NY, 1994): 245–59; J. M. Burke and Margaret C. Jacob, "French Freemasonry, Women, and Feminist Scholarship," *Journal of Modern History* 68 (1996):513–549; J. A. M. Snoek, "The Adoption Rite, its Origins, its Opening up for Women, and its 'Craft' Rituals," *Journal for Research in Freemasonry and Fraternalism* (hereafter *JRFF*) 4 (2013): 24–43.

to the genre, though unfortunately there is a marked paucity of scholarship relevant to Scottish Freemasonry.[3]

As it now stands, the majority of British Masonic histories are written from English perspectives, and as such are largely unrepresentative of eighteenth-century Scottish Freemasonry and its distinctive legacy.[4] A recent four-volume set edited by Róbert Péter, titled *British Freemasonry, 1717–1813*, offers a wonderfully candid look into English, Irish, and Scottish Freemasonry. Drawing significantly on primary source material, including lodge records, manuscripts, and newspaper and periodical articles, the volumes seek to reassert the importance of Freemasonry as a relevant source of scholarship within the wider context of eighteenth-century associationalism. Included in this compendium is a thorough historiographic essay, discussing much of the current and more topical scholarship aimed at focusing on the wider impact of British Freemasonry as a holistic movement. However, as Péter laments, "research into eighteenth-century Freemasonry in the British Isles has been largely Anglocentric. ... No scholarly monograph has been produced on the history of eighteenth-century Scottish Freemasonry in English."[5] Péter's bibliography is meticulous, but the dearth of Scottish material is striking in terms of how little has actually been produced when compared to the relatively recent publication of so many books and articles devoted to English Freemasonry. For example, Ric Berman has lately published several wonderfully informative and carefully researched books on Freemasonry, but they are decidedly English in their scope and complexion.[6]

---

3   For example, the *JRFF* (2010); International Conferences on the History of Freemasonry (2007–2013): and the Canonbury Masonic Research Centre at the University of Sheffield (1999–2010). See also Andrew Prescott, "The Study of Freemasonry as a New Academic Discipline," in *Vrijmetserarij in Nederland*, ed. A. Kroon (Leiden, 2003), 5–31.

4   See M. D. J. Scanlan, "The Origins of Freemasonry: England," in *Handbook of Freemasonry*, eds. H. Bogdan and J. A. M. Snoek, 63–81; J. Hamill, *The Craft: A History of English Freemasonry* (Wellingborough, 1986).

5   Róbert Péter, ed., *British Freemasonry, 1717–1813. Volume I: General Introduction and Institutions* (London, 2016), xx. I am grateful for Péter's work, as it is ground-breaking in its range, detail, and thoroughness. Though the historiographical references are by no means exhaustive, they provide a scrupulous dissection of current trends in Masonic scholarship. Since the completion of my PhD, numerous books, papers, and articles have been published on Freemasonry, which Péter catalogues carefully and provide a starting point for any student of Freemasonry. Sadly, very few contributions have been made since 2006 in the area of Scottish Freemasonry.

6   Ric Berman, "The London Irish and the Antients Grand Lodge," *Eighteenth–Centu-*

Until the recent publication of Péter's four-volume set, there existed no consolidated, thorough primary source reader for students of Masonic history.[7] The abundance of unsubstantiated material is challenging, leading Masonic historian David Stevenson to lament the "historical ghetto" into which Freemasonry "has all too often been consigned by the narrow historical outlook of many masons combined with the unreasoning prejudice of professional historians."[8] Masonic historians Knoop and Jones, in no uncertain terms, assert that "there are undoubtedly numerous gaps in the history of freemasonry, but to fill them, not by the successful search for new facts, but by the use of imagination, is to revert to the mythical or imaginative treatment of the subject."[9] As such, Freemasonry has become the "happy hunting-ground of wildly imaginative and uncritical writers."[10]

Masonic histories are frequently useful not because of their accuracy, but because of their interest. In 1723 (reprinted in 1738), Scottish minister James Anderson published the *Constitutions of the Freemasons*.[11] In addition to Anderson's rather inflated discussion of the genesis of Freemasonry, the *Constitutions* enumerates the laws and etiquette freemasons should observe and addresses sundry other topics such as lodge music, poems, and toasts. More recent endeavors, however, have been made to dispel such extraordinary historical narratives.[12] Frances Yates asserts that the

ry Life 39 (2015): 103–130; *Schism: The Battle that Forged Freemasonry* (Brighton, 2013); *The Foundations of Modern Freemasonry: The Grand Architects—Political Change and the Scientific Enlightenment, 1714–1740* (Brighton, 2012).

7   P. Y. Beaurepaire, "Researching Freemasonry in the Twenty–first Century: Opportunities and Challenges," *JRFF* 1 (2010): 249–257.

8   David Stevenson, *The Origins of Freemasonry: Scotland's Century 1590–1710* (Cambridge, 1988), 2.

9   Douglas Knoop and G. P. Jones, *The Scope and Method of Masonic History* (Oldham, 1944), 9; See also Stevenson's *Origins*, 1–5, for further discussion on the problems of masonic historiography.

10   Frances Yates, *The Art of Memory* (London, 1966), 294–295. Margaret Jacob echoes the claims of Yates, writing that "much of what has been written on Freemasonry is worthless and every library is filled with non-scholarly literature on the subject," *The Radical Enlightenment: Pantheists, Freemasons and Republicans* (London, 1981), 7.

11   James Anderson, *The Constitutions of the Freemasons* (repr., London, 1976).

12   For additional masonic historiography, see Mary Ann Clawson, *Constructing Brotherhood: Class, Gender, and Fraternalism* (Princeton, 1989), esp. 53–83; Steven C. Bullock, *Revolutionary Brotherhood: Freemasonry and the Transformation of the American Social Order, 1730–1840* (Chapel Hill, 1996), esp. 9–49; Robert Freke Gould, *Gould's History of Freemasonry Throughout The World, Vols. 1–6* (New York, 1936),esp. *Vol. 2*, 295–408; *Freemasonry on Both Sides of the Atlantic*, eds. William Weisberger, S. Brent Morris, and Wallace McLeod (New York, 2002), esp. 3–278; Bernard E. Jones, *Freemason's Guide and Compendium* (New York, 1950); Douglas Knoop and Gwilym

"origin of Freemasonry is one of the most debated, and debatable, subjects in the whole realm of historical inquiry. One has to distinguish between the legendary history of Freemasonry and the problem of when it actually began as an organized institution."[13] At one time, David Murray Lyon's *History of the Lodge of Edinburgh* (1900) was accepted as the authoritative text on Masonic history.[14] Like Anderson's *Constitutions*, much of the content is vague and often based purely on conjecture and speculation. Although unreliable, facts are hidden among the fiction; for all its shortcomings, Lyon's *History* contains sections and chapters that are useful. Knoop and Jones have made concerted efforts to write both an accurate and objective history of Freemasonry. They published *The Genesis of Freemasonry* in 1947 and attempted to clearly establish the organization's operative roots.[15] David Stevenson notes that although their study "may be criticized in some respects, their work provides a strong and essential foundation for masonic history, vastly superior to what had preceded it."[16]

Also problematic is the overabundance of biased works written by "insiders," those freemasons who seek to distance the fraternity from political and religious movements and beliers, and who "rarely bracket out their biased view of Freemasonry as a harmonious and universal brotherhood."[17] Alternatively, writings overtly critical of Freemasonry are often panned as inaccurate, or motivated by spite. And, as Péter has pointed out, much of the historical record has become obfuscated by self-serving accounts that are purely speculative though often "repeated and ... unquestioned even in academic scholarship."[18] As recent as 2011, Péter notes, David Stevenson asserted that British academics were disinclined to embrace the study of Freemasonry because of "ignorance and negative stereotypes of the movement and ... the excessive secrecy of freemasons in the past."[19]

Stevenson, in his books *The Origins of Freemasonry: Scotland's Century 1590–1710* and *The First Freemasons: Scotland's Early Lodge and their*

Peredur Jones, *The Scottish Mason and the Mason Word* (Manchester, 1939); and *A Short History of Freemasonry to 1730* (Manchester, 1940).

13 Frances Yates, *The Rosicrucian Enlightenment* (London, 1972), 266.

14 David Murray Lyon, *History of the Lodge of Edinburgh (Mary's Chapel) No. 1, Embracing An Account of the Rise and Progress of Freemasonry in Scotland* (London, 1900).

15 D. Knoop and G. P. Jones, *The Genesis of Freemasonry* (Manchester, 1947).

16 Stevenson, *Origins*, 3.

17 Péter, "Historiography of Freemasonry in the British Isles in Light of Recent Scholarship," *General Introduction*, xv.

18 Ibid., xv.

19 David Stevenson, "Four Hundred Years of Freemasonry in Scotland," *Scottish Historical Review* 9 (2011): 280–295.

Members, precisely charts the gradual development and growth of both operative and speculative freemasonry in Scotland.[20] These two histories are the first of their kind to offer a definitive and historically sound starting point for the study of eighteenth-century Scottish Freemasonry—and, according to Stevenson, modern British Freemasonry—in a wider historical environment.[21] Although he provides the first comprehensive listing of Scottish lodges, their archival holdings, and a close examination of their histories from 1590 to 1710, no extensive study of eighteenth-century lodge records has been attempted. Historian Margaret Jacob does acknowledge that Scottish lodges do contain a wealth of information that offer brief glimpses of the transition from operative to speculative—or non-operative—Freemasonry. According to Jacob, the richness of these records and minutes "has led the historian who has worked most extensively with them, David Stevenson, to argue that the freemasonry bequeathed to the eighteenth century was a Scottish invention."[22] A critical problem, however, is the varied quality and completeness of lodge archives, as some are much more detailed and carefully preserved than others.[23] Péter, too, echoes these sentiments, and he additionally notes that there is a distinct lack of organized, bibliographical information to aid in the perusal of research material.[24] Despite such inconsistencies, Stevenson's research has played an important role in illus-

---

20   David Stevenson, *The Origins of Freemasonry: Scotland's Century 1590–1710* (Cambridge, 1988) and *The First Freemasons: Scotland's Early Lodges and their Members* (Aberdeen, 1988).

21   However, some historians dispute this. For example, masonic historian John Hamill situates the emergence of modern freemasonry in England. As Péter notes, in the second edition of *The Craft: A History of English Freemasonry* (Addlestone, 1994), he appears to intentionally discount Stevenson's research. See also See J. A. M. Snoek, "The Earliest Development of Masonic Degrees and Rituals: Hamill versus Stevenson," in *The Social Impact of Freemasonry on the Modern Western World*, ed. M. D. J. Scanlan (London, 2002), 1–19.

22   Margaret Jacob, *Living the Enlightenment*, 35–28.

23   During my six-year study of lodges across Scotland, I found lodge records, minutes, and archives in varying states of preservation: often, lodges are fiercely protective of documents and are unwilling to loan them out for digitization or personal use. As was the case with all the lodges studied, I was required to examine minutes in-house, was not allowed to photocopy, and in one particular instance I was asked not to return to the lodge as my presence was not welcome. Such experiences do little to dispel the somewhat enigmatic, guarded aura surrounding the fraternity.

24   Péter, "Historiography," xiv. Some do exist, however. See R. A. Gilbert, "The Role of Bibliography in Masonic Research," *AQC* 103 (1990): 124–149; A. Faivre, *Access to Western Esotericism* (Albany, NY, 1994), 311–314; T. Stewart, "European Periodical Literature on Masonic Research: A Review of Two Decades of Achievement," in *Freemasonry on Both Sides of the Atlantic*, eds. Weisberger, Morris, and McLeod, 805–936.

trating the significance of Scottish Freemasonry as a form of association during the seventeenth and early-eighteenth centuries. This monograph deviates from the Anglo-centric Masonic approach and—following the example of Stevenson's works—endeavors to render a rich discussion and analysis of individual Scottish freemasons and lodges based largely on lodge archives, and their broader significance to the eighteenth-century associational movement.

Scottish Freemasonry has too often been viewed from a strictly Masonic context that frequently ignores its wider impact and influence on Enlightenment culture and sociability. A broader contextualization offers a clearer representation of recruitment patterns among provincial and metropolitan lodges, and reveals the similarities and differences existing among Freemasonry and other eighteenth-century clubs and societies. As such, analysis of Masonic membership, organizational characteristics, and ideological concerns will provide a clearer understanding and purpose of Masonic lodges and their attraction to a wider cross-section of Scottish society during the 1700s. Concentrating solely on Scottish organizations and furthering Arthur Williamson's view that Freemasonry ultimately emerged from "Scottish culture and social self-consciousness,"[25] Davis D. McElroy's *Scotland's Age of Improvement: A Survey of Eighteenth-Century Literary Clubs and Societies* (1969) is an invaluable resource for a general study of the abundant organizations in Scotland during the Enlightenment.[26] McElroy's research is a central part of this monography, as it provides a broad contextual basis for the discussion of the wider patterns of voluntarism associated with eighteenth-century Scottish Freemasonry. Not confined exclusively to Scotland, Peter Clark examines numerous clubs and societies throughout Britain. In his book *British Clubs and Societies 1580–1800: The Origins of an Associational World*,[27] Clark approaches the associational world from several different angles. He explores the reasons for joining a club and the cultural and social needs and expectations that they served, and considers how the nature of these societies changed over the course of two centuries. There is a section on English Freemasonry that provides general membership analyses of Masonic lodges and

---

25   Arthur H. Williamson, "Number and National Consciousness: The Edinburgh Mathematicians and Scottish Political Culture at the Union of the Crowns," in *Scots and Britons: Scottish Political Thought and the Union of 1603*, ed. Roger A. Mason (New York, 1994), 188–212.

26   Davis D. McElroy, *Scotland's Age of Improvement: A Survey of Eighteenth-Century Literary Clubs and Societies* (Washington, 1969).

27   Peter Clark, *British Clubs and Societies 1580–1800: The Origins of an Associational World* (Oxford, 2000).

follows their growth and expansion throughout the eighteenth century, but Clark's discussion of Scottish Freemasonry is negligible at best.

One of the most influential works on European Freemasonry and the masonic impact the social and political culture of the Enlightenment is Margaret Jacob's *Living the Enlightenment: Freemasonry and Politics in Eighteenth-Century Europe* (1991).[28] Published 10 years after *The Radical Enlightenment: Pantheists, Freemasons and Republicans* (1981), it offers a striking and vivid account of the rise and development of eighteenth-century European Freemasonry.[29] Furthermore, Jacob raises interesting questions about the origins of the society and how it changed and evolved after its transportation from Britain to Europe. The "radical Enlightenment," or evolution of Freemasonry, is further examined through the rather fascinating debate between Jacob and Jonathan Israel. Each articulates a specific viewpoint, acknowledging to varying degrees the impact of Continental lodges on other European lodges, and lodges in England. Specifically, Jacob and Israel question to what extent the freemasons promoted radical political ideas, and whether or not the exclusivity and intolerance of Continental lodges made their way to Britain.[30]

Finally, very little is known about the relationship between Scottish Freemasonry and the British government during the late-eighteenth and early-nineteenth centuries. Again, Berman's influential book *The Foundations of Modern Freemasonry: The Grand Architects—Political Change and the Scientific Enlightenment, 1714–1740* is notable for its examination of the interplay among—as the title suggests—English freemasons and the government, but it largely neglects the rich and at times fascinating interaction among Scottish masons and the government. In exploring the ways in which freemasons reacted to the political stresses brought about by the onset of the French Revolution and the enactment of parliamentary legislation aimed at regulating secret societies, this thesis addresses an important yet largely unknown aspect of eighteenth-century freemasonry.

---

28   Margaret C. Jacob, *Living the Enlightenment: Freemasonry and Politics in Eighteenth-Century Europe* (Oxford, 1991). Also see Jacob's *The Radical Enlightenment.*

29   See Paul Turnbridge and C. A. Batham, "The Climate of European Freemasonry 1750–1810," *AQC* 83 (1970). The authors suggest that "the rituals and instructions [from Britain] were transmitted solely by word of mouth and as a result underwent considerable modifications," 248.

30   J. I. Israel, *Enlightenment Contested: Philosophy, Modernity and the Emancipation of Man, 1670–1752* (Oxford, 2006), 864–865; Margaret Jacob, "The Radical Enlightenment and Freemasonry: Where We Are Now," *REHMLAC* 5 (2012): 11–24.

Central to any analysis of freemasonry is its relation to other groups. Radical organizations, though, comprise a different strand of topics, as these associations were often politically or religiously motivated. Jacob addresses these factions, as many were pseudo-masonic in that they imitated or closely fashioned their own unique rituals and ceremonies after the freemasons. Elaine W. McFarland's *Ireland And Scotland In The Age Of Revolution* (1994) looks at the role of organizations in fostering ideas of revolution.[31] She discusses the problems which seditious societies such as the United Irishmen (who, as we shall see, were to be implicated in the Maybole Trial of Sedition in 1800) posed for the government. McFarland also considers the government response to their revolutionary ideas; ultimately, the disciplinary measures aimed at eradicating these organizations severely impacted British freemasons, especially those in Scotland.

The motivations behind the formation of popular societies were much more than just the opportunity to debate issues, discuss topics of interests, or engage in convivial celebrations. The un-stated purpose of most eighteenth-century Scottish clubs was the verbalization of "a Scottish viewpoint" and the improvement of Scottish society.[32] Roger Emerson has suggested that during the beginning of the eighteenth century—amid the growing realization of the need for professional education—the new population of the learned and educated "became numerous enough to change the institutional mix in the country."[33] Although intellectual clubs had existed since the 1680s, a new emphasis was placed upon the structure and objectives of such societies. During the first half of the eighteenth century, Freemasonry was already an old-established part of Scottish and British culture. Its secrecy sometimes evoked skeptical feelings, but Freemasonry did not normally provoke the extreme anti-masonic attitudes prevalent in Europe.[34] Its organization and development were such that it had always precluded any serious accusations of treason or sedition from

---

31   E. W. McFarland, *Ireland and Scotland in the Age of Revolution* (Edinburgh, 1994).

32   Roger Emerson, "The Enlightenment and Social Structures," in *City and Society in the 18th Century*, eds. Paul Fritz and David Williams (Toronto, 1973), 121.

33   Roger Emerson, "The Contexts of the Scottish Enlightenment," in *The Cambridge Companion to the Scottish Enlightenment*, ed. Alexander Broadie (Cambridge, 2003), 19.

34   British freemasonry did receive some criticism during the eighteenth century, although it was infrequent and principally confined to England and Europe. See S. N. Smith, "The So-Called 'Exposures' of Freemasonry of the Mid-Eighteenth Century," *AQC* 56 (1943): 4–36; Knoop and Jones, "An Anti–Masonic Leaflet of 1698," *AQC* 55 (1942): 117–118; N. B. Spencer, "Exposures and Their Effect on Freemasonry," *AQC* 74 (1961): 142–145. Spencer notes that "considering the number of exposures, it is marvellous that they have had so little effect on the Craft," 145.

the public and the government. However, as the second half of the eighteenth century progressed and the French Revolution exercised a significant influence over political thought, British Freemasonry was targeted by a suspicious government intent on monitoring the activities of secret societies. As such, heavy-handed legislation passed in the 1790s to stamp out radical groups transformed Scottish Freemasonry from a convivial, charitable association into an organization characterized by intense political rivalries and power struggles. The friction among Scottish freemasons during the end of the century was directly caused by government legislation as well as problems stemming from the formation of the Grand Lodge of Scotland in 1736. Smoldering inter-lodge disputes combined with accusations of treason triggered a decade of conflict which severely damaged the reputation of Scottish Freemasonry and exposed its vulnerable organizational structure.

In exploring the changes in Scottish lodges between the years 1725 and 1810, several related questions will be considered in this study. First, what was the nature of early eighteenth-century Scottish Freemasonry and how did it change in the years following the creation of the Grand Lodge of Scotland? Second, what are the essential similarities and differences between English and Scottish masons, and how did they affect the progression of eighteenth-century Scottish lodges? Third, what were the roles and functions of the Grand Lodge of Scotland? Fourth, what are the broader patterns of voluntarism among freemasons, and what are the similarities and differences of the fraternity when compared to other eighteenth-century clubs and associations? Lastly, what caused the conflicts among Scottish freemasons during the 1790s, and why was the Grand Lodge of Scotland unable to effectively contain the turmoil among its lodges?

The advantage of the present study is that it draws directly on previously unused, or otherwise unknown, lodge records which offer a candid look into masonic life. This monograph contains an unusual amount of essentially inaccessible evidence, examining original eighteenth- and nineteenth-century lodge records and minutes from 14 masonic lodges across Scotland and England.[35] As such, this book is significant not just for the interpretation it offers, but also for the evidence it has uncovered and brings into the public domain for the first time. Perhaps most importantly, it reveals that the history of eighteenth-century Scottish Free-

---

35 Where appropriate, punctuation and spelling have been modernized to improve clarity and structure. Unless notes, excerpts from lodge records and minutes remain faithful to the original manuscripts.

masonry was most influenced by four major events: the formation of the Grand Lodge of Scotland in 1736; the passage of the Unlawful Oaths and Secret Societies Acts in 1797 and 1799 by the British government which attempted to eradicate radical groups; the Maybole Trial of Sedition in 1800; and the Masonic Secession of 1808.

Chapter 2 will examine the creation of the Grand Lodge of Scotland in 1736 and the development of Scottish Freemasonry between the years 1736 and 1740. The Grand Lodge of Scotland considerably affected the overall structure and character of lodges: as it steadily increased its power and authority, it attempted to acquire complete control of Scottish Freemasonry. Close examination of lodge records reveals the changing attitudes of Scottish lodges—in particular those which were inherently operative—toward the Grand Lodge. Despite the looming turmoil of the 1790s, the Grand Lodge of Scotland ushered in an era of expansion, conviviality, and notoriety for Scottish Freemasonry. Chapter 3 focuses on the development of Scottish Freemasonry and the Grand Lodge of Scotland between the years 1740 until 1790, arguably the pinnacle of the fraternity, especially for Edinburgh lodges. Boasting a wide variety of artisans, *literati*, and government figures, and with its steadily-increasing number of lodges, Freemasonry—under the steady, if not staid—gaze of the Grand Lodge became one of the most popular associations of eighteenth-century Scotland.

While clubs and societies appeared and thrived in Scotland during the 1700s, other nations boasted their own array of clubs and societies. After 1789, however, certain groups assumed the mantle of political radicalism. Chapter 4 will outline the climate of growing hostility toward British and European Freemasonry in the years leading up to and following the outbreak of the French Revolution, the intrusion of the Grand Lodge of Scotland and national politics into lodge life, and the impact of Masonic and governmental legislation aimed at eradicating the perceived threats of secret and seditious societies on British Freemasonry. This chapter will also consider the alleged and actual links between radical organizations and the freemasons, and what were the ultimate ramifications of their self-imposed adherence to secrecy and rituals during a time of heightened skepticism of such practices.

The presence of national politics in lodges and the concomitant loss of lodge autonomy directly caused two major Scottish legal cases at the beginning of the nineteenth century. Both incidents culminated in courtroom battles and created further tensions among masons, in addition to fueling the growing public and national demand for increased openness in Masonic activities. Chapter 5 explores the first of these important yet poorly understood cases, the Maybole Trial of Sedition in 1800, which involved two West Coast lodges, wild accusations of Illuminati infiltration, and charges that radical Irish societies were using Masonic lodges as covers for seditious activities. The second legal battle occurred in Edinburgh itself, pitting two lodges against one another and eventually ending in what modern masonic historians have labeled the Masonic Secession of 1808. Chapter 6 examines Masonic protocol in relation to political issues and the observance of proscribed laws. Sparked by a political debate, the Masonic Secession of 1808, or the Great Masonic Rebellion, was the culmination of a century of change among freemasons in Scotland. As we shall see, the Rebellion manifested the extreme resentment of some Scottish lodges toward one another and triggered an intense questioning of the political and personal motivations of the Grand Lodge of Scotland, all of which nearly caused the complete collapse of Scottish freemasonry.

CHAPTER TWO

"Antient Lustre in This Kingdome":
The Grand Lodge of Scotland,
Operative Freemasonry and the Early
Characteristics of Scottish Lodges

Peter Clark—in his study *British Clubs and Societies 1580–1800* (2000)—particularly emphasizes the role of Freemasonry in "fostering social harmony, serving to unite different social, as well as political and religious groups," and its effective deployment of "all the… levers of recruitment, marketing, and organization."[1] Clark explains that through publicity, self- promotion, and the creation of a central governing body, Freemasonry became "the biggest association in the British world."[2]

Although largely based on English evidence, there are several broad similarities between Clark's conclusions and the progress of eighteenth-century Scottish Freemasonry: the creation of a central Grand Lodge, a penchant for conviviality, adherence to a system of constitutionalism, overt respect and loyalty for the political establishment, varying degrees of Newtonian intellectual influence, and a clear, recognizable presence in the community.[3] Regardless of certain parallels, the extent to which Scotland integrated these elements into lodges differed significantly from England.[4]

The Beginnings of the Grand Lodge System

As the model for all British Grand Lodges, the Grand Lodge of England also provided, according to William Heckthorn, "an inspiration and ex-

---

1 Clark, *British Clubs*, 319; 348.

2 Ibid. See pages 309–348 for a discussion of British Freemasonry and its functions, characteristics, and politics.

3 David Stevenson argues that in order to correctly situate the origins of Scottish Freemasonry, the "relevant English evidence must also be examined. When this is done, it immediately becomes apparent that the English evidence is very different from the Scottish," *Origins* 213–233. For a discussion on Scottish Masonic lodge membership in Edinburgh, see Lisa Kahler, "Freemasonry in Edinburgh 1721–1746: Institutions and Context," Unpublished Thesis (St. Andrews, 1998).

4 See Lisa Kahler, "The Grand Lodge of Scotland and the Establishment of the Masonic Community," in *Freemasonry on Both Sides of the Atlantic*, 112–115, for a discussion on the English influence. Kahler's observations are concerned with the ceremonial and ritualistic aspects of Freemasonry, not the broader thematic concerns such as Newtonianism, religion, and loyalism.

ample to the world-wide Masonic movement of the eighteenth century."[5] Developed at a time when clubs and societies were becoming progressively more fashionable, it was formed because interest in Freemasonry "was beginning to awaken and spread."[6] Initially conceived for sociable purposes[7] and designed as a "corporate meeting of the representatives of its constituent lodges,"[8] the Grand Lodge of England expanded its powers and, in 1721, "claimed the right to control the creation of new lodges and served as the final authority in Masonic matters."[9] Harry Carr explains that the newly formed Grand Lodge was indeed a manifestation of its own time, necessitated by the burgeoning interest in voluntarism:

> In the sense that no organization of that kind had ever existed before, the Grand Lodge was certainly a new management, although from the very limited aims that are indicated in its earliest records any suggestion that it was consciously trying to 'remodel' the Craft would seem to be an exaggeration. Everything in the fragmentary English records—and in the far more plentiful and continuous Scottish records—goes to show that there had not been any break (or break-down) in the Craft.[10]

The Grand Lodge of England quickly recognized the need for a clearly defined system of regulations, "not merely in respect of the new central authority, but also with regard to the rapidly increasing membership of the Order."[11] Providing a set of rules which closely resembled British politics and constitutionalism would reinforce its legitimacy and dispel any doubts regarding the political loyalties of the freemasons.[12]

---

5   William Heckthorn, *The Secret Societies of all Ages* (New York, 1965), 21–22.

6   T. O. Haunch, "The Formation," in *United Grand Lodge of England 1717–1967* (Oxford, 1967), 49. See also T. O. Haunch, "Grand Lodge 1717–1751," AQC 42 (1966): 264–270.

7   Jones, *Guide and Compendium*, 166–167. See also Bullock, *Revolutionary Brotherhood*, 15; Harry Carr, "Three Phases of Masonic History" AQC 77 (1964): 260; Haunch, "Grand Lodge 1717–1751," 264–270.

8   Haunch, "The Formation," 61.

9   Bullock, *Revolutionary Brotherhood*, 15.

10   Carr, "Three Phases," 261.

11   Lionel Vibert, "Anderson's Constitutions of 1723," AQC 36 (1923): 36.

12   Ibid., 11.

Such was the immediate context for James Anderson's *Constitutions of the Freemasons* (1723). Born in Aberdeen in 1679 and educated at Marischal College, Anderson graduated MA in 1698 and subsequently studied theology for four years, suggesting that he was preparing himself for a career in the Presbyterian ministry.[13] His connections with Freemasonry are unclear at best, and there is no definitive explanation as to the origins of the relationship between Anderson and the Grand Lodge of England. What is clear, however, is that the newly-formed Grand Lodge was ambitious in its search for elite patronage and a codified system of rules. Until 1717, oral histories and medieval documents which were collectively referred to as the "Old Constitutions" or "Old Charges" had provided the foundation for any existing standards of administration. The basic purposes of the *Constitutions* were twofold: to establish a historical account of Freemasonry largely based on the Old Testament of the Bible and to reconstruct an elite Masonic lineage.[14] Anderson's work was not only an "opportune piece of invented tradition from the point of country ideology; it also bespoke a desire not to move too far away from the Christian past."[15] Lending itself to a more congenial and open-minded atmosphere in which members could meet, Freemasonry's "prohibition of overt political discussion and its espousal of natural religion and rational tolerance among good men of all persuasions made it an ideal vehicle for diffusing the non-partisan patriotism of Country ideology among the emerging professional and entrepreneurial elements of provincial society."[16]

In effect, his imagination had conjured up an ingenious instance of Masonic propaganda which fused constitutional and religious history.[17] By

---

13   See David Stevenson, "James Anderson (1679–1739): Man and Mason," in *Freemasonry on Both Sides of the Atlantic*, (New York, 2002), 199–205 for an in-depth discussion of Anderson's early life. For more biographical information on Anderson, see also Chetwode Crawley, "The Rev. Dr. Anderson's Non-Masonic Writings, 1712–1739," *AQC* 18 (1905): 28–42; A. L. Miller, "The Connection of Dr. James Anderson of the 'Constitutions' With Aberdeen and Aberdeen University," *AQC* 36 (1923): 86–103; Edward Newton, "Brethren Who Made Masonic History," *AQC* 78 (1965): 130–145.

14   See Anderson's *Constitutions*, 1–23. The 1738 edition contains a much more detailed lineage, accounting for the first 142 pages.

15   John Money, "Freemasonry and Loyalism in England," in *The Transformation of Political Culture: England and Germany in the Late Eighteenth Century*, ed. Eckhart Hellmuth (Oxford, 1990), 258.

16   Ibid., 257.

17   Stevenson comments on the alacrity which characterized the Grand Lodge's actions: "The new constitutions made fast progress: they had been commissioned, written, re-

1721, Anderson had completed the first edition of the *Constitutions*, although due to a dispute among several members of the Grand Lodge its publication was delayed until 1723.[18] What emerged, according to Roberts, was "worthless."[19] His assertion is shared by Edwards, who maintains that

> ... it cannot be said that either the form or content of the *Book of Constitutions* show many effects of the spirit of inquiry, or rationalism, or of modern historical method. Indeed, though the first two editions of the *Constitutions* stand at the parting of the ways between the old Freemasonry and the new ... it seems that they look backward in form and in spirit to what is popularly considered medievalism rather than forward to eighteenth-century enlightenment and method.[20]

Other historians also share this disparaging view, characterizing Anderson's work as "almost entirely rubbish" and "mumbo-jumbo to which modern masons only give veneration of lip-service because it is tradition to the Craft."[21]

Seen in an eighteenth-century Masonic context, however, its implications are much clearer. Stevenson reasons that the numerous invented passages and false historical claims comprising Anderson's *Constitutions* were intended to convey the impression that Freemasonry offered "an escape from competitive pressures and rivalries into brotherhood, with the legitimacy of having been highly respected from ancient times."[22] This theory is also communicated by Roberts, who states that "in the eighteenth cen-

---

vised and approved for publication in a period of six months. With a noble grand master providing publicity and numbers of lodges and masons growing rapidly, it seems that the need for a published summary of the non-secret aspects of freemasonry was seen as a priority," "James Anderson," 208.

18 See Stevenson, "James Anderson," 208–216 for a detailed discussion on this dispute.

19 Ibid., 218.

20 Lewis Edwards, "Anderson's Book of Constitutions of 1738," *AQC* 46 (1933): 357.

21 J. M. Roberts, *The Mythology of the Secret Societies* (London, 1972), 19.

22 Ibid., 219–220. This sympathetic view of Anderson's *Constitutions*—which ignores its historical and grammatical shortcomings—is not accepted by all historians. For example, Jacob views the *Constitutions* as "an extraordinary example of political propaganda," *Radical Enlightenment*, 130. Other historians consider his work "imaginative, fantastic, and unhistorical," Alfred Robbins, *AQC* 23 (1910): 22.

tury much more weight was given to these legends ... and they were influential in shaping both the characteristic Masonic ideology and the image of masonry formed by its detractors. As a guide to the positive history of Freemasonry, on the other hand, they are valueless."[23]

Although the organization and development of the Scottish Grand Lodge were both modeled after the Grand Lodge of England,[24] the actual formation of each governing body, according to Gould, was "wholly dissimilar."[25] The four lodges that gathered in Edinburgh in 1736, having "taken into consideration the great loss that Masonry has sustained thro the wont of a Grand Master," determined that a Grand Lodge was necessary in order to restore Freemasonry to "its antient lustre in this Kingdome."[26] In theory, the lodges envisioned—as no doubt did the founding lodges in England— the new Grand Lodge as a conduit for the gradual development and progression of speculative Freemasonry. In practice, however, the specific motivations behind the creation of the Scottish Grand Lodge differed from its English predecessor. Ostensibly, the main contributing factor to the amalgamation of Scottish lodges into a national system of Masonic governance was envy over the success of the Grand Lodge of England.[27] Scottish masons "envied the éclat"[28] given to English masons and were critical of their own operations, which were carried out "without patronage or display."[29] Restoring Scottish Freemasonry to its "antient lustre" was another way of stating that as England possessed a Grand Lodge, so Scotland needed and wanted one as well.[30] Gould accurately conveys this rationale, offering

---

23 Roberts, *Mythology*, 19.

24 Kahler, "The Grand Lodge of Scotland," 112.

25 Gould, *History of Freemasonry Vol. 3* (New York, 1936), 243. Margaret Jacob echoes this claim that modern, or speculative Freemasonry, "may have indeed been invented in Scotland and then exported south; but what returned to Scotland in the early eighteenth century, in a reverse migration from England, was quite different."

26 Kahler, "The Grand Lodge of Scotland," 94. The four lodges were Mary's Chapel, Canongate Kilwinning, Kilwinning Scots Arms, and Leith Kilwinning, all located in Edinburgh.

27 See also Gould, *History of Freemasonry Vol. 3*, 249; Lyon, *Mary's Chapel*, 189; Kahler, "The Grand Lodge of Scotland," 94.

28 J. Stewart Seggie, in *Annals of the Lodge of Journeymen Masons No. 8* (Edinburgh, 1930), 71.

29 Ibid.

30 Bullock maintains that Ireland and Scotland were "imitating the London body's penchant for fabricating tradition" by setting up "grand lodges that claimed the same powers as the early speculative order," *Revolutionary Brotherhood*, 15. Stevenson notes that

further support to McElroy's assertions that many Scottish organizations looked to English models for guidance and direction:

> By the year 1727, within a decade of the formation of the Grand Lodge of England, southern ideas had permeated to the northern capital [Edinburgh] and were quickly engrafted on the Masonry of Scotland. The innovations are known to have taken firm root in Edinburgh as early as 1729 and their general diffusion throughout the Scottish kingdom was a natural consequence of the erection of the Grand Lodge of Scotland ... In proceeding with the history of the Grand Lodge of Scotland, the remark may be expressed, that if any surprise is permissible at the establishment of that body in 1736, it can only legitimately arise from the circumstance that the Masons of Edinburgh allowed the Brethren in York, Munster and Dublin to precede them in following the example set at London in 1717. If any one influence more than another conduced to the eventual erection of a governing Masonic body for Scotland, it may be found in the fact that, within the comparatively short space of thirteen years, six prominent noblemen, all of whom were connected with the northern kingdom had filled the chair of the Grand Lodge of England.[31]

In addition to divergent motivations, the Scottish Grand Lodge was confronted with markedly different responsibilities. The Grand Lodge of England, for example, was founded by the only four English Masonic lodges in existence. Having completely severed the link with operative masonry, it was essentially a speculative organization.[32] Such a severance with

---

the "Scottish system of permanent lodges was crowned with a grand lodge. Just as English masons had adopted so much from Scotland in earlier years, so by the 1720s the results of this burst of creativity in England were influencing the practices of Scottish lodges. England had become dominant in the development of freemasonry within Britain," *Origins*, 231.

31 Gould, *History of Freemasonry Vol. 2*, 376–377.

32 Harry Carr, "Grand Lodge and the Significance of 1717," *AQC* 79 (1966): 290. Bullock further explains that "the new grand lodge took on powers quite different from previous trade practice. New genealogies stressed the speculative group's continuity with the past. The rituals themselves, the ultimate evidence for connection with

the operative element of the craft inevitably permitted a smooth—if not unopposed—creation of a Grand Lodge system. Any fears of a resulting clash between old customs and traditions with modern progressiveness and a new vision of Freemasonry were soon dispelled. As the new Grand Lodge had little or no connection with working masons, and "no operative influences played any part in its creation," there were "no operative objectives in its programme. It came into being at a time when the operative craft lodges had virtually disappeared and when the transition from operative to speculative masonry had almost run its full course."[33]

Scotland, however, attempted to consolidate an already active and varied group of 49 lodges.[34] According to Seggie, the new Scottish Grand Lodge had to simultaneously "embrace and be acceptable to every existing type of Lodge" and consider the "jealousies rife amongst the old Operative Lodges and their offshoots."[35] Indeed, as Kahler has noted, the Grand Lodge

> recognised the existence of operative lodges and was keen to attract them, and keep them, in the Masonic community. It also indicates that the Grand Lodge recognized the operative roots of the organization, and was willing to acknowledge these origins ... Its establishment provided the impetus for the transition from operative to accepted lodges, but did not require a fundamental change in what the operative lodges had been doing all along ... there is no evidence to suggest that the Grand Lodge discriminated against operative lodges. It attempted to create a cohesiveness between the lodges by establishing common regulations which all joining lodges were required to follow.[36]

Although the lion's share of the 49 lodges were actually self-serving, operative institutions, others were either making the transition to or exclusively practicing speculative Freemasonry. Stevenson maintains that "the

---

antiquity, changed dramatically by severing the vital link with the actual trade of masonry," *Revolutionary Brotherhood*, 15.

33 Ibid.

34 Clark, *British Clubs*, 310.

35 Seggie, *Journeymen Masons*, 46.

36 Kahler, "The Grand Lodge of Scotland," 108; 114.

great majority of Scottish lodges until the early eighteenth century (and in many cases long beyond that) ... were stonemasons."[37] This argument is echoed by Kahler, who writes that "the primary business of the operative lodges had been to control the trade and regulate the working lives of their members."[38]

Rules and regulations were also particular to individual lodges and occasionally specified with whom the members could or could not work. No. 1(3) Aberdeen Lodge, in a minute dated September 30, 1730, stated that a local journeyman mason,

> notwithstanding of the kindness shown him by the Masters of our Lodge, hath engaged work of his own which is highly prejudicial to our publick concern. Therefore we the under subscribers doe hereby unanimously consent and agree that none of our fraternity shall work with him as journeyman, nor employ him as such when we can be served by our own, or work conjunctly with him in any work.[39]

The Grand Lodge of Scotland was also presented with another formidable problem: as lodges were spread across a wide geographical area and often isolated from one another, there was "nothing at all to act as a link ... except the visitation of Brethren from one Lodge to another," and the conditions of the lodges in various parts of the country "made casual co-ordination impossible."[40] Unlike England, where evidence suggests active contact among lodges, Scottish minutes before 1740 offer little indication of lodge interaction and communication.[41] By 1747, however, the Grand Lodge of Scotland had addressed this problem. As will be explained in greater detail in Chapter 3, the office of Provincial Grand Master enabled lodges outside of Edinburgh to correspond with the Grand Lodge and afforded an accessible and convenient method of collecting subscription monies, charitable donations, and other mandatory fees.

---

37   Stevenson, *Origins*, 215.

38   Kahler, "The Grand Lodge of Scotland," 114.

39   No. 1(3) Aberdeen Lodge Minutes, September 23, 1730.

40   Robert Strathern Lindsay, *A History of the Mason Lodge of Holyrood House (St Luke) No. 44 Holding of the Grand Lodge of Scotland with a Roll of Members, 1734–1934* (Edinburgh, 1935), 46.

41   Clark, *British Clubs*, 331.

The Grand Lodge of Scotland

Despite the best efforts of the four Edinburgh lodges to create an institution that would satisfy everyone, the manner in which the central governing body emerged would dog its existence for almost a century from its inception.[42] According to Lyon, there was an overall "disorganization that was prevalent in the Craft at the date of the erection," and the Grand Lodge itself held "indistinct notions" regarding its functions and role in Scottish Freemasonry.[43]

Three separate incidents occurred during its formation and development which reinforce Lyon's claims: first, the sending of invitations announcing the Grand Election and the formal establishment of the Grand Lodge; second, the ordering of lodges on the Grand Roll of Scotland; and third, the handling of a communication sent by Maybole Lodge to the Grand Lodge in 1737.[44] Ultimately, these three events precipitated widespread indifference toward the Grand Lodge and prevented many lodges from acknowledging it as the supreme governing body in Scotland; several lodges "never joined the Grand Lodge at all, while others did so and retired, though of the latter some renewed their allegiance."[45] Although the Grand Lodge was the authoritative Masonic body, for years it waged a war of attrition with the much older, venerable lodges in Scotland.

Its official recognition as the putative head of Scottish Freemasonry and the election of the first Grand Master were held on November 30, 1736, St. Andrew's Day, at Mary's Chapel Lodge in Edinburgh.[46] Only 4 out of 49 Scottish lodges, however, were involved in the detailed planning of such important events. Furthermore, these four lodges were located in Edinburgh, attesting to the initial solidarity and exclusiveness of their endeavors. According to Lindsay, members of the Canongate Kilwinning Lodge in Edinburgh composed a letter which expressed their objections

---

42 Kahler, "The Grand Lodge of Scotland," 108. Kahler explains that "it is likely that the introduction of some type of governing board would have been distasteful to the existing lodges, particularly the older, primarily operative lodges," "The Grand Lodge," 94. See also E. Macbean, "Formation of the Grand Lodge of Scotland," *AQC* 3 (1890): 183.

43 Lyon, *Mary's Chapel*, 192.

44 For further discussion on numerous other disputes that occurred during the Grand Election, see Kahler, "The Grand Lodge of Scotland," 99–101.

45 Gould, *A Concise History of Freemasonry* (London, 1903), 275.

46 Freemasons traditionally held elections on St. Andrew's Day.

"to the permanent seat of Grand Lodge being in Edinburgh as likely to give an undue preference to the Lodges on the spot."[47] They also opposed the planned fixed registration fee for operatives and speculatives, arguing that operatives "should be left ... to pay what they can afford."[48] However, the letter—because it "raised points on which the whole scheme might be wrecked"—was suppressed "until Grand Lodge was fairly launched."[49]

From the beginning, the core group made a concerted effort to "convince the other lodges of what they considered the importance" of establishing a Grand Lodge and "allay any doubts that the lodges might have" regarding its functions.[50] It is possible, however, that the imminent Grand Lodge had no concise vision as to what its functions would be. Indeed, as its rudimentary framework was built on dim perceptions of what the Grand Lodge of England actually did, it is not difficult to conclude that the organizational proceedings and the years immediately following the formation of the Grand Lodge of Scotland would be fraught with disagreements and ambiguities. Carr states that the invitations sent by the four founding lodges "contained no hint of government by the Grand Lodge, nor any suggestion that the lodges, all existing by inherent right, might be yielding up any of their self-governing powers to a new authority."[51] Attributing the omission of such details to Masonic duplicity would be simple and convenient, and indeed would offer a solid justification for much of the conflict during the 1790s. However, such a view ignores the fact that the lodges composing the nascent Grand Lodge did not foresee the future expansion and popularity of Scottish Freemasonry, nor did they consider the finer details of the style and content of Masonic government.

In any event, the invitations for the Grand Election which were sent on 20 October suggest that there was a deliberate attempt to defend their unilateral decision to impose a structural and organizational hierarchy upon Scottish lodges. Kahler proposes that the founding four not only omitted other freemasons from the planning process, but they also failed to invite every known Scottish lodge.[52] The apparent justification for selec-

---

47   Lindsay, *Holyrood House*, 292.

48   Ibid.

49   Ibid.

50   Kahler, "The Grand Lodge of Scotland," 94.

51   Carr, Harry, *Lodge Mother Kilwinning, No. 0. A Study of the Earliest Minute Books, 1642–1842* (London, 1961), 215.

52   Kahler, "The Grand Lodge of Scotland," 94.

tive inclusion is that only "regular lodges" were to be included in the proceedings.[53] A mere 22 days were allowed for the delivery and subsequent return of the invitations, thus reducing the number of lodges that might attend and possibly reject the idea of the Grand Lodge. [54] By November 11, 1736, only seven lodges had responded to the invitation.[55]

Four other lodges with surviving minutes for the year 1736—No. 1(3) Aberdeen, No. 3 Scoon & Perth, No. 8 Journeymen Edinburgh, and No. 25 St. Andrew—do not refer to the invitation or the subsequent formation of the Grand Lodge. Taking into consideration the relative nonexistence of inter-lodge contact and the inefficiency of the eighteenth-century postal system, this lack of acknowledgement is not surprising.[56] However, given that they recorded other communications from the Grand Lodge relatively soon after its establishment, it is peculiar that the inauguration is not mentioned in their lodge minutes, if indeed the invitations were received. For example, an entry in the minute books of No.1(3) Aberdeen almost 1 year after the Grand Lodge's formation stated, "There was Produced by the Right Worshipful Master a Letter address'd to him from the Grand Lodge at Edinburgh with Proposealls concerning the building of the Hospitall of the Royall Infirmary."[57] No. 3 Scoon & Perth lodge minutes even suggest that no communication was established with the Grand Lodge until nearly 4 years after its inception. In a minute entry dated December 8, 1740, the lodge noted that "it was unanimously agreed to by the Lodge That application be made to the Grand Lodge at Edinburgh for a new Charter to this Lodge That thereby they may have Communication with the Grand Lodge."[58]

One further example will suffice to illustrate the argument that communication among lodges was—if not infrequent—selective at best. No. 8

---

53 Ibid., 95. Kahler claims that the term "regular" is intentionally ambiguous and "it is possible that the lodges may have used it as an excuse to avoid inviting lodges they did not want to include," Ibid.

54 Acknowledgment of the invitation was expected by 11 November 1736.

55 These lodges were Glasgow, Lanark, Greenock, Jedburgh, Melrose, Journeymen, and St. Bride's at Douglas. Ultimately, 33 lodges were present at its inception, although it is unclear as to how many of these actually received or acknowledged the invitation.

56 Kahler, "The Grand Lodge of Scotland," 95. See also Amelia H. Stirling, A Sketch of Scottish Industrial and Social History (London, 1906), 40–41.

57 No. 1(3) Aberdeen Lodge Minutes, 7 July 1737.

58 No. 3 Scoon & Perth Lodge Minutes, 8 December 1740.

Journeymen Lodge in Edinburgh, which regularly attended Grand Lodge meetings, documented its first mention of the Grand Lodge on December 27, 1743. Alluding to subscription fees and general dues, the lodge stipulated that "for this day and the like to be Continued for the future that each member shall bear and pay an equall proportion of the whole Expenses of this days entertainment whether they be present or absent and also an equall proportion of the Charges of the Grand Lodge."[59]

With the exception of No. 3 Scoon & Perth, these lodges were operative, a fact which may support Seggie's conclusion that jealousies were "rife amongst the old Operative Lodges."[60] Initially, at the founding of the Grand Lodge, precedence was determined by the order in which the representatives of the 33 lodges in attendance entered the hall.[61] Whereas this question of primacy was not particularly significant to the Grand Lodge of England, it was of paramount importance in Scotland.[62] Freemasons, especially operatives, intensely coveted their antiquity, and some even viewed the creation of the Grand Lodge and the emergence of speculative Freemasonry in earnest as the "death-blow given to the operative character of masonry in Scotland."[63] It is more likely, however, that the gradual waning of operative Freemasonry was due, in large part, to population increase and the rising importance of industry and trading. Indeed, Freemasonry gradually outgrew "the narrow machinery of government which had suited it so admirably two or three centuries earlier."[64]

Uncertainty ruled the events, as the initial ordering of the lodges based on the sequence of entrance was overturned one year later when the Grand

---

59   No. 8 Journeymen Lodge Minutes, 27 December 1743.

60   Seggie, *Journeymen Masons*, 46.

61   Lionel Vibert, "The Early Freemasonry of England and Scotland," *AQC* 43 (1930): 217.

62   Ibid. Referring to the founding four lodges of the Grand Lodge of England, Vibert notes that they "seem from the very commencement to have settled the order by which they were to stand; possibly they had traditions to go by ... In no single instance did a Lodge come forward and make claim to a higher place on the roll by reason of its having been in existence before its recognition," 217. Here again, as the Grand Lodge of England did not have the quandary of satisfying so many different types of lodges, the numbering process occurred without controversy.

63   William Hunter, *Incidents in the History of the Lodge Journeymen Masons, Edinburgh, No. 8* (Edinburgh, 1884), 63.

64   "The Grand Lodge," 114, quoting Harry Carr, *The Mason and the Burgh* (London, 1954), 62.

Lodge resolved that "all the Lodges ... should be enrolled according to their seniority, which should be determined from the authentic documents they produced, and in accordance with this principle."[65] This is significant as Mary's Chapel was a founding lodge of the Grand Lodge of Scotland. As it played such an important role in the creation of the Grand Lodge, Mary's Chapel was seemingly safe as the oldest lodge on the Grand Roll of Scotland. The questioning of the initial numbering further suggests an imbalance of power and the inability of the core group to enforce judgments and rulings. Ultimately, Mary's Chapel—having produced minutes extant from 1599—was designated as the oldest lodge in Scotland and Lodge Kilwinning, having supplied records from 1643, was relegated to number two.

Not satisfied with its ranking, Kilwinning objected on the grounds that the Grand Lodge had failed to examine all the pertinent evidence attesting to its precedence.[66] Kilwinning's claims were based on the assertion that it existed at the erection of Kilwinning Abbey in c.1140, and partly on the First Schaw Statutes, issued on December 28, 1598 by William Schaw, Master of Works for King James VI. These regulations established a system of lodges, regulated the trade and working practices of masons, and provided for the election of lodge officials. In no uncertain terms, the statutes command obedience to "the hale auld antient actis and statutes maid of befoir be ye predicessrs of ye maisonis of Kilwynning."[67] Consequently, Kilwinning resumed its independence from the Grand Lodge of Scotland. In doing so, it continued the practice of granting charters to new lodges irrespective of the Grand Lodge's disapproval which was, according to Gould, "inconsistent ... with its profession of adhesion to the new regime."[68] In 1806, the Grand Lodge of Scotland entered into negotiations with Kilwinning Lodge in an effort to resolve the long-standing dispute over lodge precedence on the Grand Roll of Scotland. Although Kilwinning renounced its right to grant charters, it was re-styled No. 0 Mother Kilwinning Lodge and placed at the head of the Grand Roll.

---

65   Gould, *Concise History*, 276.

66   See Lyon, *Mary's Chapel*, 260–265.

67   David Stevenson, *Origins*, 34–44.

68   Gould, *History of Freemasonry Vol. 2*, 313. Kilwinning's refusal to surrender its charter-granting privileges and acknowledge the authority of the Grand Lodge occurred in 1744.

Mary's Chapel, although still No. 1 on the Grand Roll, was second behind No. 0 Mother Kilwinning and the Grand Lodge of Scotland now was the only Masonic body in Scotland with the power to create new lodges. Dissatisfied with the outcome of the dispute, Mary's Chapel agitated for the reform of the system of precedence as well as the entire organizational structure of the Grand Lodge. As will be shown, the issue of seniority would become an even more acrimonious and volatile subject in the early-nineteenth century, ultimately contributing to the Masonic Secession of 1808.

The final incident during this period which clearly illustrates the disorganization of the early Grand Lodge involved No. 14 St. John Lodge in Maybole.[69] A query sent from No. 14 to the Grand Lodge of Scotland on January 12, 1737 posed several questions regarding entrance fees, the regulation of wages and, most importantly, proper discipline for improper conduct. The members expressed their concerns over such "irregular brethren as belong to no particular Lodge, yet meet in private and enter Masons at such low rates and in such irregular methods as is a scandal to be mentioned among Masons" and "through want of due direction both act and speak unmannerly in public and private meetings."[70] The term "irregular," as used by No. 14, refers to those masons who were admitted to a lodge that was not registered on the Grand Roll and practiced Freemasonry without the consent or authority of the Grand Lodge. Clark notes, "a serious constraint on Modern lodges and their membership policies was competition ... from irregular lodges,"[71] which were essentially illegal and may have charged lower admission and subscription fees. According to Lyon, these items "were never reported upon by the committee to whom they were remitted."[72]

The communication is significant because it deals with several key issues that closely mirror the events directly responsible for the Maybole Trial of Sedition in 1800. First, in 1797, Lodge Maybole accused No. 264 Royal Arch Maybole of sedition, namely for admitting irregular masons and allowing them to conduct illicit meetings. Consequently, two nascent

---

69   St. John Maybole is now No. 11 on the Grand Roll of Scotland.

70   Lyon, *Mary's Chapel*, 192.

71   Clark, *British Clubs*, 325.

72   Ibid.

degrees of Freemasonry—Royal Arch and Knights Templar—appeared in Maybole in the 1790s and at the time were not sanctioned as official and recognized Masonic degrees.[73] Secondly, the Grand Lodge largely ignored the concerns of Lodge Maybole and the members of the Royal Arch and Knights Templar lodges continued their illegal meetings.

Early Development of Scottish Lodges

Despite the problems of lodge diversity and the inevitable resistance to such a sudden and extensive transformation, Kahler asserts that the Grand Lodge of Scotland was the "catalyst in the transition of the Scottish lodges" from operative to speculative masonry.[74] Although the advent of a Grand Lodge system in Britain did facilitate growth and change, Masonic development in Scotland was somewhat more gradual and conservative than in England.[75] In England, where Freemasonry was almost entirely speculative, being a member of a lodge was fashionable and thus lent itself to continual Masonic expansion. And the English Grand Lodge effectively promoted the society, as illustrated from the increasing number of lodges. By 1740, London alone contained 113 lodges, compared with only six in Edinburgh. All told, by 1740 English lodges numbered 168, while Scotland had 64.[76]

Despite such initial disparities in numbers, Scottish lodges were chartered with increasing speed and apparent enthusiasm for the association. Closer examination of the data reveals that by 1766, the Grand Lodge of Scotland had chartered or sanctioned the formation of 176 lodges.[77] After

---

73 Lodge Royal Arch Maybole is now No. 198 on the Grand Roll of Scotland.

74 Kahler, "The Grand Lodge of Scotland," 112–114.

75 Stevenson explains that the English "did not, of course, passively adopt Scottish masonry wholesale. Though they adopted so many Scottish practices they began immediately to adapt them to suit their own needs. Here the fact that most English freemasons had no connection with the operative craft became highly important ... rituals were based on Scottish practices, but they were soon elaborated and altered. The Scottish two degrees were extended to three, perhaps hastening and completing an evolutionary practice begun in Scotland," *Origins*, 231.

76 See Clark, *British Clubs*, 309–317 for a detailed analysis of English lodges. For a listing of Scottish lodges, their inception dates and locations, see Grand Lodge of Scotland, *Chartulary and List of Lodges and Members: 1736–1799* (Edinburgh, 1736–1799), 1–6.

77 Lodge totals reflect military lodges, dormant lodges, amalgamations, and lodges chartered by Kilwinning.

the same period of approximately 30 years in existence, Scottish lodges were more numerous than those in England.[78]

The expansion of Scottish lodges can be attributed to the important presence of operative and the gradual development of speculative Freemasonry. Despite such growth, a problem contributing to the relative isolation of lodges and lack of Masonic communication was the paucity of promotion through the newly established Grand Lodge. Clark writes that the underlying themes of Masonic literature were "improvement and enlightenment, with a stress on merit as the measure of men, education, and the joys of fraternal association; in sum a utopian world detached from political, religious or ascribed social status."[79] Although the Grand Lodge of England was particularly successful in its marketing and endorsement of such themes, George Draffen argues that "Scotland seems to have been singularly unsuccessful in attempts at Masonic journalism," making only "fourteen attempts to produce a Masonic periodical since the year 1797."[80]

As Clark asserts, English Masonic literature was an effective means of education for freemasons, serving as a conduit for such Enlightenment ideas as self-improvement and education. Yet in Scotland, this same process was lacking, even though it has been claimed by Kahler that Scottish freemasons were teaching and receiving such themes.[81] Given the pronounced emphasis of the founding lodges on facilitating the triumphant re-emergence of Scottish Freemasonry as a respected association, it is ironic that they had no plan to effectively implement and achieve this objective.

As the number of lodges and masons multiplied and flourished, a new, problematic issue presented itself. Encouragement of the formation of speculative lodges through the prompt issuance of charters inevitably meant sources of competition to already-established operative in-

---

78 Grand Lodge of Scotland, *Consolidated List*, 1–6. See John Money, "Freemasonry and Loyalism in England," 255–260 for a description of the growth rate of Freemasonry in England during the eighteenth century.

79 Clark, *British Clubs*, 335–336.

80 George Draffen, "Scottish Masonic Periodicals," *AQC* 92 (1979): 191–198.

81 Kahler argues that "while the surviving minutes [of Scottish lodges] give no indication that the [Newtonian and Enlightenment] ideas Jacob discusses were also being debated in the Edinburgh lodges, it is well documented that Newtonian ideas had been taught in Scotland from the 1680s" and thus "it is plausible that Scottish masons were also being influenced by new ideas spread by visitors from outside Scotland. It is also plausible that they were spreading their own ideas to visitors as well," 114.

stitutions. The arrival of speculative masonry would also have enticed non-stonemason members, as they would have more influence and status than in an exclusively operative lodge. To protect their interests and effectively ensure their continual dominance within the lodge, operative masons sometimes limited the number of non-operative admissions and restricted their participation in lodge affairs. As English freemasons had no natural connection with the operative roots of masonry, "they were not hampered in developing the craft by the conservative insistence of operative masons on sticking to traditional practices" and thus "were free to remodel masonry as they wished."[82] In Scotland, however, belonging to an operative lodge was necessary for employment and facilitated economic solidarity among its members. Operative lodges also legislated for journeymen masons, or itinerant masons who travelled from place to place in search of labor. Beginning in 1737, No. 25 Lodge St. Andrew made provisions to exact immediate payment from any "jurneman that is imployed out of the loge in the amount of one shilen Scotts money."[83] Admission to the lodge was granted to the journeyman only after the lodge gave the "first offer [of employment] to the members of the said Loge" and the journeymen made payment of one shilling.[84]

The creation of a Grand Lodge and the introduction of a new era of Freemasonry relying almost entirely on symbolic representation of the stonemason craft initiated a growing awareness among operative masons of the imminent changes to the structure and nature of the fraternity. Consequently, lodge policies were amended to safeguard their status. For example, the Master of No. 6 Old Inverness St. John's Kilwinning observed that

> all or most of the operative Brethren were either working in the Country or employed in the publick Worke at the Point of Ardeneir, and for that Reason, he thought it unnecessary to Conveen the few Geometrical Brethren who live in the Burgh, as no Business could be conducted or Settled in the absence of the operative Brethren, and more particularly that he thought it a hardship that any of them should be called from their Work at any Time.[85]

---

82 Ibid., 231.

83 No. 25 Lodge St. Andrew Minutes, December 28, 1737.

84 Ibid.

85 No. 6 Old Inverness St. John's Kilwinning Lodge Minutes, November 1, 1752.

As the majority of operative records were concerned with the regulation of work and trade, any business was strictly handled by the operative members. Speculative—or in the case of No. 6 Inverness, Geometrical—masons were excluded from business decisions for practical reasons because they were untrained as stonemasons. This entry also clearly illustrates that the employment and welfare of operatives took precedence over lodge meetings, as well as over the discussion of lodge affairs. In addition to the well-being of the members, this November minute entry accounts for seasonal travel and the convenience of the operative members. The survival of the lodge depended on the success of the operative masons in securing employment, the admission of new members to the lodge, and the subsequent collection of entry fees and dues; the influence and impact of the few Geometrical members in the lodge were negligible. By deferring the discussion of lodge business, the lodge was essentially protecting the authority of its operative members.

Occasionally, the division between old and new unified working stonemasons against the perceived corrosive influence of speculative freemasons. No. 8 Journeymen Lodge in Edinburgh, for example, stipulated in its constitution that the lodge should contain no more than 11 non-operative masons at any one time. Exceeding this number threatened the stability of the lodge and created a certain apprehension over the possible diminution of operative authority and control.[86] The actions of No. 8 Journeymen Lodge coincide with David Stevenson's claim that "the stonemason majority of lodge members might fluctuate between pride that others ... wanted to join their organization and were willing to pay fees for the privilege" and "disillusionment at finding that admitting new types of members was changing the character of the lodge and that there was a danger that the newcomers might take over control of it."[87] In an entry dated November 10, 1763, the lodge in no uncertain terms expressed its skepticism over the admission of too many non-operative masons:

> The Lodge having taken under their consideration the present state they are now in with respect to their Constitution as an Operative Lodge, They find that through inadvertency of their managers there are now about fifteen non operatives received into their community

---

86 Stevenson, *Origins*, 197.
87 Ibid.

tho by the Rules of the Lodge they ought not to exceed eleven. Beside that there are severall non operatives who have enter'd and allowed themselves to be scored out by running Three years in arrear of Quarterage. And That by an act in the Books members may again Claim to be received although scored out upon payment of a small donation and by gone Quarters and Absences. Therefore they being Apprehensive of the prevailing power of the Non Operatives a Danger they Cannot too Cautiously avoid Considering how many Operative Lodges have been overwhelm'd by that Faction, Did and hereby Do Statute and Ordain that non operatives shall not be received in to this Lodge Untill that number already received be reduced below Eleven and that all and every member whether Operative or Non Operative that are presently resting three full years Quarter accounts are hereby declared scored out and deprived of all priviledges as a member and never again to be received upon any condition whatever.[88]

By the end of the eighteenth century, it was clear that No. 8 was intent on maintaining operative dominance in all lodge affairs. On December 20, 1787, the members "agreed to receive unoperative members as Master Masons on them paying each one pound five shillings sterling but to have no vote nor Benefits from this Lodge."[89]

Notwithstanding individual lodge regulations, further efforts were made to accommodate operative Freemasonry. The Grand Lodge of Scotland, from 1739 to 1740, instigated four new policies affecting operative ma-

---

88 No. 8 Journeymen Lodge Minutes, November 10, 1763. The full provision in the Lodge Constitution states that "in all time coming There should not be admitted above Eleven persons in all into the numbers of the lodge that are not Operative Masons, but have agreed that when those eleven are made up on the Lodge, and when any of their number dyes or goes our of the Lodge, It shall be in the power of the Lodge to make up the forsaid number by one or more But not to acceed the number now agreed on. And any of those to be admitted for the future are to bring in a Petition to the Lodge at their private meeting and the same to be approven of by the whole Lodge before any such person shall be entered that is not an Operative, and it is also agreed upon that none of those eleven shall carry any publick office in the Lodge," 6 November 1753.

89 Ibid., 30 December 1787.

sons which included offering patronage to the son of a stonemason; lowering the cost of admission fees for operatives; purchasing a set of stonemason tools; and deciding that the "masters of the Lodge of Edinburgh and the Journeymen, along with an additional master from another lodge, were to serve as examiners for ... visiting members as are Strangers to the Grand Lodge and who are desirous to attend' the meetings."[90] Special dispensations were also made for operative masons on the annual St. Andrew's Day Festival. Tickets for the festival cost two shillings, but operatives were only required to pay half the sum, or one shilling.[91]

The Grand Lodge was also instrumental in setting up a hospital for operative masons during the construction of the Royal Infirmary in Edinburgh. The hospital, or "masons Cell," was a room appropriated "in the Hospitall for the Reception of one or more infirme Masons ... into which Cell all Masons belonging to such Lodges as have acknowledged the Grand Lodge, are to be without definition receiv'd."[92] Admission into the Cell was conditional on acknowledgement of the Grand Lodge, again illustrating not only the territoriality of operative masons, but the early designs of the Grand Lodge to control the operative element. However, the financial strain of the hospital proved too much of a burden, as construction of the Cell had "been put off from time to time," principally due to the lack of support for the project.[93] By 1750, the mason's cell was discontinued.

According to Kahler, the implementation of these policies and the concerted effort to accommodate the stonemasons suggests that the Grand Lodge "recognized the existence of operative lodges and was keen to attract them, and keep them, in the Masonic community. It also indicates that Grand Lodge recognized the operative roots of the organization, and was willing to acknowledge these origins."[94] Despite such attempts to protect the interests of operative masons, the excerpt from the minute books of No. 8 Journeymen Lodge regulating the number of speculative entrants underscores the assertions by historians that the creation of the Grand Lodge and the ushering in of speculative masonry

---

90 Kahler, "Grand Lodge of Scotland," 108.
91 Grand Lodge of Scotland Minutes, November 15, 1749. This practice continued throughout the eighteenth century.
92 No. 1(3) Aberdeen Lodge Minutes, July 17, 1737.
93 Ibid., November 30, 1750.
94 Ibid.

were, indeed, the "death-blow" given to operative Freemasonry.[95] Some lodges charged higher entry fees for non-operatives, further magnifying an over-arching sense of operative individualism,[96] while others, according to Stevenson, "seem to have experimented with allowing gentlemen into their lodges, not liked the long-term results, and therefore excluded them."[97]

Operative lodges, for example No. 1 Mary's Chapel, No. 1(3) Aberdeen, No. 6 Inverness, and No. 25 St. Andrew—at least until the 1750s—rarely recorded non-operative admissions. The majority of entered apprentices were stonemasons, wrights, baxters, merchants, and deacons from other incorporations.[98] One finds occasional references to servants, but none were employed in poor trades such as "peddling or hawking,"[99] as lodges discouraged such activities. A fine example is recorded in the minutes of No. 1(3) Aberdeen Lodge, when the "Right Worshipful Master Reported that he had Reprimanded John Aikenhead mason for begging and horning In town and had threatened him with imprisonment But that he had promised to behave for the future."[100] Musicians were intermittently admitted as members, although as Clark notes they served as "prime sponsors of lodge sociability."[101]

By 1740, however, evidence suggests that operative lodges were aware of the financial boons accorded with the arrival of speculative members.

---

95 Hunter, *Journeymen Masons*, 63.

96 See G. W. Speth, "Scottish Freemasonry Before the Era of Grand Lodges," AQC 1 (1886–1888): 191. Speth writes that "In many cases the gentlemen paid higher initiation and office fees. A very unusual name for them was Geomatics, whilst the masons by trade were called Domatics. The Geomatics were also known as Gentlemen masons, Theoretical masons, Architect masons, and Honorary members. There was always a sharp distinction drawn between these and masons by trade, which so far does not appear to have obtained in England."

97 Stevenson, *Origins*, 216.

98 No. 1 Mary's Chapel Lodge Minutes, November 24, 1740.

99 Clark, *British Clubs*, 321.

100 No. 1(3) Aberdeen Lodge Minutes, September 1, 1755.

101 Clark, *British Clubs*, 321. On September 23, 1740, No. 1 Mary's Chapel recorded that "upon application to them by John Palma musician, he was admitted and reased ane entered apprentice gratis for the benefit of his musick to the Lodge which he promised and engaged to perform att all their meetings in tyme coming during his residence in this city without other fee or reward and also to pay the ordinary dues for the use of the entered and Grand Lodge."

No longer comprised solely of operative members, membership lists included mathematicians, ministers, surgeons, and students. One lodge even recorded the admission of a "teacher of dancing."[102] As professional representation became increasingly important, the rise of "gentle recruitment"[103] was embraced by numerous lodges, although some were more successful than others in attracting patronage in order to raise the "social threshold of membership."[104] No. 25 St. Andrew, for example, realized the benefits of admitting gentlemen into the lodge. On December 10, 1767, the members

> having taken into their Serious Consideration the present state of the Lodge, found it to be in Such Condition that it is but few Members that is fitt for Carrying the Office of Master. Not for Those in capacity of Being good Measons but Want of ability and Interest to promot the Prosperity of the Lodge Which is there Chief End. And for Which they are willing to Dispence with any Gentleman in this Neighbourhood that is Properlie Tallied And Adopted As Ane Incorporate Member of Said Lodge.[105]

The minute further states that gentlemen shall be entitled to all of the benefits of operatives. Although initially charged higher entrance fees, a stipulation made December 12, 1797 set identical admission fees for gentlemen and operatives, stating "no difference should be made in future of the dues to be paid by Brethren at their entries, whether they be mechanical men or not, but that they all should pay the same, namely one pound one shilling sterling."[106]

As stonemasonry began to decline toward the end of the eighteenth century, operative lodges such as St. Andrew began to rely more and more on non-operatives not only for financial support, but also to increase lodge membership. These trends support Stevenson's observation that the admission of gentlemen masons was a direct result from either "changes in policy within the lodge or changes in attitudes of non-operatives to

---

102 No. 25 Lodge St. Andrew Minutes, January 10, 1783.

103 Clark, *British Clubs*, 321.

104 Ibid., 324.

105 No. 25 Lodge St. Andrew Minutes, December 10, 1767.

106 Ibid., December 2, 1797.

the lodges."[107] The attitude of non-operatives to new speculative lodges is one which reflected a strong devotion to the belief that "freemasonry ha[d] always claimed to have grown out of the practices and beliefs of stonemasons."[108]

Though the Grand Lodge was purportedly created to facilitate the union of Scottish lodges while simultaneously allowing operative and speculative masons to retain and promote individual customs, it did not immediately achieve this harmonious merger, as operatives continued to harbor feelings of resentment toward non-operatives. Notably, these sentiments did not exist before the establishment of the Grand Lodge, suggesting that only after the creation of a centralized Masonic government which endorsed speculative masonry and attempted to accommodate the remaining operative masons did such attitudes of suspicion and distrust begin in earnest. Indeed, lodges involved in the founding of the Grand Lodge of Scotland—for instance No. 1 Mary's Chapel—emphasized their operative roots and prohibited non-operatives from taking part in the election of lodge officers. In a minute dated December 24, 1753, several members

> protested for themselves ... In regard [that] as the lodge being constitutionally an Operative Lodge, and uniformity in use to be represented by an Operative Brother, they judg'd in departing from their Constitution to Elect an Honorary Member however worthy unto that office, and thereupon they left this meeting and declined to Concur in any further proceedings ... as this [No. 1 Mary's Chapel] Lodge is the most Ancient Lodge upon the Rolls of the Grand Lodge, and by their records appears to be originally and Constitutionally an operative Lodge, Strictly connected with the operative Brethren of the Craft, [the lodge] thought it was most agreeable to the Spirit and Constitution of this Lodge To have all due regard In Electing their master and officers to the Worthy Operative Brethren.[109]

---

107 Stevenson, *Origins*, 197.

108 Ibid., 216.

109 No. 1 Mary's Chapel Lodge Minutes, January 17, 1754.

The new Masonic community which began in Edinburgh and "quickly widened to include other Scottish lodges, lodges in London and in England, and foreign lodges,"[110] in fact was a slowly developing phenomenon. Although visitations occurred, frequently the delegations were from lodges in relatively close proximity to one another. For example, No. 6 Old Inverness did not receive a deputation from a lodge other than the Grand Lodge of Scotland and No. 43 Fort William until 1758.[111] Other operative lodges followed similar patterns. No. 8 Journeymen in Edinburgh regularly received visitations from other Edinburgh lodges such as Mary's Chapel, Canongate Kilwinning, Canongate and Leith, Leith and Canongate, St James, and New Edinburgh Kilwinning. Only in 1793 did a reference to a lodge outside Edinburgh—No. 13 Torpichen Kilwinning of Bathgate—appear in the minutes.[112] As Kahler argues, speculative lodges may have been "more receptive to the idea of a Masonic community in which lodges from other locations visited one another," as opposed to operatives, which "were still mired in the traditional idea of the lodge as an autonomous entity."[113]

The differences between operatives and speculatives also manifest varying motivations among Scottish and English freemasons for joining a lodge. The reasons for becoming a member of a particular club or society, whether Masonic or otherwise, were as numerous and varied as the individuals and personalities comprising their membership: general fellowship and drinking, political and religious discussion, taking part in sports, and social and national improvement.[114] Clark argues that eighteenth-century British clubs and societies attempted to erase class and social boundaries by creating an atmosphere characterized by diverse eco-

---

110 Kahler, "The Grand Lodge of Scotland," 112–114.

111 No. 6 Inverness Lodge Minutes, December 27, 1758. The visiting lodge was No. 4 Glasgow Kilwinning.

112 No. 8 Journeymen Lodge Minutes, June 24, 1793. Evidence of gradually widening circles among operative lodges is evident in the minutes of No. 30 Stirling as well. Minutes record that a gentleman from South Carolina visiting on December 27, 1754. On February 18, 1758, "Masons from the Lodge of Dunfermline, Dundee, and St. Giles Edinburgh matriculated at Stirling." The first mention of a lodge outside of Scotland was not until March 10, 1809, when a Peter King of No. 483 Lodge of Ireland was admitted as a member to the lodge.

113 Kahler, "Grand Lodge of Scotland," 108.

114 See Corey Andrews, "Club Life and Convivial Society in Mid-eighteenth Century Edinburgh," *Social History of Alcohol and Drugs* 22 (2007): 68, for the importance of drinking and alcohol in clubs and societies.

nomic and occupational backgrounds. However, Broadie maintains that eighteenth-century societies were predominantly male, as women were not among the "first rank of contributors."[115] And Freemasonry was no exception, although the brotherhood was ostensibly open to "all creeds and classes."[116] In banning women, the "lodge licensed itself as another all-men's drinking club."[117] Indeed, this assortment of backgrounds, motivations, and interests is what Clark acknowledges as "one of the distinctive features of British associational life."[118]

Despite such varying motivations and backgrounds, Margaret Jacob writes that "the reforming and utopian tendencies within eighteenth-century British Freemasonry generally never obscured the more typical and widespread masonic dedication to harmony, moderation, conviviality, and social cohesion within the lodge."[119] In London, English Masonic publicists emphasized "the ritualistic and fraternal aspects of food, drink, and song," which occupied "a central place in every masonic evening."[120] Clark echoes these assertions, noting that "lodges were, of course, major arenas of male conviviality and heavy drinking."[121] This English context also highlights other social aspects of Freemasonry, where "business contacts and applied mathematics, not to mention good food, drink and song, became the stuff of social cohesion, and to this combination of esoteric philosophy, merry-making and useful practice one can easily see why devotees of the new science ... were drawn in increasingly large numbers."[122] Eighteenth-century English Freemasonry blended these elements to create a balanced environment which provided both

---

115 Broadie, *Scottish Enlightenment*, 29.

116 Marie Mulvey-Roberts, "Hogarth on the Square: Framing the Freemasons," *British Journal for Eighteenth-Century Studies* 26 (2003): 251–252.

117 Ibid. Clark also states that "British freemasonry, like most eighteenth–century societies, was exclusively male," *British Clubs*, 320. See also James Van Horn Melton, *Rise of the Public*, 258–259.

118 Ibid., 1–25. Also see Bullock, *Revolutionary Brotherhood*, 9–10; James Van Horn Melton, *Rise of the Public*, 254; See Roberts, *Mythology*, 26. Roberts writes that "in joining lodges ... the freemasons were only doing what many other men of their time were doing: the early eighteenth century was a great age for the formation of small assemblies and clubs for social enjoyment."

119 Jacob, *Living the Enlightenment*, 65.

120 Ibid., 67.

121 Clark, *British Clubs*, 325.

122 Jacob, *Radical Enlightenment*, 109.

an intellectual and group setting where freemasons "expressed new ways of organizing and thinking about the nature of society" and provided a "powerful language for the changing ideas of the Enlightenment."[123]

Margaret Jacob suggests that eighteenth-century Freemasonry was also appealing because of its apparent contact with a "universal and ancient wisdom made manifest in the mathematical and architectural skills displayed in those early artisan achievements."[124] Modern Freemasonry "looked backward as well as forward,"[125] and it was this "peculiar combination of modern science and ancient religion that ... lay at the heart of the new Masonic fraternity."[126] As David Stevenson explains, the "transformation from late Renaissance to early Enlightenment was an evolutionary one, the new values being linked to the old," as "alchemical and Hermetic quests gave way to 'modern' science and Newtonianism."[127]

Freemasons also embraced the Newtonian model of the universe, with its emphasis upon power and benevolence, the importance of "order, stability, and the rule of the law," and the "possibility of creating perfect harmony in human society."[128] Mary Ann Clawson gives a definition of Newtonian principles as it applied to early eighteenth-century Freemasonry:

> The Newtonian flavor of Masonic rhetoric, with its frequent references to God as the Universal Architect, has often been noted and Freemasonry seen as an institution permeated with the values of the early Enlightenment ... Reflection upon God's plan in the natural world could be used as a guide to God's plan for the moral world ... Especially, contemplation of the physical order could reveal the importance of social order and harmony.[129]

---

123 Bullock, *Revolutionary Brotherhood*, 35.

124 Jacob, *Radical Enlightenment*, 115.

125 Melton, *Rise of the Public*, 253.

126 Bullock, *Revolutionary Brotherhood*, 9.

127 Stevenson, *Origins*, 232.

128 Jacob, *Living the Enlightenment*, 57. Hyland also writes that "the term 'Newtonian' represents a view of nature as a universal system explicable in terms of mathematical reasoning, divinely created and ordered," *The Enlightenment. A Sourcebook and Reader* (London, 2003):38.

129 Clawson, *Constructing Brotherhood*, 65–73. See also Margaret Jacob, *The Newtonians and the English Revolution 1689–1720* (Ithaca, NY, 1976). Clawson's discussion of Newtonianism is confined to English Freemasonry; she ultimately concludes that

Clawson's utopian, idyllic definition coincides with Jacob's claim that modern Freemasonry owes a major debt to the Newtonian Enlightenment.[130] Its influence upon Scottish lodges, at least as specifically recorded in minute books, is negligible. Significantly absent are the "frequent references to God as the Universal Architect," as lodges begin to integrate such language well after 1700.[131] For example, it was only in 1740 that No. 6 Old Inverness used phrases such as "God as the Great Architect" and "God as the Grand Master" in its bye-laws, stating that it is the "bounded duty of all masons" to behave themselves, "especially whyle in the Lodge as in the sight of the Great Architect and Grand Master of the Universe."[132] Even words such as honor, harmony, benevolence, and order did not see widespread inclusion in lodge minutes until the late eighteenth century.

This disciplined, utopian world did, however, broadly reveal itself in the lodges through rituals, degrees, ceremonies, and the creation of a fictive family. The Masonic idea of brotherhood, claims Bullock, built upon and "powerfully expressed the ideas of the early Enlightenment, especially its order, simplicity, and social harmony."[133] To achieve and preserve stability within the lodge, freemasons elected a hierarchy of officers, collected entrance fees and dues to ensure sufficient funds, and established a fixed schedule of meetings.[134] In conjunction with the management and running of lodge affairs, codes of conduct and morality were also implemented by which freemasons might govern themselves. No. 1(3) Aberdeen, for example, prevented intoxicated members from entering meetings so that they would not "behave themselves indecently or turbulently so as to disturb the harmony of the Lodge."[135]

"the Grand Lodge of England was an organization dominated by this popular Newtonianism," *Constructing Brotherhood*, 65–66.

130 Jacob, *Radical Enlightenment*, 109. In particular, Jean Theophile Desaguliers was responsible for the dissemination of Newtonian ideas. See especially pages 122–126. See also William Weisberger, "J.T. Desaguliers: Newtonian Experimental Scientist," in *Freemasonry on Both Sides of the Atlantic*, 243–275.

131 Clawson, *Constructing Brotherhood*, 66.

132 No. 6 Inverness Lodge Minutes, March 25, 1740.

133 Bullock, *Revolutionary Brotherhood*, 26.

134 No. 1 Mary's Chapel Lodge Minutes, December 27, 1708; No. 3 Scoon & Perth Lodge Minutes, January 14, 1729; No. 8 Journeymen Lodge Minutes, November 1, 1709.

135 No. 1(3) Aberdeen Lodge Minutes, December 6, 1739. See No. 25 Lodge St. Andrew Minutes, December 28, 1737.

Lodges, however, were not always the ordered, harmonious milieu so often portrayed by historians. Though rules and regulations were put into place to prevent disputes, minutes record financial disagreements, arguments with business associates, quarrels with other lodges over the order of processions, and occasionally even physical conflicts. For example, No. 25 St. Andrew recorded the following incident on December 20, 1803:

> A complaint was brought against Brother John Weymss Sinor by Brother James Adamson for very rude and unbecoming usage at a meeting of the committee on the 6th current. When Brother Weymss in consequence of some altercation betwixt him and Brother Adamson respecting an extravagant charge made by Brother Weymss for recuping a few articels of houshold furniture that belonged to the late James Thomson lodge Tyler and for charging 7/6 of Kings duty which was not accounted for nor intimation thereof given by Brother Weymss to the excuse of the said Brother Weymss took Brother Adamson by the nose and twisted it with great violence.[136]

The majority of debates, though, were caused by financial problems within the lodge and the inconsistent attendance of members.[137] For instance, records from No. 3 Scoon & Perth frequently chronicled poor attendance and the consistent dwindling of lodge funds caused by the failure of members to pay entrance fees and dues.[138] Any disagreements, however, were largely internal and seldom made public, and disputes were also quickly settled by the lodges without interference from other Masonic bodies such as the Grand Lodge of Scotland. This was imperative, as any disruption could potentially jeopardize lodge stability and hinder its ability to provide—in the case of operative lodges—employment for its members.

---

136   No. 25 Lodge St. Andrew Minutes, December 20, 1803.

137   A major problem experienced by lodges in Scotland and England was recurring financial debt, exacerbated by the "high drop-out rate, poor attendance, and subscription arrears," Clark, *British Clubs*, 325.

138   No. 3 Scoon & Perth Lodge Minutes, June 2, 1729:"... the Members that are absent at this quarterly Meeting and the former on the third Day of March are to Give In their excuse next meeting quarterly or to be liable to the Masters Determination of their fine and otherways as the Master pleases." The lodge also recorded that on March 3, 1740, the members "Conveend with the Master the other members" and drew up a "Roll of the whole members of the Lodge in order to know who are deficient in their annual payments."

Rules and regulations often prevented conflict and were largely determined by lodge composition. The fact that most English lodges were speculative and embraced Newtonianism precluded the admission of operatives.[139] Although English freemasons "extolled the moral values enshrined in Masonic symbolism," they usually "had little or no interest in going slumming by actually associating with working men."[140] In general, they were concerned with the quest for order and harmony, social exclusivity, religious tradition, and placed great emphasis on "decorum and civility."[141]

Societies that emphasized manners and etiquette were influential and popular in early eighteenth-century England. In 1701, Sir Francis Grant published *A Brief Account Of The Nation, Rise, and Progress, of The Societies, For Reformation of Manners &c. In England and Ireland: With A Preface Exhorting to the Use of Such Societies In Scotland*, in which he alludes to several books cataloguing various societies of the same ilk. Yet the existence of such societies in Scotland appears negligible, as Grant states that it is his intention to "excite and encourage these in this Kingdom of Scotland, to imitate so laudable an example. And may it not be hoped, that the Wise and sober part, of the Nation, would promote so good a design, and encourage and assist any, who would enter into such societies for Reformation."[142]

As we have seen, however, operative lodges still existed in Scotland throughout the eighteenth century. Although they did legislate for attendance, general behavior, and the regulation of the mason trade to ensure the success of the lodge through the timely collection of fees and election of capable officers,[143] they did not address the need for "table manners, literally on forks, plates, and napkins."[144] Here again, the operative ele-

---

139 Jacob, *Radical Enlightenment*, 109. Jacob argues that "by the 1720s, the membership lists of various London lodges were heavily bourgeois, although many lodges did include, and indeed sought out, aristocratic leadership," 116.

140 Stevenson, *Origins*, 216.

141 Ibid.

142 Sir Francis Grant, *A Brief Account of the Nation, Rise, and Progress, of the Societies, for Reformation of Manners &c. in England and Ireland: With a Preface Exhorting to the Use of Such Societies in Scotland* (Edinburgh, 1701), 4–5.

143 Jacob, *Living the Enlightenment*, 67. See Stevenson, *Origins*, 208: "The main functions of the early Scottish lodges have already been discussed. They performed the rituals of initiation and identification ... Most of them attempted to regulate the operative mason trade to a great or lesser extent."

144 Ibid.

ment of many Scottish lodges influenced the inculcation of Newtonian and Enlightenment principles. Indeed, the Grand Lodge of England was influenced by Newtonianism and as it was created before widespread development of Freemasonry in that country, dissemination of such Enlightenment principles was more manageable.[145] According to Ferrone, "the Great Lodge of London, inaugurated in 1717, from its inception carried out this task quite well."[146]

Scottish lodges did possess individual constitutions or rules and regulations that addressed the particular needs of lodge members. Anderson's *Constitutions,* however, were rarely mentioned. For example, No. 3 Scoon & Perth recorded on September 2, 1735 that the lodge "Borrowed up a large quarto book Intitled the Constitutions of the free masons Dedicated to the Duke of Montague."[147] Although there was no immediate need for self-promotion or advertisement, "there was a need for standardization and up-dating if Freemasonry was to be a coherent product attractive to new—and socially superior—members."[148] However, as the Scottish Grand Lodge attempted to circulate and publicize such ideas to an operative-dominated society, it is not surprising that Newtonian ideas and Anderson's *Constitutions*—which were so popular among the speculative lodges in England—were not as prominent in Scotland.

Eighteenth-Century Scottish Lodges as Models for Improvement

Certainly, Scottish Freemasonry was similar and different to its English counterpart. As we have seen, each exhibited certain qualities, more specifically the encouragement of social harmony, unity, and of course conviviality. Contextualizing Freemasonry in terms of the wider evolution of associations in eighteenth-century Scotland reveals several parallels and differences between the pattern of Masonic activity and voluntarism in general. By way of introduction, McElroy provides the following definitions for the somewhat interchangeable and thus confusing terms of club, association, and society:

---

145 Clawson, *Constructing Brotherhood,* 65–66.

146 Vincenzo Ferrone, *The Intellectual Roots of the Italian Enlightenment. Newtonian Science, Religion, and Politics in the Early Eighteenth Century* (Atlantic Highlands, NJ, 1995), 74. See also Jacob, *Radical Enlightenment,* 111–137.

147 No. 3 Scoon & Perth Lodge Minutes, September 2, 1735.

148 Stevenson, *Origins,* 206.

... an association was usually a more businesslike affair than either a club or a society; and there was probably a further inclination to regard a society as being a slightly more sedate and purposeful organization than those which one familiarly referred to as a 'club' ... the clubs, literary and otherwise, generally met in taverns, and they were characterized by a convivial disregard for formality ... By way of contrast, most of the organizations which bore the title of 'society' or 'association' had a more sober purpose, a more businesslike procedure, and a more formal method of choosing candidates for admission.[149]

Eighteenth-century Scottish Freemasonry incorporated characteristics of all three. Although masons met in taverns and frequently engaged in convivial celebrations, they did promote the more "sedate and purposeful" endeavors of charity and philanthropy. And, as Clark has noted, such diversity allowed Freemasonry to ultimately become the largest and most influential association in the British world.[150]

As the intellectual capital of eighteenth-century Scotland, Edinburgh was certainly Smollet's hot-bed of genius. Clubs and societies began to flourish, and although men and women had widely different interests, a myriad of organizations accommodated most if not all leisure pursuits and provided social settings which facilitated intellectual stimulation and instruction. Freemasonry was no exception. From the 1740s, it began to emerge as a major facet of public life, and its impact as a federal organization was fully realized throughout the remainder of the eighteenth century. During the first half of the eighteenth century, however, even after the creation of the Grand Lodge of Scotland, most lodges were independent entities, many of these being operative. Each possessed its own system of rules and regulations, and speculative lodges and masons were—as some historians have argued—intruders among what was traditionally an operative organization. However, as McElroy astutely notes, "the title of an organization is not always a good description of its type and purpose,"[151]

---

149 Davis Dunbar McElroy, "The Literary Clubs and Societies of Eighteenth-Century Scotland, and their Influence on the Literary Productions of the Period from 1700 to 1800," PhD Thesis (Edinburgh, 1952), 8.

150 Clark, *British Clubs*, 319; 348.

151 McElroy, "Clubs and Societies," 10.

and classification largely hinges on the reason for which it was organized. Although it is convenient to assert that early lodges existed primarily to regulate the stonemason trade or simply reveal esoteric secrets to non-operatives, early eighteenth-century Scottish Freemasonry can generally be defined as an improvement society.

At this time, Scotland was "acutely aware of her 'backward' state and, prompted by pride and a desire to share in the good things of life, she resolved to 'improve' herself, and to bring herself abreast of the times by imitating and emulating her traditional enemy, the English."[152] As such, three characteristics manifested themselves during this era of heightened emphasis on self-development: the need for prosperity through improvement; acceptance of English societies as models for imitation; and the emergence of the voluntary association as a device for furthering these national aspirations and for promoting the wider acceptance of the English models.[153]

For instance, the Edinburgh Society for the Reformation of Manners was based on a similar society in London, and the Society in Scotland for the Propagation of Christian Knowledge mirrored the structure of the English Society for the Propagation of the Gospel. Much like these organizations, the creation of the Grand Lodge of Scotland was facilitated by the creation of the Grand Lodge of England. As we have seen, "the union and incorporation of the Scottish Lodges into one organized body was due rather to the influence which the erection and successful career of a kindred institution in England would naturally have upon its northern neighbours."[154] The term improvement, therefore, "was much more than an economic slogan, for it represented a national attitude of mind which recognized Scotland's true situation and embodied, in that recognition,

---

152 Ibid., 13–14.

153 Ibid., 15. See Clark, *British Clubs*, 86–87: "In the case of Ireland and Scottish masonry, the London grand lodge had a decisive effect on their evolution during the 1720s and 1730s, promoting the creation of similar central structures."

154 Lyon, *Mary's Chapel*, 181. Lyon further states that the influence was "rendered all the more potent by the fact that more than one Scottish noble had been called to preside in the Grand Lodge of England." Clark echoes this statement: "Whatever the background, there can be no question that after 1717 the London grand lodge performed a key role in promoting the advance and organization of English freemasonry, setting a pattern quickly copied in Ireland and Scotland through the establishment of their own grand lodges," *British Clubs*, 311.

the resolve to equal, if not to exceed, the accomplishments of her more prosperous and more productive neighbours."[155]

The inclusion of the term "improvement" in the title of clubs and societies and in mission statements also evinced this national attitude of cultural and economic advancement. A good example of one such society is The Honourable the Improvers in the Knowledge of Agriculture in Scotland, an organizational precursor of the agricultural revolution that would transform agrarian lifestyles and methods of farming throughout Scotland.[156] Another case in point is the Society for Promoting the Reading and Speaking of the English Language in Scotland, illustrated the preoccupation of literary Scots with the "problem of form, and that in reaching a solution to that problem they had resolve, as they had in other fields, to follow the English example."[157] And the Select Society, affirming its purpose, maintained that it strove for "the mutual improvement in the art of speaking of its members."[158]

The formation of the Grand Lodge of Scotland and the existence of numerous Scottish lodges reflect the all-purpose aspirations of cultural and societal development of the aforementioned societies and also exemplify what Davis McElroy has called "a deep desire among the Scottish people to improve their nation through voluntary co-operative effort."[159] Interestingly, as least for freemasons, such a noble aspiration was unwritten. Although English freemasons boasted the somewhat rambling and verbose *Constitutions*, freemasons in Scotland had no official set of constitutions until 1836. Repeated attempts, however, were made to establish a formal book of rules, although it never materialized. In 1740, the Grand Lodge ordered "7 copies of William Smith's Small Constitutions anent Masonry Unbound, for use by the Grand Lodge."[160] Apparently some collection of rules and regulations existed as of 1756, for the Grand Lodge resolved to inspect them "so far as they judge them either inexpedient or

---

155 McElroy, "Clubs and Societies," 23.
156 See T. C. Smout, *A History of the Scottish People, 1560–1830* (London, 1998), 271–281.
157 McElroy, "Clubs and Societies," 166.
158 Select Society. *Resolutions of the Select Society for the Encouragement of Arts, Sciences, Manufactures, and Agriculture* (Edinburgh, 1755), 2.
159 McElroy, "Clubs and Societies," 18.
160 Grand Lodge of Scotland Minutes, August 6, 1740.

defective, to propose Such Alterations or Additions As they judge may conduce to the Advantage of the Craft."[161] By 1762, a certified body of law was ordered to be compiled, though a minute on August 4, 1766 noted that the commission "ha[d] been hitherto neglected."[162]

Unlike other Scottish improvement societies, Scottish freemasons also possessed no mission statement. For example, the Society for the Reformation of Manners in Scotland (1701), a self-proclaimed paragon of moral rectitude, endeavored to rectify what it perceived as the "gross Ignorance, Atheism, Popery and Impiety wherewith the Highlands and Islands of Scotland abounded, which was chiefly owing to the poverty of the People, whereby they were rendered unable to get their Children instructed in the Principles of Religion and Virtue."[163]

Although this venture failed, the aspirations of its founders were not abandoned, and in 1709 the society was reorganized and renamed the Society in Scotland for Propagating Christian Knowledge. After a brief period of restructuring the new society, "who after diverse Conferences with the Undertakers, published Proposals for a Subscription, for propagating Christian Knowledge, not only in the Highland and Islands of Scotland but in foreign Parts, to which was annexed an Obligation, to be subscribed by such as were willing to promote such laudable work."[164] Essentially, its purpose was to "found schools 'where religion and virtue might be taught to young and old' in the shape of reading, writing, arithmetic, and religious instruction,'" in an effort to reform and improve—especially in the Highlands—Scottish culture.[165]

It was not until 1723 that a movement for national improvement embedded itself in the consciousness of the Scottish people, although by this time individual Masonic lodges had already taken an active interest in maintaining order and stability during meetings and the overall health and improvement of their members. Though not advertised as an improvement society, close examination of lodge rules and bye-laws re-

---

161 Ibid., November 30, 1756.

162 Ibid., 5 January 1762; August 4, 1766.

163 William Maitland, *The History of Edinburgh: From its Foundation to the Present Time* (Edinburgh, 1753), 471.

164 Ibid., 417–420.

165 Smout, *Scottish People*, 434.

veals the similarities among the masons and reformation societies. For instance, freemasons implemented systems of rules, fines, and penalties to maintain order within the lodge, especially during meetings. As indicated above, Scottish masons did legislate for general attendance and behavior, although several lodges established specific guidelines concerning the unruly conduct resulting from the consumption of too much alcohol. Journeymen Lodge No. 8 in Edinburgh asserted "if any member gets drunk and interrupts the Business of the Society by his Stupidness in not observing the regulations, he shall be liable to a fine of six pence ... and if after being rebuked in a civil manner he still pursist in making a noise, he shall be put out and not admitted that evening."[166]

Provisions were also established to prevent intoxicated members from entering the Lodge, as when the members of Aberdeen No. 1(3) set forth the following stipulation on December 6, 1739, unanimously agreeing that

> if any member of this Lodge shall come into the Same under Liquor or tho Sober behave themselves indecently or turbulently so as to disturb the harmony of the Lodge or Stop the business thereof, they shall subject to what fine the Lodge pleases to impose upon them and be instantly turned out of the Doors for that night, by the Stewards, or make such other Satisfaction as to the Lodge shall seem proper.[167]

Other lodges, such as Old Inverness St. John's Kilwinning No. 6, imposed obligatory fines of one shilling if "any Brother [come] into the Lodge drunk or taken with liquor" and expulsion from the Lodge "until he become sober."[168]

Rules and regulations, in addition to discouraging the excessive consumption of alcohol and considering the welfare of all members, were also established to deter members from engaging in other harmful or disruptive activities, just as early eighteenth-century interventionist societies attempted to control the proliferation of "prostitutes [and] disorderly houses."[169] Journeymen Lodge in Edinburgh maintained "if any member

---

166 No. 8 Journeymen Lodge Minutes, October 24, 1783.

167 No. 1(3) Aberdeen Lodge Minutes, December 6, 1739.

168 No. 6 Inverness Lodge Minutes, December 6, 1739.

169 Clark, *British Clubs*, 64.

lying badly, and his trouble found to be the consequence of the Venereal disorder, or quarrelling and fighting, or any other intemperance which tends to the destruction of the human frame, he shall receive no benefit from the Lodge and shall be excluded forever."[170] One lodge even prohibited debating or quarrelling, and ardently declared "none of the Members of this Lodge shall curse, swear or blaspheme the Holy name of God."[171] Individual improvement and emphasis on high moral suasion was a consistent theme for Masonic lodges throughout the entire eighteenth century, as No. 6 Inverness recorded on February 3, 1795 that "a number of the Brethren of this Lodge having some time ago Expressed a wish that there should be a Master Mason meeting held monthly for the purpose of Lecturing for the Improvement of the Brethren."[172]

Other Edinburgh clubs and societies established similar rules. The Easy Club, in the introduction to its *Journal*, stated "On ye second day of their Meeting after some deliberation it was Unanimously determined their Society should go under the name of the Easy Club designing thereby that their denomination should be a Check to all unruly and disturbing behaviour among their members."[173] In language comparable to the masons, the all-female Fair Intellectual-Club affirmed in its laws "That altho' different Principles and Politicks shall be no Hindrance to the Admission of Members into our Club ... none shall presume to urge these directly or indirectly in our Meetings on Pain of Censure."[174]

Stonemasons, Shipmasters, and Shoemakers

As Clark observes, "both public improvement and self-improvement were clearly vital strands in the social discourse of Hanoverian freemasonry."[175] Scottish lodges, through the implementation of various rules and regulations, created a social and familial setting characterized by harmony, conviviality, moderation, and camaraderie. Despite differenc-

---

170 No. 8 Journeymen Lodge Minutes, October 24, 1783.

171 No. 27 St. Mungo's Lodge Minutes, February 6, 1729.

172 No. 6 Inverness Lodge Minutes, February 3, 1795.

173 McElroy, "Clubs and Societies," 36. On the Easy Club, see Alexander M. Kinghorn and Alexander Law, eds., "The Journal of the Easy Club," in *The Works of Allan Ramsay* Vol. 6 (Edinburgh, 1945–74); Alexander Law, "Allan Ramsay and the Easy Club," *Scottish Literary Journal* 16 (1989): 18–40.

174 Ibid., 54.

175 Clark, *British Clubs*, 336.

es among operatives and speculatives and the apparent disorganization that typified the creation of the Grand Lodge of Scotland, Scottish Freemasonry was an influential improvement society for both its members and the community. In addition to policies that regulated the health and well-being of masons while attending lodges, members also contributed to the welfare and interest of the public. Along with public processions and a charity fund available to widows and orphans, operative masons were frequently involved in numerous building projects.[176]

Along with its diversity of activities, a key contributing factor to Freemasonry's success was its occupational diversity. Not limited to stonemasons, lodges were composed of men from many different backgrounds, attracting its rank and file from the upper, middle, and occasionally lower classes. The occupational returns for Ancient Dundee No. 47 illustrate the assortment of professions present within the lodge and the range of stratification, from shipmasters and shoemakers to writers and officers of the excise. Only two returns are recorded in Grand Lodge of Scotland's *Chartulary and List of Lodges and Members: 1736–1799*, an inconsistency that plagued most lodges in Scotland. Indeed, as Clark writes, "analysis of the membership is not without its problems. Occupational descriptions are a precarious source at the best of times; in this period their meaning is often fluid."[177] A brief examination of the recruitment patterns of Dundee No. 47 manifests several wider trends present among Scottish lodges.

Table 2.1 and Appendix 1 show the number of members and professions in 1745 and in 1770. A comparison of the two years shows that there is no significant attempt to recruit gentlemen masons among the ranks of the lodge, suggesting that classicism and the elitist bias of some Edinburgh lodges were not prevalent in Dundee. Professional representation was negligible, and despite the Masonic penchant for conviviality and celebratory events and the role of victuallers as "prime sponsors of lodge sociability,"[178] few if any are present. Tradesmen, however, are well-rep-

---

176 Margaret Jacob, referring to the Lodge in Dundee, notes that "by the 1730s the local masons are actively involved in promoting public works projects, contributing generously in 1739 to a fund for building a workhouse for beggars and other poor. In 1730 guildsmen and burgesses had joined in petitioning the magistrates to build a new prison, with a local mason promptly volunteering to take down the old one for a modest fee," *Enlightenment*, 41.

177 Clark, *British Clubs*, 320.

178 Clark, *British Clubs*, 321.

resented, and given Dundee's geographic location as a port-city, by 1770 seafaring members—including mariners and shipmasters—accounted for 31 percent of lodge composition. In 1745, the lodge recorded only one mason, and in 1770 no masons were listed.

Figures 2.1 and 2.2 provide a tangible representation of recruitment patterns within the Dundee lodge. Between 1745 and 1770, several interesting trends are apparent. Although the percentage of tradesmen declined by almost 20 percent, victualling and seafaring trades accounted for 33 percent of the overall membership. Significantly, no gentlemen were recorded in 1770 and professional trades declined from 13 to 6 percent.

Unlike the steady rise of gentlemen and landowners characterizing London lodges after 1768, the Dundee lodge exhibited a marked decrease of professionals and gentlemen.[179] Certainly, only a partial picture emerges as no data is available between 1745 and 1770. However, lodges frequently were tardy in their returns, and 1770 may well represent the combined membership data from 1746 to 1770. If this is indeed the case, No. 49 only admitted an average of 1.5 members over a 14-year span; the lodge itself was chartered in 1745, and the initial membership total was 16. Similar to Clark's analysis, few if any stonemasons were recorded among the Dundee lodge ranks, and the overall impression of the returns for No. 47 is that the majority of members belonged to the "middling and lesser trades," without the "shift towards the middle- and upper-classes over time, underlined by the decline of lesser trades."[180]

This assertion is supported by a comparison with recruitment patterns from the Ancients in England. From 1751 to 1755, the Ancients exhibited a small proportion of elite members and a high percentage (72.9) of major trades, comparable to the significant representation of tradesmen in the Dundee lodge. Allowing for the limited samples, the evidence suggests that provincial Scottish lodges were more akin to the trends present within the Ancients; the greater elitism present among Modern English lodges is reflected among some Scottish lodges, but only in Edinburgh. Indeed, such findings "raise general questions about the pace and extent of social and class segregation in [Scottish] society"[181] in the eighteenth century.

---

179 See Clark, *British Clubs*, 319–325 for a full analysis of eighteenth-century London and provincial English lodge occupational returns.

180 Ibid., 321.

181 Ibid., 323.

Conclusion

The upsurge of Masonic popularity and prominence during the mid-1700s closely parallels the cultural achievements of Scotland after 1740. Individual lodges ultimately contributed to the erection of the Grand Lodge of Scotland, and from this institution Scottish Freemasonry reached a level of prominence previously unseen. Such was the case with Scottish culture, especially in academics and arts. With David Hume, Adam Smith, Robert Burns, and Robert Adam among the nation's best and brightest minds, a new era of cultural and intellectual advancement was ushered in. Indeed, as moral reform societies and organizations diminished in importance, new elements of continuity in associational activity appeared and developed. Drawing upon "this concentration of intellectual greatness in so many different fields,"[182] the age of improvement gradually gave way to the age of advancement.

The academic and intellectual vigor produced new forums for discussion and debate, and Enlightenment sociability in the form of clubs, societies, and organizations became extremely popular. Among these societies were literary groups which, according to McElroy, existed as "organizations of learned men who combined for the purpose of exchanging ideas on any subject which was of interest to themselves, to the other members, or to mankind at large."[183] Other variations included scientific societies, philosophical and convivial clubs, and organizations concerned with horticulture and fishing. Whatever the interest, eighteenth-century clubs were composed of men from varying backgrounds, and an underlying and common consideration of form allowed men of the eighteenth century to meet "with mutual benefit, irrespective of their primary interests."[184] Many of the members of prominent and selective organizations, for example the Select Society and the Society of Belles Lettres, and the Newtonian Society, were also freemasons, raising pointed questions about the attraction of lodges and what they offered to the Scottish *literati*.[185]

---

182 Smout, *History*, 470.

183 McElroy, "Clubs and Societies," 1.

184 Ibid., 6.

185 See Belles Lettres Society, *Roll of the Members of the Belles Lettres Society* (Farmington Hills, 2005); On the Select Society, see Roger Emerson, "The Social Composition of Enlightenment Scotland: The Select Society of Edinburgh, 1754–1764," *Studies on Voltaire and the Eighteenth Century* 114 (1973): 291–329.

Although elite patronage surely added to the luster of the society, it is impossible not to suspect that the extraordinary development of Scottish Freemasonry was, in large part, due to the Grand Lodge of Scotland. Notwithstanding esthetic differences among operatives and speculative masons and various organizational difficulties experienced by the early federal system, the years 1740 until 1785 witnessed a remarkable period of Masonic growth and complexity. In addition to an ever-increasing geographical sphere of Grand Lodge influence, lodges acquired individual complexions and, in some cases, eccentricities. It is likely that the organization received motivation from the success of its English counterpart and gained a particular stimulus from the interest in clubs and societies. Regardless of the source of its inspiration, Freemasonry developed into a highly visible, highly influential society that impacted Scottish culture throughout the eighteenth century.

CHAPTER THREE

"Revival of the Grand Lodge": Enlightenment, Evolution, and Expansion

For most of the early eighteenth century, Scottish Freemasonry operated much as it had done before the creation of a Grand Lodge. This was made possible by the ambiguity of Grand Lodge powers and the long-established traditions of operative masons that were reluctant to adopt or accommodate speculative freemasonry. By 1740, however, the nature and complexion of the Grand Lodge began to change, and this transformation resulted in significant lodge growth and Masonic expansion. Some historians have asserted that the Grand Lodge impact on Scottish lodges between 1740 and 1790 was unimpressive. According to Gould, there were "few events to chronicle"[1] during this period, a fact that has led Stevenson to argue that the Grand Lodge was not paramount to the development of Scottish Freemasonry up until 1789:

> ... in the first place, while there existed a network of lodges there was no grand lodge supervising the movement, and after the decline and fall of the general wardens there was no other central authority presiding over the Masonic movement. But, without denying the importance of grand lodges in the spread and development of freemasonry, it is difficult to see the existence of a grand lodge as an essential of freemasonry ...[2]

Stevenson's assertions are valid in that they emphasize the survival and continuation of Scottish lodges for centuries without a Grand Lodge. Given, however, the cultural and social development of Enlightenment Scotland and the burgeoning interest in clubs and societies, the gradual demise of the stonemason trade, and the controversy surrounding secret societies during the 1790s, it is highly improbable that Scottish Freemasonry could have endured such change and upheaval without the guidance and powers of a Grand Lodge. Certainly, its relationship with the government fully prevented the indiscriminate inclusion of Freemasonry

---

1   See Gould, *History of Freemasonry Vol. 3*, 376–392, esp. 384–392.
2   Stevenson, *Origins*, 215.

under the original terms of the Secret Societies Act. Furthermore, the increasing number of lodges throughout the eighteenth century, geographical expansion, the organizational changes in the association, and the functioning of the Grand Charity all suggest that Scottish Freemasonry was immensely influenced by a centralized system of Masonic government.

From Great Loss to Revival

In 1736, four lodges gathered in Edinburgh to discuss the "great loss"[3] Freemasonry had suffered due to the non-existence of a Grand Lodge. By 1740, this attitude was replaced by feelings of optimism among Scottish freemasons; no longer concerned with loss, masons now spoke of the "revival of the Grand Lodge."[4] The years following its creation were fruitful, the product of the founding lodges' prediction of Masonic renewal: despite an initial period of stagnancy, lodge numbers increased dramatically after 1750, and they continued to grow well into the 1790s. By 1800, more than 300 lodges were functioning, with provincial lodges accounting for almost 76 percent of the aggregate numbers.

The increase in Masonic lodges was also accompanied by a general trend among masons to seek private premises for lodge meetings. Compared to the Grand Lodge's decision to build a Freemason's Hall, this pattern occurred quite early in the century. Of the lodges studied, those that chronicled the plans, preparation, and construction of new buildings were all operative: No. 1(3) Aberdeen, No. 3 Scoon & Perth, No. 6 Inverness, No. 8 Journeymen, and No. 30 Stirling. Each erected private lodges between 1750 and 1765, and though geographically spread across Scotland, the close proximity of the dates suggests that lodges began the transition to private premises at approximately the same time.

Until the construction of the private buildings, these lodges met in the houses of the various members. The Journeymen Lodge frequently complained of "the Inconveniency of their not having a proper place of their own to keep the Lodge in;"[5] consequently, their meetings were held in either the Kings Arms Tavern or the building occupied by Mary's Chapel. As such, the members unanimously agreed to take "the under story of their own Land in Hodge's Close on Black Friars Wynd presently pos-

---

3   Gould, *History of Freemasonry Vol. 3*, 243.
4   Grand Lodge of Scotland Minutes, May 21, 1740.
5   No. 8 Journeymen Lodge Minutes, December 27, 1752.

sess'd by Robert Clark their Tennant," who is to be "warn'd to remove against Whitsunday and His House to be fitted up after that Term for a Convenient Lodge for this Society to meet in for the future ... and that non be admitted to the Society but one of a trade or occupation different from Journeymen masons."[6]

No. 3 Scoon & Perth also recorded the details of its decision to purchase a building and renovate it. On December 15, 1760, "the Committee appointed for inspecting ... houses reported that they had inspected the Said houses" and they agreed "that the first flat above the Shops and brewseat will make a very handsome and Commodious Lodge and preparing Rooms the next of which is eight pounds Stirling, The Lodge is of opinion that it would Sink their Stock to purchase the Said flat."[7] Similarly, on December 27, 1767, No. 6 moved to have "a Lodge Erected and Built ... as such a Building would not only be a necessary and beneficial ornament, But contribute much to the increase of Masonry." No. 30 Stirling also bemoaned its itinerant state, as it met in the houses of its members. Discussing this issue on January 29, 1751, the lodge resolved to begin plans on a new lodge:

> being mett in the house of Brother Hicksons and having taken into Consideration that the said Lodge had hitherto got no proper Lodge or meeting place of their own, And it having been by some of the members present represented to them, That the Seven Incorporated trades of the Burgh of Stirling under the Direction of their Conveener Court, were about to erect a house or fabrick at the head of the nether Hospital Garden, Which house the Lodge thought would be very convenient and remote place for Holding their Lodge or meetings.[8]

Occasionally, lodges recorded the redecoration of its rooms. For example, No. 1(3) Aberdeen Lodge listed extensive restorations which were to occur, employing the talents of a local painter and utilizing many colors to esthetically improve the lodge:

---

6   Ibid. Roman Eagle Lodge, chartered on February 7, 1785, frequently met in Wall's Oyster Booth in Edinburgh. See Brian Cowan, *The Social Life of Coffee: The Emergence of the British Coffee House* (New Haven, CT, 2011), for more on the development and trajectory of associationalism and coffee houses.

7   No. 3 Scoon & Perth Lodge Minutes, December 15, 1760.

8   No. 30 Stirling Lodge Minutes, January 29, 1751.

> ... It was Unanimously Agreed to Paint the Chair...of a
> Stone Colour in Oil with Chacilite Base, to paint the Plas-
> ter of the Walls a Light bleu in Size, To paint the Archi-
> trave of a Syrean or Redish Marble Colour, The Frize a
> plain white, of the Cornish a Dove Colour all three in Oil,
> The East Window Pelasters Architrave of a white veined
> Marble, The Gallery of the Cartuses Mahogany Colour
> Architrave Frise and Cornish of Different Colours as the
> Painter thinks Neatest, The Doors Mahogany Colours.[9]

These developments point to a general upswing in expansion during the mid- to late-eighteenth century, as the small houses of members could not accommodate growing attendance. Accompanying this development was the Grand Lodge requirement that lodges remit specific information to be recorded in official registries, for example dates of charter trans-fers and lodge locations. Clark warns of the limitations associated with official lists, however, as they "may count lodges which were moribund, while omitting active lodges which had neglected to pay their dues to grand lodge."[10] Furthermore, high turnover rates were prevalent among lodges and warrants could be recycled, a practice which would be used during the turmoil created by the Secret Societies Act.[11] Notwithstanding such shortcomings, it is evident from Grand Lodge records that Scottish Freemasonry between the year 1740 and 1790 experienced a period of marked growth and development.

As Table 3.1 shows, overall totals increased by an average of 77 lodges during the three periods listed from 1736 until 1785. By 1800, the Grand Lodge of Scotland had chartered almost the same number of provincial lodges as the Modern Grand Lodge of England.[12] Although this average growth rate dropped to 24 percent by 1800, external factors, such as the French Revolution and government legislation, aimed at suppressing se-cret societies certainly affected lodge growth.

---

9   No. 1(3) Aberdeen Lodge Minutes, December 10, 1773.

10   Clark, *British Clubs*, 309.

11   See Chapter 4 for a discussion on the Secret Societies Act and charter-granting privi-leges. Also see Clark, *British Clubs*, 319, for further details on the limitations of lodge records and distribution.

12   Clark, *British Clubs*, 310. The number of Provincial Modern Lodges in 1800 stood at 263. For the remainder of the chapter, percentages of Scottish lodges will not include lodges abroad or those which are military in origin. Military lodges were often peripatet-ic, their records were incomplete, and frequently the lodges had no fixed meeting place.

Unlike English Freemasonry, however, the metropolitan impetus—at least from a numerical standpoint—was negligible. Clark's analysis of English lodges shows that by 1780, almost 35 percent of all Modern lodges were located in London; and, by 1807, lodges in London accounted for almost 50 percent of all Ancient lodges.[13] In comparison, only 7 percent of Scottish lodges were operating in Edinburgh by 1800, though the city had the second largest population in Scotland.[14] Figure 3.1 illustrates the disparity among lodge numbers in Edinburgh and provincial lodges; at the close of the century, colonial and military lodges surpassed those found in Edinburgh by a ratio of almost 3:1.

Social stratification may have contributed to the large numbers of lodges concentrated in other regions of Scotland. Lodge composition varied greatly from Edinburgh to other areas, and classicism and elite bias may have influenced lodge growth outside of the city. Also, operatives were still an integral part of many lodges, and it is highly possible that potential members who were stonemasons or tradesmen left Edinburgh in search of support from the middling and artisan groups in cities such as Dundee, Perth, and Inverness.

Just as the "diffusion of freemasonry was regionally based, so there was no automatic percolation down the [Scottish] urban hierarchy."[15] Similar to Edinburgh, other cities manifested the same pattern of high population concentrations but low Masonic lodge representation. For example, by 1800, only 18 lodges had been chartered in the city of Glasgow, and its population exceeded 83,000.[16] The operative centers of Dundee and Aberdeen represented a meagre 4 percent of lodges in Scotland. All said, by the beginning of the nineteenth century, the provincial capitals of Edinburgh, Glasgow, Dundee, and Aberdeen made up only 17 percent of the complete total of Scottish lodges.

Provincial Expansion

Despite the unimpressive urban numbers, provincial Britain and Scotland proved to be highly successful in establishing Masonic lodges and maintaining them throughout the eighteenth century. Though many clubs and

---

13 Ibid., 313.

14 Smout, *Scottish People*, 243.

15 Clark, *British Clubs*, 314.

16 Smout, *Scottish People*, 356.

societies enjoyed pronounced visibility and attracted much social attention, they often faded into obscurity within several years. During the early 1700s, societies and organizations were mostly concentrated in urban
areas such as London and Edinburgh. However, the British metropolitan
impetus "had a growing, if less direct, impact on provincial developments
in other areas," as groups—including the freemasons—migrated from
traditionally urban capitals to regional towns and cities.[17]

Such evolution and progress can be attributed to active recruitment from
artisans and the middle class. As shown by the analysis of Dundee No.
47, the lodge embraced a wide variety of occupations, although the majority of its members were either tradesmen or seafaring men. Stonemasons were poorly represented, corroborating Clark's assertion that the increased proclivity of British clubs and societies to recruit members from
artisans and middling social groups "stemmed in part from the declining
importance of older organizations like the gilds."[18] In Scotland and Britain, the elitist voluntary associations of the early 1700s no longer dominated the club scene. Ultimately, social needs, the locations of towns, and
the growing importance and role of artisans and tradesmen affected the
demographic and geographic division of Masonic lodges.

The distribution of Freemasonry "seems to have been affected both by
institutional and external factors."[19] According to Clark, two of the major
factors shaping lodge growth were the establishment of a Grand Lodge
system and the creation of Provincial Grand Lodges and Provincial Districts. By 1740, the Grand Lodge of Scotland recognized that the geographic distribution of old-established lodges and the inevitable establishment of new lodges required more than just a central governing body
in Edinburgh.[20] To properly collect dues and subscription fees, monitor Masonic activities, ensure proper operation of lodges, and maintain
communication and correspondence among its constituents, the Grand
Lodge created several Provincial Districts across Scotland.

---

17   Clark, *British Clubs*, 67.

18   Ibid., 83.

19   Ibid., 318.

20   See Haunch, "The Formation," 71. Haunch, referring to the Grand Lodge of England,
     notes that "entries in minutes in the later 1720s show the ever-widening sphere of
     influence of Grand Lodge: a letter from the Provincial Grand Lodge at Chester dated
     April 15, 1727 (the first note of such a body) expressing 'most Cheerful Obedience
     and Extensive Gratitude to our Superious in London and Westminster,'" Ibid.

Little is actually said in the Grand Lodge of Scotland minutes concerning the obligations of the Provincial Grand Masters. Macbean offers the following summary of duties:

> The Provincial Grand and District Grand Masters are appointed for a term of not more than five years, by commission from Grand Lodge—not by the Grand Master, as in England. They nominate their own Deputy And Substitute Masters, Wardens, Secretary, and Chaplain. The other offices are filled up by the Provincial Grand Lodge, so that you will observe the Provincial Grand Master can dispense more patronage than the supreme Grand Master himself. Certain of the officers, as in Grand Lodge, can only retain their position for two consecutive years.[21]

These roles and responsibilities were not so clearly delineated in 1738, when Anderson's *Constitutions* first mentioned the Provincial Grand Master. Nine years later, the Grand Lodge of England alluded to the office of Provincial Grand Master, although as one historian has noted his status was defined as that of the Deputy Grand Master, and "there is no mention of [the] Provincial Grand Lodge and its Officers at all. Grand Lodge did not apparently know or care whether these existed or not."[22] What is clear is that Provincial Grand Masters and Districts were found particularly necessary, due to "the extraordinary Increase of the *Craftsmen*, and their travelling into distant Parts, and convening themselves in Lodges."[23]

In 1739, the Scottish Grand Lodge recorded that it had granted a Provincial Commission to the "Worshipful Alexander Drummond Esq. present Master of the Lodge Entitled Greenock Kilwinning Impowering him to visit the Severall Lodges in the Countys therein mentioned who Acknowledge the Jurisdiction of the Grand Lodge," and "such Lodges as hereafter shall be regularly Constituted by Authority thereof as often as their regular meetings will admit at least once in the year with Select other

---

21   Edward Macbean, "Formation of the Grand Lodge of Scotland," *AQC* 3 (1890): 195.

22   W. Bathurst, "The Evolution of the English Provincial Grand Lodge," *AQC* 79 (1966): 216.

23   Ibid., 217. Also see Aubrey Newman, "The Contribution of the Provinces to the Development of English Freemasonry," *AQC* 117 (2004): 68–82.

powers in manner therein mentioned and Conform to Instruction given therewith."[24] Neither the counties nor the specific powers of Drummond are mentioned. However, a minute entry from May 21, 1740 verified that Drummond, referred to as the "Grand Provincial Master of the Western Lodges," had visited the lodges of Kirkintilloch and Kilsyth.[25] The only other District to be specifically named was the Stirling District. On February 6, 1745, the Grand Lodge of Scotland reported that it had received a letter from the Master of Stirling Lodge No. 30, stating that the members

> stood much in need of a Provincial Master for that part of the country not on account of any irregularities amongst them, But for want of due instruction in some parts convening the craft. Which being considered by the Grand Lodge They nominated and appointed their worshipful brother John Callender of Craigforth, Esq., To be Provincial Master of that District for the ensuing year and thereafter until another be named in his place for the said Lodge of Stirling and other Lodges in that county.[26]

The Provincial System existed in theory more than in practice. Aside from the Western and Stirling Districts, apparently no other territorial demarcations were created. And the geographical ambiguities were part and parcel of the vague notions surrounding the overall duties of the Provincial Grand Master. As such, the system was allowed to stumble along until 1747, when a concerted effort was made to clearly establish provincial boundaries and Grand Masters for each newly created territory. On August 5, 1747, the Grand Lodge proposed that "Lodges throughout the Kingdom should be classed into particular Districts or divisions and

---

24 Grand Lodge of Scotland Minutes, February 7, 1739.

25 Ibid., May 21, 1740. The minute states that as the lodges are "are generally all operative Brethren, and have but very Small funds for their poor, they are not in a Condition to pay the Regulation dues for new Constitutions being Two Guineas to the Grand Lodge ... Which being considered by them, They for the Ease and Encouragement of Operative Lodges in the Country Statute and Ordain That the Said two Lodges and others in their Circumstances shall apply for patents [and] in time coming shall only pay to the Grand Lodge the dues of Confirmations and Ratifications being half a Guinea each, and not as new Constitutions, And that the Clerk give them out accordingly in those Terms."

26 Ibid., February 6, 1745.

some particular person within such District or division who is a reale [il-legible] to the brotherhood be wrote to and [illegible] to advertise [these resolutions to] the members of the other lodges in their respective divisions."[27] Table 3.2 breaks down the 10 Masonic Districts as created by the Grand Lodge of Scotland.[28]

As of August 5, 1747, 82 lodges existed or had been chartered in Scotland, but only 59 are listed in various Districts. There are several possible explanations why 23 lodges were omitted from the initial classifications: two lodges were chartered by No. 0 Kilwinning and had not been officially recognized by the Grand Lodge;[29] 12 were unlocated, extinct, dormant, had no official charter, or had withdrawn from the Grand Lodge;[30] No. 1(2) Melrose remained independent until 1891, and thus was not included on the Grand Roll. The remaining seven lodges excluded seem to have been oversights. For example, it was reported in 1740 that Alexander Drummond had visited Kilsyth; this lodge, however, was not listed among the Districts.[31] Also, Clark's assertion that lodges which had failed to pay annual dues were struck from the Grand Roll may also account for the omissions.[32]

Much like the Provincial System of England, the indistinct notions of purpose and direction prevented the Scottish Provincial Districts from accomplishing its main goals of creating a network of inter-lodge communication and linking regional lodges more closely with the Grand Lodge of Scotland. Seemingly more interested in establishing Scottish Freema-

---

27 Ibid., August 5, 1747.

28 The original minutes only list the District Number and the lodges within each District. For purposes of clarity and analysis, I have added the actual areas included in each District.

29 Moortown of Garron (April 8, 1734), No. 51 Loundon Kilwinning (March 14, 1747).

30 A Lodge at Haughfoot (c. 1702), No. 14 United Lodge of Dunkeld (c. 1737, chartered August 1, 1757), No. 17 Ancient Brazen (November 30, 1737), St. Bride's Douglas (1736), Strathaven (1736), Sanquhar (1736), Mariaburgh (1736), Kirkcaldy (1736), The Virgin Lodge (1736), Aitcheson's Haven (1736), New Tarbet (1738), Lesmahagow (1741), A Lodge in Isle of Islay (May 19, 1742), Lodge Pitterfrand (November 30, 1743).

31 The remaining lodges were No. 20 St. Machute (December 27, 1736), No. 22 St. John Kilwinning at Kilmarnock (April 13, 1737), No. 32 St. John at Selkirk (December 27, 1736), The Lodge of Goollen (February 8, 1738), No. 40 St. Thomas at Arbroath (December 1, 1740), and No. 50 Inverary St. John (February 23, 1747).

32 Clark, British Clubs, 309.

sonry outside of Britain, the Grand Lodge encouraged overseas expansion more than the creation and maintenance of a properly organized Provincial System. It quickly acknowledged the request of Alexander Drummond who, having recently moved to Turkey, wished to "propagate the art and science of masonry in those parts of the world where he hath already erected some mason Lodges."[33] Having carefully considered the request, the Grand Lodge determined that it would

> Give & Grant Warrant for a Provincial Commission to Expand and given out to the said Alexander Drummond with power to him and other nominated and commissioned by him to Constitute and erect mason Lodges one or more in any part of Europe or Asia bordering upon the Mediterranean seas, and to superintend the same, or any other Lodges already erected in those Parts of the world for the utility and prosperity of masonry. And to report his diligences to the Grand Lodge with his conveniency Providing they be not thereby [illegible] in trouble and expences.[34]

Networking was also prominent in North America. Owing to the popularity of clubs and societies, the expansion of the empire, and the influx of Scottish migrants, organizations began to appear in important American cities such as Philadelphia and Boston.[35] A branch of the Glasgow-based Tuesday Club—founded by Scotsman Alexander Hamilton—was established in Annapolis, Maryland, and many ceremonies and rites of the club were copied.[36] Masonic lodges were no exception, as lodges were chartered in the Virginia cities of Port Royal Crosse, Hampton, Petersburg, Tapahannock, Fredericksburg, and Norfolk. Other lodges appeared in Charleston, South Carolina; Boston, Massachusetts; and Philadelphia, Pennsylvania.[37]

---

33 Grand Lodge of Scotland Minutes, November 30, 1747.

34 Ibid.

35 Clark, *British Clubs*, 139.

36 Ibid., 87.

37 Kilwinning Port Royal Crosse Lodge (December 1, 1755), St. Andrews-Boston (November 30, 1756), Hampton Lodge (1757), Blandford Lodge-Petersburg (September 9, 1757) Tapahannock Kilwinning (June 3, 1758), Fredericksburg (July 21, 1758), Union Kilwinning-South Carolina (November 30, 1759), St. John-Norfolk (August 8, 1763), St. John–Philadelphia (December 15, 1773).

By 1754, though, it was clear that the Provincial System required a codified set of rules and regulations. Recognizing the need to effectively promote a "more regular Correspondence with ... Lodges [in Scotland]," the Grand Lodge of Scotland granted "Provincial Commissions for visiting and corresponding with Such Lodges and Recommended to the masters of the Lodges present to Condescend upon proper pursuant for Executing these Commissions."[38] Two years later, a list of the responsibilities and duties of the Provincial Grand Masters was adopted, and the 10 initial Districts were amalgamated into six. Ostensibly, the resolutions of February 2, 1756 would lend some semblance of orderliness and consolidation to the growing number of lodges, and a complete list of lodges and a Provincial Grand Master to collect dues and fees would provide additional revenue to the Grand Lodge.

> ... In order to have the affairs of the Grand Lodge put upon a better footing it would be proper and Necessary That provincial Grand Masters Should be appointed to visit the Several distant Lodges, Examine their books to report the following particulars. To witt –
>
> 1st. The names of their present master and other officers
>
> 2nd. The day of their Annual Election
>
> 3rd. The place and time of their Stated meetings
>
> 4. The Number of their Members
>
> 5. The State of their Funds
>
> 6. To take up a list of their members to be Inrolled in the Grand Lodge Books and the dues thereof being 2 shillings Each with power to Compound for bygones if they See Cause.
>
> 7. To get proper Proxys from them to represent their Lodges at the Grand Election on St Andrews day and at the quarterly Communication, by whom they will be acquainted of what passes there from time to time.
>
> 8. That the Provincial Grand Masters Return their Reports in writing to the Secretary of the Grand Lodge who or the Clerk Shall Ingross them in a Book to be kept for

---

38   Grand Lodge of Scotland Minutes, February 6, 1754.

> that purpose, and on Receipt of any money deliver the
> Same to the Grand Treasurer to be Stated in his Account.

A clear and concise set of responsibilities and purposes having been established, the Grand Lodge mapped out the following geographic classifications and the lodges in each District (see Table 3.3). Despite several
omissions, it is assumed that the Districts as created in 1747 encompass-
ing Edinburgh and Midlothian; Perth and Kinross; Stirling, Farlkirk, and
West Lothinan; and Orkney remained the same. Interestingly, all lodges
omitted from the initial Districting with the exception of the Selkirk lodge
were again excluded, raising the possibility of human error, non-payment
of lodge arrears, dormancy, or extinction.

Although it would be fair to conclude that those lodges listed in the 1747
classifications would, unless erased from the Grand Roll, remain in their
respective Districts, a closer examination reveals that some were either
unintentionally omitted or intentionally left out. For instance, a comparison of the Glasgow Districts in 1747 and 1756 shows that Kilwinning,
Lodge of Glasgow St. John, Greenock Kilwinning, Dumbarton Kilwinning, Coltness, and Kilbride were present in the initial Districting, but
were noticeably absent from the 1756 classifications. Notwithstanding
lodges chartered abroad or by other Grand Lodges, the Grand Lodge of
Scotland neglected to list 10 lodges which were created or chartered from
1747 to 1756, and of these six were chartered by No. 0 Kilwinning.[39]

Despite the redistricting and the appointment of Provincial Grand Masters, the Grand Lodge failed to take the necessary steps to ensure the
smooth functioning of, what can fairly be called at this stage, a provincial scheme. Although several structural changes were made overseas and
various provincial officers were added,[40] it is evident from Grand Lodge

---

39   Cessnock Kilwinning (January 21, 1748), Paisley Kilwinning (August 5, 1749),
      Airdrie Kilwinning (December 20, 1749), Campbeltown Kilwinning (November 30,
      1752), No. 57 St. John Kilwinning (February 6, 1754), Provan Kilwinning (Decem-
      ber 3, 1754), No. 65 Stonehaven (August 6, 1755), and No. 66 St. Ninian (November
      12, 1755).

40   Grand Lodge Minutes, March 15, 1768: Florida Governor James Grant was appoint-
      ed Provincial Grand Master over the Lodges in the "Southern District of North Amer-
      ica." On February 6, 1769, James George Verchild, Esq., was appointed "Provincial
      Grand Master for the Leeward Caribbean Islands viz. St Kitts, Nevis, Montserat, and
      Antiqua," Grand Lodge of Scotland Minutes, February 6, 1769. In a Grand Lodge
      communication dated May 31, 1769, Joseph Warren is named as the Provincial Grand

minutes that the Districts were not in communication with one another, let alone the central Masonic government in Edinburgh. Through the
end of the eighteenth century, the Grand Lodge continually implored the
Provincial Grand Masters to visit the lodges under their supervision and
to transmit an annual register of officers and members.[41] Furthermore,
masons complained of the small number of Provincial officers,[42] and the
officers themselves criticized the boundaries of their Districts, prompting
further discussions on reshuffling the lodges contained in each.[43]

Masonic Boom: Provincial Expansion and Geographic Distribution

The Provincial Grand Lodge is rarely mentioned in Grand Lodge minutes
from 1756 until the end of the century. At best, it was an ambitious yet
inadequate attempt to reorganize Scottish Freemasonry into a highly-or-
ganized, complex network of lodges and officers. In reality, the Provincial Grand Lodge had little overall impact on the development of eighteenth-century Scottish Freemasonry.

Despite these limitations and inefficiencies, the establishment of Districts and Provinces is important for two reasons: it manifests the Grand
Lodge's desire to expand regionally and overseas and to promote Freemasonry through the encouragement of a network of communication
among lodges. This closely mirrors the broader goals of British Enlightenment clubs and societies to develop a "web of dependent or linked bodies, in order to insure greater public recognition and the dissemination of
ideas," and to also move "steadily away from the earlier heavily metropol-
itan-centred picture to a more polycentric pattern."[44] Much like the Scot-

Master over lodges in Boston, Massachusetts, and Provincial Wardens are mentioned
for the first time. The Provincial Grand Secretary is referenced for the first time on
February 23, 1771. The Provincial Grand Master of Jamaica is alluded to on May 17,
1771, but it is unclear as to the identity of this person.

41 Grand Lodge of Scotland Minutes, January 18, 1770.
42 Ibid., May 3, 1784.
43 Ibid., May 2, 1785. This entry mentions a Southern District, and after "John Stewart
Younger, Esq., of Allan banch, was named Provincial Grand Master of the Eastern
District, he stated that that there were only two or at most three Lodges in that Corner
of the Country which could properly fall under his Cognisance as Provincial Grand
Master ... Remit to the Committee to consider and divide the Northern part of Scotland into [several] Districts as they shall think proper, and to suggest [list] persons to
be appointed Provincial Grand Masters therein."
44 Clark, British Clubs, 98; 87–88.

tish version of the Society for the Propagation of Christian Knowledge, the Grand Lodge of Scotland was created to keep pace with the overall development of Freemasonry in England and Ireland and contribute further to the overall expansion of masonry throughout Britain via the close correspondence among the various Grand Lodges.

Analysis of the lodges in each Scottish District reveals interesting geographical trends and provokes questions concerning Masonic membership in urban versus provincial areas. Unfortunately, the details of the Provincial System in Scotland are dubious at best. George Draffen, in *Scottish Masonic Records*, records 14 Scottish Masonic Districts (Table 3.4).

The accuracy of his classifications is uncertain, as Grand Lodge minutes do not record the creation of the Glasgow City and Caithness Districts. Furthermore, those Districts designated as Ayrshire, Lanarkshire, Argyll and the Isles, and Banffshire, were created much earlier than Draffen indicates.[45] The Grand Lodge configurations of 1747 and 1756 encompass these four areas, and by 1756, 11 major Districts had been specified or existed (Table 3.5).[46]

Unlike English Freemasonry and other British societies, Scottish Masonic lodges did not boast an influential metropolitan impetus. According to Clark, as late as 1760 "the majority of Modern [English] lodges were located in the capital, while most Ancient [English] lodges at that time were also London based."[47] At roughly the same time, only 15 percent of Scottish lodges were located in Edinburgh and, by 1800, the Edinburgh District represented a meagre 11 percent of all lodges (Table 3.5).

Despite the overall lackluster showings, by 1750 Edinburgh had the second highest number of lodges, closely following the Western District (Figure 3.2). As the Western District encompassed more territory than any other District, it is not surprising that throughout the eighteenth century it accounted for the highest number of lodges. Compared to English data for the same period, however, smaller towns were significantly underrepresented.[48]

---

45 See Tables 3.2 and 3.3. By 1756, each of these four districts had been created, contrary to the dates given by Draffen.

46 For the purposes of analysis, I have designated District 11 as the Western Isles.

47 Clark, *British Clubs*, 313.

48 Ibid., 309–319.

As Figure 3.2 illustrates, the number of lodges for the remaining nine Districts was similar, with the exception of the Highlands which made up 11 percent of the aggregate total. The largest concentrations of lodges were geographically dispersed across Scotland; by 1750, Edinburgh and Midlothian, the Western Lodges, and the Highlands made up 51 percent of all lodges.

This pattern changed dramatically in 1765. The amount of new lodges dropped by 36 percent, as all Districts with the exception of Fife and Aberdeen and Angus showed reductions in new charters (Figure 3.3).

The Edinburgh, Western, and Highland Districts also witnessed sharp falls in lodges, although smaller Districts were better represented. The Fife District reported eight new lodges, compared to only six for Edinburgh. From 1766 until 1800, the results are strikingly similar to the findings in the first two periods. Although Scottish Freemasonry endured a decline in new lodges, by 1785 the number had again risen to 81 (Figure 3.4). However, the Edinburgh and Metropolitan District was again beset by a perpetual downturn, as new lodges dropped from six to five.

Dumfries and Galloway saw the largest increase, and the Western District doubled its total from the previous 14 years. During this period, the Western District made up over one-fourth of the total (26 percent), while the Districts of Dumfries and Galloway (16 percent), Edinburgh (12 percent), Aberdeen and Angus (12 percent), and The Highlands (9 percent) rounded out the five largest Districts. Mirroring the lower number of chartered lodges from 1751 to 1765, the number of new lodges per District again fell by 36 percent, although this is almost certainly attributable to the Secret Societies Act of 1799 and the Revolutionary turmoil during the final decades of the eighteenth century (Figure 3.5).

The final analysis shows that during the eighteenth century, Scottish Freemasonry ebbed and flowed. Overall representation in the smaller Districts was fairly consistent and stable, with fluctuations paralleling the general rise and fall of numbers throughout the century. Certainly, between 1736 and 1800, Scottish Freemasonry did expand in terms of new lodges and Provincial Districts. Figures 3.6 and 3.7 suggest, however, that with the exception of noticeable spikes in the larger Districts, the broader picture is one of early gains overshadowed by a gradual decline from 1736 to 1800.

Comparing the numbers from 1736 to 1765 and 1766 to 1800, the evidence supporting a general decline of lodges is even more apparent. Despite modest increases for the Districts of the Western Lodges (21 percent), Dumfries and Galloway (10 percent), and Aberdeen and Angus (1 percent), and no change for Perth and Kinross, lodges in the remaining Districts decreased by an average of 50 percent, with the Edinburgh and Metropolitan District showing the largest reduction at 68 percent. As Figure 3.8 reveals, by 1800 the heaviest concentrations of lodges appeared in the Western District, Dumfries and Galloway, Aberdeen and Angus, Edinburgh, and the Highlands (Figure 3.8).

Although arguably the 1760s and 1770s appear to be the apogee of Scottish Freemasonry in terms of new lodges, the results manifest more sobering trends. As we have seen, lodge totals and patterns of creation were inconsistent even among the larger Districts. Population was no solid indicator of regional representation, as the largest city had the largest decline in new lodges from 1736 to 1800. Finally, Masonic concentrations were skewed toward the central, west, and north of Scotland, as these regions represented 78 percent of complete lodge totals.

Cultivating Diversity: Occupational Recruitment and Social Stratification

In terms of distribution, Masonic lodges steadily moved away from traditional urban centers. As we have seen, the majority of masons were found in the Western District, and this can be attributed to its large territorial area. Overall, the larger Districts contained the highest number of lodges, although urban capitals such as Aberdeen, Dundee, and Glasgow accounted for a small percentage of lodge totals. Unlike other clubs and societies, which relied on Edinburgh for members, inspiration, and entertainment, Freemasonry migrated to other areas of Scotland, reflecting the late Georgian Britain trend of movement away from major commercial centers to industrial and dockyard cities. Certainly, the location of lodges influenced memberships, as large portions of the members were from artisan or middling backgrounds. The fragmentation—especially along class and social lines—alluded to by Clark was occurring among Scottish masons: lodges assumed identities of their own, resulting mainly from provincial expansion and occupational diversity.[49]

---

49   Clark, *British Clubs*, 77.

The Grand Lodge of Scotland was singularly successful in its recording of occupations for Masonic lodges. There are gaps in return years, and occasionally lodges do not report occupations; those that meticulously documented vital statistics provide important data which reflect significant recruitment trends. Although the limitations of occupational returns and membership lists were mentioned in the discussion of No. 47 Dundee, careful analysis contributes greatly to the understanding of Masonic sociability. Specifically, the information helps to answer the lingering questions posed by historians concerning recruitment, social stratification, and "how far it [freemasonry] matched the broad pattern of social banding, with clusters of elite, middle-rank, and artisan social groups, which were discernible for other types of British association."[50]

Concentrating on lists procured from lodges in this study, including No. 2 Canongate Kilwinning, several recruitment patterns are immediately visible.[51] First, there is a direct correlation between professional variety and lodge location in or near Edinburgh (Figure 3.9). Those lodges located north and west of Edinburgh generally recorded fewer occupations. Statistically more significant is the evidence showing that operative lodges— No. 1(3) Aberdeen, No. 6 Inverness, and No. 8 Journeymen—reported fewer occupations on average than other lodges.

From a regional standpoint, the average number of occupations is surprisingly similar, as the mean number for Edinburgh lodges was 32.5, compared to 21.5 for the provincial lodges. Looking more closely at the occupational categorization, it is clear that the specialized lodges in Edinburgh—or lodges that appealed to a specific occupation or trade— were more likely to be less diversified. For example, the extant returns of Journeymen Operative Lodge show that 83 percent of its members were stonemasons, while a small percentage (7 percent) were gentlemen. Records for No. 1(3) Aberdeen reveal that stonemasons accounted for one-third of total membership; 145 of the 282 entrants between 1736 and 1751 were tradesmen, and only 22 were gentlemen. In the entirely-specu-

---

50 Ibid., 320.

51 Lodge occupations are analyzed for No. 1 Mary's Chapel, No. 1(3) Aberdeen, No. 2 Canongate Kilwinning, No. 6 Inverness, No. 8 Journeymen, No. 30 Stirling, No. 47 Dundee, and No. 160 Roman Eagle. The data compiled includes the years 1736– 1770, as lodges such as No. 47 reported occupational listings only twice, thus raising the possibility that they encompass the large gaps in between returns.

lative Roman Eagle Lodge, 77 percent of its members were doctors, and only 5 percent were tradesmen (Appendix 1).

The results suggest that provincial lodges recruited heavily from artisan and middling classes, as tradesmen accounted for 60 percent of the membership, and only 44 percent in Edinburgh. These numbers mirror the high percentage of artisanal trades comprising the Ancient lodges in England during the 1750s.[52] Further examination of the totals shows that Edinburgh lodges recruited greatly from the professional class (30 percent) compared to only 12 percent for provincial lodges. However, regional lodges showed a higher proportion of military (28 percent) compared to only 3 percent for Edinburgh, and each was composed of an almost equal percentage of gentlemen (see Figures 3.10 and 3.11).

Clearly, although there was a greater concentration of lodges outside of Edinburgh, membership numbers were much higher in the capital. Between 1736 and 1757, No. 1, No. 3, No. 8, and No. 160 enrolled over 1,000 members; in contrast, the four provincial lodges registered 326 members, or roughly one-third of the Edinburgh totals. By way of comparison, the average number of men joining Lodge St. Andrew Lodge annually between 1727 and 1788 was only 2.5, with only 151 total members entering the lodge during this 61-year span.[53] Membership analysis also reveals that only 30 new members were added to the lodge roles between the years 1727 and 1757. Between 1737 and 1757, Canongate Kilwinning admitted 632 members, averaging almost 32 per year, highlighting the disparity among overall recruitment for Edinburgh and regional lodges.

The data need careful qualification, as they represent single years in some cases, and relatively continuous returns for most of the eighteenth century in other examples. What is striking is that each lodge in this study was largely dominated by one category, and location seemed to affect lodge composition. Early lodge returns from Edinburgh reveal social complexions represented almost entirely by major trades, although by the mid-eighteenth century elite groups were more prominent in the capital. These findings are similar to Clark's data on Modern Lodges in London, which show Freemasonry's early inability to attract fashionable support but steadily attracting elite patronage and gentlemen by the 1760s.[54]

---

52   Clark, *British Clubs*, 322–323.

53   No. 25 Lodge St. Andrew Minutes, 1727–1757.

54   Ibid., 321.

In aggregate, the data show that lodges maintained a great deal of autonomy over recruitment. Critical analysis of who joined the lodges and overlapping club membership reveals that at least some Edinburgh lodges were socially biased toward the respectable classes. Although it is difficult to quantify any trends of exclusivity and elitism in other lodges represented in this study, it is clear that a high proportion of masons outside of Edinburgh were artisans. Combining major trades, military, seafaring and victualling, and comparing the percentages to professional and gentlemen composition, the results signal regional reliance on middling classes and tradesmen, similar to recruitment patterns in the north of England (Table 3.6).[55]

Provincial lodges exhibited more consistency in the recruitment of major tradesmen. Although the sample size is small, it is geographically diverse, and several arguments may be advanced regarding lodge heterogeneity and exclusivity. Regional evidence suggests that there was no noticeable shift toward redefining lodges along elitist lines. Obviously, the lodges were artisan in nature, and it would seem that membership characteristics were more a product of geography and social composition of towns rather than recruitment bias. This does not seem to be the case, however, in Edinburgh. Having a large and diverse population from which to recruit, lodges often assumed identities of their own based solely on exclusivity of profession, elite members, or overlapping membership with other clubs or societies (Table 3.7). The Roman Eagle lodge is a good example, as it was composed almost entirely of doctors and, until 1794, its minutes were recorded entirely in Latin. Another example is No. 2 Canongate Kilwinning lodge, as many of the leading *literati*, political figures, and gentlemen of Edinburgh joined, making it the most elite and prominent lodge in the capital. Much like lodges in England, membership and character varied, manifesting an assortment of occupations and social complexions. As Clark notes,

> To a considerable extent, then, the composition of eighteenth-century freemasonry conforms to the broad pattern of social banding [prevalent] in other types of associations. But it also had a pluralistic character, reflecting both the slow and confused pace of class formation and

---

55 Ibid., 322–323.

the commercial and institutional realities of organizing lodges at the local level.[56]

A *"Chearful Glass and Song"*

From the 1740 until the late 1780s, Scottish Freemasonry expanded territorially, socially, and culturally. Provincial Districts in Scotland and abroad illustrated an over-arching desire of the Grand Lodge to clearly establish masonry as a world-wide movement. As Districts differed in size and composition, so too did lodge memberships and occupations, which often defined its overall cast and nature. However, it was in Edinburgh where Freemasonry made its most impressive showing. Not simply an idiosyncratic society possessing supposed ancient lore and secrets, yet more than just a convivial club, Freemasonry attracted the attention of many men. During the mid-eighteenth century, the organization began to define itself by the growing organizational prowess of the Grand Lodge and its social and philanthropic activities. Beginning in 1770, however, there was a general move away from unincorporated to incorporated societies such as the Royal Society of Antiquaries, the Royal Society of Edinburgh, and the Highland and Agricultural Society of Scotland.[57] As a consequence, organizations became much more stratified, and the jejune affairs which once proved to be so entertaining now gave way to societies gaining in cachet:

> ... there was a natural and unpreventable drawing away from the egalitarianism of such unincorporated societies ... which drew members from the middle and upper ranks of society and all the professions [resulting in] an unmistakable division upwards: aristocrats, intellectuals, and scholars separated themselves and gathered together in societies which were no longer open to those in the middle ranks of society. This threw the middle ranks on their own resources insofar as literary societies were concerned. Moreover this division was accompanied by a growing democratization of the Scots middle class.[58]

56 Ibid., 325.
57 McElroy, *Age of Improvement*, 87.
58 Ibid.

By the 1780s, freemasonry had survived where other societies had failed or were declining, and many of Edinburgh's elite found cause to join the fashionable freemasons. As Masonic occupational returns and lists show, however, lodge memberships were often a fusion of tradesmen, professionals, and gentlemen. Thus, two major questions emerge: during a period when clubs and societies failed and others restricted membership, how did Scottish Freemasonry endure the ebb and flow of lodges and members, and what attracted elite patronage to a traditionally middle class organization?

Freemasonry was popular for several reasons, although it successfully blended the elements of associations to create an organization accessible to all ranks of society. During the first half of the eighteenth century, it existed primarily as an improvement and charitable organization, although as the nature of enlightenment sociability changed, so too did the masons. The reasons for joining a particular club or society were as numerous and varied as the individuals and personalities comprising their membership: general fellowship and drinking, political and religious discussions, taking part in sports, or social and national improvement. This assortment of backgrounds, motivations, and interests certainly influenced Enlightenment sociability, and the varying reasons for joining an organization necessitated several shifts in Masonic perspective. As such, Freemasonry enthusiastically embraced diversity, and its popularity subsequently stemmed from a predilection for conviviality, its economic benefits, and the pursuit of public and self-improvement.

Scottish Lodges are often depicted as social clubs epitomized by their conviviality and the incorporation of arcane rituals and ceremonies into lodge meetings. Moreover, minutes detailing lodge banquets, processions, drinking, music, and song do not appear frequently until the mid- to late-eighteenth century. Davis McElroy writes that the Cape Club "was popular at least in part for many of the same reasons that the Masonic lodges were so popular in Scotland: it was convivial, secretive, ritualistic, and democratic."[59]

Certainly, notorious carouser James Boswell enjoyed his evenings at the No. 2 Canongate Kilwinning Lodge. And Robert Burns, member of Canongate Kilwinning, joined the convivial Tarbolton Bachelor's Club

---

59   McElroy, *Age of Improvement*, 147.

and the Crochallan Fencibles, for a "large part of the *esprit de corps* of the Crochallans was spirits, and Burns had a dangerous thirst."[60] Other prominent Scottish freemasons who joined the Fencibles were Sir William Dunbar, William Smellie, Henry Erskine, Alexander Gordon, and Alexander Wight. And included among the members of two popular drinking societies—the Cape Club and the Poker Club—were James Aitken of No. 2 Canongate Kilwinning,[61] Thomas Erskine, 6th Earl of Kellie of St. Giles' Lodge, Dugald Stewart, and Reverend William Roberston.

One interesting convivial society, ostensibly a "club composed of lawyers and literary men, whose bond of union was their friendship for Henry Dundas ... who met at Perves's tavern in Parliament Square,"[62] was the Feast of Tabernacles. Lawyer and antiquary Andrew Crosbie, a member of St. Luke's, and founder and First Fellow of the Society of Scottish Antiquaries, was a member; Henry Dundas was also a member, although his association with the freemasons is ambiguous.[63] And finally, although much more vulgar and ribald than the masons, the Beggar's Benison was supported by Edinburgh Kilwinning associate Chambre Lewis, who was the Benison's Grand Master and a Scottish Customs Officer.[64]

---

60 Ibid., 150. The Fencibles were based on the practice of citizens banding together against "dangers arising from invasion during the American War." However, it was a drinking society; the name Crochallan "came from an old Gaelic song, 'Cro chalien, or Colin's cattle,' sung by Dawney Douglas, landlord of the taern where the club met." The Bachelor's Club–organized by Burns in 1780–apparently used as a model a debating club in Ayr." See Corey Andrews, *Literary Nationalism in Eighteenth-Century Club Poetry* (Lewiston, NY, 2004), and Stephen Brown, "Robert Burns, the Crochallan Fencibles, and the Original Printer of *The Merry Muses of Caledonia*," *Studies in Scottish Literature* 38 (2012): 92–107. On the Cape Club, see Rhona Brown, "Literary Communities and Commemorations in the Edinburgh Cape Club," *Journal for Eighteenth-Century Studies*, Special Issue on *Networks of Improvement* 38 (2015): 525–539, and Hans Hecht, ed., *Songs from David Herd's Manuscripts* (Edinburgh, 1904).

61 Ibid., 145. Aitken, who suggested the members adopt "fanciful knighthoods," assumed the title "Sir Poker."

62 John Ramsay of Ochtertyre, *Scotland and Scotsmen of the Eighteenth Century* (Edinburgh, 1888), 448.

63 See Michael Fry, *The Dundas Despotism* (Edinburgh, 1992), 168.

64 Grand Master of Beggar's Benison 1755–1761; Customs Officer, Assistant Comptroller of the Customs in Scotland, 1736–1746, then Collector of Customs at Leith until 1770; See David Stevenson, *The Beggar's Benison: Sex Clubs of Enlightenment Scotland and their Rituals* (East Linton, 2001), 153. The Beggar's Benison was a well-known sex club during the Enlightenment. See also McElroy, *Age of Improvement*, 153.

These examples illustrate that, at least for some members, drinking, merriment, and general fellowship were leading reasons for joining a Masonic lodge as well as other societies. The drinking and socializing that characterized other clubs and English lodges during the early decades of the eighteenth century do materialize in Scottish lodges.[65] Underutilized as historical sources, minutes and records from Masonic lodges throughout the eighteenth century provide frequent and sometimes candid allusions to the geniality and gaiety of their meetings. After the conclusion of business, such as the examination of candidates for initiation into the fraternity, petitions for charity, and purchases for the lodge, meetings regularly ended with a blend of music, drinking, and singing, as was often found at non-Masonic societies. For example, a treasurer's report for No. 25 St. Andrew on December 27, 1769 listed numerous expenditures, including "coals for the lodge, candles, payment for the fiddlers, the flambeau carriers, for rum, brandy, sugar, drink for the fiddlers, a pair of compasses, 8 bottles of punch, and 13 bottles port."[66] No. 3 Scoon & Perth recorded similar payments "totaling £9 6 shillings to make up the dinner and aquavita and honey."[67] And meetings at Ancient Lodge No. 49 in Dundee concluded "in the usual harmony agreeable to the Principles of the Craft" after having "drunk the ordinary Tostes" and ending with a "chearful glass and song."[68]

Toasts were an important part of the meeting, as at other gatherings of clubs and societies, attesting to the unity of the members. Although Cockburn brands healths and toasts as "special torments" and "prandial nuisance[s],"[69] they nevertheless constituted a principal part of Masonic meetings, customarily signifying the closing of the lodge. Recipients and the order of toasts varied, acknowledging the Master of the Lodge and his officers, members in attendance, visiting lodges, the Grand Lodges of Scotland and England, and the King. Mary's Chapel No. 1 in Edinburgh, upon settling sundry lodge matters, toasted "the common and ordinary healths ... such as 'The King and the Craft,' The Grand Master, and his deputy, Grand Wardens and other officers of the Grand Lodge, The Grand

65   Mark Wallace, "Music, Song and Spirits: The Lighter Side of Scottish Freemasonry," *History Scotland* 4 (2004): 38–44.

66   No. 25 Lodge St. Andrew Minutes, December 27, 1769.

67   No. 3 Scoon & Perth Lodge Minutes, December 27, 1766.

68   No. 49 Antient Lodge of Dundee Lodge Minutes, February 6, 1789.

69   Henry Cockburn, *Memorials of His Time* (Edinburgh, 1971).

Master of England and several others suitable to the occasion."[70] Some Lodges, such as St. Luke's No. 44 in Edinburgh, observed a toasting protocol: "every Master Mason should sitt still in their seats during a Toast, except when their own Lodges are drank to, but the Entered Apprentices and fellow Crafts must rise up and stand at every Toast."[71]

Davis McElroy writes that the Scottish desire for national improvement resulted in the proliferation of societies which promoted cultural and social development. Necessary to the achievement of this national improvement was a continual emphasis on camaraderie and the integration of common aspects of institutional life, such as songs and music, into clubs and societies. Songs and music were central features of Masonic meetings, the culminating elements of a night spent with mirth and jollity. Combining toasts and music, Roman Eagle Lodge No. 160 in Edinburgh, "what with eating and drinking and appropriate conversation ... passed the time with much good humour and sparkling wit till past eight o'clock in the evening; Finally, after several songs in Latin, French, Italian, English, and Gaelic, the Lodge was closed in the usual manner."[72] Embracing a penchant for the flamboyant, Roman Eagle hosted a lavish Masonic Ball at the Kings Arms Tavern,

> where a brilliant numerous and respectable company attended, amounting to Fifty Brethren attired in full Dress, and their proper Insignia ... the Band in the 4th North British Militia favoured the Company with several German and Polish Airs upon the Piano Forte, the Lodge's Military and violin Bands performed this evening. Brother Gardner performed many fine Scots Airs upon the flute, which were well receiv'd—upon the whole a finer sight or more happy company could not be, the room was lighted with 149 wax lights—the company retired into a small side room where an elegant cold collation was prepared, with all sorts of wines and spirits [and] fruits and the company broke up at 4 o'clock A.M.[73]

---

70   No. 1 Mary's Chapel Lodge Minutes, June 26, 1740.

71   Lindsay, *Holyrood House*, 69.

72   No. 160 Roman Eagle Lodge Minutes, August 1, 1785.

73   Ibid., February 27, 1801.

Not confining their convivial and celebratory tendencies to the lodges, and in some ways helping to moderate suspicion from some quarters about their covert and supposedly conspiratorial activities, freemasons frequently participated openly in public events. Manifesting the popularity, pageantry, and spectacle of Freemasonry, Peter Clark notes that "masonic processions tended to be bigger and better than those of other associations."[74] Following the laying of the foundation stone for the New City Exchange in Edinburgh on September 17, 1753, for example, *The Ladies Magazine* of Edinburgh published an account of the procession, recounting the splendor and circumstance surrounding the event. Upon completion of the ceremony, no fewer than six hundred and seventy two Masons, consisting mainly of the city's academic, legal, and ecclesiastical establishments, proceeded through a "very magnificent triumphal Arch, in the true Augustine Stile," and

> marched to the Palace of Holy-Rood House, in the Manner as from the Chapel, amidst such immense Crowds of People, and innumerable Multitudes of Spectators from the Windows and Tops of Houses, as never were known in this City on any Occasion; and notwithstanding the hazardous Situation which the Curiosity of many led them to, the Whole concluded without the least Accident happening to any.[75]

Masons also processed on feast days and civic occasions—such as the laying of the Foundation Stone for the New College in Edinburgh on November 16, 1789—and these events often served as a conduit for publicity, attesting to the solidarity and mutuality of freemasons with each other and the general public. Processions may have displayed the orthodoxy and authority of Freemasonry, but they also exhibited the individuality and, in some cases, the sheer eccentricity of many lodges. At the laying of the Foundation Stone for the New Criminal Jail in September 1815, for example, Roman Eagle Lodge No.160 in Edinburgh recorded the following description of the ceremony:

> Grand and imposing as the whole Procession appeared to the Thousands assembled untill the appearance of

---

74   Clark, *British Clubs*, 327.
75   No. 1 Mary's Chapel Lodge Minutes, September 17, 1753.

the Birds of Jove preceeded by their officer, a Gigantic Form armed in a complete coat of Mail Mounted on a Milk White Charge. All Eyes were instantly turned towards the Lodge Roman Eagle and the Skies reecho'd the Shouts of the admiring multitude on the arrival of the Procession. By this time the clouds, which had obscured the Morning were dissipated by the God of Day who now shine forth with all his Splendor Exposing to the View of Thousands one of the Grandest Lights ever seen in this Island ... Every part which afforded an opportunity of Viewing the Light of the new Building was cover'd by Spectators whose Eyes were still attracted to the officer of the Roman Eagle Lodge, who proudly Peer'd above the Brethren.[76]

Feast days, such as St. Andrew's Day (30 November) and the Festivals of St. John The Evangelist (27 December), and St. John The Baptist (24 June) also offered the opportunity for masons to adorn themselves in Masonic habiliments and process through the town. For example, Ancient Stirling No. 30 agreed on December 20, 1775 "that a procession should be made on St. Johns day from Stirling Castle to the Trades Hall with lighted Flambeaus and appointed Brother Alexander Young to Commission Thirty Flambeaus for Said purpose and likewise to procure Thirty sober men from the garrison to Carry them, all to be paid by the Lodge."[77] Similarly, Ancient Lodge No. 49 in Dundee proposed to "have a Procession on St John's day this year [1797]. It was likewise agreed that after said Procession the Lodges are to attend a Sermon in the English Chapel."[78]

The Grand Lodge of Scotland also held processions on designated days. Upon the election of its office bearers for the ensuing year at the Grand Election on November 30, 1803—St. Andrew's Day—and following the installation of the newly chosen officers, everyone in attendance "walked in procession from the New Church Aisle to the Tron Church where an Excellent and appropriate Sermon was preached to them by the Reverend Mr. David Ritchie one of the ministers of St. Andrews Church Ed-

76   No. 160 Roman Eagle Lodge Minutes, September 1815.
77   No. 30 Ancient Stirling Lodge Minutes, December 20, 1775.
78   No. 49 Ancient Lodge Dundee Lodge Minutes, December 11, 1797.

inburgh from a passage in the Hebrews 'Let Brotherly Love continue.'"[79] Messages expounded upon the virtues of freemasons, and the foregoing sermon title reflects themes and tenets of the fraternity, such as harmony and brotherly love.

Eighteenth-century freemasons also ventured into other areas of entertainment, including the theatre. Minutes and records refer to members attending plays as well as dramas specifically written for and about freemasons. For example, on December 27, 1768 Inverness No. 6, after the conclusion of a procession involving several other Lodges, discussed a plan of "going to the Play tomorrow night ... when they took one hundred forty half Crown Tickets and are to meet at the Lodge by 4 o'clock [and proceed] therefrom to the Play House in Procession with Musick and Flambeaus."[80] Masonic plays appeared in Edinburgh toward the end of the eighteenth century, and the Grand Lodge of Scotland recorded on February 4, 1793 that "it was proposed by Right Worshipful Brother Inglis Master of St Luke's Lodge, that there should be a Mason's Play in the New Theatre ... Right Worshipful Substitute Grand Master Brother Thomas Hay ... named Wednesday evening when he hoped there would be a numerous attendance."[81] The proliferation of such plays and events spilled over into public advertising, forcing the Grand Lodge to discuss the problem that

> of late Plays and other public amusements had been advertised in the newspapers and hand Bills as being sanctioned by them when this [was] understood no such authority had been granted. The Grand Lodge therefore resolve that in future no play or other public Exhibition shall be allowed to appear in the newspapers unless it has the authority of the Grand Lodge and the Signature of the Grand Secretary or Grand Clerk attached to it.[82]

Lodges even employed the talents of ventriloquists to provide entertainment for the members. Although aiming to promote social harmony

---

79   Grand Lodge of Scotland Minutes, November 30, 1803.

80   No. 6 Inverness Lodge Minutes, December 27, 1768.

81   Grand Lodge of Scotland Minutes, February 4, 1793.

82   Ibid., May 5, 1806.

among members, freemasons maintained a well-balanced blend of regulations and conviviality, preserving order while allowing the members to
enjoy themselves. On January 20, 1804, Roman Eagle

> ... Had a very numerous meeting and were highly en-
> tertained by Brother Henry and brother James Bryson,
> brother Short and two or three more brethren from the
> Circus. A Brother ... from the Circus entertained the
> brethren with his skill in Ventriloquism which gave gen-
> eral satisfaction. Brother Henry and James Bryson enter-
> tained the brethren with Several musical performances;
> Brother Henry imitated the singing of several kinds of
> birds particularly the canary, Black-bird, and Nightin-
> gale: He also imitated the crying of a suckling pig, in
> a complete and masterly manner; He likewise played
> some favourite pieces on the piano-forte sometimes ac-
> companying it with his voice, and joined in chorus by
> the whole Lodge. And [as a] Grand Overture, which he
> accompanyed by the imitation of Several birds, to the as-
> tonishment of all present.[83]

Historians have asserted that "one of the most engaging qualities of Scottish social life during the eighteenth century is its lack of the rigid rules
of decorum that we still very much take for granted."[84] Freemasons did
invoke rules and regulations, although these largely applied to general behavior during lodge meetings, attendance policies, and the payment of
subscription fees and other monies. However, convivial diversions often
precluded the need for such restrictions, as the tempers of masons at their
feasts and celebrations were improved so as to enhance "that quality of ef-
fervescent participation in the social frolic which is a genuine mark of the
eighteenth-century social demeanor."[85] Ultimately, men of letters and the
social elite of eighteenth-century Scotland were drawn to the cordial and
delightful Masonic receptions, for they made "the *literati* less captious

---

83 No. 160 Roman Eagle Lodge, January 20, 1804. Clark asserts that "Masonic feasts had
an extensive music programme, and singing was equally important on lodge nights,
sometimes accompanied in the first-rate lodge by 'a concert of French horns and other
instruments,'" *British Clubs*, 326.

84 McElroy, "Clubs and Societies," 494.

85 Ibid.

and pedantic then they were elsewhere ... [and] improved the members more by free conversation."[86]

The Impact of Masonic Charity

Despite the attractions of music, drinking, and song, Clark asserts that Freemasonry had its greatest impact "in the area of philanthropy."[87] A fundamental purpose of lodge funds, charitable activities were multivarious. Although as Clark has asserted lodge charity is difficult to quantify, it is clearly evident from minutes and records that a substantial proportion of lodge funds went toward the relief of the poor and indigent. Upon entry to the lodge, new members were often required to contribute on "behoof of the poor of the lodge."[88] Sums varied from lodge to lodge, as members of No. 1 Mary's Chapel paid "nyne pounds Scots money for his admission for the use of the poor."[89] In 1751, members of No. 1(3) Aberdeen paid a "half a Crown into the Box Master for behoof of the Poor yearly,"[90] and in 1787 the sum was two shillings six pence.[91] Some lodges, for example No. 3 Scoon & Perth, charged different fees for operatives and speculatives. Making such a distinction, the lodge resolved on December 8, 1740 that "in all time coming every apprentice Shall pay at his Entry as fellows viz The operative and working ones Ten shillings sterling and the non-operatives or dry handed apprentice twenty shillings Sterling at least for the use of the poor brethren."[92]

By 1744, the amount was half a guinea for all new members,[93] and in 1749 an extra charge of half a Crown was required of all members absent from stated meetings.[94] The amount of money for the charity fund had fallen by over half of the sum required in 1740, as all masons upon admission were to pay in only five shillings, or one Crown.[95] Not requiring a specific

---

86 Ibid., 496.
87 Clark, *British Clubs*, 337.
88 No. 1 Mary's Chapel Lodge Minutes, December 28, 1741.
89 Ibid.
90 No. 1(3) Aberdeen Lodge Minutes, December 27, 1751.
91 Ibid., January 10, 1787.
92 No. 3 Scoon & Perth Lodge Minutes, December 27, 1740.
93 Ibid., December 31, 1744.
94 Ibid., January 10, 1749.
95 Ibid., November 30, 1757.

amount, No. 27 St. Mungo's stipulated that members "shall conform to the tenor of their obligations; give to the poor strangers such charity as their low circumstances and necessity require and our abilities will admit, they giving account of themselves to be true and lawful Masons."[96]

In several instances, lodges were compelled to restrict monetary assistance due to financial deficiencies. For example, No. 1(3) maintained that as many of the members had failed to pay their dues, the lodge hereby

> Prohibite[d] and discharge[d] the Lending of any money whatsoever to any Person or Persons whatsoever without the Warrant and Authority of the Master and other Officers of the Lodge or a Majority of them, And that no money be lent to any Brother or member of the Lodge on any amount whatsoever, unless Such Member find ane Extranear or Stranger to the Lodge of sufficient Credite bound justly for the same.[97]

In addition to the non-payment of subscription fees and annual monies, charitable gifts were also limited due to members failing to contribute to the lodge's relief fund. As this was a recurring problem for much of the eighteenth century, lodges often urged its members to settle their outstanding debts. Emphasizing the importance of Masonic charity, No. 1(3) Aberdeen recorded that

> As there is a very great deficiency in the Funds of the Lodge of Aberdeen arising from the neglect of payment of the Annual Contribution by a number of their members—and as these Contributions are entirely appropriated for the use of the Poor and the principal fund for their support it is earnestly entreated you will pay the sum, as under noted, and due by you on or before the thirty first day of July next.[98]

Ultimately, the Aberdeen Lodge divided its charity into three classes: "1st Domatic and Geomatic Masters 2nd Domatic and Geomatic Fellow Crafts 3rd Domatic and Geomatic Apprentices—One third to Apprentices, Two

---

96   No. 27 St. Mungo's Lodge Minutes, February 6, 1729.
97   No. 1(3) Aberdeen Lodge Minutes, February 7, 1743.
98   Ibid., March 14, 1783.

Thirds to Fellow Crafts, and a sum equal to both to a Master Mason."[99] To replenish its coffers, No. 1(3) occasionally required members who had broken various rules and regulations to contribute to the poor box,[100] while petitions were infrequently "paid from a Collection made by the Brethren from their private pockets in order to Save the publick Funds."[101]

Although beneficiaries included the sick and, as Clark lists, "those adversely affected by bad weather, brethren imprisoned for debt, and others suffering from losses from fires," operative lodge charity was frequently given to members who were physically incapacitated due to work-related accidents. Such beneficiaries included Brother David of No. 8 Journeymen, who "mett with the misfortune of a brokin arm which has rendered him incapable of working for himself and family;"[102] "James Brown present Depute Master [of No. 8] having a considerable time ago mett with the misfortune of a Broken legg and much crushed in Boddy;"[103] and Brother James Mack of No. 1 Mary's Chapel, "an operative Craving the Charity of the Lodge In respect he was disabled from work by a fall from a house."[104]

Lodges also provided for members unable to work as a result of old-age and disease. Aberdeen No. 1(3) records a vivid entry detailing the circumstances of Brother Peter Forsyth, "who is now an old man, uncapable of earning a Liberty had by reason of the Gout, and who by his Representation given into the Lodge was and is willing to Deprive his whole subjects both Heritable and moveable on their allowing him such a Consideration as they In their goodness should be pleas'd to Appoint for his support during his Life."[105] Monetary dispensations, however, were not the only source of charity. A good example of non-fiscal assistance is re-

---

99   Ibid.

100 Ibid., January 10, 1749. No. 1(3) recorded that "Alexander Fraser not only drunk but gave very good offense to the Lodge by opprobrious Language and after being him ordered out, Contrair to the good rules and decent decorum of the Lodge broke open the door thereof and entered in the same in a very rude and unmannerly way for which he was fined in five shillings sterling to be put into the poor box."

101 No. 1(3) Aberdeen Lodge Minutes, December 27, 1770.

102 No. 8 Journeymen Lodge Minutes, November 10, 1746.

103 Ibid., November 5, 1771.

104 No. 1 Mary's Chapel Lodge Minutes, December 15, 1760.

105 No. 1(3) Aberdeen Lodge Minutes, August 6, 1772. The lodge also recorded on March 25, 1747 that several brethren applied for charity, who "on account of their old age and Infirmity ... were not able to work for their bread."

corded in the records of No. 8 Journeymen Lodge in Edinburgh. John Turnbull, the oldest member of the lodge, intimated to the lodge that he was "in grate want of the Nessarys of Life."[106] Subsequently, the members supplied him with a "Cart of Coals ... one peck of meal per week during the winter Quarter,"[107] and a "new Coat and ... a pair of shoes and a shirt which the Lodge unanimously agreed to."[108]

Scottish Masonic lodge charity, similar to the philanthropic practices of English lodges, "was also disbursed more widely, to the local poor and needy causes at home."[109] In Edinburgh, No. 8 Journeymen met on September 10, 1762 to discuss "the State of the widows at present upon the Societys Expence," ultimately concluding that they were "to be paid at the rate of Five shillings quarterly."[110] Also taking an interest in education, No. 8 introduced a scheme for apprenticing boys to masters, although this venture seemed to be singularly unsuccessful and was quickly abandoned. Lodge minutes recount that George Stewart, apprentice of Charles Watkins—a barber and wigmaker in Edinburgh—"did not incline to the trade he was bound to, neither had his business to give him."[111] Allegedly, "the boy was not well guided, who is now lying in his masters Home with a swelled face and a hurt to his gut on the north loch."[112]

Toward the end of the eighteenth century, St. Andrews Lodge No. 25 also adopted a wider variety of philanthropic efforts, voting to support "the Voluntary Subscription [for the French Revolution] that is presently going on for the defence of the country,"[113] and voted several guineas towards the construction of "a Hall for the Masons of Scotland," stating that "as the funds of this Lodge [are] but small they agreed that five Guineas would be as much as they could possibly give from the funds.[114]

Charity was also a major function of the Grand Lodge and, like other associations and lodges, its philanthropic concerns extended into many

---

106 No. 8 Journeymen Lodge Minutes, December 27, 1804.

107 Ibid.

108 Ibid., February 15, 1805.

109 Clark, *British Clubs*, 337.

110 No. 8 Journeymen Lodge Minutes, September 10, 1762.

111 Ibid., December 18, 1759.

112 Ibid.

113 No. 25 Lodge St. Andrew Minutes, March 24, 1798.

114 Ibid., December 27, 1798.

areas of the community. For instance, on June 19, 1758, the Right Worshipful Master of No. 1 Mary's Chapel Lodge in Edinburgh asserted that

> The Right Worshipful Master Represented to the Lodge That the Edinburgh Society for improving of Arts, Agriculture, and Manufacturing has already been of great Service to this Country in general; and if properly supported will still be of more. That this has induced all true Lovers of their Country to Contribute accordingly to the best of their abilities towards the Support of this Society. That as there is at present a General Contribution for this purpose among all the Lodges in Town by order of the Grand Lodge, She hoped that the Antient Lodge of Marys Chapel would not be behind hand in this matter but show to the world That freemasons are always as ready to Join in every laudable measure for the Service of their Country and to Contribute thereto according to the best of their abilities, as they are to relieve and support one another. That for his part he was willing to Contribute a Guinea out of his own private pocket over and above what the Lodge should give. The Lodge unanimously agreed to give five pounds five shillings sterling to the said Society, and hereby order their Treasurer to pay the same accordingly and take credit therefore in his accounts, together with the masters Guinea which he instantly gave to the Treasurer for that purpose.[115]

In addition to supporting other improvement societies in Edinburgh, the Grand Lodge—much like the Grand Lodge of England—apprenticed poor boys to tradesmen or masters in a lodge.[116] On May 21, 1740, the Deputy Grand Master of Scotland sent a letter to the Grand Master, "concerning the binding of Some poor operative Mason an apprentice for the freedom of the City of Edinburgh and Incorporation of Mary's Chappell. And he being one Alexander Ramsay ... Bind the said Boy for the Freedom of the Said City and Incorporation and Agreed to accept of him as an Apprentice for Eight Years."[117] It seems, however, that Ramsay's

---

115 No. 1 Mary's Chapel Lodge Minutes, June 19, 1758.

116 See Clark, *British Clubs*, 338.

117 Grand Lodge of Scotland Minutes, May 21, 1740, excerpted from the Gild Court

apprenticeship was hardly supported, for within six months the Grand Lodge wished to be "relieved of the obligation of providing the apprentice with clothing and appealed to the lodges in and around Edinburgh to furnish clothing for him."[118] Unfortunately for Ramsay and the lodges that apparently helped him for 2 years, his apprenticeship came to a distasteful end. On August 3, 1742, the Grand Lodge reported that Alexander Ramsay "had Turned altogether vilious and had been guilty of Severall very discommendable practices" and "declared that he should never have the freedom of the City by his Indentures."[119]

Similar to other Scottish lodges, the majority of Grand Lodge charity was designated for the relief of widows, orphans, and injured or sick freemasons. For example, charity was given to "a poor distressed Woman with two Children on her Breast;"[120] "a poor destitute orphan wanting both father and mother and but about six years of age;"[121] and the widow of a poor operative brother in Glasgow "who had five small children, all at the point of starving."[122] Charity petitions varied, as appeals ranged from a "a poor man sorly afflicted with the flux"[123] who was given 10 shillings; five guineas allotted to a mason of Fort William whose home was "burnt to ashes,"[124] and an application made by "Brother William Young present Master of the Lodge of St. Nicholas at Aberdeen, to the Grand Secretary, setting forth that he in the prosecution of his business had been in Ireland and was so far in his return home, but that he was in great Strait for want of money to help him, having been Shipwreck'd, and Lost his All,"[125] who was presented with four pounds to help offset his losses. Prisoners of war were also the beneficiaries of Grand Lodge charity. Grand Lodge minutes present an extraordinary account of a meeting held on October 10, 1759, during which the Charity Committee, "taking into their Consideration the distressed Case of the French Prisoners presently in the Castle of Ed-

Books of Edinburgh.
118 Ibid., December 1, 1740.
119 Ibid., August 3, 1743.
120 Ibid., May 19, 1742.
121 Ibid., February 3, 1748.
122 Ibid., August 3, 1743.
123 Ibid., November 14, 1750.
124 Ibid., July 10, 1765.
125 Ibid., October 30, 1771.

inburgh," voted 10 guineas toward their relief "in purchasing Cloaths and other necessaries for them But in the first place in supplying the necessitys of Such as may be Brother Masons Amongst them."[126] A group was appointed to "Enquire into and Inspect the Condition and Situation of these Prisoners Particularly Such of them as they shall find to be free Masons And to Report their Opinion as to their Number and Necessity with their first Convenience."[127]

"An Age Sunk in Barbarism": Social Reform and Intellectual Endeavors

As we have seen, freemasons fostered a greater sense of public awareness and social networking through multiple memberships among Scottish clubs and dedication to charitable activities. With the ranks of lodges composed of so many bright, ambitious, and intelligent minds, it is difficult to exclude the possibility that Masonic lodges in some way contributed to the pursuit of knowledge and social reform. Lodge minutes, though at times meticulous, are often selectively so and thus any conclusions regarding intellectual endeavors must be based on what survives or what has been recorded.

It has been argued above that Scottish lodges were not heavily influenced by Newtonianism, nor was it a prevalent theme throughout Scottish Masonic discourse or readily discernible in lodge minutes.[128] However, records do attest to the continual emphasis on personal development. Although examples are scarce, evidence suggests that freemasons did engage in debates and discussed pertinent issues of the eighteenth century. Indeed, "both public improvement and self-improvement were clearly vital strands in the social discourse of Hanoverian freemasonry."[129] For the freemasons, much like Scottish literary clubs and societies, a "rigid and immutable definition of subject-matter was not a feature of the eighteenth-century literary society. On the contrary, there was a decided tendency to include an ever increasing range of subjects."[130]

---

126 Grand Lodge of Scotland Minutes, October 10, 1759. See also Clark, *British Clubs*, 338.
127 Ibid., November 11, 1759.
128 See Chapter 2, 46–48.
129 Clark, *British Clubs*, 336.
130 McElroy, *Age of Improvement*, 73.

Critical to this analysis is the issue of vails, or giving drink-money to servants, which gripped the country in 1760. This seemingly insignificant issue of social reform sparked a debate that pitted master and servant against one another, and divided Edinburgh along class and cultural lines. As McElroy contends, "the class which was to be deprived of an accustomed and cherished source of income was far from meek in their resentment at the attack on their privileges."[131] Championing the cause of the abolition of this alleged pernicious custom was the Edinburgh Society for Encouraging Arts, Sciences, Manufactures, and Agriculture. During a meeting in 1759, the society debated the following questions: "What is the best and most equal way of hiring and conducting servants? and, what is the most proper method to abolish the practice of giving of vails?"[132] The conflict soon reached epic proportions, with dramas being staged ridiculing the servant class, the *Edinburgh Magazine* condemning the plays, and finally the Select Society entering the dispute on January 29, 1760. By February 5, 1760, its members adopted the following binding resolution:

> The Select Society having taken into consideration the practice of giving vails, or drink-money to servants, and being convinced that this custom, unknown to other nations, is a reproach upon the manners and policy of this country, has a manifest tendency to corrupt the morals of servants, to obstruct the exercise of hospitality, and to destroy all social intercourse between families; the members did unanimously agree to exert themselves the utmost, in order to remove this publick nuisance.[133]

Resolutions from other societies and organizations followed, including the Company of Hunters, Clerks to the Signet, Heritors of Mid-Lothian, Society of Advocates, and the Grand Lodge of Scotland on behalf of Scottish masons. Emulating the Select Society, the Grand Lodge recorded on February 4, 1760 that

> It having been thereafter Represented to the Grand Lodge That as an Honourable Body of Gentlemen in

---

131 Ibid., 161.

132 Ibid.

133 Originally printed in *Scots Magazine*, January 1760, 42–43; reprinted in McElroy, *Scottish Clubs*, 163–164.

this Country had Entered into a determined Resolution against Giving Vails to Servants which being a pernicious practice and Detrimental to Society the Grand Lodge would Consider of the Same Whereupon the Grand Master and Grand Lodge Recommended to the Committee to make up a Scroll of a Resolution against this Practice and Report the same to the Grand Master.[134]

Consequently, the following "Scroll of Advertisement" was prepared by the Grand Secretary and approved by the Grand Master, and at "his desire published in all the Edinburgh News Papers for Notification to the General Lodges":

> A Quarterly Communication of the Grand Lodge of Scotland, lately held in Mary's Chapel, having taken into their consideration, the prevailing practice of giving vails, or drink money to servants, did unanimously *resolve*, to do everything in their power to remove the same.
>
> The zeal of Free masons for the welfare of the publick, and their readiness to promote every laudable purpose, will easily prevail on them to endeavour to discourage this practice, as by it the virtues of many servants have been destroyed and their pride and licentiousness increased; and, besides, as it has a tendency to obstruct that kind hospitality and disinterested friendship which the fraternity always wish to diffuse. The *Grand Lodge,* reckon themselves obliged to declare to all under their jurisdiction, their dislike of any custom prejudicial to the principles of Masons, and to *require* the officers of every lodge in Scotland, to intimate and recommend the above resolution in the first meeting, after it comes to their hands.
>
> By command of the Right Honourable, and Most Worshipful DAVID Earl of Leven and Grand Master Mason of *Scotland.*
>
> Alexander McDougal, G. Secretary[135]

---

134 Grand Lodge of Scotland Minutes, February 4, 1760.

135 Walter Ruddiman, John Richardson and Company, *Caledonian Mercury,* March 3, 1760.

This resolution was forwarded to all lodges, and by 1762 the practice of distributing vails was abolished. To be sure, the freemasons played their noble part in agitating for social reform and helping to moderate drinking among the servant class. It must be noted with some humour and irony, however, that the masons clearly wanted to distinguish themselves as exemplary models of temperance and fortitude, though as we have seen lodges often prided themselves on their lavish celebrations replete with fiddlers, flambeaus, and ample amounts of alcohol. It is quite possible that this apparent conflict of interests and the occasional overindulgence in alcohol led the Grand Lodge to consider integrating sermons into their festivals. As one Scottish officer quipped, delivering sermons had "long been a practice in many considerable Towns in England, Ireland, and America ... In this Country that practice has not yet been adopted, although it may perhaps be more necessary than in any of the Countries already mentioned."[136]

The academic activities and exploits of Scottish masons also made them the object of praise. The eclectic Roman Eagle Lodge, whose minutes were recorded in Latin from 1785 to 1794, attracted the attention from the respected eighteenth-century teacher and writer George Chapman. Chapman was born in 1723 in the parish of Alvale, Banffshire. He studied at Aberdeen, and is perhaps best known for his *Treatise on Education*, which appeared in 1782. Having received critical attention for its pageantry at local processions and conducting lodge meetings entirely in Latin until the end of the eighteenth century, Chapman—intrigued by No. 160—offered his praise and admiration to the lodge. On January 2, 1786,

> The Roman Eagle Lodge having been regularly opened in accordance with the rules of the Craft and in working order, a letter which had been recently received by the Master and of which a copy is appended was, at the Master's request, read to the Lodge by the Chaplain.
>
> Copy: - George Chapman to John Brown
>
> When I heard that a Masonic Lodge had been regularly founded by you in which the Latin tongue should be employed chiefly with the purpose of bringing back that ancient Language, which the Schools of this country have

---

136 Grand Lodge of Scotland Minutes, February 6, 1786.

almost driven into banishment, and of applying it to our domestic affairs and daily speech, I could not refrain although a [illegible] from writing this [cut off] such noble efforts.

To you, Learned Sir, and to your Brethren, I wish happiness and prosperity; and my prayer is that the beautiful Tongue which you are so zealously and nobly cherishing may hold never-ending music in Scotland, the purest stronghold of hard-pressed Scholarship (Humanitas). As a token of my regard from you, I have sent you a Treatise which I wrote on the education of the Young, and as you to take the gift, so much as it is, in good part.

Continue, Honoured Sir, as you have begun, and recall Academic youth from Barbarism to the refinement of [illegible] letters. Farewell.

Meldmeria, Banff

On the motion of the Master, the above George Chapman Accepted Mason (a man equally distinguished in culture and scholarship at the head of Letters in Scotland, and standing alone amongst us after Crookshanks in an age sunk in barbarism) was—if he should be a mason as he appears to be—unanimously admitted an honorary member of the Lodge.[137]

The Bureaucratic Reformation

Clark correctly asserts that, in addition to members, conviviality, and elite patronage, a "key factor influencing the social clientele of a lodge (as with other voluntary associations) was the admission charge ... Charges varied considerably between lodges, mirroring different markets and lodge aspirations."[138] Certainly, the constant increases in lodge dues and fees reflect such attitudes. Aberdeen Lodge No. 1(3) raised admission fees for operative and nonoperative masons no less than four times between

---

137 No. 160 Roman Eagle Lodge Minutes, January 2, 1786

138 Clark, *British Clubs*, 325.

November 1, 1725 and December 28, 1749. In 1725, dues for admission fees for operative entered apprentices were 12 shillings Scots annually.[139] Speculative masons were required to pay six guineas over and above the 12 shillings, reinforcing not only the operative status of the lodge, but also the division present among members during the first half of the eighteenth century.[140]

Lodge admission fees clearly fluctuated, and often decreased, as speculative mason admission fees had fallen to one guinea by 1776.[141] Occasionally, lodges would offer special dispensations to certain groups. For example, in December 1800, the members of No. 49 Ancient Dundee resolved that "all Military Gentlemen should be pass'd and raised for half the Lodge dues but not intitled to any benefit from the Funds."[142] Other lodges also showed a marked increase in admission fees. St. Andrews charged only one shilling in 1737, but by 1797—as the funds of the lodge had "now become of some consequence"—raised the sum to one pound one shilling sterling.[143] Another good example is No. 8 Journeymen in Edinburgh. Originally, the lodge stipulated in its bye-laws that "none shall come into be members with that Company after the date hereof [1 November 1709] Except they pay five shillings for their Donation and Six pence each Quarter except the Winter Quarter."[144] By 1783, the entry fee for entered apprentices had risen to 15 shillings.[145] Only 3 years later, the entrance fees had more than doubled to two pounds.[146] Compared to Mary's Chapel, the fees are relatively high, as No. 1 charged one shilling six pence for new entrants.[147]

---

139 No. 1(3) Aberdeen Lodge Minutes, November 1, 1725.

140 Ibid., December 27, 1735.

141 Ibid., January 27, 1776.

142 Ibid., December 5, 1800.

143 No. 25 Lodge St. Andrew Minutes, December 12, 1797.

144 No. 8 Journeymen Lodge Minutes, November 1, 1709.

145 Ibid., May 9, 1783. This same trend is apparent in the minutes of No. 6 Inverness. On April 7, 1772, the lodge recorded "that the Dues of an Entered Apprentice shall from this time be one pound one shilling Sterling over and above the Grand Lodge dues And that of a Fellow Craft and Master Mason ten Shillings and Sixpence Sterling for each Degree for the Benefit of the publick funds of the Lodge." Five years later, the lodge "unanimously agreed upon that no opearative Mason shou'd be admitted without paying One Guinea and the ordinary dues of the Lodge," February 7, 1777.

146 Ibid., October 20, 1786.

147 No. 1 Mary's Chapel Lodge Minutes, April 16, 1759.

Overall, the fees charged by speculative lodges were comparable to those fees required by operative lodges. In 1729, No. 27 Glasgow St. Mungo's charged "Five Merks of money and one shilling Sterling to the Secretary and another shilling like money to the Tyler, besides a moderate treat to the Quoram present, and four Merks Money foresaid to the Lodge at passing."[148] However, by December 1769, the admission fee had been raised to one pound one shilling, with an additional one pound contributed to the general use of the lodge, presumably charity and entertainment.[149] The total fees which amounted to two pounds one shilling were essentially the same as those charged by No. 8 Journeymen Lodge in Edinburgh.

Although lodges controlled all dues and admission fees, by 1780 the Grand Lodge of Scotland began to demand a minimum entrance charge. Roman Eagle Lodge minutes bear this out, as the Master read a "New Regulation anent the Entries and requiring payment of their Arrears"[150]:

> Worshipfull Brother,
>   The Quarterly Communication, held here of this date considering that the cause of so many Lodges being in arrears to the Grand Lodge, was owing to their entering members, either upon acceptance or for Triffling sums which often tended to the hurt and ruin of these Lodges; they therefore resolved, that all Lodges holding of the Grand Lodge do enter no apprentice in time coming under ONE GUINEA at least, and prohibited and discharged all Lodges holding of the Grand Lodge of Scotland from entering any apprentice below said sum.
>   They also resolved, that all Lodges in arrears to the Grand Lodge do on or before St. John's day in December next, pay up their arrears, otherwise the Lodges neglecting so to do will be thereafter struck off from the roll of the Grand Lodge, and receive no benefit therefrom in time coming.
>   It is therefore hoped that your Lodge will comply with the above resolutions of the Grand Lodge, by trans-

---

148 No. 27 Glasgow St. Mungo's Lodge Minutes, February 6, 1729.

149 Ibid., December 27, 1769.

150 No. 160 Roman Eagle Lodge Minutes, November 6, 1780.

mitting a list of your intrants, with money for discharg-
ing the same forthwith.

By order of the Quarterly Communication
[Signed] Will Mason Grand Secretary[151]

Roman Eagle resisted the declaration, stating that "they [members] are
of Opinion that advancing of ones entry would be attended with hurt instead of Service;"[152] the rather pusillanimous justification of its actions
suggests that the lodge may have expected reprisals for its refusal. Other
lodges were dissatisfied with the ruling. In a letter dated August 7, 1780,
St. James' Lodge in Edinburgh "entreated the Grand Lodge to allow their
lodge and all Operative Lodges in Scotland to adhere to the previous admission fee [of two shillings six pence]."[153] Although Grand Lodge had
previously allowed operatives to pay other costs at a reduced rate—namely tickets for the St. Andrew's Day Feasts—it resolutely stated that the new
entrance fee was to be strictly observed by everyone.[154] As a conciliatory
gesture, however, a circular was sent to solicit opinions over the proposed
(and at this stage unilaterally-imposed) increase. Apparently, only 32 letters were sent, and the Grand Secretary reported that "fourteen Lodges
were for adhering to the resolution of the Grand Lodge, that nine were
against it, and nine ... took no notice of the resolution."[155] Unimpressed by
the bureaucratic posturing of the Grand Lodge, over half of the surveyed
lodges either opposed the resolution or simply did not respond.

Clearly, however, the letter from the Grand Lodge outlining the mandatory entrance fee of one guinea and threatening noncompliant lodges with
expulsion points to organizational and bureaucratic shifts in the central
governing body. Just as the Modern Grand Lodge of England had "man-

---

151 Ibid. Interestingly, the Grand Lodge recorded the following minute on February
    11, 1780: "Upon reading a Petition of the Master, Wardens, and Brethren of the
    Journeymen Lodge Edinburgh Praying for the reasons therein set forth That the
    Grand Lodge would pass a law prohibiting all the Lodges in and about Edinburgh
    from admitting any person an apprentice into their Lodge under one Guinea at
    least of entry money." However, no mention was made of No. 8 in its official man-
    date.

152 Ibid., November 13, 1780.

153 Grand Lodge of Scotland Minutes, August 7, 1780.

154 On November 18, 1767, Grand Lodge stated that operatives should pay only one shil-
    ling for tickets, while all other masons would pay the full price of two shillings.

155 Grand Lodge of Scotland Minutes, February 5, 1781.

aged to assert its authority over most local lodges"[156] by the mid-1780s, the Grand Lodge of Scotland had instituted a series of policies that re-defined its position as the real and tangible head of Scottish Freemasonry. The progression of the Grand Lodge from its purely titular position to the central Masonic bureaucracy of Scotland began in earnest in the mid-eighteenth century with the dispensation of charity and monitoring of all dues and arrears. Initially, petitions for charity were made to the Grand Lodge and, more often than not, were approved without question. By 1750, and continuing until 1767, the Grand Lodge passed nine regulations which completely altered the application process and ultimately restricted the number of people who qualified for financial assistance. Several of the early resolutions asserted that no charity petitions would be received from lodges that did not regularly remit monies due to the Grand Lodge for new admissions.[157]

With the advent of the Grand Charity Committee in 1754 which consisted of the "Grand Master, Deputy Grand Master, Substitute Grand Master, Grand Wardens, and all persons who have held these offices at any time, with the masters of the Several Contributing Lodges or their representatives, who are always to be attended by the Grand Secretary, Treasurer, and Clerk,"[158] new restrictions were put into place. Most extraordinary was the decision of the Grand Lodge to reserve the right to charge interest on charity—even monies allocated to widows, orphans, or sick and injured masons.[159] Ostensibly, the major factor contributing to the implementation of such a drastic measure was the nonpayment of dues and admission fees owed by lodges, a recurrent and frustrating problem that dogged Scottish Freemasonry throughout the entire eighteenth century. Additionally, when petitions were made, they had to be certified by the Grand Master and Grand Wardens and presented to the Substitute Grand Master or Grand Secretary 10 days before the committee met; and no more than 20 shillings were appropriated unless otherwise decided by the Charity Committee. Whether or not a consequence of the flood of official procedures, the custom of Grand Masters contributing upwards of 10 pounds at their induction gradually faded into obscurity.

---

156 Clark, *British Clubs*, 342.

157 Grand Lodge of Scotland Minutes, November 26, 1753.

158 Ibid., February 6, 1754.

159 Ibid.

The Committee continually implored lodges to pay their dues, with little overall success. By 1757, the Grand Lodge reported that "the Charity fund was now so much sunk that there was none to bestow on the necessitous or those in distress."[160] In an effort to dispel the lack of concern surrounding the payment of arrears and bolster the dwindling charitable funds, the Grand Lodge stated that that all of the lodges in Edinburgh

> and within 12 miles of the city are required before St. Andrews Day 1768 to settle their debts with the Grand Lodge, and the same is to apply to future debts (to be paid on or before St. Andrews Day during the preceding year). Any lodges refusing or neglecting to do so will be expunged from the Grand Roll. Lodges further than 12 miles from Edinburgh are to be given more time to pay arrears, although the same conditions and penalties apply (they are allowed to make partial payment). If any of the Lodges in Scotland shall happen to be struck off the Rolls of the Grand Lodge, no application for Charity should thereafter be regarded from any Brother belonging to such Lodge.[161]

As Appendix 2 shows, the large number of suspensions attests to the gravity of the situation and the zeal with which the Grand Lodge pursued lodges in arrears. The Grand Lodge stipulated that lodges refusing to comply "should be Understood to have Abandoned the Grand Lodge and be by them disowned accordingly."[162] Consequently, on November 6, 1771, 8 expulsions and 51 suspensions were handed down; lodges in and about Edinburgh had until 30 November to settle their accounts while lodges at a greater distance had until 27 December, and "those that may be more remote" had until the next Quarterly Communication in February 1772. If overdue fees were not paid, their charters would be revoked and they would be struck from the Grand Roll.[163] Overall, 59 lodges were affected by the actions of the Grand Lodge, accounting for almost one-third of all lodges in Scotland, or 32.7 percent. The list of expulsions and suspensions is nondiscriminatory: old-established as

---

160 Ibid., November 14, 1757.
161 Ibid., November 10, 1767.
162 Ibid., June 20, 1759.
163 Ibid., November 6, 1771.

well as newly-chartered lodges are listed. The oldest lodge recorded is Edinburgh Kilwinning Scots Arms (1736), also the first to be named on the registry of expulsions. The most recently erected lodge at that time—Rutherglen Royal Arch (1769)—is the last lodge to be named. Although precedence was utilized to recognize lodges for their history and prestige, it is clear that the Grand Lodge pursued all lodges in arrears with equal determination.

This surge of authority was accompanied by an attendant increase in correspondence with the Grand Lodge of England. The English Grand Lodge, as Clark explains, had claimed almost complete authority over its lodges. Almost certainly, the Grand Lodge of Scotland was aware of the scope and extent of its power and wished to establish an advantageous link with its English counterpart. Not only would this prove beneficial in any disputes, but a mutual correspondence with England would advance the cause of Freemasonry throughout Britain. On November 4, 1772, Grand Secretary of England William Dickey sent a letter to the Grand Lodge of Scotland stating that he would be

> very Punctual in All Matters between Our two Grand Lodge, and doubt not of the same Care on your Side, for notwithstanding the wise Regulations laid down for the Government of the Craft in general, at times there may be Occasion to Expel unruly Members, in that case it is Absolutely Necessary that we should give each other Compleat Notice, in order to render them Incapable of Imposing on the Worthy Brethren of the Fraternity; the good Consequences Attending it, the Antient Craft would soon Experience.[164]

Seemingly preparing for the conflict that would embroil Scottish and English masons during the Secret Societies Act controversy of 1799 and the Masonic Secession of 1808, both Grand Lodges agreed to defend the principles of Freemasonry and prohibit or check any disturbances that would threaten the stability of the fraternity. As a symbolic gesture, the Grand Lodge of Scotland resolved on the annual St Andrew's Day Feast that "it was of Opinion that the Motherly intercourse and Correspondence which the Right Worshipful the Grand Lodge of England was

---

164 Ibid., November 4, 1772.

desirous to Establish would be serviceable to both Grand Lodges, and productive of Honour and Advantage to the Fraternity in General."[165]

The expansion of control was reinforced by three additional organizational developments within the Grand Lodge. First, there was a significant consolidation of power among Grand Lodge officers. Although the terms of the Grand Master of Scotland were considerably shorter than those of the Moderns in England, it was increased from one year to two; on several occasions, the Grand Master of England served as the Grand Master of Scotland.[166] Second, and similar to the Grand Officers of the Modern Lodge in England, "there was a parallel tendency for senior officers to serve for extended periods."[167] In Scotland, John Douglas acted as Substitute Grand Master from 1737 to 1751, while Nathaniel Spenser held this office between 1776 and 1781. William Mason was Junior Grand Warden from 1774 to 1794, James Hunger was the Grand Treasurer between 1765 and 1779, and Robert Meikle functioned as the Grand Clerk from 1779 to 1794. Although the Treasurers, Chaplains, and Clerks rarely advanced further through the Masonic hierarchy, their roles were very important and clearly delineated. On February 4, 1760 the Grand Lodge recorded that "for some time past there had been a Confusion in Carrying on the business of the Grand Lodge betwixt the Grand Secretary and Clerk So that it was not easily Understood what was the Proper business or Department of either and therefore Prayed the Grand Lodge would Consider the said matter and Appropriate the proper business to each."[168] As such, the Secretary was given license over the Grand Seal and charged with keeping it and "applying it to respective documents."[169] Other duties included answering "all such Letters as he may receive in relation to Questions or any other Matters of the Grand Lodge,"[170] and recording minutes and all monies paid to the Treasurer.

Although the duties of the Secretary, Clerk, and Treasurer overlapped, it was ultimately asserted that the Clerk would make inventories of all the jewels and clothing and lodge these lists with the Treasurer. The Clerk

165 Ibid., November 30, 1772.
166 The term of the Grand Master of Scotland was lengthened on November 30, 1756.
167 Clark, *British Clubs*, 343.
168 Grand Lodge of Scotland Minutes, February 4, 1760.
169 Ibid., February 15, 1759.
170 Ibid., February 8, 1762.

was also expected to record all monies paid in and fees owed, and document lodge names and issuance date of all charters. By 1807, the Grand Lodge observed that the Grand Clerk is "the person who is regularly intitled to declare the state of any vote in the Grand Lodge being of course held from his official situation as beyond all suspicion of partiality."[171] And whereas the Clerk recorded monetary transactions, it was the duty of the Treasurer to collect entry fees, present receipts for expenditures, purchase new items for the Grand Lodge, and pay out charity. Essentially, a system of check and balances was established whereby officers were able to constantly monitor each other's actions.

Finally, the "pressure for more centralist control"[172] manifested itself in the form of increased demand for a Freemasons' Hall in Edinburgh. Serving chiefly as a "symbol of the enterprise ... the only way the building could be funded was through the enforcement of ... levies on local lodges."[173] Initially, this project was to be financed by voluntary subscriptions, with each lodge donating what it could reasonably afford.[174] However, by 1806, the Grand Lodge was intent on raising the money and completing the project and regularly sent letters to lodges "on the subject of building a hall for their accommodation and soliciting ... aid for that undertaking."[175] No. 8 Journeymen was quite benevolent, donating nine pounds 21 shillings from May 16 to October 17, 1806. Clearly, these developments signaled the transformation of Scottish Freemasonry into a "well-organized, federal association, with a great deal of its power concentrated in the hands of grand lodge."[176]

Conclusion

The nature of eighteenth-century Freemasonry is characterized by constant adaptation and conversion from a charitable, convivial club into a much-respected, powerful, and influential organization. Indeed, it still maintained its early features of philanthropy, self-improvement, and general merriment. By the end of the 1700s, however, Freemasonry had

---

171 Ibid., June 19, 1807.

172 Clark, *British Clubs*, 342.

173 Ibid.

174 No. 8 Journeymen Lodge Minutes, January 31, 1799.

175 No. 6 Inverness Lodge Minutes, March 25, 1806.

176 Clark, *British Clubs*, 343.

grown on a scale unrivalled by any other society, manifesting its remarkable ability to synthesize the traits and aspects of many organizations and successfully market itself to the public.

Freemasonry, for all its secrecy, mysteries, and assortment of occupations and lifestyles, succeeded and survived where other societies declined and disappeared. Unlike other organizations, it did not exclude members based on cultural or economic standing. And the copious minutes allow a candid look at the social mechanisms that allowed Freemasonry to grow, expand, and compete with academic, literary, and scientific associations. The organization exhibited a durability and resilience not demonstrated in other societies, whereas other associations rose in popularity, reached a pinnacle, and gradually were consigned to the societal and associational graveyard of indifference and disinterestedness, Masonic lodges endured. McElroy notes that the prominent Select and Edinburgh societies failed because of "a gradual diminishing of interest in the members of the society which was their common parent, the Select Society of Edinburgh ... When the Select Society began to suffer from the increasing lack of interest and the non-attendance of its members, its dependent societies likewise suffered from lack of support."[177] Elaborating on this underlying principle of demise, McElroy argues, "the process of decay and dissolution ... was a gradual one brought about by failing interest among its members, by its being too expansionist in forming subsidiary societies, by the demands made on its members for repeated contributions, and by the natural shocks that such institutions are heir to."[178]

Although Freemasonry faced similar problems throughout the century, its longevity surely can be attributed to its inclusiveness, organizational competence, the myriad intellectual, economic, and social benefits it offered, and the freedom of lodges to form their own identity based on who joined. Yet the problems which plagued other associations—for example the Select and Edinburgh Societies—would eventually beset the associational behemoth that was Freemasonry. The massive consolidation of power and continual growth, the vulnerability of the Grand Lodge facilitated by the emergence of new, unsanctioned concordant orders, and flagging interest in clubs and societies resulted in derisive, internal conflicts.

---

177 McElroy, *Age of Improvement*, 180.
178 Ibid., 187.

Even more influential were politics, eschewed by other societies principally because of their potentially destructive effects. Despite the Masonic proscription of political discussions, it steadily found its way into lodges. Combined with a suspicious government and a fragile political state, Freemasonry's relatively unproblematic existence was surely over.

CHAPTER FOUR

"Behind Closed and Guarded Doors": Political Suspicion, Masonic Suppression, and The French Revolution

According to F.R. Worts, British Freemasonry from the years 1717 to 1780 has long been regarded as weak, "not only in its organiza tion but in the more important fundamental principles on which to build an enduring structure."[1] These values, claims Worts, were belief in God and a constant emphasis on order and stability.[2] Subsequently, Freemasonry became "primarily a social institution which provided good fellowship."[3] As we have seen, however, Scottish lodges established and enforced rules and regulations to ensure proper organization and became a popular destination for all members of society. Worts' generalized description also hides three very distinct and divergent periods in the history of Scottish Freemasonry: 1700–35, the pre-Grand Lodge era; 1736–89, the formal establishment of the Grand Lodge, the emergence of Freemasonry as a popular Enlightenment society, and the consolidation of Grand Lodge power; and 1790–1808, an era defined by the national impact of the French Revolution and the increased presence of a central governing Masonic institution.[4] Similar to Money's classification of English Freemasonry, this final period was characterized by a "complex balance between ultimately conflicting tendencies which temporarily coincided."[5] Freemasonry was forced, as a result of the French Revolution, to reconcile the secrecy and mystery surrounding the society with an urgent need to appear open and loyal to the government.

---

1   F. R. Worts, "The Development of the Content of Masonry During the Eighteenth Century," *AQC* 1965 (78): 1.

2   Ibid.

3   Ibid., 2; 14.

4   These classifications are based on my research and reflect four important and influential periods in the development of eighteenth-century Scottish Freemasonry.

5   John Money separates eighteenth-century English Freemasonry into three main periods: 1717–1750, marked by the formation of a Grand Lodge and the establishment of London as the center of Masonic activity; 1751–1775, the development and growth of Freemasonry outside of London; and 1776–1800, the suspicion surrounding secret clubs and societies. "Freemasonry and Loyalism," 255–256.

During this final and significant phase, the entire nature of Freemasonry changed. Although masons largely avoided political and religious discussions and "repeatedly insisted on the nonpolitical aims of their lodges,"[6] the intense revolutionary struggles of the late-eighteenth and early-nineteenth centuries did stimulate several political conflicts which were directly responsible for the Maybole Trial of Sedition and the Masonic Secession. Other Scottish clubs and societies—such as the Fair and Intellectual Society—also banned political discussions, especially during the turbulent years of the eighteenth century. And The Easy Club explicitly stated that "the Club shall never be acters or intermedlers in politicks as a Society."[7] By way of explanation, McElroy notes that apparently "the members were somehow made uneasy by politics and hence decided to give them up forever."[8]

In several instances, these fears manifested the vulnerability of associations to undesirable divisions created along political and party lines. Historians attribute the failing membership of the Speculative Society to the "political conditions of the time ... The French Revolution [and] some circumstances in the state of Scotland ... caused even the association of a few young gentlemen assembling weekly for private debate, under the control of an ancient established College, to be looked upon by many with no very kindly eye."[9] In a time when the "revolutionary atmosphere feeling ran high and the fear of an explosion which would wreck the society was well founded as ensuing events proved," the majority of the members decided that it [Speculative Society] "should be cautious in admitting as subjects of discussion or debate, the political topics of the day."[10]

Contrary to the political skepticism of some organizations, others—for example the Dialectic and Logical Societies—permitted such discussions. At a meeting of December 10, 1791, the society debated the following question: "Will the Revolution of France be of more Advantage than disadvantage to Europe?" Ultimately, the members "decided unanimously in the affirmative."[11] When the Logical Society and the Juridical Society

---

6   Melton, *Rise of the Public*, 252.

7   McElroy, *Age of Improvement*, 17–18.

8   Ibid., 18.

9   Ibid., 112.

10 Ibid.

11 Ibid., 114.

merged in 1797, the Logical Society flourished, while the Juridical Society languished for one reason: "the Logical permitted political debates and the Juridical did not."[12] Indeed, any society which discouraged such considerations would be unattractive to those potential members who wanted to discuss affairs of the state. However, McElroy notes that the "French Revolution and its consequences brought all political discussion among the young men in these debating societies under suspicion."[13]

Unfortunately for Scotland, the French Revolution was a watershed event in terms of the nature of Enlightenment sociability. Michael Lynch astutely observes that the "new strains brought on by the French Revolution were undermining the closed world of the literati."[14] He further notes that

> the Select Society had faded in popularity at the seeming height of its influence, in the early 1760s. A generation later, the Speculative Society, home of most of the later literati, saw attendance at its meetings decline after 1789; the proposal in 1794, supported by Walter Scott and Francis Jeffrey, that the Society be allowed to discuss 'the political topics of the day', split it asunder. Politics had infiltrated the world of the clubs ... The unique atmosphere which for almost a century had stimulated and cosseted the brilliant world of the literati dissolved.[15]

It was this infiltration that was responsible, as Lynch asserts, for the demise of various associations; it was also this intrusion that was to blame for the near-collapse of Scottish Freemasonry. Although Koselleck maintains that masons rejected political and religious discussions, mainly to "convince the government that the secret society was harmless and deserved toleration," politics soon became an integral part of the society.[16] Furthermore, "under their common rule in the sign of virtue they had no need of political tricks and external constructs such as the balance of power. The inner union along guaranteed happiness."[17] Pressured by a

---

12 Ibid., 130.

13 Ibid.

14 Michael Lynch, *Scotland: A New History* (London, 2000): 349–350.

15 Ibid., 350.

16 Koselleck, *Critique and Crisis*, 73–74.

17 Ibid., 75.

government intent on eradicating any traces of treason among clubs and societies in Britain, however, freemasons were forced to make politics a central issue.

Constitutionalism, Loyalism, and Politics

The rise of politics coincided with an upsurge of loyalism as an expression of opposition to reformist organizations and, especially in the 1790s, "its more aggressive manifestations united around the war-cry 'Church and King!'"[18] In effect, British freemasons intensely emphasized their extreme patriotism and reverence for the "craft's sense of its own past, real and invented," and the "King as its symbol, head, and chief protector."[19] This ideological belief and trust in both the King and constitution played a vital role in establishing a political basis for lodges and contributed to a general standardization of laws and regulations. Lodge constitutions, texts, and rituals were all heavily influenced by "proto-parliamentary themes" such as electing officers by vote, discussing lodge business and issues in debates, imposing fines and penalties on members who violated rules, and keeping detailed minutes of all lodge transactions.[20] James Van Horn Melton assesses the political and ideological shift in British Freemasonry:

> By the 1790s English freemasonry had become thoroughly domesticated. The rhetoric of liberty and brotherhood that had hitherto dominated the language of the movement gave way to a conspicuously patriotic discourse, one that stressed respect for national tradition and loyalty to church and king. Here the loyalist tone of British freemasonry mirrored more broadly the patriotic mood that pervaded British political culture at the end of the eighteenth century.[21]

This sense of loyalism was also apparent in Scotland. Speeches, prayers, and toasts that paid homage to the government and its leadership were

---

18 Clive Emsley, *Britain and the French Revolution* (London, 2000): 40. See also Harry Dickinson, "Popular Loyalism in Britain in the 1790s," *Transformation*, 503–534.

19 Melton, *Rise of the Public*, 265–266.

20 Ibid., 258.

21 Melton, *Rise of the Public*, 267. Jacob writes that lodges were "enamored of British constitutionalism" and "encouraging of enlightened and strong central government," *Radical Enlightenment*, 110. On the politicization of English Freemasonry, Berman, *Foundations*.

often extensively recorded in lodge minutes.[22] For example, during a dedication ceremony for the Barracks in Aberdeen in 1794, the Grand Chaplain prayed that the building might "be so happily finished, as to become a commodious edifice for the temporary residence of British Soldiers, the brave defenders of our King, our Constitution, our Religion, our liberties and our Laws."[23] No. 1(3) also equated freedom with the establishment. In a prayer given on July 7, 1801 at the laying of the foundation stone of the bridge over the Denburn River, the chaplain for the lodge prayed that the people might maintain their "Liberty, the happy order and good Government which we enjoy under our gracious King, our excellent Constitution and our equal laws."[24]

Masonic loyalism was also conveyed through letter writing. In correspondence, especially to the government and the King, freemasons expressed their sentiments about a variety of public issues and continually declared their intense support for the Crown. A fine example is a letter of 1800 from the Grand Lodge of Scotland to George III. Characterized by overzealous flattery and ornate language, the freemasons asserted their steadfast allegiance:

> We your Majesties most dutiful and Loyal Subjects The Grand Master and other officers of the Grand Lodge of Scotland with the Masters and Proxies of Lodge and their Wardens in Grand Lodge Assembled, approach your Majestys Throne with reflection of Horror in common with all your other affectionate Subjects on the possible event of a recent attempt upon the Sacred person of your Majesty which but for the proof of that atrocity we should for the honor of humanity have doubted the reality. The miserable person who made this wicked attack on a life so justly precious to the whole community must according to our feelings have either been vested by the Supreme Being with the greatest affliction to which

---

22 Lionel Vibert notes that the "Kings in Scotland very much encouraged the Royal art, Lodges were there kept up without interruptions for many hundred years, and the old toast among Scots Masons was 'God Bless the King and the Craft,'" "Anderson's *Constitutions* of 1723," 49.

23 No. 1(3) Aberdeen Lodge Minutes, June 24, 1794.

24 Ibid., June 24, 1794.

our Nature is liable or be of a description of men (if such are entitled to the appellation) of which we are fully convinced there exists not another solitary Individual throughout the Extended Dominions of your Majesty.

The Magnanimity displayed by your Majesty on so trying an occasion will ever in recollection fill the eyes of your faithful Subjects with tears of gratitude as establishing your entire confidence on your affectionate People as having an effect pleasing. We are well aware to your Majesty of preventing many and serious mischiefs among the great concourse of your Subjects then assembled whose fears were alive for the safety of their beloved Sovereign. We take this opportunity of assuring your Majesty of the purity and simplicity of our Ancient order and of our sincere attachment to the Glorious Constitution of our Country founded on a basis which from its stability cannot be shaken by Foes foreign or Domestic, and conclude with our most anxious wishes for the long continuance and prosperity of your Majestys Reign, and for the permanent unimpaired and undisturbed felicity of your Majesty—and of every branch of your illustrious House.[25]

Style and tone were carefully chosen and crafted in such a way as to portray freemasons as the most reliable supporters of church and state. Letters were even sent to the King congratulating him on the marriage of family members and anniversaries of his accession. Such letters were not exclusive to freemasons. As Michael Fry notes, many organizations and public societies were "urged to send in loyal addresses to George III. More than 400 immediately did so, and many continued to at every excuse: by 1796 the King was sick of the sight of them, and ordered that they should be sent straight to [Henry] Dundas without bothering him."[26]

This outpouring of respect, however, was a new departure in the period after 1789. After all, Anderson's *Constitutions* of 1723 stated that freemasons should be "resolv'd against all Politicks, as what never yet conduc'd

25   Grand Lodge of Scotland Minutes, June 9, 1800.
26   Fry, *Despotism*, 168.

to the Welfare of the *Lodge*, nor ever will."[27] The Grand Lodge of Scotland recognized that "it was at all times unbecoming of them as a Body to interfere with Politics," but at the same it considered "Loyalty to the King and Submissions to the Laws to be duties incumbent On all."[28] Though such expressions of devotion strengthened public perceptions of the fraternity, the timing of their appearance suggests that the masons were attempting to bolster their image while simultaneously safeguarding themselves against government suspicion of secret societies.[29]

Revolutionary Attitudes and Suspicion

In addition to toasts, speeches, and letters, surviving lodge minutes also attest to the increase of political discussions and ideas, even though they were effectively banned by the *Constitutions*. For example, on St. John the Baptist's Day in June 1806, No. 6 Old Inverness recorded that upon the conclusion of the meeting, it was "moved by a Brother, and unanimously approved of, that the Secretary be instructed to engross after these Minutes the Patriotick Songs ... and thereby increase the Harmony of Masonry."[30] One particular song set to the music of "In The Garb of Old Gaul" expressed the lodge's opposition to the revolution while firmly establishing its confidence in the ability of the government to prevent any threats of revolt or rebellion. C. M. Jackson-Houlston, referring to "In the Garb of Old Gaul," writes that the original "song of robust patriotism" was published in 1765 and referred to "wresting Canada from the French. After invoking the 'sons of old Scotland' to defy the 'Corsican Tyrant,' the song recounts the heroism of the undefeated Fingal, and the Scots defeat of 'the Danes and fierce Saxons,' and celebrates Caledonia 'valiant, unconquer'd and free—a very selective version of history that cuts to the assertion that 'Now united with England, our int'rests are join'd.'"[31]

---

27 James Anderson, *Constitutions*, 54. The section on politics also stipulates that "... no private Piques or Quarrels must be brought within the Door of the *Lodge*, far less Quarrels about *Religion*, or *Nations*, or *State Policy*."

28 Grand Lodge of Scotland Minutes, November 30, 1795.

29 Michael Fry notes that Dundas heard that "a network of Scottish societies already had 300 members, including ordinary workers, whom they [Friends of the People] could attract because they set much lower subscriptions than their English counterparts. Dundas thought he would make himself useful to the Government by dealing in person with this," *Despotism*, 168.

30 No. 6 Old Inverness Lodge Minutes, June 1806.

31 From a paper entitled "'You Heroes of the Day': Ephemeral Verse Responses to the

No. 6 Old Inverness adapted the words of the song, presumably, to contrast the superior political stability of Britain to the crumbling revolutionary machine in France. The chorus provides a rousing patriotic message:

Then round the loved standard let each Volunteer
Well accouter'd & armed in firm courage appear
To shew the regicides of France that freedom alone
Will thrive in the nations where George fills the throne.[32]

Two verses follow which reiterate the ardent allegiance of the masons, offer an unflattering description of the fate of Robespierre, and praise the bravery of the British people:

When Wilson the Standard unfolded displays
Acclamations are heard and Repeated Huzzas
While Robertspeare is doomed & died married to shame
Good Magistrates are nich'd in the Temple of Fame

No terror a threatened invasion can breed
In the man fired for conquest or bravely to bleed
Enthusiasts we'er all for our country and our laws
What coward would fly death in so glorious a cause?[33]

Another incident of orthodox patriotism is recorded in the minutes from Roman Eagle Lodge No. 160 in Edinburgh. On January 14, 1808, the lodge reported that

> After the Grand Master Elect retired the Depute Master ... made a very appropriate and Expressive Speech to the Brethren, wherein he pointed out to them the very Elegant manner in which the Room was fitted up this Evening for the reception of the Grand Lodge, The Brethren will easily conceive the beautiful manner in which the Orchestra was Decorated so completely with Green Branches and Illuminated with One Hundred

---

Peace of Amiens and the Napoleonic Wars 1802–04," given at Oxford-Brookes University in 2003. Houlston references R. Ford, *Song Histories* (Glasgow, 1900): 242–247.

32   No. 6 Old Inverness Lodge Minutes, June 1806.

33   Ibid.

and twelve variegated [candles], in the ... Room were placed the Busts upon proper Pedestals of the immortal ... Charles James Fox, Lord Nelson the Hero of the Nile and of Trafalgar, probably there never were in any country two Men of equal celebrity and Virtue. The Lodge in a very proper manner drank ... to their remembrance in usual Masonic Form, The Room was full and the Musical Entertainment was great.[34]

Some lodges, such as No. 27 St. Mungo's in Glasgow, endeavored to keep politics from entering into lodges. For instance, in a minute dated November 4, 1788, the lodge noted that although "this being the Night appointed by the Magistrates for Celebrating the Memory of the Revolution in 1688 ... The Night was spent in the greatest Harmony & Politicks intirely excluded the Walls of our peacefull habitation. No toast was given that Could be offensive to either Whig or Torry & Consequently the Grand design of Masonry was strictly adhered to."[35]

Notwithstanding repeated affirmations of loyalty to the Crown and the attempts of masons to proscribe political discussions, it is clear that some Scottish lodges were associated with radical and seditious societies. Wartski argues that freemasons in the United Kingdom espoused "many divergent opinions and sentiments," and thus it was quite possible that some supported government reform.[36] Nevertheless, as Wartski reasons, the fact that masons "met behind closed and guarded doors and deliberated in secret" suggested a comparison with revolutionary societies in Britain and Europe.[37]

No. 8 Journeymen Operative Lodge in Edinburgh, for example, was involved in an incident which exemplified this gradual opening-up to political questions. On November 22, 1793, the lodge agreed to rent its

---

34   No. 160 Roman Eagle Lodge Minutes, January 14, 1808.

35   No. 27 St. Mungo's Lodge Minutes, November 4, 1788.

36   L. D. Wartski, "Freemasonry and the Early Secret Societies Act" (Monograph, Grand Lodge of Scotland): 19.

37   Ibid. For further discussion on European attitudes toward Freemasonry, see Jacob, *Living the Enlightenment*, esp. 23–32, and *Radical Enlightenment*; Kosselleck, *Critique and Crisis*, 62–98; Melton, *Rise of the Public*, 262–270; Roberts, *Mythology*, 58–90; A. Mellor, "Eighteenth-Century French Freemasonry and the French Revolution," *AQC* 97 (1984): 105–114; Turnbridge and Batham, "The Climate of European Freemasonry 1750–1810," *AQC* 83 (1970): 248–255.

premises for unspecified reasons to the radical organization the Friends of the People. Led by their lionized and demonized vice president Thomas Muir and relying on Thomas Paine's *Rights of Man* (1791) to express their beliefs in universal suffrage and annual parliaments, the Friends actively communicated with the London Corresponding Society (LCS), a "leader among [the] new generation of reform clubs."[38] The objectives of these revolutionary bodies were to communicate with similar societies and to "publish literature with the object of stirring up people to its ideals all over the country."[39] While it is not apparent that Muir was a freemason, he did correspond with Hamilton Rowan, who was a member of the First Volunteer Lodge of Ireland and Secretary of the Dublin Society of United Irishmen. E. W. McFarland suggests that one cannot rule out Freemasonry "as an additional contact medium at this stage, given its role among other Enlightenment influences on radicalism."[40]

In 1792, the Friends held their first Convention in Edinburgh.[41] Shortly thereafter, during the King's Birthday Riots, effigies of Henry Dundas were burned and the Lord Provost's house was attacked by anti-government demonstrators.[42] McFarland notes that although Scotland was pacific during the 1780s, the rising tide of revolutionary and reform societies in England swept northwards after 1789 causing numerous disturbances, leading Dundas to assert that the Friends were to blame for much of the unrest.[43] Dundas was so concerned about the action of the Friends, in fact, that he lamented the inefficacy of parliament in checking the "indiscriminate process of the association," and asserted it would ultimately "spread the fermentation of the Country to such a height, that it will be impossi-

---

38 Benjamin Weinstein, "Popular Constitutionalism and the London Corresponding Society," *Albion*, 34 (2002): 38. See also H. T. Dickinson, ed., *British Radicalism and the French Revolution 1789–1815* (Oxford, 1985): 9–13.

39 Wartski, "Secret Societies Act," 4.

40 McFarland, *Ireland and Scotland*, 75.

41 During the Convention of 1792, Muir read an address from the United Irishmen in Dublin. Due to apparent seditious undertones of the message, Muir was subsequently "found guilty of sedition and sentenced to transportation to Botany Bay," Dickinson, *British Radicalism*, 21. See also Kenneth J. Logue, *Popular Disturbances in Scotland, 1780–1815* (Edinburgh, 1979), 11–16.

42 John Stevenson, "Popular Radicalism and Popular Protest," in *Britain and the French Revolution 1789–1815*, ed. Harry T. Dickinson (London, 1989), 69. See also Logue, *Popular Disturbances*, 133–143.

43 McFarland, *Ireland and Scotland*, 81–82.

ble to restrain the effects of them. They stop at nothing, it would appear they intend to either murder myself or burn my house."[44] Indeed, following formation of The Friends of the People in July 1792, numerous societies began to appear in September 1792 such as the Dundee Friends of the Constitution and the Glasgow Associated Friends of the Constitution.[45]

Propagating reformist ideas in imitation of the French, the Friends' radicalism caused much alarm not only within the British government, but among Masonic lodges.[46] On November 4, 1793, the Grand Lodge of Scotland met to discuss the actions of the Journeymen. Thomas Hay, the Substitute Grand Master of Scotland, intimated that

> he understood some of the Lodges in and about this City had been in the practice of allowing certain persons styling themselves "The Friends of the People" to assemble in their Lodges, whose deliberations it was said were of a turbulent and Seditious tendency, and from the station in life of the greatest part of the people composing these Meetings, these Lodges could reap but very little pecuniary aid toward their funds. Therefore he moved, that these Lodges be in future prohibited from allowing any such meetings to be held in their said Lodges of the delegation before Mentioned.[47]

After the Grand Lodge communication of 4 November was issued, the Journeymen met on November 22, 1793 "for the purpose of Considering A Minute of the Grand Lodge about letting the Lodge room to the Society of the Friends of the People."[48] Upon deliberation of the Grand Lodge's decision, the members ultimately resolved "That the Lodge room should be Let to the highest bidder and for that purpose to advertise it in the Edinburgh News papers."[49] Notwithstanding the Grand Lodge's resolution, No. 8 Journeymen allowed the meeting to take place on December 5, 1793. Lord Provost Thomas Elder, accompanied by several constables,

---

44   Ibid.

45   Ibid., 66–73.

46   Henry W. Meikle, *Scotland and the French Revolution* (London, 1969), 86–111.

47   Grand Lodge of Scotland Minutes, November 4, 1793.

48   No. 8 Journeymen Lodge Minutes, November 22, 1793.

49   Ibid.

forcibly disbanded the assembly; shortly thereafter, numerous members of the Friends were arrested and charged with sedition.[50] On December 7, 1793, the Grand Lodge of Scotland held a meeting to discuss the conduct of No. 8. During the meeting,

> it was Represented by the Substitute Grand Master that the Journeymen Mason Lodge of Edinburgh ... had subjected their Lodge to persons calling themselves the "Friends of the People," and wished to know how the Grand Lodge would dispose of the matter. Whereupon it was Resolved to call by public advertisement in the newspapers, a General Meeting of the Grand Lodge to Consider the Matter, and ordered Circular Letters should be sent to the whole members or Committee of the Journeymen Mason Lodge requesting their attendance upon Thursday next at seven o'clock in the Evening, which was accordingly done, and cards sent to that effect.[51]

Subsequently, the Grand Lodge suspended five members of No. 8 for permitting the Friends to meet in their lodge. In an overt magnanimous gesture, the Grand Lodge acknowledged that it would "repone the whole members, and admit them to their free stations in the Lodge, they always behaving properly in time coming agreeable to the rules of the Craft."[52]

The overall links between Freemasonry and radicals are tenuous at best. No membership roles for the Friends of the People exist; thus, it is highly problematic to argue that freemasons were actively involved with the radical association. However, there is evidence which suggests that at least some members of Masonic lodges were affiliated with other revolutionary groups. In Dundee, three members of St. David's Lodge were involved with the Dundee Friends of Liberty and the Perth and Dundee Radical Society. Among the most famous members of the Friends of Liberty was George Mealmaker, also a leader of the United Scotsmen; Mealmaker was arrested in 1797 and tried for sedition.[53] Among Mealmaker's colleagues

---

50   Seggie, *Journeymen Masons*, 83–87. The members were also "sentenced to transportation ... for a period of fourteen years."

51   Grand Lodge of Scotland Minutes, December 7, 1793.

52   Ibid.

53   See Ferguson, *Scotland, 1689 to the Present: The Edinburgh History of Scotland Volume 4* (Edinburgh, 1965), 261.

in the Friends of Liberty were James Yeoman, baker, and a member of St. David's.[54] Members of both the Perth and Dundee Radical Club and St David's Masonic lodges included William Bisset, a "rich" founder, and one Mr. Crichton, who is listed as Patrick Crichton.[55] And in Edinburgh, James Thomason Callender—member of the Canongate and Leith, Leith and Canongate Lodge—is listed as a member of the radical Canongate No. 1 Society of the Friends of the People.[56] An outspoken critic of what he perceived as Britain's "imperialist foreign policy,"[57] Callender published several pamphlets agitating for parliamentary reform and a return of the British constitution to "its original purity."[58]

Robert Burns, freemason and member of St. David's Tarbolton and Canongate Kilwinning, suffered from what McElroy calls "revolutionary fever."[59] During the 1790s, appetites increased among young Scottish men for revolutionary literature, and often such curiosity placed them "in social and political hot water."[60] Burns admired Tom Paine, and briefly entertained the idea of joining the Friends of the People although there is no clear evidence linking him with the radical group. It seems as if the revolutionary fervor aroused the political sentiments of Burns, not the Masonic lodges of which he was a member.[61]

As we have seen, these few sympathizers, known radicals, and the incident involving No. 8 Journeymen and the Friends of the People do not, of course, definitively link Scottish freemasons with radical and subversive societies. It does, however, suggest that the members of at least three

---

54 See Richard G. Gallin, "Scottish Radicalism 1792–1794," Unpublished Thesis (New York, 1979), 249.

55 Ibid. See also Corey Andrews, "Paradox and Improvement: Literary Nationalism and Eighteenth-Century Scotland Club Poetry," Unpublished Thesis (Ohio, 2000), 97.

56 Gallin, "Scottish Radicalism," 248.

57 John Brims, "Scottish Radicalism and the United Irishmen," in *The United Irishmen: Republicanism, Radicalism and Rebellion*, ed. Kevin Whelan (Dublin, 1993), 152.

58 Ibid.

59 McElroy, *Age of Improvement*, 100–101.

60 Ibid.

61 Although not a known freemason, Colonel William Fullerton—member of the Ayrshire Parliament and a key figure in the debate over Grand Lodge's authority—joined the Whig Club on November 4, 1788 and was also a member of the Friends of the People. However, "alarmed at the excesses of the French Revolution, he became 'heartily ashamed' of the Friends and on 6 February 1793" severed ties with the association, Thorne, *History of Parliament*, 843–845.

lodges were susceptible to the ideas of reformist groups, as they allowed the Friends to use their premises in open defiance of the Grand Lodge.[62] Certainly the members of No. 8 were familiar with the Friends, as that society had held conventions in Edinburgh and the arrest and trial of Thomas Muir was a much-publicized event in the city. The actions of No. 8 also illustrate that operative lodges had embraced a much more liberal and broader view of the craft. The admission of nonoperative masons became more frequent and, in some cases, fees owed by operative masons upon their admission to a lodge were now actually higher than those monies owed by speculative masons. For example, No. 1(3) Lodge Aberdeen recorded on December 27, 1790 that the

> Entry money to be paid in future by Geomatic Masons, including cloathing, shall be Two pounds Ten shillings sterling, besides the usual contribution to the Mortification fund, Clerk and officers Fees. And That the Money Appropriate for drink and entertainments to the Candidates shall be Abolished and done away—And That there shall be an additional sum of Five shillings upon every Operative Mason to be paid on his being entered an Apprentice And that the usual money Appropriate for Entertainment to the Lodge by Operatives, shall be applied to the Funds of the Lodge, on their going through the different steps; And That Members of other Lodges shall pay, when Initiated into this Lodge whither Geomatics or Operatives, the respective dues as above which motion was readily and unanimously agreed to by the Lodge and ordained to be entered and Recorded as a Rule to be Observed in time coming, in this Lodge.[63]

Moreover, operative minutes were no longer dominated by the regulation of labor and trade, financial matters, and the election of officers. Rather, operative lodges began to record detailed descriptions of public processions, correspondence from the Grand Lodge and, as we have seen, controversial political issues.

---

62 Most strikingly, the Grand Lodge minute implicated several lodges in Edinburgh who were apparently involved with the Friends of the People.

63 No. 1(3) Lodge Aberdeen Minutes, December 27, 1790.

This altercation typifies the tensions present between the Grand Lodge of Scotland, its lodges, and the government during the final years of the eighteenth century. In the politically volatile climate of the 1790s, it was imperative that the Grand Lodge demonstrate its intolerance of insubordination and reaffirm the loyalty of freemasons to the church and state. Although the suspensions of the Journeymen masons were eventually reversed, the same patterns of harsh penalties and ultimate reconciliation would re-emerge during the Maybole Trial of Sedition in 1800 and the Masonic Secession of 1808. As the concerted effort to stamp out revolutionary threats and treasonable societies increased, however, the Grand Lodge's ability to arbitrate these disputes was impaired by a conflict of interests: wanting to appear strong in the face of discord, yet at the same time not wanting to alienate constituent lodges and bring about further controversy. The decision by No. 8 Journeymen to allow the Friends to meet in their lodge also manifests two further trends which will become much more apparent in subsequent chapters: the inability of the Grand Lodge to enforce its decisions and the propensity of lodges to act on their own accord. Indeed, these two patterns greatly reinforced the role of the Grand Lodge of Scotland as a figurehead of Scottish masonry, not a central ruling body. As such, it was ill-prepared to defend freemasons in general against the swirl of revolutionary accusations that surfaced during the end of the eighteenth century.

The Government Crackdown

Between the years 1792 and 1799, Parliament took the war against radicalism to a new level, reflecting the government's determination to "crush ... democratic opponents wherever they emerged."[64] Faced with perceived threats from subversive organizations and a dramatic increase of revolutionary sentiments in Britain, the government launched a campaign to eradicate all traces of sedition, treason, and sympathies for reformist societies. O'Gorman correctly notes that Pitt's legislative policies "acquired several different forms and operated on several different levels."[65] Pitt's first method of implementing this repressive policy was to "utilize exist-

---

64   Roger Wells, *Insurrection: The British Experience, 1795–1803* (Gloucester, 1983), 44.

65   Frank O'Gorman, "Pitt and the 'Tory' Reaction to the French Revolution 1798–1815," in *Britain and the French Revolution 1789–1815*, ed. H. T. Dickinson (London, 1989), 30.

ing disciplinary mechanisms as strongly as possible."[66] This meant involving the magistrates and warning them in 1792 to monitor any seditious literature and to prevent—and if necessary, quell—any disturbances. Pitt also implemented a system of local informants and spies to monitor public mood and sentiments.

The second method of policy enforcement was the mobilization of the legal system. Intent on setting an example through the harsh sentences imposed on prominent radical figures, Pitt was successful in intimidating and forcing into submission numerous seditious leaders. Through harassment, threats, prosecutions, and "legal compulsion and social prejudice," Pitt's policy achieved its goal of stamping out popular dissent.[67] However, the "*third* and complementary element in the government's repressive reaction to domestic radical agitation: its use of Parliament and parliamentary enactments," had the most significant impact on societies and the freemasons.[68]

The first piece of legislation designed by the government for the purpose of regulating clubs and societies was The Friendly Societies Act of 1793, which allowed the government to monitor organizations in Britain. Under the guidelines of the Act, clubs and societies would be registered as benefit and philanthropic associations. Ostensibly, the government justified the Act as a means to create a list of friendly societies. In practice, however, the Friendly Societies Act prevented registered associations from being incorporated and allowed the government to scrutinize the activities of the associations. Membership lists submitted to the government provided personal information on each affiliate, thus giving officials a wealth of personal information as the Pitt administration waged its war against seditious activities.

The Friendly Societies Act was discussed in Aberdeen Lodge No. 1(3). In a minute dated December 6, 1793, the lodge recorded the following extract which was also advertised in the *Aberdeen Journal*:

> The said day there was laid before the meeting by the
> Committee Appointed by the Society for drawing up
> Rules and Regulations in terms of the late Act of Parlia-

---

66 Ibid.

67 See O'Gorman, "Britain and the French Revolution," 31–32.

68 Ibid., 32.

ment for the relief and protection of Friendly Societies, a Report of said Committee with a copy of Rules, orders and Regulations to be observed in future by this said Society And which orders, Rules and regulations having been read over to the Meeting and deliberately considered, were by a very great Majority Approven of And the Lodge Did and do hereby make, ordain, and constitute the said Rules, which are hereby appointed to be engrossed in this Sederint book as Constitutional and Fundamental Laws, Orders, and Regulations of this Society, to be observed in all time coming. Repealing hereby, and Rescinding all former Rules, Orders, and Regulations made and Established in this Society.[69]

Although lodges such as No. 1(3) Aberdeen readily accepted the stipulations of the Act, its existence as a secret society made them susceptible to any legislation aimed at preventing the meeting of any organizations with real or imagined treasonable or seditious purposes.

Despite "limited legislative solutions to the problems of the 1790s," Prime Minister William Pitt earnestly believed that any discontent would ultimately be "checked by its own excess, and by the steadiness of Government."[70] Dogged by ethical quandaries and a reluctance to pursue any course of action that would infringe upon personal liberty and freedom, Pitt was acutely aware that any legislative measures had to be justified as "necessary and temporary sacrifices for the long-term defence of British freedoms."[71] Henry Dundas, however, recognized the "evident signs ... of a very turbulent and pernicious spirit having pervaded numerous and various descriptions of persons" in Britain.[72] He endorsed swift action against radical societies, suggesting that "whatever is to be done, ought to be done right"[73] and, according to Cockburn, engaged in a "general witch-hunt

---

69 No. 1(3) Aberdeen Lodge Minutes, December 6, 1793.

70 Michael Duffy, *The Younger Pitt* (Harlow, 2000), 148. Pitt "adhered throughout to a high-minded belief in virtuous government," 91.

71 Ibid. Duffy remarks that Pitt's concern with public opinion meant that "his measures were marked by restraint rather than intemperance or panic," 45.

72 Fry, *Despotism*, 159.

73 Ibid. Unlike Dundas, Pitt sought to "drive a wedge between the moderates who distanced themselves from the violence in France and accepted the limitations that Parliament imposed on their activities, and the irreconcilable extremists who after 1795

against anyone tainted with dissent."[74] Although his campaign in England to suppress revolutionary societies is hardly remembered, in Scotland "he has gone down as an ogre of repression."[75] Unlike Pitt, who declared it his "mild and forgiving policy to separate the misguided from the criminal,"[76] Dundas strove to enforce the laws with stringent retribution.

Dundas' zealous pursuit of radicalism in Scotland is typified, not least of all, by his handling of the trial of Thomas Muir. In 1793, the Friends of the People held their second convention in Edinburgh. Despite Muir's calls for universal suffrage and annual Parliaments, it was clear that support for his ideas had begun to wane, as many of the delegates in attendance expressed their support for the constitution.[77] Dundas was intent on mobilizing the legal system by prosecuting prominent radical reformers such as Muir;[78] upon the conclusion of a trial that was, as Dickinson claims, "unjust and vindictive," Muir was found guilty and sentenced to fourteen years' transportation.[79] After Muir's hearing and his subsequent transportation, radicalism in Scotland "disintegrated."[80] Despite this decline, Dundas acted as though the "threat remained palpable" and subsequently "intensified the repression, exploiting the fevered atmosphere of the war."[81] This increased concern with the supposed threat of French-inspired revolution resulted in the most important element in the government's reac-

developed a conspiratorial, underground, extremist fringe ... Like the rest of the Draconian legislation of eighteenth-century England with its plethora of capital offences, 'Pitt's Reign of Terror', as the radicals branded it, was intended to deter rather than punish," Ibid., 152.

74 Fry, *Despotism*, 172.

75 Ibid., 154. Fry notes that the "assessments of his [Dundas's] conduct during these years have usually stressed its expediency, arguing that whatever masks he had worn earlier now dropped to reveal the monster of depraved cynicism beneath ... Still, one effect of the threat to his conceptions posed in the 1790s was certainly to make him respond in kind," 172–173.

76 Duffy, *The Younger Pitt*, 150–152.

77 Ibid.

78 O'Gorman, "Pitt," 31. O'Gorman notes that through harassment, threats, prosecutions, and "legal compulsion and social prejudice," Dundas achieved his goal of stamping out popular dissent and radical societies.

79 Dickinson, *British Radicalism*, 21–22; 31–32; 38.

80 Fry, *Despotism*, 172. After the trial of Thomas Muir and his subsequent transportation, radicalism was "more or less finished, as we know in retrospect, for a good twenty years," 174.

81 Ibid., 172.

tion to domestic radicalism which was, according to O'Gorman, its "use of Parliament and parliamentary enactments."[82]

As Britain was quickly becoming a refuge for French exiles seeking to escape the revolution, the Alien Act of 1793 delayed the entry of all foreigners into the United Kingdom until they were issued a passport.[83] Two years later, following the suspension of *habeas corpus* in 1795,[84] the government passed the Treasonable and Seditious Meetings Acts, collectively referred to as the Gagging Acts. As Fry maintains, Dundas made a "particular fuss about the Treason and Sedition Bills of 1795, introduced to clear up the legal controversies arising from the recent trials by declaring such offences indeed to be criminal in Scotland, just in case they were not so already."[85] The Treasonable and Seditious Practices Act defined as treason any

> compassings, imaginations, inventions, devices, or intentions which might be published, printed or written and which might endeavour by force or constraint, to compel him or them to change his or their measures or counsels, or in order to put any force or constraint upon, or to intimidate, or overawe, both houses or either house of parliament.[86]

Essentially, the Act protected the King, constitution, and government from defamation.[87] The second of the Two Acts, the Seditious Meetings Act, "banned meetings of more than fifty people whose object was either to petition Parliament on or to discuss any alteration of the establishment in church and state."[88] Wells asserts that of the two Acts, the Seditious Meetings Act was "much more insidious," as it "equated the attenders of political meetings (even those held in a field) with visitors to disorder-

---

82 O'Gorman, "Pitt," 31–32.

83 Ibid., 29.

84 Ibid. Pitt was more hesitant in his decision to suspend *habeas corpus*. Duffy writes that "during the debates on the suspension of habeas corpus in May 1794, he declared that 'prosecution, in no instance, ought to extend beyond what the real necessity of the case required,'" *The Younger Pitt*, 149.

85 Fry, *Despotism*, 172.

86 O'Gorman, "Pitt," 32.

87 Wells, *Insurrection*, 44.

88 O'Gorman, "Pitt," 32.

ly houses, and gave the local Bench arbitrary powers over suspects who could be simply packed off."[89]

The Alien Act of 1793, sudden suspension of *habeas corpus*, and the passage of the Gagging Acts have led historians to question the motives that lay behind the approval of such extreme actions and legislation. Wells dismisses the "blinkered approach" of those liberal historians who claim simply that the "laws eroding political liberty were unnecessary, because the revolutionary element was either non-existent, or impotent."[90] Yet he also is skeptical of the claims that Pitt's apparent paranoia was "based on fears of what might occur rather than what was actually happening."[91] Whether excessive or inspired by untenable threats, it is clear that more legislation in stricter and much harsher forms resulted from the inadequacy of earlier measures.[92] An attack at Parliament on George III by the London Corresponding Society on October 29, 1795 prompted the government to pass the Unlawful Oaths (1797) and Secret Societies (1799) Acts, both of which proved to be problematical to Freemasonry.[93] The Unlawful Oaths Act was significant, for the swearing of oaths was the basis by which the working class organized successfully and ensured both secrecy and solidarity. Fearing that such assemblies would incite revolutionary activities, the Unlawful Oaths Act stipulated that

---

89 Wells, *Insurrection*, 45.

90 Ibid, 28–29.

91 Ibid.

92 Ibid.

93 William Earl of Ancrum, then Grand Master of Scotland, read the following letter on November 30, 1795 before the Grand Lodge of Scotland which was afterwards sent to the King: "Most Gracious Sovereign, We your Majesty's most dutiful subjects the Grand Lodge of Scotland, humbly request permission to approach you Majesty, with the most sincere expressions of that attachment, and Loyalty, for which our Antient and respectable order, has ever been distinguished. Your Majesty's late deliverance from the hands of wicked and sanguinary men, while it recalls to us the recollections of your Majesty's virtues, impresses us with Gratitude to that Providential care, which by watching over your Majesty's Life, has averted the most alarming calamities from your people. We on this occasion witnessed the interposition of Heaven for the safety of your Royal Person, that it may never cease to extend its Guardian protection to your Majesty, and to your Illustrious House is our united Prayer," Grand Lodge of Scotland Minutes, November 30, 1795. See Shelia Lambert, ed., *House of Commons Sessional Papers of the Eighteenth Century* (Wilmington, DE, 1975), 33–35. This letter was sent the same day that "An Act for the safety and preservation of His Majesty's Person" was sent to committee in the House of Commons.

any person is guilty of a felony and liable to heavy punishment who in any manner or form administers or
causes to be administered, or aids or assists at, or is present and consents to the administering or taking of any
oath or engagement purporting or intended to bind the
person taking it to engage in any mutinous or seditious
purpose, or to disturb the public peace, or to be of any
society formed for such a purpose or to obey the orders
of any committee or body not lawfully constituted, or
of any commander not having authority by law for that
purpose, or not to inform or give evidence against any
associate or other person or not to reveal any unlawful
combination or any illegal act done or to be done or any
illegal oath or engagement or its import, or who takes
any such oath without being compelled to do so.[94]

While Masonic initiations involved compulsory oaths and obligations,
they were not seditious or mutinous. Ultimately, the freemasons were not
directly implicated under this Act. To allay suspicion, however, the Grand
Lodge of Scotland and the Ancient Grand Lodge of England "in view of
the prevalent excitement, resolved to hold no procession on St. Andrews
Day, and it was recommended to Brethren, who might visit one another
on the occasion, to pass as privately through the streets as possible, so that
there might be no cause given for raising a tumult or noise in the street."[95]
In addition to prohibiting all public Masonic processions, the Ancient
Grand Lodge of England resolved

> That it be recommended to His Grace the Duke of Atholl
> Right Worshipful Grand Master of Free Masons of En-
> gland according to the Old Constitutions to inhibit and
> totally prevent all public Masonic Processions—and
> all private meetings of Masons of Lodges of Emergen-
> cy upon any pretence whatsoever and to suppress and
> suspend all Masonic Meetings except the regular stated
> Lodge Meetings and Royal Arch Chapter which shall be

---

94 See Lambert, *House of Commons Sessional Papers*, "A Bill for more effectually preventing the administering of unlawful oaths," *Vol. 103*, 433–435.

95 See Lindsay, *Holyrood House*, 246. Significantly, there were no Grand Festivals from
1799 to 1802.

held open to all Masons to visit duly qualified as such. That when the usual Masonic Business be ended the Lodge shall then disperse, the Tyler withdraw from the Door of the Lodge room and formal restraint of Admission shall cease. The above Resolutions being submitted to this Committee they were unanimously approved of and confirmed. Ordered that the Grand Secretary shall immediately give Notice to every Lodge under the Ancient Constitution also to the Grand Lodges of Scotland and Ireland etc. etc. of these proceedings.[96]

The immediate effects of the legislation were minimal at best, only calling into question the secrets contained within and the substance of Masonic oaths. It did not insinuate that freemasons shared the radical tendencies of such factions as the Friends of the People and the London Corresponding Society. Two years later, however, Freemasonry would be directly affected by the passage of the Secret Societies Act, the most "sweeping of the legislative measures introduced by Pitt's government to forestall the threat of a revolution."[97] In a speech delivered to the House of Commons on April 19, 1799, Pitt listed the names of those radical associations that he believed posed the greatest risk to domestic stability, including clubs and societies, such as the freemasons, that were secretive by nature.[98] By name, the government outlawed the London Corresponding Society, the United Englishmen, United Scotsmen, United Irishmen, and the United Britons. Pitt justified the legislation by emphasizing the continual need to oppose seditious societies:

> We must proceed still farther, now that we are engaged in a most important struggle with the restless and fatal spirit of Jacobinism, assuming new shapes, and concealing its malignant and destructive designs under new forms and new practices. In order to oppose its effect, we must also from time to time adopt new modes, and

---

96 See Library and Museum of Freemasonry, Antient Minute Book No. 4, May 6, 1799.

97 Andrew Prescott, "The Unlawful Societies Act of 1799," Conference Paper, Canonbury Masonic Research Centre (London, 2000), 1.

98 See Gould's *History of Freemasonry Vol. 3*, 394–395; Fred L. Pick and G. Norman Knight, *The Freemason's Pocket Reference Book* (London, 1983), 344–345; Seggie, *Journeymen Masons*, 253–257.

assume new shapes ... These marks are wicked and illegal engagements of mutual fidelity and secrecy by which the members are bound; the secrecy of electing the members; the secret government and conduct of the affairs of the society; secret appointments unknown to the bulk of the members; presidents and committees, which, veiling themselves from the general mass and knowledge of the members, plot and conduct the treason—I propose that all societies which administer such oaths shall be declared unlawful confederacies.[99]

By July 1799, the government had passed the Secret Societies Act, or "An act for the more effectual suppression of societies established for seditious and treasonable purposes; and for the better preventing treasonable and seditious practices," which effectively regulated and policed Freemasonry in Scotland. In no uncertain terms, the Act emphatically declared that

a traitorous conspiracy had long been carried on with the persons from time to time exercising the power of government in France to overturn the laws, constitution and government and that in pursuance of such design, diverse societies had been instituted ... All and every of the said societies [that require] an unlawful oath or engagement ... shall be deemed guilty of an unlawful combination and confederacy.[100]

Although arguably Masonic oaths fell "outside the scope of [the] bill since they were not seditious," stipulations set forth by the Act demanded public initiations which would immediately result in the forced exposure of Masonic oaths, rites, and rituals.[101] Additionally, the government placed severe restrictions on printing, mandating that all printers or vendors of printing presses register themselves with the Home Office, maintain accounts of all transactions, and record the name and address of the printer or publisher on the "title and end papers of all books."[102]

---

99 Quoted in Prescott, "Unlawful," 3.

100 Lambert, *House of Commons Sessional Papers Vol. 120*, 365–384.

101 Prescott, "Unlawful," 5.

102 Ibid., 4.

The Fate of the Freemasons and the Loss of Power

The parliamentary debate surrounding the inclusion or exclusion of the freemasons in the Secret Societies Act is well documented. As Prescott notes, "such wide-ranging legislation was bound to create problems by inadvertently catching in its net harmless and respectable activities," and "many of these difficulties became apparent when the bill came to committee on 6 May [1799]."[103] During its second reading on 30 May, Pitt received a request for a meeting with Masonic representatives, including Lord Moira and the Duke of Atholl, to discuss the Act as it related to the freemasons.[104] The Modern Grand Lodge of England recorded the details of the discussion, noting that the Prime Minister "expressed his good opinion of the Society and said he was willing to recommend any clause to prevent the new act from affecting the Society, provided that the name of the society could be prevented from being made use of as a cover by evilly disposed persons for seditious purposes."[105] Exemptions for the Grand Lodges of England and Scotland were added at the committee stage of the bill, but only after much controversy and debate. The exclusion clause resolutely stated that

> Nothing in this act contained shall extend, or be construed to extend, to prevent the meetings of the Lodge or society of persons which is now held at Free Masons Hall in Great Queen Street in the County of Middlesex, and usually denominated the Grand Lodge of Freemasons in England, or of the Lodge or society of persons usually

---

103 Ibid.

104 Moira was the Acting Grand Master of the Grand Lodge of England, and Atholl was the Grand Master of the Ancient Grand Lodge of England.

105 Cited in Prescott, "Unlawful," taken from Library and Museum of Freemasonry, Minutes of the Hall Committee Minute Book No. 4, July 23, 1799. Prescott also includes the following minute entry from the Antient Grand Lodge Minute Book No. 4, June 5, 1799: "Upon hearing the report of the Right Honourable Deputy Grand Master respecting the proceedings relative to a Bill now pending in parliament for the suppression of private meetings of societies and now containing a clause granting a privilege to the Grand Lodge of Free Masons of England according to the Old Constitutions and to all subordinate lodges under them to be exempted from the penalties and operation of the said Act. It was resolved unanimously that the thanks of the Grand Lodge be given to the Right Worshipful Grand Master the Duke of Atholl for his uniform and unremitting attention to the Honor and Interest of the Ancient Craft and particularly for his care and exertions in the instance of the bill now pending in parliament from the operation of which the Ancient Craft is by a clause in the said bill exempted."

denominated The Grand Lodge of Masons in England, according to the Old Institution, or of the Lodge or society of persons which is now held at Edinburgh, and usually denominated The Grand Lodge of Free Masons of Scotland, or the meetings of any subordinate lodge or society of persons usually calling themselves Free Masons, the holding whereof shall be sanctioned or approved by any one of the above mentioned lodges or societies.[106]

Grenville expressed his doubts as to the efficacy of the clause, stating that "though he did not mean to propose setting it aside, yet it did not appear to him to be fraught with that clearness and certainty which he could wish," as "what the clause provided was of an anomalous nature, and new to the functions of parliament."[107]

The Scottish Grand Lodge's inclusion was guaranteed by a letter sent from Henry Dundas to Grand Master Sir James Stirling, stating that he had received Stirling's letter

> respecting the Free Masons of Scotland. The exception has already been made in their favour. Indeed if it was to be introduced in favour of the Lodges in England it was impossible that those who are acquainted as I am with the approved Loyalty and respectability of the Lodge in Scotland could have been inattentive to their Interests and Character.[108]

It was, perhaps, Dundas' association with Freemasonry and his influence over Pitt that prevented the masons from being explicitly named as a seditious society. Pitt and Grenville were not freemasons. If, however, Dundas was indeed a freemason,[109] it was expected—if not predictable—that the masons would be protected under the Secret Societies Act. There is no conclusive evidence establishing Dundas as a freemason; however, as a member of the Feast of Tabernacles and Mirror Club, he would surely have known that his fellow club members—including Alexander Aber-

---

106 Ibid., f. 35. Prescott, reproduced in facsimile form in F. William Torrington, *House of Lords Sessional Papers Session 1798–9 Vol. 1* (New York, 1974), 192–218.

107 Quoted in Prescott, "Unlawful," 7–8.

108 Grand Lodge of Scotland Minutes, August 5, 1799.

109 See Fry, *Despotism*, 184.

cromby, Andrew Crosbie, Cosmo George 3rd Duke of Gordon, Lord Hailes, Henry Mackenzie, and George Home of Wedderburn were freemasons. As such, the possibility exists that he may have been a member of a Masonic lodge in Edinburgh.

Eventually the government passed the amendment, and the Grand Lodges of Scotland and England "energetically circularized secretaries of lodges reminding them of their obligations under the act" and provided "pre-printed forms for the necessary declarations and returns."[110] Owing to an "odd side effect of the hasty way" in which the amendments had been passed, however, only those lodges which existed before July 12, 1799 were protected under the legislation, thus precluding the warranting of new lodges.[111]

For the Grand Lodge of Scotland, the revocation of its charter-granting privileges was perhaps the most important consequence of the Secret Societies Act. As Appendix 4 shows, it engaged in a detailed correspondence with the government between November 1799 and March 1803 regarding its charter-granting powers. The extracts reveal not only the sense of urgency present among the Grand Officers during the conflict over charter-granting privileges, but also the extent to which the Scottish Grand Lodge relied on the English Grand Officers to assist them in the matter. Issuing charters was a tangible method of illustrating the popularity of the organization; and symbolically, the ability to grant charters was one of the great powers of Scottish Freemasonry. Taking away such authority thus effectively prevented Masonic growth and development. Moreover, all lodges in Scotland—including the Grand Lodge—now possessed the same fundamental abilities.

The debate surrounding the restoration of its charter-granting privileges began on November 25, 1799. At a Grand Lodge meeting, Past Master William Inglis of St. Luke's Lodge expressed his concern over the Secret Societies Act and the inability of the Grand Lodge to grant new charters:

> He [Inglis] had considerable doubts whether under the
> Act passed in the present Session of Parliament entitled
> "An Act for the more effective suppression of Societies
> Established for Seditious and Treasonable purposes," the

---

110 Prescott, "Unlawful," 10.
111 Ibid.

Grand Lodge had powers to Grant New Charters. He Therefore Moved that a case be made out and laid before The Lord Advocate of Scotland for his opinion and advice upon the Subject. And should His Lordship be of Opinion that the Grand Lodge under the above Act had not Powers to Grant such Charters he moved that the Grand Lodge should Solicit his Lordships assistance in an application to Parliament (should this appear necessary) for remedying this defect as well as for vesting certain Powers in the Grand Lodge which would naturally benefit their poor.[112]

The "certain powers" Inglis refers to are charitable and philanthropic activities. Not being able to grant charters to new lodges would mean a reduction in the funds remitted to the Grand Lodge of Scotland for the relief of the poor and indigent. These concerns were echoed by the Duke of Atholl. Fearing that the Secret Societies Act would weaken the charitable capabilities of Freemasonry, Atholl stated that the "Masonic system was founded on the most exalted system of benevolence, morals, and charity, and many thousands were annually relieved by the charitable benevolence of masons. The very laudable and useful charities must necessarily be quashed did the bill pass into a law, as recommended by the Noble Earl [of Radnor]."[113] Following the initial meeting and the decision to enlist the help of the Lord Advocate, the Grand Lodge reconvened and appointed a committee to "draw up a Memorial and case ... respecting the Question whether the Grand Lodge had powers under the late Act of Parliament to Grant charters of Constitution and Erection."[114]

---

112 Grand Lodge of Scotland Minutes, November 25, 1799.

113 Quoted in Prescott, "Unlawful Societies Act," 9. See R. G. Thorne, *History of Parliament: The Commons 1790–1820* (London, 1986), 826–832. Notably, Radnor, or Lord Folkstone, William Pleydell Bouverie, "voted his approval of Pitt's removal from office, 7 May [1802]," 827.

114 Grand Lodge of Scotland Minutes, February 2, 1800. The full minute reads "It was then stated that the committee appointed by the Meeting of 25th November last in compliance with the order of that meeting had directed the Grand Clerk to draw up a Memorial and case which they had laid before the Lord Advocate of Scotland for his opinion respecting the Question whether the Grand Lodge had powers under the late Act of Parliament to Grant Charters of Constitution and Erection and that the Lord Advocate had given a clear opinion that the Grand Lodge had not powers under that Act to Grant New Charters and that it would be necessary to apply to parliament for such alterations of the Law as might appear necessary. And after reading the memorial

The committee met on February 28, 1800 and prepared a case addressing the "two great objects anxiously wished to be attained," which were the recognition of "their former powers of Grand Charters of Constitution and Erection to new Lodges" and the assignment of *"persona standi in judicio* regarding which doubts at least are entertained."[115] According to the memorial, obtaining "the interference of the Legislature in their favour" was the "only possible mode of accomplishing the ends in view."[116]

The minute entries listed in Appendix 4 are significant in that they reveal the determination and resolve of the Grand Officers—notably the Grand Clerk and a special Committee formed for the purpose of resolving the charter-granting issue—to rectify the situation. No less than four entries meticulously outlining the progress of the Grand Clerk and the Committee were recorded between November 25, 1799 and August 8, 1800, and each account is more detailed and characterized by a heightened sense of anxiety and uncertainty. By January 23, 1801, despite numerous letters to the government and the Grand Lodge of England, "nothing had been done in consequence thereof."[117] Subsequently, the committee decided to discuss further actions with the Grand Master of Scotland, the Earl of Dalkeith:

> In Consequence of the Appointment of the General Committee of the Grand Lodge of 28 January last the Select Committee waited upon the Grand Master and Explained to him the purpose of their visit, and after

and case with the opinion of the Lord Advocate there on it was stated by the Right Worshipful Brother Inglis Master of St Luke that he as one of the committee appointed for that purpose had waited on the Lord Advocate at the Consultation, that tho his Lordship had not so Expressed in his opinion yet his Lordship had spared him and the other Brethren of the Committee that should the Grand Lodge deem an application to Parliament necessary he would most cordially give them every assistance in his power towards obtaining such alterations as might tend to the advantage of the Grand Lodge and the Good of the country. Brother Inglis therefore moved that full and ample powers should be given to the same Committee to take such steps as they think proper by application to Parliament or otherways for obtaining the great object in view as stated in the case and opinion, of which copies are ordered to be herein engrossed, which motion being approven of was unanimously agreed to, and the Memorial and Case with the Lord Advocates opinion."

115 Grand Lodge of Scotland Minutes, February 28, 1800.

116 Ibid.

117 Ibid., January 23, 1801. Copies of the case had been sent to Henry Dundas, the Duke of Atholl, the Earl of Dalkeith, and the Lord Advocate.

reading to his Lordship the Minutes of the Grand Lodge
relative to an application to Parliament for an alteration
of the late Act regarding Mason Lodges—The Right
Honorable and Most Worshipful The Grand Master approved of the Steps that had already been taken on points
so interesting to the Craft, and informed the Committee that he intended to be in London by the first of next
month, when he would most assuredly take the earliest
opportunity of Communicating with the Duke of Athole
Grand Master of the Ancient Fraternity of Free Masons
in England, with whom it was his Lordships opinion
the Grand Lodge here should by all means endeavour
to cooperate in the application to Parliament and that
he should likewise make it his business to lay the matter before His Majesties Ministers. In the mean time His
Lordship requested to be put in possession of extracts
of the whole proceedings of the Grand Lodge relative to
the above business which the Committee appointed to
the Grand Clerk to transmit to the Grand Master with all
convenient dispatch.[118]

As the debate over charter-granting privileges continued, the Grand
Lodge of Scotland became increasingly reliant on assistance from the
Grand Lodge of England. The Committee reported that "as the Grand
Lodge of England according to the information of the Committee stands
in the same predicament as that of Scotland, an application should be
made to her thro the present Most Noble Grand Master for their joint
and hearty cooperation."[119]

While in London, Dalkeith received numerous letters from the Grand
Clerk repeatedly impressing upon him the importance of the matter and
urging him to enlist the counsel of the Grand Lodge of England. A letter
sent to London on February 11, 1801 went unanswered, and the committee sent yet another letter on April 3, 1801 reminding Dalkeith of his
promise to "Communicate with his Majesties Ministers regarding the
Application to Parliament for an Extension of the Powers of the Grand

118 Grand Lodge of Scotland Minutes, February 11, 1801.
119 Ibid., February 28, 1800.

Lodge with regard to granting Charters."[120] Eventually, on August 9, 1801, Dalkeith informed the committee that he had "received an Answer from the Government relative to the Granting further powers to the Grand Lodge of Scotland to this effect, 'that it is not expedient to allow more Lodges to be established at the present moment.' Have the goodness to communicate this information ... so that it may be laid before the Grand Lodge."[121]

Even as the Scottish Grand Lodge continued to correspond with the government and the Grand Lodge of England, it was still unable to achieve any compromise over the restoration of its right to grant charters. During this entire affair, Wartski notes that both Grand Lodges of England had discovered a loophole in the exemption clause. Essentially, it was adhering to the government's ban on issuing new charters; instead of warranting new lodges, however, "it sought for the old Charters of dormant Lodges and assigned those to the new Lodge, in a flagrant pretence that the new Lodge was merely a continuation of the dormant Lodge."[122]

The Grand Lodge of England warned its Scottish counterpart not to pursue the matter of warranting new lodges. On March 2, 1803, one day before the letter from Lord Advocate Hope was received containing his decision regarding the creation of lodges, the Grand Lodge of England wrote to the Scottish Grand Lodge, asserting that

> it has however occurred that since this matter first engaged your attention public affairs have become too critical for the agitation of this question at this moment. It

---

120 Dalkeith replied to this communication, although no definite answer was given to the question of granting charters: "Great George Street April 9th 1801—Sir I have never lost sight of the business relative to the application to Parliament to grant more extensive powers to the Grand Lodge of Scotland. But I beg to observe to you that for some time after my arrival in Town it was not very clear who were and who were not his Majesties Ministers and I did not know to whom with propriety to apply. After that period a stop was put to all public business in consequence of the Kings Illness untill I heard that his Majesty had considerably regained his strength I did not Judge it proper to add any thing to the business that was of necessity to come before him, and I do not think any Minister at liberty to give any Answer to an application of the importance of mine without taking his commands on the subject. I shall now lose no time in bringing the business foreward. I am your obedient servant [signed] Dalkeith," Grand Lodge of Scotland Minutes, April 9, 1801.

121 Ibid., August 9, 1801.

122 Wartski, "Secret Societies Act," 28.

has been thought advisable to defer the application to a season of profound Tranquillity when every objection on the score of external alarm may be removed. In the propriety of this delay we have no doubt but your will concur with us.[123]

Despite the advice of the Grand Lodge of England not to persist with its decision to "take the opinion of the Kings Counsel hire, whether or not they are at liberty now to resume their former powers of granting warrants for Erecting and Establishing new lodges," the Grand Lodge of Scotland wrote to Lord Advocate Hope asking for a final explanation of the Act's implications.[124] The ambiguity surrounding this privilege was finally clarified when the Lord Advocate delivered his judgment in response to the query of the Grand Lodge:

> The Act of Parliament quoted is not limited either in its principal or in its enactments to the continuance of the War; and not being in any other shape made temporary nor having been since repealed it of course remains still in force and therefore it is not lawful or competent for the Grand Lodge to grant Charters to new Lodges.[125]

Legislative Consequences and Lodge Reaction

Although effectively taking away a large measure of power from the freemasons, the 1799 act "seems to have been appreciated by the Grand Lodges, which perhaps felt that it gave them some standing in law and also provided a potential means of proceeding against lodges acting irregularly."[126] Indeed, this interpretation would be critical during the Masonic Secession; Prescott cites Murray Lyon's account of the dispute between the Grand Lodge and Mother Kilwinning and states that the recognition of this new power "is particularly evident in Scotland where the 1799 act provided the Grand Lodge with the means to take legal action against seceding lodges."[127] In all probability, the motivation behind the revoca-

---

123 Grand Lodge of Scotland Minutes, March 2, 1803.

124 Ibid., February 10, 1803.

125 Grand Lodge of Scotland Minutes, March 3, 1803. [Signed] Lord Advocate Clerk Hope, letter sent to Grand Lodge of Scotland, St. Andrews Square March 1803.

126 Prescott, "Unlawful," 16.

127 Ibid.

tion of charter-granting privileges arose from Foreign Secretary William Grenville's view that "the idea of self-regulation raised serious constitutional difficulties; it seemed to him inappropriate that Grand Officers should be given statutory authority effectively to license Masonic lodges when parliament itself had no control over how those grand officers were appointed."[128] Prescott also asserts that the Duke of Norfolk took exception to the Foreign Secretary's remarks and "deplored the idea of setting aside the exempting clause, as tending to their [freemasons'] annihilation."[129] Grenville clarified his position, stating that he did not intend to remove the clause. Rather, he wanted to implement a better method of regulating lodges. As part of the exclusionary clause, Grenville proposed that an amendment should be added requiring all lodges to

> make affidavit before two or more magistrates of the particular place where the lodge was held, and of the number and names of its members. That these accounts should be transmitted to the clerk of the peace, who should, once a year at least, furnish a general account of the whole within his district, to the magistrates sitting in -quarter sessions, who should be empowered, in case of well-founded complaints against any particular lodge, to suppress its meetings.[130]

Compulsory certifications before a magistrate ensured the regulation and constant monitoring of Masonic meetings. According to Grenville, the "objects and purposes of such lodges as should be permitted to meet, should be declared to be purely Masonic, and only for the avowed objects of the institutions, the principal ends of which he conceived to be those of charity and benevolence."[131] Furthermore, the submission of a comprehensive listing of all lodge members is a provision originating from the intention of authorities to "keep tabs on exactly who were meeting as Masons, so that an immediate clamp could be applied if those considered undesirable by them surfaced among the names."[132] No. 6 Old Inverness recorded the following sworn declaration in its minutes of September 10, 1799:

---

128 Ibid, 8.
129 Ibid.
130 Ibid., 10.
131 Ibid., 9.
132 Wartski, "Secret Societies Act," 29.

Before passing of the Act of Parliament entitled 'An act for the more effectual suppression of societies established for seditious and treasonable purposes' the said Lodge 'The Old Kilwinning Lodge of Inverness number Eight of Scotland,' has been usually held under the Denomination of a Lodge of Free Masons and in conformity to the Rules prevailing among the Lodge of Free Masons in this Kingdom all which is truth as the Deponents shall answer to God [Signed] Farquhar MacDonald Alexander Macdonnell. Declaration: ... That the said Lodge is distinguished by the above name and designation. 2nd That the Lodge met within the mason Lodge of Inverness and the usual days of meeting are Lady Day which holds on the Twenty fifth day of March summer St John's, which holds on the Twenty fourth day of June St. Andrews which holds on the Thirtieth day of November and St Johns which holds on the Twenty seventh day of December, and that when urgent business concerning the Craft require it they meet on other days.[133]

The Grand Lodge of Scotland immediately communicated the government's requirements to all lodges, "asserting its province as the head of the Masonic Body in Scotland, from whom all regular Lodges hold their right of meeting by Charter, to take effectual steps for enforcing observance of the law before decided."[134] Failure to comply with the demands of the government and the Grand Lodge would result in the deletion of an insubordinate lodge from the Grand Roll and the revocation of all its Masonic rights. Before the passage of the Secret Societies Act, the loss of Masonic privileges principally meant not being recognized as an official Scottish lodge. After its enactment, however, any lodge struck from the Grand Roll forfeited the "countenance and protection" of the Grand Lodge and thus was in danger of being suppressed by the government.[135]

---

133 No. 6 Inverness Lodge Minutes, September 10, 1799.

134 Grand Lodge of Scotland Minutes, August 5, 1799.

135 Ibid., August 8, 1800: "... Several of the Lodges in this Country however, have not yet complied with the resolutions of the Grand Lodge ... Those Lodges therefore that have not yet come forward are hereby directed to send up a Statement of their situation ... Should this opportunity be neglected and no offer of composition made betwixt and the 10th day of January 1801 the Grand Lodge is determined to send a proper officer

As we have seen, the Grand Lodge suspended and expelled lodges for much less; thus, it is apparent that the Scottish Grand Lodge was ready and willing to delete lodges from the Grand Roll.

The majority of lodges make no reference to the Act of Parliament, but those that did clearly supported the new legislation. No. 49 Dundee Lodge reported that it had received a letter from the Grand Lodge of Scotland on August 22, 1799 requesting that "two Members belonging to this Lodge shall Make Oath before a Magistrate that our said Lodge was in being before said Act of Parliament was pass'd as to Societies Meeting. Agreeable to which, the Meeting appointed Brothers John Scott and Peter Geddes to make such affidavit."[136] No. 1(3) Aberdeen also reported having received a communication from the Grand Lodge, and thereafter appointed several members to

> see the injunctions mentioned in the said Act complied with, by getting the Certificate required, Lodged with the Clerk of the Peace of the County of Aberdeen, and also a Certified List of the names and designations of the present members of this Lodge, Name of the Place, and days of meeting to be at same time Lodged with the Justice of Peace Clerk in terms of said Act of Parliament, And that as soon as possible.[137]

---

thro every Lodge of Scotland that may be in Arrear in order to ascertain not only the circumstances and situation of every Lodge but likewise to know what Lodges are still in Existance in order that a proper Roll may be made up, and none permitted to stand thereon but such as are deserving of the Countenance and protection of the Grand Lodge."

136 No. 49 Dundee Lodge Minutes, August 22, 1799. No. 198 Roman Eagle Lodge also reported having received a communication from the Grand Lodge respecting the Act of Parliament, August 21, 1799: "The Master in the Chair he Informed the meeting that they were called together In Consequence of Some notice from the Grand Lodge of Scotland. A Letter from Mr. John Clerk Substitute Grand Master ... narrated in last minute And a printed letter was produced from the Grand Lodge of Scotland with Acts and Statutes Contained in the Act of Parliament Annent free Mason Meetings, August 21, 1799."

137 No. 1(3) Aberdeen Lodge Minutes, September 6, 1799. A subsequent meeting on December 27, 1799 noted that "a Certificate from the Clerk to the Justices of Peace of the County of Aberdeen, showing that a List of the Members of this Lodge had been given in to him, in terms of the late Act of Parliament, along with a Certificate Agreeable to the directions of said Act. Which Certificate was ordered to be transmitted by the Secretary to the Grand Lodge at Edinburgh in Obedience to the Grand Secretarys letter of the 12ᵗʰ August last ingrossed in the Sederint of the Sixth of September last," Ibid.

Not all lodges, however, felt that the requirements were fair and practical. On St. John's Day, December 27, 1799, the secretary of No. 25 St. Andrew read a letter from St. John's Cupar Fife Lodge pertaining to the recent declarations by the Grand Lodge of Scotland. The letter complained "of the late resolutions of the Grand Lodge as being in their opinion troublesem and expensive and that the Lodge of St Johns Cupar Fife would wish some of the adjacent Lodges to join with them in getting clear of the burden."[138] Although St. John's Cupar attempted to convince other freemasons in the area of the inconvenience caused by the Act, it appears that the lodge garnered little support. The members of No. 25 expressed their concern over the opinion of the Cupar lodge, asserting that

> they had at all former periods readily complied with every Act of Parliament and they with much chearfulness agreed with the present and were much surprised that the Lodge of St Johns could make any objections to an Act of Parliament especially when it was giving such indulgences to masons and attended with no very trifling expence.[139]

Conclusion

Prescott argues that the Secret Societies Act was largely "an exercise in closing stable doors after horses had fled."[140] The radical societies that the government attempted to suppress continued to meet, and the societies who fell outside the scope of the Act from the onset were placed under extreme pressure to comply. Organizations inevitably discovered means to circumvent the legislation, and those who chose to act in accordance with the law forfeited rights, privileges, and powers, in large measure to preserve their relationship with the government and safeguard themselves against undue persecution. Although Pitt's government was intent on limiting the influence of radical groups through a "formidable array of repressive legislation," the "irony of these policies is that they helped to create the very problem that they were designed to solve."[141] The legisla-

---

138 No. 25 Lodge St. Andrew Minutes, December 27, 1799.

139 Ibid.

140 See Prescott, "Unlawful," 10–12.

141 Ibid., 17. O'Gorman writes that "The Acts had little effect ... They were rarely enforced ... Historians have argued for nearly 200 years about the legitimacy and justifiability of

tion forced radical organizations underground, and as "long as protests remained open and within the law it was safe. When it was placed outside the law ... it became dangerous."[142]

Historians have questioned the force of radicals in Scotland as well as the legitimacy and the overall impact of the repressive legislation. Fry comments that

> Scotland's history contained little preparation for a secular radicalism. Previous accounts, seeking its roots, have too glibly lumped it together with the reforming movements in counties and burghs, as part of a universal democratic awakening ... Reformers, in contradistinction to radicals, owed nothing to foreign revolutionary inspiration ... The radicals were unsuccessful in rousing the masses with them.[143]

If this is indeed the case, much then still hangs on the question: "was there really a danger of revolution or, possibly, of insurrection in the 1790s? With the benefit of hindsight we can, of course, argue that there was not."[144] Masonic emphasis on charity and self-improvement did little to sustain its image or position among the upper-echelons of the government. Although it was eventually reclassified as an organization unlikely to pose a threat to the stability of the country, it suffered much at the hands of the legislation. Certainly, as lodge trends indicate, numbers steadily plummeted throughout the 1790s. Accompanying the reduction in lodge numbers due to the revocation of charter-granting powers was a

---

Pitt's repression of radicalism. Some have pointed to the draconian nature of the legislation against reformers, who were undeniably loyal and well-intentioned, and the considerable, and often extremely unpleasant harassment and intimidation directed against innocent reformers ..." "Pitt," 33–34.

142 Malcolm Thomis and Peter Holt, *Threats of Revolution in Britain 1789–1848* (London, 1977), 17. Gould argues that "the various Acts passed between 1799 and 1810, under which all combinations were forbidden and heavy penalties for infraction from time to time enforced, drove those trades whose organizations did not disappear to more secret organization ... All over England and Scotland the skilled craftsman continued to hold the fortnightly meeting of his trade club at the public-house, and the records and rules of some of these clubs have survived," *History of Freemasonry Vol. 1,* 156.

143 Fry, *Despotism,* 174.

144 O'Gorman, "Pitt," 33–34.

decrease in new members, and thus a reduction in charitable funds. Furthermore, Masonic autonomy was compromised, as it—more specifically the Grand Lodge of Scotland—was now answerable to the national government.

McElroy and Clark each raise interesting points in their respective studies of clubs, societies, and freemasons, with both coming to similar conclusions. McElroy notes that "not until the end of the century did social clubs seek their own buildings, and even then some of their arrangements seem strange to an age in which conviviality in the old style [was] dead."[145] Clark echoes this argument, particularly emphasizing the role of the Secret Societies Act:

> By 1800 ... there were signs that freemasonry was becoming less open ... There was a growing trend towards local lodges renting or building dedicated premises, instead of gathering in public drinking houses. Government action against seditious societies led to the [Secret] Societies Act in 1799 ... By then the formative age of freemasonry was surely over.[146]

The demise of the "formative age" of Freemasonry is a direct consequence of the government's reaction toward seditious clubs and societies, and the ramifications for freemasons were huge. Government ministers convinced themselves of an imminent threat and imposed various pieces of legislation that were, as Harry Dickinson writes, "serious infringements of civil liberties."[147]

Repressive legislation was often ineffective or rarely implemented, and although it did succeed to a certain degree in checking the ostensible threat of rebellion, the government's determination to eradicate seditious and treasonable organizations caused serious Masonic turmoil during the early years of the nineteenth century. Once again, allegations of involvement in the dissemination of revolutionary ideas resurfaced, triggering fresh fears of Masonic ambitions to subvert the establishment. Although the masons categorically denied the veracity of such claims and affirmed their

---

145 McElroy, *Age of Improvement*, 144.

146 Clark, *British Clubs*, 349.

147 Dickinson, *British Radicalism*, 41.

allegiance to preserving the stability of the government, internal political turmoil threatened to erode the public image so carefully crafted by the eighteenth-century freemason.

The government crackdown on treasonous and seditious societies during the 1790s caused a shift in the nature of the Grand Lodge of Scotland. Suddenly, the vagueness which once surrounded the extent of its power and authority was resolved. It was much less a reactive body and became much more proactive during the years of the French Revolution, demanding compliance from lodges in all matters relating to the legislation passed by the government and imposing strict fines and penalties for noncompliant lodges. Although it initially made no concerted effort to take complete control of Scottish Freemasonry, by the end of the eighteenth century the Grand Lodge attempted to solidify its status as the sole governing Masonic body in Scotland. Such designs met with strong resistance from lodges and ultimately caused the Masonic Secession of 1808.

It has been claimed that the Grand Lodge's formation "stripped the self-sufficient lodges of a great deal of autonomy," as it "endeavoured, with mounting success, to impose a centralist regime on local lodges through the return of membership lists and rising dues to grand lodge."[148] Whether or not the Grand Lodge imposed a centralist regime on constituent lodges is a matter of historical interpretation; as we have seen, though, the Grand Lodge of Scotland did require membership lists and the prompt return of annual fees, threatening noncompliant lodges with expulsion.[149] Although Bullock remarks that the Grand Lodge of England sought to remove all sovereignty from individual lodges, other historians have noted that the four lodges which founded the Grand Lodge of England in 1717 "were not prompted by ambitious motives. They were not seeking to promote their own status and they had no intention of submitting all their lodges to a new authority, nor did they persuade others to do so."[150] Some lodges did not recognize the Grand Lodge of England as a major ruling

---

148 Bullock, *Revolutionary Brotherhood*, 339; 15. Contrary to Bullock's assertions that the Grand Lodge of England claimed authority over all British lodges, it never had any power over Scottish lodges.

149 James Heckthorn writes that "... in the third and fourth decades of the [eighteenth] century, its authority was more widely accepted ... By 1740 it was an accepted and well-known feature of English life," *Secret Societies*, 21–22.

150 Carr, "Grand Lodge of Scotland and the Significance," 291.

authority, "about which little was known," and feared they may "lose their independence."[151] These reservations were largely unfounded, however, as the Grand Lodge did not control or dictate "the internal management of private lodges."[152]

Despite such conflicting views, this pursuit of dominance over ordinary lodges is a trait that emerged in the history of the Grand Lodge of Scotland. As an improvement society existing primarily to promote charitable concerns, freemasons were one among many associations of that ilk during the Enlightenment. By the 1750s, the Gran d Lodge of Scotland recognized that the association had burgeoned and expanded, essentially transforming the nature and structure of Freemasonry. Although managing the fraternity for the greater part of the eighteenth century, by the 1790s it wielded a great deal of power and eventually became an authoritative, federal organization.

---

151 A. R. Hewitt, "The Grand Lodge of England: A History of the First Hundred Years, 1717–1817," *AQC* 80 (1967): 212.

152 Ibid.

CHAPTER FIVE

"I Dub Thee In the Name of the Father, Son, and Holy Ghost": The Unlawful Oaths Act and the Maybole Trial of Sedition

During the Masonic controversy surrounding the Secret Societies Act, one figure, in particular, was responsible for securing the exemption clause for the freemasons. According to Hamill, Lord Moira—representing the Grand Lodge of England and acting on behalf of the Grand Lodge of Scotland—ultimately "saved Freemasonry from extinction."[1] Moira led a delegation which met with William Pitt to discuss the Masonic exemption clause; ultimately, the deputation influenced the Prime Minister to introduce a series of stipulations exempting Freemasonry from the Act.[2] Emphasizing the impending consequences of the legislation, more specifically the loss of charitable funds, the Earl of Moira "was able to point out to the Prime Minister the implications of the proposed Act, and brought persuasion to bear upon Pitt to amend it."[3]

Despite Moira's successes, he nevertheless initiated a series of events that would further aggravate the continuing power struggles among Scottish freemasons. Moira wanted to extend the scope of the amendment to make Grand Lodge's control over granting charters "*legally* binding rather than merely constitutionally binding."[4] In a letter of 1808 to the Sheriff Depute of Edinburgh, Moira stated that

> the exemption in favour of Masonic meetings was admitted into the Act in consequence of my assurances to Mr. Pitt that nothing could be deemed a lodge which did not sit by precise authorisation from the Grand Lodge, and under its superintendence. I have pledged myself to His Majesty's Ministers that should any set of men attempt

---

1   J. M. Hamill, "The Earl of Moira, Acting Grand Master 1790–1813," *AQC* 93 (1980): 34.

2   Ibid.

3   Wartski, "Secret Societies Act," 22.

4   Ibid., 34.

to meet as a lodge without sanction, the Grand Master, or Acting Grand Master (whomsoever he might be), would apprise the civil authority.[5]

Not all Scottish lodges, however, willingly accepted this proposed expansion of authority. In a petition to Colonel William Fullarton[6]—Member of Parliament for Ayrshire—Lodge Kilwinning argued that as it and several other lodges existed independently of the Grand Lodge, it should be specifically exempted from the terms of the Act. Fullerton, who "had the ear of Mr. Pitt ... persuaded the Prime Minister further to amend the Bill to exempt 'all Lodges declaring upon oath before a Justice of the Peace that they were freemasons.'"[7] As a consequence, all references to the Grand Lodge were deleted, ultimately thwarting what Hamill refers to as "Moira's attempt at strengthening the power of Grand Lodge."[8] Furthermore, Lodge Kilwinning continued to grant charters to other lodges, irrespective of Grand Lodge's claim that it alone was entitled to this privilege.

Had Moira succeeded, any lodge erected without the approval of the Grand Lodge would have been subject to criminal prosecution.[9] It seems, however, that Moira was unaware of the changes made to the amendment which, as Seemungal says, "eliminated the necessity of [Masonic lodges] being under any Grand Lodge."[10] Moira's misinterpretation of the amendment would ultimately contribute to the Masonic Secession of 1808. Wartski writes that "as the representative of the Premier Grand Lodge, Lord Moira urged the exemption from the Act of Lodges, authorized and directly superintended by a Grand Lodge, and he undoubtedly believed that Pitt agreed to the alteration in that form. This left the unattached Scottish Lodges in danger of oblivion, a result possibly intended by Moira."[11] Consequently, the Grand Lodge believed it possessed full legal and constitutional authority over Scottish freemasons. Thus misinformed, it was clearly willing to pursue charges of sedition against individual Masonic lodges.

---

5   Ibid.

6   See Thorne, *History of Parliament*, 843–845.

7   Lionel A. Seemungal, "The Edinburgh Rebellion 1808–1813," *AQC* 86 (1973): 323.

8   Hamill, "Moira," 34.

9   Ibid., 33.

10 Seemungal, "Rebellion," 323.

11 Wartski, "Secret Societies Act," 22.

The Threat of "Illuminism"

Moira's misreading of the amendment and the debate over the Masonic exemptions were not the only sources of contention among freemasons and the government during the 1790s. The controversies also included questions over the political aims of the society and the extent to which its actions and deliberations might be influenced by seditious European organizations. Freemasonry, as it appeared in Europe, was "first articulated in postrevolutionary Britain" and the "form of the lodge became one of the many channels that transmitted a new political culture, based upon constitutionalism, which gradually turned against traditional privileges and established, hierarchical authority."[12] In Europe, Jacob argues, Freemasonry did play a major role in nurturing and promoting revolutionary ideas. Though built upon the British model, Continental Freemasonry had become politically and socially subversive and posed a clear threat to all forms of organized religion:

> Whether we are examining the literature of British Freemasonry ... or entering individual lodges on the Continent ... one major point needs to be stressed: These were political societies, not in a party or faction sense of the term but in a larger connotation. Within the framework of civility and in the service of an imagined social cohesion, the lodges practiced a civil administration, derived from British political practice and tradition. Predictably in a British context lodges were, on the whole, remarkably supportive of established institutions, of church and state. Yet they could also house divisive, or oppositional political practices. They could be loyalist to the Hanoverian and Whig order, yet they could also at moments show affiliation with radical interests, whether republican or Jacobite, and, possibly by the end of the century, Jacobin. Whatever the political affiliations of their members, the eighteenth-century masonic lodges were at the heart of a new secular culture, created in the century and fashioned to operate within the confines of its social ranks, privileges, and degrees.[13]

---

12 Jacob, *Living the Enlightenment*, 51.

13 Ibid., 50–51. See also Robert Clifford, *Application of Barruel's Memoirs of Jacobinism, to the Secret Societies of Ireland and Great Britain* (Farmington Hills, 2005), 1–50.

Despite Jacob's assertions, Jeremy Black maintains that although some cynics perceived Freemasonry to be a dissident faction intent on fomenting radical activities and, occasionally, blamed the society for the French Revolution, most lodges existed purely for sociable reasons. While certain Masonic beliefs, such as "man's ethical autonomy, capacity for moral improvement and common rationality, the exclusiveness and yet universal pretensions," had potentially radical connotations it was essentially "no more radical in practice than several other aspects of European thought in this period."[14] David Stevenson correctly reasons that frequent misuse of the word "Masonic" to describe "anything combining radical ideas and secrecy ... was illogical and confusing."[15] This confusion ultimately allowed detractors of the masons to formulate conspiracy theories which asserted that "Freemasonry was one of the great causes of the French Revolution."[16] Although there was little tangible evidence to substantiate such allegations, British Freemasonry became the object of much scrutiny and suspicion.

In 1797, amid claims of Jacobin lodges in France and seditious and treasonable activities among German freemasons, John Robison—eminent mechanical philosopher and professor of natural philosophy at the University of Edinburgh—published *Proofs of a Conspiracy Against All the Religions and Governments of Europe, Carried on in the Secret Meetings of the Freemasons, Illuminati, and Reading Societies, Collected from Good Authorities.*[17] Convinced that all of Britain stood on the brink of revolu-

---

14 Jeremy Black, *Eighteenth-Century Europe* (Basingstoke, 1999), 496–497.

15 Stevenson, *Origins*, 1–12.

16 Jacob, *Living the Enlightenment*, 9–10; Abbe de Barruel published a work entitled *Memoires pour servir a l'Historie du Jacobinisme*, or *Memoris, Illustrating the History of Jacobinism* (London, 1798), which condemned Freemasonry. He did, however, distinguish between British and French Freemasonry, separating the goals, aims, and circumstances of each. For an additional discussion on Freemasonry and the French Revolution, see A. Mellor, "Eighteenth-Century French Freemasonry and the French Revolution," *AQC* 97 (1984): 105–114. Michael Kennedy, in *The Jacobin Clubs in the French Revolution: The First Years* (Princeton, 1982), dismisses Barruel's claims, stating that a "tremendous amount of research has been done in recent years on Freemasonry; and while, unfortunately, only a small proportion pertains directly to the clubs, it is now possible to discard a number of once-popular theories about their masonic origins. Today, only the most imaginative minds could describe the masons as conspirators who established the clubs as part of a grand design to subvert the Church and the Monarchy," 5.

17 John Robison, *Proofs of a Conspiracy Against All the Religions and Governments of*

tion based on the French model, Robison claimed that secret societies throughout Europe were conspiring to overturn governments and inspire social upheaval. Firminger argues that Robison was seized by a panic that "the whole system of society was in progress of demolition by the French Revolution," and thus he "strayed from more accordant subjects to look for the causes of all the confusion." [18] Ultimately, he traced alleged conspiratorial crimes to the machinations of freemasons:

> Being at a friend's house in the country during some part
> of the summer 1795, I there saw a volume of a German
> periodical work, called *Religions Begebenheiten, i.e.* Reli-
> gious Occurrences; in which there was an account of the
> various schisms in the Fraternity of Free Masons, with
> frequent allusions to the origin and history of that cel-
> ebrated association. This account interested me a good
> deal, because, in my early life, I had taken some part in
> the occupations (shall I call them) of Free Masonry; and
> having chiefly frequented the Lodges on the Continent,
> I had learned many doctrines, and seen many ceremo-
> nials, which have no place in the simple system of Free
> Masonry which obtains in this country ... I had also re-
> marked, that the whole was much more the object of re-
> flection and thought than I could remember it to have
> been among my acquaintances at home. There, I had
> seen a Mason Lodge considered merely as a pretext for
> passing an hour or two in a sort of decent conviviality,
> not altogether void of some rational occupation. I had
> sometimes heard of differences of doctrines or of cer-
> emonies, but in terms which marked them as mere fri-
> volities. But, on the Continent, I found them matters of
> serious concern and debate ... But all the splendour and
> elegance that I saw could not conceal a frivolity in every
> part. It appeared a baseless fabric, and I could not think
> of engaging in an occupation which would consume
> much time, cost me a good deal of money, and might

---

*Europe, Carried on in the Secret Meetings of the Freemasons, Illuminati, and Reading Soci-
eties, Collected from Good Authorities* (Edinburgh, 1797).

18   W. K. Firminger, "The Romances of Robison and Barruel," AQC 50 (1937): 31–69.

perhaps excite in me some of that fanaticism, or, at least, enthusiasm that I saw in others, and perceived to be void of any rational support.[19]

Robison himself had been initiated in Lodge La Parfaite Intelligence at Liège in March 1770. Despite his Masonic affiliations, he believed that Continental Freemasonry, as was particularly found in Germany and France, was potentially subversive. His doubts were first circulated in the *Anti-Jacobin Review*, a conservative and loyalist monthly journal to which he regularly contributed. Similar to the ideas espoused in *Proofs of a Conspiracy*, the *Anti-Jacobin* "set out to refute what it considered to be the dangerous doctrines of sedition being fervently circulated in the country."[20] Robison did not directly accuse British freemasons of being seditious, but he did remark that

> the homely Free Masonry imported from England has been totally changed in every country of Europe, either by the imposing ascendancy of French brethren, who are to be found everywhere, ready to instruct the world; or by the importation of the doctrines, and ceremonies, and ornaments of the Parisian Lodges. Even England, the birth-place of Masonry, has experienced the French innovations; and all the repeated injunctions, admonitions, and reproofs of the old Lodges, cannot prevent those in different parts of the kingdom from admitting the French novelties, full of tinsel and glitter, and high-founding titles.[21]

Although he asserted that British Masonic lodges were vehicles only for passing the time in merriment, Robison nevertheless retained some suspicions regarding their association with radical groups. He does note that no definitive link exists between European and British lodges, but Robison does not dismiss the possibility that Continental ideas of revolution did penetrate the British Masonic models of constitutionalism and loyalism.

---

19   Robison, *Proofs*, 1–3.

20   Emsley, *Britain and the French Revolution*, 18. For an in-depth discussion of Jacobinism, see Augustin Cochin, "The Theory of Jacobinism," in *Interpreting the French Revolution*, ed. Francois Furet (Cambridge, 1981), 164–204.

21   Robison, *Proofs of a Conspiracy*, 9.

Indeed, the debate over Freemasonry's contribution to revolutionary sentiments and activities has been taken up by many historians. According to Jacob, Jacobite sympathies may have existed in some British lodges, although they were much more prominent in Continental lodges.[22] Kennedy argues that there is no proof to substantiate the influence of French Masonic lodges on the revolution; he does, however, concede that "one cannot deny that the clubs [i.e. revolutionary societies] owed much to the lodges."[23] Contrary to such views, Thomas Munck maintains that "although the Masons did promote international and cross-social contacts which were essentially non-religious and in agreement with enlightened values," they can hardly be described "as a major radical or reformist network in their own right."[24] Notwithstanding varying perceptions of Freemasonry, it is clear that by the 1790s the society's turbulent and increasingly controversial existence in Europe had undermined confidence that British Freemasonry was neither a subversive or revolutionary organization.

A major cause of this change of opinion was the Order of Illuminati, founded by Adam Weishaupt in May 1776 in Bavaria. Weishaupt was a student at the University of Ingolstadt and by the age of 22 he was elected Professor of Canon Law of the same University, a position long held by Jesuits. It was his hatred of the Jesuits which ultimately formed the ideological foundation of the order he founded. Initially styled the Order of Perfectibilists and later changed to the Illuminati, the main goal of the society was to eradicate political and religious tyranny while simultaneously emphasizing morality and virtue.[25] This program for restructuring society became known as Illuminism, which Weishaupt attempted to blend with Freemasonry to ensure his Order's success. Ostensibly to

---

22 Jacob, *Living the Enlightenment*, 54.

23 Kennedy, *The Jacobin Clubs*, 5–8.

24 Thomas Munck, *The Enlightenment, A Comparative Social History 1721–1794* (London, 2000), 70. See also Roberts, *Mythology*, 114–145; Heckthorn, *Secret Societies Vol. 1*, 205–314; *Gould's History of Freemasonry Vol. 4*, 357–360; A. E. Waite, *A New Encyclopedia of Freemasonry, Vol. 1* (New York, 1921), 385–388.

25 Black writes that "In 1785 all secret societies, including the Freemasons and Illuminati, were banned by Karl Theodor of Bavaria and in 1787 evidence that purported to demonstrate a plot by the latter was published ... In an age bred on notions of conspiracy, it is not surprising that Freemasonry and other movements aroused acute fears ... ," *Eighteenth-Century Europe*, 399–400; See also Ulrich Im Hof, "German Associations and Politics in the Second Half of the Eighteenth Century," in *Transformation*, 215–216.

dispel any doubts as to the aims of the Illuminati, he joined Lodge The-odore of Good Counsel in Munich in 1777. His radical political stance drew criticism, however, and the Order's association with Freemasonry encouraged detractors' efforts to increasingly tarnish the reputation of the masons.

This was why The Order of the Illuminati was cited during the debate over the Secret Societies Act of 1799. The suspicions the Illuminati provoked stemmed from their beliefs as well as their secrecy, and in an age "bred on notions of conspiracy, it is not surprising that Freemasonry and other movements aroused acute fears."[26] The Earl of Radnor expressed his skep-ticism about the activities of the freemasons,[27] asserting that

> their meetings were, in other countries at least, made subservient to the purposes of those Illuminati who had succeeded in the overthrow of one great government, and were labouring for the destruction of all others. This he conceived to have been proved in a work some time since published by a very learned Professor and he was desirous to guard against any similar practices in this country.[28]

Questioning the integrity of the society, Radnor further declared that "not being himself a mason, and having heard that they administered oaths of secrecy," he did not know "whether in times so critical as the present, it was wise to trust the freemasons any more than any other meetings."[29] Although the masons, as we have seen, professed their loyal-ty to the crown, some doubts still lingered in parliament about their re-liability and allegiance.[30] Radnor had good cause to worry: Stewart links

26 Ibid.

27 Quoted in Prescott, "Unlawful," 8. For a wider explanation of the Illuminati, their doctrines and impact on the European Enlightenment, see Robison, *Proofs*, 100–271; 360–496; Barruel, *Memoirs Vol. 3*; Vernon Stauffer, *New England and the Bavarian Illu-minati* (New York, 1919), 142–228.

28 Ibid., 8. Prescott proposes that "this was the first point at which Robison's famous 1797 anti-masonic work was mentioned in the course of the 1799 legislation."

29 Ibid.

30 Several documents were sent to the Home Office citing Masonic irregularities. The letters included the names of freemasons who were members of the United English-men, the United Scotsmen and supported the "Cannibalian government in France." See also Koselleck, *Critique and Crisis*, 62–97, esp. 86–97.

United Irishmen founder William Drennan with the Illuminati, stating that his "idea [of brotherhood] seems to be closer to that of the Illuminati in Bavaria ... The Illuminati, too, were merely a schismatic branch of European Freemasonry."[31]

These feelings of Masonic uncertainty created by Robison's allegations of an association between the Illuminati and freemasons were not confined to Continental Europe and Britain. In the United States, Robison's book generated criticism of English lodges, prompting George Washington Snyder to express his misgivings about the freemasons to President George Washington. Although Washington believed that the doctrines of the Illuminati may have spread to the United States he doubted that Masonic lodges had been corrupted by the organization. On October 24, 1798, Washington wrote to Snyder, stating that it was

> not my intention to doubt that, the doctrines of the Illuminati, and principles of Jacobinism had not spread to the United States ... The idea I meant to convey, was, that I did not believe that the *Lodges* of Free Masons, in *this* Country had, as *Societies*, endeavoured to propagate the diabolical tenets of the first, or pernicious principles of the latter (if they are susceptible of separation). That individuals of them may have done it, or that the *founder*, or *instrument* employed to found, the Democratic Societies in the United States, may have had these objects; and actually had a separation of the *People* from their *Government* in view, is too evident to be questioned.[32]

It was this alleged connection between the Illuminati and Freemasonry and the geographical reach of its influence which aroused the suspicions of Robison as well as James Robertson, a Benedictine monk in Galloway—so much so, in fact, that they each wrote to the Lord Advocate. Robison warned Robert Dundas of the potential subversive influence not only of the Illuminati, but European freemasons as well:

---

31 A. T. Q. Stewart, *A Deeper Silence: The Hidden Roots of the Irish Movement* (London, 1993), 177.

32 From *The Writings of George Washington from the Original Manuscript Sources, 1745–1799*, ed. John C. Fitzpatrick (Washington, 1939).

January 1798

My Lord

What I wished to inform your Lordship of is thus some time ago an invitation was given to the Fraternity of Free Masons in Scotland to hold a Correspondence with the Grand or Royal Lodge of Berlin. This was decorated with every Ornament and full of pompous titles, and conceived in terms of the highest import for Scotch Masonry. It was conceived as particularly addressed to the most advanced Order of Masonry (tho' I rather suppose it addressed to the National Lodge). This is supposed to be what they call the Royal Order of St. Andrews—professing what they call the Masonry of Rose Croix Tau the Letter, and thus it was from a Lodge professing the same Masonry. The simplicity of the fraternity in this Country has made us indifferent as to all the parties on the Continent, but of late we are also seized with the desire of innovation, and becoming fond of the high degrees of masonry. But we are quite ignorant of the life made of them abroad. I know that this System was continued by Swedes and the Duke of Sudermannia had a great hand in it. Under the most inoffensive exterior, I know that the cosmopolitical doctrines are most zealously taught, and that the whole of this Order is engaged in the Schisms of Illumatism. I firmly believe that this Invitation to a Correspondence is with a view to make proselytes. It were to be wished that it could be prevented. One way occurs to me, to publish the whole secrets of the Order, which are in my possession, but this is very disagreeable to me, because altho' I came under no obligation to consult them, the person who sent them to me, when he quitted Russia in haste, expected that they would be kept.

What makes me trouble your Lordship just now is the Letter which accompanies this. By it you will see that it is highly probably that a bad use is already made of Free Masonry in this Country. I remember hearing of the story of a detachment being spared by the French because they were Brethren but it was not supposed to be authentic by the foreign [illegible]. It would be of some use to inquire of our officers who were on the spot such as Major Tytler now at Stirling who was then an Aid de Camp, and must have known more than an ordinary battalion officer. If the Story could be proved to be false, it might put an End to the use made of it in Galloway and probably in other places.

I have sent your Lordship a pamphlet which I had a few weeks ago from Lord Auckland which confirms my Suspicions about the Swedish Masonry. I am respectfully

Your Lordships ms. Obedt. Servt.,
[Signed] John Robison[33]

Robertson's letter in January 1798 addresses issues similar to those raised by Robison. Robertson had attended seminary in Ratisbon, Germany, and after he was professed in 1778 he served on missions in Buchan, Edinburgh, and Galloway.[34] Having briefly revisiting Ratisbon in 1788, he returned to Scotland in 1789. By 1797, he was in Galloway when he composed the following letter to Dundas, which drew upon his recent and personal knowledge of Continental Freemasonry:

My Lord,

Permit a Stranger to congratulate you & the world on your late performance. If any thing can save us, it can only be men who have courage to unmask such horrors, at no small risk to their own lives. Providence I trust will work for the preservation of such useful Persons.

The writer of this happened to be at Ratisbon in the year 1788 when the discovery of illumination was quite fresh. I was told that one of those wretches had been struck dead with lightning & that it was by papers found on him the discovery was made. They shew'd me the tree where he was thunderstruck. A Singular interposition of

---

33 Letter from John Robison, (Laing MSS II 500), reprinted with the permission of the University of Edinburgh Library.

34 Mark Dilworth, "Two necrologies of Scottish Benedictine Abbey's in Germany," *IR* 9 (1958): 191.

Providence, I pass'd afterwards by Munich where I was presented with the System & Correspondence publish'd by the Elector's Authority: which I brought to Edinburgh where I think I lent it to Lord Elliock. But nobody there would believe it they treated it as a dream of the senseless Bavarians. I was laugh'd at in Munich, when I maintain'd that Scotch Masonry was not tinctured with Illumination. They assur'd me they had proof of a Correspondence with Scotland. In Galloway where I now live I can assure you Sir, that the Masons are uncommonly active in recruiting, having frequent & numerous meetings: they scruple at nobody however worthless which shews no good design. I believe the bulk of them is led by the nose but there is nothing good at bottom. I have this from very good Authority, that the Masons give out that when the Robespierrists had pass'd a decree to give no quarter to the English, a whole Regiment was saved by Masonry. I think it is said of the Inniskilling Dragoons, They were surrounded, as the story goes, by the French & were going to be cut to pieces, when the commanding officer stept forward & made some of the Mason's signs to the French, which their Commander observed & return'd: then the firing ceas'd & both parties retreated.

The circulation of this tale by the Masons to procure recruits has an obvious meaning, & therefore I presum'd it not unworthy [of] your notice. I think I had once the honor of being presented before your Couch, but you must have forgot that long ago ere now. May you arise from it more vigorous than ever & the health of your body equal the power of your mind.

I am with the most sincere Veneration
Sir

Munches near	Your most obedt. Sert.
Dumfries	[Signed] James Robertson Priest
8 Jan. 1798[35]	

---

35 Letter from James Robertson (Laing MSS II 1769–1770), reprinted with the permission of the University of Edinburgh Library.

Both Robison and Robertson clearly refer to the same military incident. Although they each were at pains to vindicate British freemasons, they do hint at the possibility of subversive activities on the West Coast of Scotland. These allusions, in turn, may well relate to an event which had occurred in Maybole in Ayrshire as recently as 1797.

The United Irishmen and "Black Masonry"

Two nascent degrees of Freemasonry, the Royal Arch and Knights Templar, had appeared on the West Coast of Scotland in Maybole during the 1790s and at the time were not sanctioned by the Grand Lodge of Scotland as official Masonic degrees. The Royal Arch and Knights Templar degrees were extensions of the three sanctioned degrees of Freemasonry—Entered Apprentice, Fellow Craft, Master Mason—and were based upon legends of the Knights of St John and the Holy Royal Arch located in Solomon's Temple in Jerusalem. Members of the Royal Arch and Knights Templar professed an interest in the higher degrees of masonry; McFarland explains that these degrees, "under a pretended connection with Freemasonry," sought to "propagate the infidelity of the French Revolution, and to evoke sympathy for the democrats in Ireland."[36]

Clark is correct in arguing that although Royal Arch and Knights Templar ceremonies were introduced in Britain, "they never developed the baroquely elaborate hierarchy of ritual degrees which became widespread in Germany, France, and other parts of Europe."[37] According to Jones, however, it appears that "some of the material brought over from France ... did contain the salient features of the Royal Arch."[38] Indeed, by the mid-eighteenth century, the degree was gaining popularity in Scotland and was practiced by several lodges, including Stirling and Glasgow.[39] Records

36 McFarland, Ireland and Scotland, 59. See Jones, Guide and Compendium, 511–512; Chetwode Crawley, "The Templar Legends in Freemasonry," AQC 26 (1900): 45–70; C. A. Cameron, "On the Origin and Progress of the Chivalric Freemasonry in the British Isles," AQC 19 (1906): 209–228; W. J. Hughan, "Origin of Masonic Knight Templary in the United Kingdom," AQC 18 (1905): 91–93; E. J. Castle, "Enquiry Into the Charge of Gnosticism Brought Against the Freemasons and Templars," AQC 19 (1906): 209–228; F. R. Radice, "Reflections on the Antiquity of the Order of the Royal Arch," AQC 77 (1964): 201–210; W. R. Kelly, "The Advent of Royal Arch Masonry," AQC 30 (1917): 7–55.

37 Clark, British Clubs, 334.

38 Jones, Guide and Compendium, 501.

39 Ibid., 496–497. Jones also asserts that "the 1750s give us uncontested records of the

from No. 30 Stirling exist from 1745, and the earliest mention of the Royal Arch Degree occurs on March 4, 1766, when "John Sawers ... prayed he might be Matriculated in this Lodge as a Brother from the Royall Arch Lodge of Said place Gratice, which the Lodge agreed to."[40]

By the early 1790s, however, allegations had surfaced which connected these higher degrees to the radical United Irishmen. Established in Belfast in 1791, the United Irishmen advocated religious toleration, parliamentary reform, and universal manhood suffrage.[41] Although initially attempting to achieve their goals by "radical persuasion and by enlisting mass support," Dickinson remarks that French exploitation of Irish resentment ultimately drove them "into the hands of the militant, republican minority."[42] Procuring Tory support and advancing beliefs and doctrines rooted in the revolutionary sentiments which threatened to overwhelm France, the creation of the United Irishmen in 1791 was essentially "a reaction against Whig diffidence and a reflection of the determination of some men to implement the democratic principles which the example of the French Revolution had carried on a tidal wave which threatened to engulf Europe."[43] The radical organization only posed a direct threat to the mainland when it realized the "importance of political subversion in Britain as a means of bringing pressure to bear on the Government there," and that military assistance from France would be imperative in bringing this revolution to Britain.[44]

The passage of the Unlawful Oaths and Secret Societies Acts was a warning to all radical groups that treason and sedition would not be tolerated;

---

making of Royal Arch masons in Ireland, Virginia, England, and Scotland. Royal Arch masonry had found its feet in the seven years ending 1759," 498.

40 No. 30 Stirling Lodge Minutes, March 4, 1766.

41 For more information on the United Irishmen and their doctrines, see Niall Ó Ciosáin, *Print and Popular Culture in Ireland, 1750–1850* (London, 1997), 132–136; James O'Connor, *History of Ireland 1798–1924* (London, 1925), 61–72; Marianne Elliot, *Wolfe Tone: Prophet of Irish Independence* (New Haven, 1989), 134–150; Frank MacDermot, *Theobald Wolfe Tone: A Biographical Study* (London, 1939), 68–89; R. B. McDowell, *Ireland in the Age of Imperialism and Revolution* (Oxford, 1979), 473–490; J. L. McCracken, "The United Irishmen," in *Secret Societies in Ireland*, ed. T. Desmond Williams, (Dublin, 1973), 58–67; Thomis and Holt, *Threats of Revolution*, 18–22.

42 Dickinson, *British Radicalism*, 46.

43 Wells, *Insurrection*, 8.

44 Dickinson, *British Radicalism*, 49. See also Marianne Elliot, "Ireland and the French Revolution," in *Britain and the French Revolution*, ed. H. T. Dickinson, 83–101.

however, militant radicals used Irish societies as fronts for their extremist activities and meetings. As British freemasons had already come under increasing scrutiny after 1789, the alleged connection with subversive Irish organizations certainly did not placate public and government suspicions. Elaine McFarland maintains that

> a familiar Irish tactic employed in Scotland was the use of Freemasons' Lodges as a cover for underground activities ... Certainly by the 1790s the Craft had acquired a reputation for advanced political principles, and the United Irishmen felt comfortable in making the most of the lodges as fronts and recruiting grounds. Scotland offered good opportunities to extend the surrogate method, with an extensive network of lodges, which were believed to be more "popular and radical" than elsewhere.[45]

The tone and nature of a lodge was dictated as much by its geographical location as its membership. Analysis shows that Scottish lodges emphasized charity and philanthropy, and largely eschewed political and religious discussion. In Ireland, however, by 1798 at least some lodges were politically polarized, causing a schism among Irish freemasons.[46] In 1797, White notes that 34 Masonic lodges in Armagh acknowledged the influence of the United Irishmen and that they "wished to wipe away the stigma,"[47] attempting to eradicate all links with the radical group. This was difficult, as lodges proved to be susceptible to the ideas of the United Irishmen. Historians have commented on this vulnerability, emphasizing the role of Freemasonry in helping to foster revolutionary ideas:

> The United Irishmen were originally conceived as a masonic secret society or "brotherhood of affection." Their oaths, tests and procedures were all grounded in masonic ritual. Because it was strictly non-denominational and because it endorsed speculative political theory relating to ideas of human perfectibility, masonry was amenable to political radicalism. In the 1790s, the United Irishmen

---

45 McFarland, *Ireland and Scotland*, 159. See also R. E. Parkinson, "Ireland and the Royal Arch Degree," *AQC* 79 (1966): 181–193; William Tait, "Early Records of the Royal Arch in Ireland," *AQC* 36 (1923): 193–194.

46 See Terence De Vere White, "The Freemasons," in *Secret Societies in Ireland*, 46–57.

47 Ibid., 51.

used masonry as an organizational and recruiting mechanism. They were so successful that the government cracked down hard on it 1797, forbidding the forming of new lodges.[48]

Political tensions were also exacerbated by religious intolerance and the rise of the Orange Order. Indeed, any account of Irish Freemasonry must include its association with Orangeism, which "took the word 'lodge' from Masonry, its members were bound by an oath of secrecy as in masonry, Masonic titles and practices were also adopted, and as Catholics were specifically excluded from its ranks, a great many Masons must have been Orangemen as well."[49] Although the purposes of the two institutions were wholly different, it is clear that Irish Freemasonry was influenced by politics and religion, and also affected the development of other organizations in Ireland.[50] Thus, the skepticism surrounding Masonic activities would have been heightened, due to radical infiltration and the intolerant religious attitudes of societies modeled after the freemasons.

William Drennan, chief architect of the United Irishmen, admired the secretive, ritualistic, and religious aspects of the freemasons. Recognizing the potential success of an organization based on Masonic tenets, he created the politically radical United Irishmen and adopted the "secrecy and somewhat of the ceremonial of Freemasonry, so much secrecy as might communicate curiosity, uncertainty, [and] expectation to the minds of surrounding men."[51] Drennan aspired to create a "benevolent conspiracy" which would ultimately draw inspiration from the Brotherhood—or Freemasonry—which would serve as

> ... a plot for the people—no *Whig* Club—no party title—the Brotherhood its name—the Rights of Men and the Greatest Happiness of the Greatest Number in

---

48   Kevin Whelan, *Fellowship of Freedom: The United Irishmen and 1798* (Ireland, 1998), 38.

49   White, "The Freemasons," 52.

50   White states that "Masons existed for the sake of masonry; the Orange Order was specifically directed towards the suppression of Catholics and the maintenance of Protestant ascendancy," 52.

51   Letter from William Drennan to Samuel McTier, May 21, 1791, Quoted in *The Decade of the United Irishmen: Contemporary Accounts, 1791–1801*, ed. John Killen, (Belfast, 1997), 13.

its end—its general and Real Independence to Ireland, and Republicanism its particular purpose—its business every means to accomplish these ends as speedily as the prejudices and bigotry of the land we live in would permit, as speedily as to give us some enjoyment and not to protract anything too long in this short span of life. The means are manifold, publication always coming from one of the Brotherhood, and no other designation.[52]

The relationship between Freemasonry and radical societies, such as the United Irishmen, is at times conspiratorial, a product of revolutionary hysteria and the "psychology of their advocates and their audiences."[53] Other times, apparent ties to extremist politics have been glossed over in an indecent attempt to conceal the "regrettable and aberrant political entanglements of the 1780s and 1790s."[54] Certainly, in Ireland, the "Masonic ethos was ... attuned to the radical cause."[55] Drennan borrowed heavily and freely from Masonic doctrine in an effort to popularize the fledgling United movement and entice potential members with pseudo-Masonic rituals, ceremonies, and the promise of solidarity and brotherhood. By the 1790s, Irish freemasons were ignoring the political and religious boundaries as established by Anderson's *Constitutions*; shrugging off chastisement by the Grand Lodge of Ireland for allowing political discussions during meetings, freemasons dissolved their lodges and reconvened as "assembl[ies] of masonic citizens."[56]

Unlike Scottish lodges, which entered into a period of decline during the final two decades of the eighteenth century, Irish Freemasonry expanded at a striking rate in the early 1780s, a trend which continued throughout the early-nineteenth century.[57] Indeed, as Smyth has argued, "sheer numbers and fashion alone help account for the influence of Freemasonry on the popular political movements of the 1790s."[58] Factoring in the

---

52 Ibid.
53 Smyth, Jim. "Freemasonry and the United Irishmen," in *The United Irishmen Republicanism, Radicalism and Rebellion*, ed. Kevin Whelan (Dublin, 1993), 167.
54 Ibid., 168.
55 Ibid.
56 Ibid., 171.
57 Ibid., 170.
58 Ibid., 171.

non-sectarian and rationalistic ideology of the society, Smyth maintains that "many of the Freemasons and Volunteers of the 1780s became the United Irishmen of the following decade."[59]

Confirming the assertions of McFarland, historians have argued that during the 1790s the United Irishmen utilized existing Masonic lodges as convenient vehicles for creating a "mass-based clandestine organisation" replete with a "centralised military structure, and the superimposition of that structure onto pre-existing networks of ... lodges."[60] Numerous members of the United Irishmen joined Masonic lodges, ushering in a period of "systematic infiltration" in order to provide access to a "ready-made lodge network."[61] These initiates included many of the Irish pioneers of the radical movement, a fact which has led A. T. Q. Stewart to speculate that William Drennan was also a freemason.[62]

Perhaps more importantly, Stewart suggests that several of Drennan's poems from the 1780s may contain imagery "connected with the higher degrees of Royal Arch Masonry, part of the ritual of the 'Antients' which continued to flourish in Irish Freemasonry."[63] Rumors alleging Irish exploitation of Masonic lodges for seditious purposes in Scotland existed as early as 1779. Lyon notes that in that year, a body of Dublin freemasons existing under the title "The High Knight Templars of Ireland Lodge," or Knights Templar, applied for and received a charter from Lodge Kilwinning in Scotland. However, according to Lyon, the "Irish Brethren subsequently erased from their Charter the word 'Lodge' ... and, surreptitiously inserting 'Encampment,' began the practice of Black Masonry,"[64] which eventually became the degree of Knights Templar.[65] Other historians agree, suggesting that masons serving in Irish regiments toward the end of the eighteenth century contributed to the introduction and practice of higher and unsanctioned degrees within Scottish lodges.[66] As Gould notes,

---

59 Ibid.

60 Ibid., 172.

61 Ibid., 173. Smyth further notes that "some lodges, useful because they provided a pretext for meeting legally, became United Irish 'fronts,'" 173.

62 Stewart, *A Deeper Silence*, 176.

63 Ibid., 176–177.

64 Gould, *History of Freemasonry Vol. 2*, 291–292.

65 Lyon, *Mary's Chapel*, 335.

66 Gould, *History of Freemasonry Vol. 2*, 291.

it was to their intercourse with Brethren belonging to regiments serving in Ireland towards the end of the last century, that Scotch Lodges owed their acquaintance with
Knight Templarism. This order, then known as Black
Masonry, was propagated, to a large extent, through
Charters issued by the High Knights Templar of Ireland,
Kilwinning—a body of Freemasons in Dublin, who
were constituted by Mother Kilwinning [in Scotland] in
1779, for the practice of the Craft Degrees, [but Lodge
Kilwinning] repudiated the existence of any material tie
between herself and any Society of Masonic Knighthood
and confessed her inability to "communicate upon Mason business" farther than the Three Steps.[67]

In addition to penetrating Masonic lodges, members of the United Irishmen were instrumental in helping to establish the United Scotsmen, and
localized branches in Dundee, Fife, and on the West Coast of Scotland
clearly were indebted to the Irish radical group for their "tests, resolutions, constitutions and links with Masonic lodges."[68] Although the majority of the United Scotsmen were Scottish, it has been suggested by
Mitchell that members of some radical societies, especially in Ayrshire,
were Irish.[69] During the 1780s and 1790s, the population of Ulster immi-
grants in Scotland increased; searching for work, they gravitated toward
Ayr and Maybole.[70] This trend did not go unnoticed by the government.
In a 1799 *Report of a Committee of Secrecy of the House of Commons*, it was
asserted that

the attempts to form a society of United Scotsmen had
made little progress till the Spring of 1797; but from the
month of April 1797 until November following (when
a discovery was made in the county of Fife, on which
George Mealmaker was brought to trial, and convicted

---

67 Ibid.

68 Emma Vincent MacLeod, "Scottish Responses to the Irish Rebellion of 1798," from
These Fissured Isles: Ireland, Scotland and British History, 1798–1848, ed. Terry Brotherstone (Edinburgh, 2004), 126.

69 Ibid. Also see Martin Mitchell, *The Irish in The West of Scotland: Trade Unions, Strikes
and Political Movements* (Edinburgh, 1998), 72.

70 Ibid., 125.

of sedition) these attempts appear to have been attended with more success, and particularly in the neighbour- hood of Glasgow, and the in the counties of Ayr, Ren- frew, Lanerk, Dumbarton, Fife, and Perth. Glasgow, and the county of Ayr, were the places in which this spirit first manifested itself, and from which emissaries were sent, into different parts of the country, for the purpose of in- creasing the numbers of the society, and disseminating what they termed, "political knowledge."[71]

Evidence, however, suggests that Scottish Masonic lodges were not hot- beds of sedition. Although it is highly possible that at least some lodges included members of the United Irishmen and Scotsmen, the overall in- fluence is negligible. Analysis of membership lists for several lodges in Maybole and the West Coast of Scotland reveal no specific links with sub- versive societies in Ireland. Comparing the roles for Maybole Royal Arch, Maybole Operative, Glasgow Royal Arch, Paisley Royal Arch, and Stirling Royal Arch with Gallin's directory of radical clubs and their members, only three names appear as members of both the freemasons and revolu- tionary clubs. John Buchanan, belonging to Stirling Royal Arch, was also affiliated with Canongate Clubs Nos. 1 and 2, although nothing more is known of his Masonic career and actions within the Canongate Clubs; William Miller, Student of Divinity and member of Maybole Royal Arch, was included among the names in the Perth Radical Association;[72] and James Boyd, member of Maybole Operative Lodge in 1792, is listed as a member of the Dunfermline Radical Club.[73]

Interestingly, the name William McTier appears in 1793 among the mem- bers of Maybole Royal Arch. This is significant, for William Drennan ex- changed letters with his sister Martha McTier and her husband Samuel McTier; it was in these letters that he intimated his admiration for the principles of Freemasonry. It is possible that in order to avoid detection, he did join Maybole Royal Arch under the name William McTier, adopt- ing the namesake of Samuel, his close friend and confidante.

---

71   Great Britain Parliament House, *House of Commons Report of Committee of Secrecy of the House of Commons* (London, 1799), 28.

72   See Gallin, "Scottish Radicalism," 248; 252.

73   Ibid., 249.

Despite these tenuous connections, it is relatively clear that few masons were members of revolutionary clubs, thus seriously preventing the advancement of a radical agenda within Masonic lodges. Furthermore, the overall United movement in Scotland was inherently weak, a testament to the "relative political, economic and social stability prevailing in Scotland."[74] As a result, the reform movement in Scotland—although possessed of some localized and insulated pockets of revolutionary activity—was not as effective at mobilizing support as in Ireland. By late 1792, many of the initial participants of the inaugural Friends of the People meeting in Edinburgh began to have "second thoughts."[75] Concerned with the ability of the society to control "the plebeian mass membership it sought to attract, and fearing that the Association would soon abandon its moderation and adopt radical, even revolutionary, policies, they withdrew their support."[76]

Sedition and the Unlawful Oaths Act

The Masonic debate over Black Masonry had first been addressed by the Modern Grand Lodge of England, almost 50 years before the Maybole case. Grand Secretary Samuel Spencer openly expressed his disapproval of the new degrees, stating that "Our Society is neither Arch, Royal Arch, or Ancient," and it is "a Society we do not acknowledge and which we hold to be an invention to introduce innovation and to seduce the brethren."[77] Opposition to the Royal Arch motivated several members of various Modern lodges to form their own independent Supreme Grand Chapter. The secretary of the rival Antient Grand Lodge of England, according to Clarke, "complained of flagrant abuses of 'this most sacred part of Masonry'" and in 1788 an investigation was conducted to verify these charges.[78] Unlike the Grand Lodge of Scotland, which condemned the degree outright, the Modern Grand Lodge of England ruled that the "no Royal Arch Masons should be made without the consent of Grand Lodge officers."[79]

---

74 MacLeod, "Scottish Responses," 131.

75 John Brims, "Scottish Radicalism and the United Irishmen," in *The United Irishmen: Republicanism, Radicalism and Rebellion*, ed. Kevin Whelan (Dublin, 1993), 153.

76 Ibid.

77 United Grand Lodge of England, *Grand Lodge*, 281.

78 Clarke, "The Formation, 1717–1813," 103–104.

79 Ibid.

The English debate over Black Masonry illustrates the early uncertainty attached to the Royal Arch and Knights Templar degrees. One historian maintains that the Royal Arch degree was "concocted by the 'Ancients' to widen the breach, and make the line of distinction between them and the Grand Lodge broader and more indelible."[80] Jones, however, tacitly disagrees with this claim, although he does state that the degree "undoubtedly suited their [Ancients'] purpose to encourage it for the purpose of accentuating the difference between themselves and their opponents."[81] Regardless of the motivations for practicing these rituals, it is evident that "not one Grand Lodge in the British Isles countenanced the Royal Arch in its earliest years."[82]

The skepticism surrounding these new degrees would be revisited in Western Scotland during the Maybole Trial of Sedition. McFarland claims that by 1797, a "contagion [which equated] Irishness with disaffection" had gripped Western Scotland.[83] As such, by 1797 Ayrshire had become one of the "first strongholds" of Irish influence.[84] And as we have seen, membership lists from radical clubs and societies offer no definitive evidence that freemasons in Maybole were members of seditious associations. Wartski, however, corroborates McFarland's assertions by claiming that "in 1796 some of the members of Maybole Lodge allied themselves with a few Masonic United Irishmen in the formation of an Assembly of Knight Templars, and clandestinely entered upon the work of Royal Arch Masonry and Knight Templars."[85]

On February 6, 1797, Lodge Royal Arch Maybole successfully applied to the Grand Lodge of Scotland for a working warrant and was designated as No. 264 on the Grand Roll. Nine days later, on 15 February, the lodge held its first official meeting.[86] The speed and alacrity with which the working warrant was granted attests to the efficiency of the Grand Lodge in establishing new lodges. The haste with which it expedited the creation

---

80   Quoted in Jones, *Guide and Compendium*, 505.

81   Ibid., 503.

82   Ibid.

83   McFarland, *Ireland and Scotland*, 157.

84   Ibid., 158.

85   Wartski, "Secret Societies," 64.

86   No. 264 Lodge Royal Arch Maybole was not officially granted a charter until November 1798.

of No. 264 also, however, prevented the Grand Lodge from considering the likely consequences of the practice of unsanctioned Masonic degrees.

Four days after the first quarterly communication of the Grand Lodge of Scotland in 1797, a letter written by an Ayrshire minister was read before the Grand Committee. The author, Reverend William Wright of Maybole, objected to the creation of Royal Arch Maybole and alleged that its members "behaved very superciliously, that they also gave out that their Lodge is of a different Order of Masonry from that of other Mother lodges, that they say they have higher mysteries in which they instruct their entrants, and that they have new and much more numerous ceremonies."[87] Reverend Wright's accusations, however, failed to arouse the suspicion of the committee and were simply passed to the Provincial Grand Master of the Southern District.[88] Eventually, as Wartski notes, "the high office bearers permitted the buck to stop passing" and the claims were ultimately dismissed.[89]

By 1799, fresh allegations of dubious lodge activities resurfaced. Quintin McAdam—then Master of No. 14 Maybole Lodge—maintained that the neighbouring Royal Arch Maybole was guilty of

> contravening the articles of its instruction by the practice of other than the degrees of St John's Masonry—that its pretended meetings for the study of the so-called higher mysteries were really held for the purpose of instilling into the minds of its entrants the principles of infidelity—that the Bible had in the Lodge been replaced by Paine's *Age of Reason* and that its teachings were altogether of a revolutionary character, prejudiced alike to the interests of Church and State.[90]

McAdam essentially claimed that No. 264 had abandoned several key points of the *Constitutions*. First, the presence of Paine's *Rights of Man* di-

---

87   Ibid., 64–65.

88   Wartski is most likely referring to the Ayrshire District. As specified in Chapter 3, page 77, this would have District 4 or the South Ayrshire District, including Maybole and Kirkcudbright and superintended by Collector Malison.

89   Wartski, "Secret Societies," 65.

90   Lyon, *Mary's Chapel*, 324. The minutes from Maybole Lodge No. 14 unfortunately no longer exist. Lyon, however, apparently had access to the records before they were lost.

rectly flouted Anderson's rule that "No private Piques, no Quarrels about Nations, Families, Religions or Politicks must be brought within the Door of the Lodge ... We are resolved against political Disputes, as contrary to the Peace and Welfare of the *Lodge*."[91] Paine's writings were dangerous in that they were a "potent polemic devoted to the notion of the sovereignty of the people, and its essential corollary—universal suffrage;"[92] furthermore, Paine's literature polarized political thought in Britain and Irish societies, as it "infused popularism into the debate started by the Revolution."[93] As *Rights of Man* had replaced the Bible in Lodge Royal Arch Maybole, the members seemed to contravene the regulation which stated that freemasons "will never be a Stupid Atheist, nor an Irreligious Libertine."[94] Furthermore, the espousal of Paine's theology was in direct opposition to the Masonic charge that masons were "never to be concern'd in Plots against the state" or implicated in *"Rebellion* against the state."[95]

It is possible, as Gray argues, that as "Masonic ritual was not standarised then as it is today, probably No. 264 members carried out their ceremonies in a different manner to those of No. 14, who being the older lodge, would feel that the young upstart lodge should fall into line and do as their elders and betters did."[96] However, it is more likely that McAdam believed that Royal Arch Maybole was "promoting the aims and objects of the French Revolution, not to mention that of the intended Irish Revolution, under the mantle of Freemasonry."[97] Gray's conclusion only addresses the issues of lodge rivalry and jealousy. If No. 264 was citing Paine— whose text was the symbol of British revolutionary politics—this was an obvious sign of genuine revolutionary views and a very clear attempt by the Maybole lodge to accuse No. 264 of radical political sentiments. The writings of Paine were so invidious to the defenders of British conservatism that the radical leader was tried and convicted of treason, branded as a traitor, and publishers of *Rights of Man* were fined and imprisoned. No. 264 faced similar penalties, as the government stipulated that the "leaders

---

91 Anderson, *Constitutions*, 147.

92 Wells, *Insurrection*, 2.

93 Ibid.

94 Anderson, *Constitutions*, 143.

95 Ibid., 144.

96 James T. Gray, *Freemasonry in Maybole, Carrick's Capital: Fact, Fiction and Folks* (Ayr, 1972), 279–287.

97 Wartski, "Secret Societies," 64.

of associations formed for the purpose of promoting parliamentary reforme" faced possible incarceration and charges of sedition and treason.[98] Paine may well have sympathized with the aims and beliefs of freemasons. According to Harrison, Paine—in his 1805 essay *Origins of Freemasonry*—"writes understandingly of the masons and contrasts masonry favourable with Christianity. He is convinced that masons are the descendants of the ancient Druids: 'Masonry is derived and is the remains of the religion of the ancient Druids ... who, by all accounts ... were a wise, learned and moral class of men.'"[99] Thus it is possible that Paine, "with his condemnation of what he regarded as ignorance, superstition and mummery would have little time for Freemasonry. The masons' secrecy and ceremonies would surely be ridiculed. Not a bit of it."[100]

The Grand Lodge of Scotland considered McAdam's allegations at a quarterly communication in May 1800 (Appendix 5). Ostensibly to settle the dispute between No. 14 and No. 264, the Grand Lodge used the meeting to employ several "neat piece[s] of footwork to dodge an awkward situation."[101] Royal Arch Maybole had been granted a working warrant in February 1797 and was officially chartered in November 1798. As such, Grand Lodge ruled that any accusations against No. 264 made prior to February 6, 1797 were inadmissible, as No. 264 was then not legally under its jurisdiction.[102] Furthermore, as "these degrees of Masonry were not sanctioned or authorised by the Grand Lodge of Scotland and consequently all of the members of the Grand Lodge [were] totally strangers to these orders of Masonry," no questions "should be put to the witness regarding Royal Arch Masonry or Knights Templars."[103] However, the Grand Lodge

---

98   George Spater, "Introduction: Thomas Paine–Questions for the Historian," in *Citizen of the World*, ed. Ian Dyck, (New York, 1988), 7. Spater also notes that "Habeas Corpus act was suspended in 1794 largely because of Paine's work," 7.

99   Harrison, "Millenarian Radicalism," *Citizen*, 82–83.

100 Ibid.

101 Wartski, "Secret Societies," 66.

102 Grand Lodge of Scotland Minutes, May 19, 1800: "A debate took place as to the Relevancy of the Charges now brought and after a considerable discussion the Grand Lodge Found that none of the Charges brought against the Members of the Royal Arch Lodge Maybole No. 264 prior to the 6th day of February 1797 the date of the Letter form the Grand Lodge authorising them to hold Mason Meetings were competent to be the subject of Investigation before the Grand Lodge because till that date they were in no shape under their Jurisdiction."

103 Ibid.

did "Find it Competent for Brother McAdam to prove by witnesses or otherways the charges subsequent to the date of the Letter form the Grand Lodge authorising them to hold meetings under their authority."[104]

Having effectively vindicated itself, the Grand Lodge then directed McAdam to provide evidence supporting the allegations of misconduct and sedition by the members of No. 264 subsequent to February 6, 1797.[105] Upon his failure to substantiate such claims, Grand Lodge then heard testimony from William Hamilton and Quintin Stewart, both of whom were members of No. 264. Each testified that the lodge practiced only the three sanctioned degrees of Freemasonry, and that Paine's *Age of Reason* or "anything Profane or Immoral, or any thing inimical to the Church or State" were all absent from lodge meetings.[106] Following their statements, several members of Royal Arch Maybole

> were then asked if they had any Evidence to adduce in Exculpation when they produced certificates from Royal Arch Lodge Ayr and from St Davids Lodge Torbolton Certifying their good conduct as Masons and also Certificates from the Minister and Elders of the parish Certifying their good conduct as Men and Christians. They also produced a Certificate from Captain Shaw Commander of the Maybole Volunteers testifying that Eighteen of the Members of that Lodge were in his Corps.[107]

Substitute Grand Master William Inglis, upon hearing the evidence attesting to the good conduct and merit of Hamilton and Stewart, "moved an Amendment to the effect that the Grand Lodge should simply find that the Charges against the Royal Arch Lodge had not been proved."[108] Despite the recommendation of James Gibson—an ardent Whig and a key figure in the Masonic Secession—that McAdam should be "censured for bringing so groundless and vexatious a Charge,"[109] the Grand Lodge

---

104 Ibid. See Appendix 5, May 19, 1800 for a full text of the entry.

105 Ibid. The full charge reads as follows: "The Grand Lodge Find it Competent for Brother McAdam to prove by witnesses or otherways the charges subsequent to the date of the Letter form the Grand Lodge authorising them to hold meetings under their authority."

106 Ibid.

107 Ibid.

108 Ibid.

109 Ibid.

ultimately expressed its "approbation of the said Masonic zeal of the said Brother McAdam" and "further recommend[ed] to both Lodges to bury their differences in oblivion and in future to Communicate together in Harmony and Brotherly Love."[110]

During the trial, both the Unlawful Oaths and Secret Societies Acts had been passed by the government and were being used with some degree of success against seditious societies. Thus, Grand Lodge's response to McAdam's accusations was influenced by its recent concern for compliance with the rules and regulations arising from the Acts. As the Maybole case was Grand Lodge's first serious challenge under these new circumstances, it was imperative to reinforce its status as the supreme Masonic body in Scotland. This was why, instead of immediately attending to the grievances of No. 14, the Grand Lodge of Scotland took urgent measures to ensure its own protection. Ultimately, this was accomplished through a series of dubious provisions, decisions, and testimonies, all designed to make Grand Lodge appear blameless and place the burden of proof upon No. 14 Maybole.

Although it seemed broadly to side with Lodge Royal Arch Maybole, a communication from the Grand Lodge suggests otherwise. And unlike the Grand Lodge minutes, No. 264 minutes are explicit during the entire ordeal and manifest the resoluteness of the members in resisting the demands of the Grand Lodge (Appendix 6). A comparison of the minute transcripts from both lodges regarding the trial reveals dissimilar descriptions of the actions of the Grand Lodge. For example, the Grand Lodge simply stated that it had ordered the "Grand Clerk to Serve the said complaint upon the Office Bearers of the said Royal Arch Lodge Maybole No. 264 and appoint them to give in Answers thereto within Ten days from this date [10 April 1800]."[111] Royal Arch Maybole, however, recorded that it had received a letter "from the Substitute Grand Master of Scotland demanding in the name by the Authority of the Most Worshipful the Grand Master us to Send in to Edinburgh the Lodges Charter under Cover to the Grand Secretary," as No. 14 Lodge Maybole claimed that the lodge "had obtained [its] Charter by unconstitutional and Illicit means."[112] Grand Lodge minutes failed to mention any of these proceedings, and it also

---

110 Ibid., May 26, 1800.
111 Grand Lodge of Scotland Minutes, April 10, 1800.
112 No. 198 Royal Arch Maybole Lodge Minutes, August 7, 1799.

omitted the fact that "Certificates from the Provincial Masters of the four Lodges in Air held on the 25th October 1798" were submitted as evidence attesting to the good character and conduct of the members of No. 264.[113] It is quite possible that as Provincial Grand Masters were appointed by the Grand Lodge, this piece of information was conveniently excluded from the trial so as to place the burden of proof on those masons not directly affiliated with the Grand Lodge. As it wanted to remain impartial, the admission of the testimonies of the Provincial Grand Masters would suggest that it supported No. 264.

The charge of illegally obtaining a charter differed significantly from the allegations of sedition. Clearly, the Grand Lodge wanted to resolve any questions over the warrant, as it had so quickly granted it to Royal Arch Maybole. It is likely that the Grand Lodge only defended No. 264 insofar as it did not find any of the Grand Officers guilty of seditious or illegal activities. As Wartski says, "Grand Lodge decided to sit on the fence, and to be all things to all men."[114] This is evident in the final verdict. After handing down its judgment of not guilty and having urged both lodges to reconcile their differences, Brother Lawrie maintains that

> the Grand Lodge of Scotland Sanctioned the three great orders of Masonry and these alone of Apprentice, Fellow Craft and Master Mason being the Ancient order of St John, But understanding that other descriptions of Masons under various Titles had crept into the Country borrowed from other Nations which he conceived to be inconsistent with the purity and true principles of the order. He therefore Moved that the Grand Lodge of Scotland should Expressly prohibit and discharge all Lodges from holding any other Meetings than that of the three orders above described under this Certification that their Charters shall be forfeited *ipso facto* in case of transgression.[115]

One week later, the Grand Lodge of Scotland decided to amend the words "that their charters shall be forfeited *ipso facto* in case of transgression" to

---

113 Ibid., May 26, 1800.

114 Wartski, "Secret Societies," 68.

115 Grand Lodge of Scotland Minutes, May 19, 1800.

the following: "that the Grand Lodge will most positively proceed on information of an infringement of this express prohibition to censure or to the forfeiture of their charters of the offending Lodge according to the circumstances of any particular case which may be brought before them."[116]

According to Wartski, Grand Lodge's inability to take one side or the other was detrimental to the final outcome of the trial. Had the affair been settled in a "more forthright and courageous manner it might just have put an end to the later distressing criminal proceedings."[117] For in addition to the complaints made to the Grand Lodge, McAdam also lodged a criminal information petition against John Andrews and Robert Ramsay, Master and Senior Warden of No. 264. Consequently, both were arrested in June 1800, arraigned before the Circuit Court of Justiciary in Ayr, and charged with sedition and the administering of unlawful oaths.

The Court Trial

The court battle that took place between June and September 1800 is interesting, not least of all because the Grand Lodge of Scotland was noticeably absent from any of the proceedings and new, extraordinary evidence was heard that had had not been presented during the previous trial. John Andrew and Robert Ramsay, the principal defendants, were charged with sedition and the administration of unlawful oaths. Appendix 7 contains the *Criminal Letters/His Majesty's Advocate/Against John Andrew* and a list of the charges against Ramsay and Andrew. The prosecution asserted that

> Whereas it is humbly meant and complained to us by our Right Trust Robert Dundas Esq. of Arniston our Advocate for our Interest upon John Andrew Shoemaker in Maybole And some time Schoolmaster there And Robert Ramsay Cartwright there That Albeit by the laws of this and of every other well governed Realm, Sedition, As Also, the wickedly & feloniously administering or causing to be administered unlawful oaths, more especially when such oaths import an obligation not to reveal or discover crimes which it is the duty of every good Citizen and

---

116 Ibid., May 26, 1800.

117 Wartski, "Secret Societies," 68. This claim is dubious, as McAdam was determined to pursue his case against Lodge Royal Arch Maybole regardless of the outcome of the Grand Lodge trial.

Loyal subject to divulge and bring to light; are crimes of a heinous nature and Severely punishable Yet true it is and of Verity that the said John Andrew and Robert Ramsay above complained on are both or one or other of them guilty actors or art and part of the aforesaid Crime or Crimes. In so far as under the Shew and pretence of a Meeting for Masonry, Some time in the course of the year One thousand seven hundred and Ninety Six, at Maybole parish of Maybole and County of Ayr; along with others their associates, most of them from Ireland, formed themselves into an illegal club or association Styling itself "The Grand Assembly of Knights Templars" or bearing some such name; which club or Association under pretence of initiating into the Ceremonies of Masonry, did admit various persons as Members, and did at said admission perform various ceremonies partly with a view to vilify and undermine the established Religion, and partly to represent the Constitution and Government of the Country As oppressive and Tyrannical.[118]

Unlike the earlier allegations made by McAdam, the accusations given before the Justiciary Court included the overt dissemination of radical Irish ideas.[119] Although Andrew and Ramsay denied being guilty of treason and sedition, Wartski claims that based on their testimonies "they were guilty at common law of administering unlawful oaths."[120] Indeed, they told Lord Justice Clerk Eskgrove[121] that while attending No. 14 Maybole they had joined the Royal Arch at St. James's Lodge in Newton Upon Ayr. Having been admitted, they were informed by the Master of No.14 that "he had no objections to it" and was "certain it could do no harm."[122]

---

118 Robert Ramsay Declaration, 1800, JC 26/305 NAS. See Appendix 7 for a complete transcript of the Robert Ramsay Declaration.

119 Ibid., 159.

120 Wartski, "Secret Societies," 68. See also Appendix 7 for the Exculpation for John Andrew and Robert Ramsay, which gives their sworn testimonies.

121 Sir David Rae of Eskgrove was elected Senior Grand Warden of the Grand Lodge of Scotland in 1807. See Lyon, *Mary's Chapel*, 327. Rae would later be named counsel for the complainers against the lodges seceding from the Grand Lodge of Scotland during the Masonic Secession of 1808.

122 *Criminal Letters/His Majesty's Advocate Against John Andrew*, September 1800, JC26/305 NAS. See Appendix 7 for a full transcript.

Subsequently, Andrew and Ramsay conferred the oaths and rituals of the Royal Arch degree upon several members of No. 14, including Quintin Stewart and William Hamilton.

The conferral, however, may have involved a member of a radical club in Kilmarnock. The transcripts for the *Criminal Letters/His Majesty's Advocate/Against John Andrew September 1800 Ayr* refer to one "Wm. Moor, an Irishman then weaver in Maybole." Gallin's list of radical clubs and members includes a William Muir, a weaver in Kilmarnock.[123] Although at best a tenuous connection, it does lend further weight to the arguments of McFarland and others that radical Irish dissidents had some influence on Masonic lodges in Western Scotland.

While Ramsay acknowledged that he could "repeat the oath or the Substance of it," he declared that he "would wish to have some time to consult with some of his other Brethren of St. James's Lodg ... whether he was at liberty to divulge it or not ... and he would rather on that account wish to decline it at present."[124] Bound by the terms of his own initiation not to reveal any details of the ceremonies,

> he understood himself bound in that manner by an oath he had taken, when he was himself initiated which he never saw committed to writing, and which he administered afterwards in the same form and tenor from his memory to those he initiated afterwards ... Being farther interrogated whether in these higher orders of Masonry there may be signs, symbols or materials used of any kind in the compleating of their instruction that he has the same objection to Exhibit and divulge, that he has stated to the condescending upon the words of his obligation Declares that he has the very same objection to the one as to the other.[125]

Having temporarily avoided the issue of administering unlawful oaths, both Andrew and Ramsay were then confronted with allegations of treason, in particular of using Thomas Paine's *Age of Reason* during lodge ceremonies. Though each admitted to having possessed personal copies of this

---

123 Gallin, "Scottish Radicalism," 251.

124 Ibid.

125 Ibid.

book, they "considered it a production of dangerous Consequence."[126] As both Ramsay and Andrew pleaded not guilty[127] to all charges, the burden of proof fell upon the two primary witnesses from the Grand Lodge Trial—William Hamilton and Quintin Stewart.

The testimonies of both Hamilton and Stewart, however, were completely unlike those previously given under sworn oath at the Grand Lodge of Scotland. Lyon writes that they "made a sweeping disclosure of what were alleged to be the secret ceremonies" of Royal Arch and Knights Templar degrees.[128] Whereas Andrew and Ramsay had declined to reveal the substance of the oaths administered during the ceremonies at No. 264, Hamilton and Stewart readily disclosed the details of the rituals.[129] Incredibly, they "suffered a remarkable resurgence of memory after the Masonic trial,"[130] offering specifics that were otherwise omitted from the Grand Lodge proceedings. Hamilton gave the following detailed description of his admission ceremony into Lodge Royal Arch Maybole:

> A pistol was fired and some person called out, "Put him to death." He was blindfolded first when brought into the room, and the covering being afterwards taken from his eyes, he was shown a stone jug in the corner of the room, and a candle burning in it. He was told by the panel that it was the representation of God Almighty in the midst of the burning bush. Andrew was Master of the Lodge, and was reading the third chapter of Exodus. The witness was desired to put off his shoes, as it was holy ground he stood on; the covering was put down again on the witness's face, and he was led under an arch, and, passing un-

---

126 Ibid.

127 Ibid. "John Andrew Shoemaker in Maybole and Sometime Schoolmaster there and Robert Ramsay Cartwright there ... [The] Pannels Indicted and Accused at the instance of His Majesties Advocate for his Majesties Interests of the Crimes of Sedition and administration of unlawful oaths in manner mentioned in the Criminal Lybell raised and prosecuted against them ... The libel being read over the panels pled not guilty."

128 Lyon, *Mary's Chapel*, 327.

129 Several records, testimonies, and verdicts cited by Lyon and Wartski are not available in the collections at the NAS, most notably Hamilton's description of the admission ceremony.

130 Wartski, "Secret Societies," 70.

der the arch, he was desired to find the Book of the Law; it was taken up by some other person in the Lodge, who was called High Priest, and who said he would explain it. The witness was desired to put money on the book to pay for explaining it to him; the book, he was told, was the Bible. The witness put money on the book as desired, and John Andrew made observations on the chapter as he read it, but the witness does not positively remember any of them. Recollects that part of the chapter where the children of Israel are said to be in bondage. The passport for a Royal Arch Mason was, "I Am that I Am." After the above ceremonies, the witness, being taken out of the room, had his coat taken off and tied on his shoulders in a bundle, and was then brought in; a carpet with a rent in it was called the veil of the temple. He was led through it, and round the room. A sword was put into his hand, and he was ordered to use it against all who opposed him as a Knight Templar. John Andrew read the fourth chapter of Exodus; the witness was desired to throw down the sword, and was told it was become a serpent; after which he was desired to take it up again, and was told it was become a rod. Andrew poured ale and porter on the floor, and called it blood. Witness was shown thirteen burning candles. One in the middle he was told represented Jesus Christ; the others the Twelve Apostles. Andrew blew out one of the candles, which he called Judas, who betrayed his Master; one of them was dim, and was called Peter, who denied his Master. Something on the table under a white cloth being uncovered, was perceived to be a human skull, which the witness was desired to take up, and view it, and was told it was a real skull of a brother called Simon Magus. Porter was poured into the skull, which the witness was desired to drink; he did so, and it was handed round the whole Knights. Andrew put the point of the sword into it, and then touched witness's head, saying, "I dub thee in the name of the Father, Son, and Holy Ghost." He took an oath "to keep the secrets of the Knights Templars, murder and treason not excepted": the penalty for revealing was that 'his body would be rooted up like a fir deal." John Andrew was Master at his admission, and at two others at which he was present. The witness's impression was that the ceremonies used were a scoffing at religion, and, though he cannot say positively, he thought they had a tendency to overturn the Government.[131]

The truthfulness of this account is clearly in question as it significantly differs from Hamilton's previous statements. Although Paine's *Rights of Man* is not mentioned, the grotesque and satirical interpretation of religion and the integration of violence and aggression were each obviously designed to compensate for its omission. Despite having told the Grand Lodge that "anything Profane or Immoral, or any thing inimical to the Church or State"[132] were absent from the lodge meetings, Hamilton now amended his account to include a fantastic story which implicated several members of No. 264 in the administration of oaths and rituals that had "a tendency to overturn the Government."[133]

By way of explanation, Wartski speculates first that McAdam, who was dissatisfied with the outcome of the Grand Lodge Trial, had conspired with Hamilton and Stewart to create this evocative account.[134] Second, he suggests that Hamilton's explicit accusation of subversion seems "like a pathetic attempt to bolster up the crumbling bastions of the sedition charge."[135] Indeed, the Lord Justice Clerk was appalled at the nature of the ceremony and "refused to believe that the ceremonies described were used in Masons' Lodges" as they were "'abominable and copious.'"[136] Eskgrove further commented that "this was a new oath introduced by the panels, and not in use before admitting Masons."[137] Ultimately, the court found that all charges were not proved.[138]

---

131 Lyon, *Mary's Chapel*, 327–329.

132 Grand Lodge of Scotland Minutes, May 17, 1800.

133 Lyon, *Mary's Chapel*, 329.

134 Wartski, "Secret Societies," 70–71.

135 Ibid.

136 Ibid., 72.

137 Ibid.

138 See Appendix 7 for the full transcript of JC26/305 NAS, *Charges read against Andrew and Ramsay: Verdict for John Andrew and Robert Ramsay*: "... having considered the

Conclusion

Remarkably, the Maybole Trial hinged on the association of No. 264 with irregular members, oaths, and illegally constituted lodges. On January 12, 1737, No. 14 Lodge Maybole presented a query to the Grand Lodge of Scotland addressing the problems of "what course shall be taken with such irregular brethren as belong to no particular Lodge, yet meet in private and enter Masons at such low rates and in such irregular methods as is a scandal to be mentioned among Masons."[139] The concerns of the lodge "were never reported upon by the committee to whom they were remitted;"[140] subsequently, no reply was given by the Grand Lodge and the matter was left unresolved.[141] Just as the Grand Lodge had failed to properly address the concerns of No. 14 in 1737, it also did not succeed in resolving the dispute in 1799.

This case illustrates several important trends that resurfaced during the Masonic Secession controversy of 1808. First, the sorts of clashes present within Scottish lodges underwent a noticeable change as a result of the French Revolution and the reactionary legislation passed by the gov-

---

Libel raised and pursued at the instance of his Majesty's Advocate ... against John Andrew & Robert Ramsay," having examined the "evidence adduced in proof of the libel and the evidence in exculpation they all in one voice find the facts Lybelled not proven." The matter was completely settled in 1805. On February 4, 1805, the Provincial Grand Master for Ayrshire reported that "he had the satisfaction to inform the Grand Lodge that thro his means that difference which had so long subsisted between the old Lodge at Maybole and the Royal Arch Lodge Maybole had been completely made up, and that these two Lodges were now on that friendly footing which all worthy Brethren should be," Grand Lodge of Scotland Minutes, February 4, 1805.

139 Lyon, *Mary's Chapel*, 192.

140 Ibid.

141 During the 1730s, the Grand Lodge of England also experienced problems with irregular masons. Whereas the Grand Lodge of Scotland entirely ignored the difficulties, the Grand Lodge of England, on March 31, 1735, addressed the "Grievance of making extranious Masons in a private and clandestine manner, upon small and unworthy Considerations, and proposed that in Order to prevent that Practice for the future: No person thus admitted into the Craft, nor any that can be proved to have assisted at such Makings shall be capable either of Acting as a Grand Officer on Occasion or even as an Officer in a private Lodge, nor ought they to have any part in the General Charity which is much impaired by this clandestine Practice," *United Grand Lodge,* 77. Furthermore, the Grand Lodge resolved that any freemason found guilty of irregularly admitting a mason would be "forever excluded from asking any Relief from the Committee of Charity, Quarterly Communications or any publick Assemblies of Masons whatsoever," Ibid., 77.

ernment in the 1790s.[142] Ultimately, financial disputes and disagreements among operatives and speculatives were overshadowed by endless wrangling over lodge precedence and charges of sedition and treason. Second, the legislation passed by parliament, though it initially offered a measure of protection to the freemasons, caused turmoil among the Scottish lodges for several years after its passage. Enacted to eradicate seditious societies, Masonic lodges actually used them maliciously against one another; not as a legitimate means to safeguard Scotland against revolution, but rather to pursue political quarrels and personal vendettas against other freemasons.

The Grand Lodge of Scotland wavered on its decisions and verdicts and simultaneously supported and condemned the defendants and plaintiffs, manifesting a lack of conviction and confidence in its own authority. In the instance of the Maybole Trial, No. 14 Lodge Maybole—not being satisfied with the Grand Lodge verdict—argued its case before the Justiciary Court in Ayr. In fact, the criminal information accusations against the Master and Senior Warden of No. 264 and the charges handed in to Grand Lodge were made at the same time, signaling a concerted effort to "deal

---

142 English Freemasonry also was not totally impervious to high profile conflicts and disputes. During the end of the eighteenth century, when the government passed the Unlawful Oaths and Secret Societies Acts and Scottish freemasons began wrangling over charter-granting privileges, English freemasons were in the process of restoring order and organization to the fraternity. In 1751, the Grand Lodge of England split into two grand lodges—the Modern Grand Lodge of England and the Antient Grand Lodge of England. Jacob describes the conflict as the "taking over of the old masonry of the operatives by gentlemen, and even nobles ... By 1751 it appears that some lodges had become battlegrounds where the meaning of equality, as well as the claim to possess the true, ancient constitution, was being adjudicated ... In general, the impulse of the ancients was decidedly reformist. Once freed from the discipline of the Grand Lodge, ancient lodges also experimented in new rituals and degrees. To add an air of respectability to these innovations, they were described as 'Scottish,'" *Living the Enlightenment*, 60–61. According to the Antients, the Moderns had drifted away from the *Constitutions* of the freemasons and effectively created a "New Mason," or speculative mason. See Knoop and Jones, *Genesis*, 242. Imbued with power that steadily grew throughout the eighteenth century, the Modern Grand Lodge—just as the Grand Lodge of Scotland would do almost fifty years later—alienated many lodges, thus causing the Grand Lodge of England to split. Ironically, the legislation passed by parliament prompted the two rival lodges to reconcile their differences, as the Secret Societies Act signaled "the need for the heads of the two Societies to act together," United Grand Lodge of England, *Grand Lodge*, 121. See also Clark, *British Clubs*, 309–319; Bullock, *Revolutionary Brotherhood*, 87–90; Clawson, *Reconstructing Brotherhood*, 75–76; Berman, *Schism*.

a fatal blow at the Royal Arch Lodge."[143] It is clear that Maybole Lodge No. 14 did not view the Grand Lodge of Scotland as the only source of authority or the final voice in Masonic matters.[144] Similar to the inconsequential presence of the Grand Lodge of Scotland during the struggle to regain its charter-granting privileges, it was effectively silenced during the hearing in Ayr.

Despite these shortcomings, it was able to argue a plausible defense of its actions. Prior to the delivery of any judgments, Grand Lodge had established several provisions to protect itself against suspicion from the government and the public. Even more alarming is the rapid manner in which the Grand Lodge severed connections with the Royal Arch degree, admonishing all members who practiced any other forms of Freemasonry than the three sanctioned degrees and threatening non-compliant lodges with exclusion from the Grand Roll.[145] The Unlawful Oaths and Secret Societies Acts were indirectly responsible for the Maybole Trial of Sedition and, as we shall see in Chapter 6, the Masonic Secession of 1808. Although each conflict was ultimately caused by disputes among rival lodges, the legislation passed by parliament allowed freemasons to pursue charges of sedition and treason outside the authority of the Grand Lodge.

Politics had, for some time, been slowly forcing its way into lodges, as is evinced by the numerous correspondences with the establishment and the election of members of nobility to the position of Grand Master. As we have seen, Anderson's *Constitutions* warned of the dangers of permitting politics and personal quarrels to enter lodges, and the consequences of each were played out in the Maybole affair. Although Jacob asserts that

---

143 Wartski, "Secret Societies," 66.

144 Notably, the Grand Lodge was absent from the court proceedings in Ayr, and mentioned only twice in the criminal letters against John Andrew. The records note only that No. 264 Lodge Royal Arch Maybole obtained a charter from the Grand Lodge of Scotland. No mention is made of the trial held at the Grand Lodge of Scotland.

145 On November 3, 1800, the Grand Lodge considered a letter from St. Andrews Lodge Cree Bridge, "regarding their being Knights Templars, and craving the Grand Lodge to take off the prohibition against that order, being practiced in their Lodge, and having been read and deliberately considered, The Grand Lodge directed their Secretary to write the Lodge of St. Andrews Cree Bridge, referring them to the resolutions of the Grand Lodge on that subject, Intimating to them at the same time, that if they did not mean strictly to adhere to these Resolutions, the Grand Lodge would not ... consider them as worthy of their countenance and protection," Grand Lodge of Scotland Minutes, November 3, 1800.

lodges had achieved some form of separation of Masonic idealism and political intervention,[146] it is clear from the numerous Acts of Parliament, the legal battles which took place in Ayr, and the impending Masonic Secession of 1808 that lodges had developed an intricate yet unstable relationship with politics.

Certainly, the French Revolution, political discussions within lodges, and the Unlawful Oaths and Secret Societies Acts did have adverse effects on Freemasonry. To a degree, though, the power of the Grand Lodge was augmented by these events. Peter Clark comments that "up to the 1750s ... the power of the grand lodge remained quite limited, confined to expelling lodges and denying members of non-subscribing lodge access to the grand charity."[147] Confronted with allegations of treason and sedition, the Grand Lodge of Scotland was forced to assert its authority; no longer restricted to expelling lodges and denying access to the grand charity, it maintained a constant intercourse with the government and initiated legal battles that would test its power over noncompliant lodges.

Despite the Grand Lodge's less-than impressive performance during the Maybole Trial of Sedition, the ordeal was a watershed event in the history of Freemasonry for two reasons. Primarily, it manifested the ability of the freemasons to survive political conflicts, unlike other eighteenth-century clubs and societies. And too, the relationship between the Grand Lodge and its constituent lodges endured an irreversible change to the nature of their relationship: freemasons, once governed by individual lodge laws, were now held accountable to higher powers. Clark accurately asserts that by the end of the eighteenth century, "the formative age of freemasonry was surely over."[148] Freemasonry, no longer an independent and novel association, was increasingly shaped by outside influences, for example noble patrons, the French Revolution, skepticism of Continental freemasons, and most importantly the government. The Unlawful Oaths and Secret Societies Acts forced masons to make politics a part of lodge life, thus disrupting the balance between the public and private spheres.

---

146 Jacob, *Living the Enlightenment*, 32.
147 Clark, *British Clubs* 340.
148 Ibid., 349.

CHAPTER SIX

"THE SCOTCH DIABLE BOITEAUX" OR THE LAME SCOTTISH DEVIL: MASONIC REBELLION AND THE RISE OF THE WHIGS

Wartski argues that the majority of the "misfortunes that befell Scottish Freemasonry in 1807 had their origins in the smouldering discontent which followed the formation in 1736 of the Grand Lodge of Scotland."[1] As we will see, Wartski is partially correct in his analysis. However, he fails to underscore the significant impact of Masonic and national politics on late-eighteenth-century and early-nineteenth-century Freemasonry.

Historically, Scottish Freemasonry has been characterized as a "pro-Hanoverian body" which "ensure[d] loyalty for the organization as a whole."[2] Indeed, as Newman says, it is "impossible in eighteenth-century terms to discount the significance of politics and the impact upon ... Freemasonry."[3] Other historians have commented that Freemasonry was principally a convivial association; indeed, lodges may have had a "political colouring," but nothing more.[4] More recently, however, historians such as Money have argued that the society retained radical associations "which almost from the start drew it into opposition politics."[5] Therefore, it "corresponded more to the populism of patriot politics than to the hierarchy of king, church, and aristocracy."[6] As we have seen, the actions of No. 8 Journeymen Lodge in Edinburgh and No. 264 Royal Arch Maybole suggest that lodges were exposed to reformist groups and vulnerable to radical, revolutionary ideas.

It would be too convenient and simplistic to conclude that all Scottish freemasons were bitterly divided along shades of political loyalty. During

---

1 Wartski, "Secret Societies," 43.
2 Newman, "Politics and Freemasonry in the Eighteenth Century," *AQC* 104 (1991): 32.
3 Ibid., 40.
4 Ibid., 44, comments by Douglas Vieler.
5 Money, "Freemasonry and Loyalism," 256.
6 John Money, "The Masonic Movement; Or, Ritual, Replica and Credit: John Wilkes, the Macaroni Parson, and the Making of the Middle-Class Mind," *Journal of British Studies* 32 (January, 1993): 372.

the early 1800s, however, a polarization of party allegiances occurred within the Grand Lodge of Scotland which ultimately spilled over into several Edinburgh lodges and resulted in the Masonic Secession of 1808. Considering the demise of operative Freemasonry, it is not surprising that social and fraternal connections established strictly for trade and building purposes gradually collapsed, eventually replaced by Whig or Tory affiliations. Certainly, traditional operative Freemasonry was dealt a damaging blow by the establishment of the Grand Lodge of Scotland and eventually expired with the advent of the French Revolution. Thus liberated from the narrow conservative views and political reservations of the operatives, and bolstered by the new measure of power granted by the Secret Societies Act, the Grand Lodge attempted to absorb all lodges into a highly politicized agenda.

Peter Clark argues that the discord which resulted from competing political ideologies during the eighteenth century created a "need for a neutral arena."[7] This came in the form of clubs and associations such as the freemasons, where political discussions were in theory prohibited, although Clark maintains that "the sound of politics was not so much excluded from ... societies as admitted with the volume turned down."[8] Despite one lodge's tenuous and questionable fraternization with the Friends of the People and several masons' associations with radical clubs, for the greater part of the 1700s Freemasonry was particularly successful in excluding politics from lodge meetings. Certainly, rules and regulations were put into place which banned political discussion. However, this "did not always work perfectly, since intense bouts of party conflict could rock even the most stable societies, leading on occasion to their dissolution."[9] The Speculative Society, as previously noted, was one such society which cast a wary eye upon all things political. McElroy claims that in the "revolutionary atmosphere, feeling ran high and the fear of an explosion which would wreck the society was well founded as ensuing events proved."[10]

In 1794, several older Tories were offended by the revolutionary attitudes and opinions expressed by the younger Whig members. An attempt to have the Whigs expelled failed, and fortunately for the Speculative Soci-

---

7   Clark, *British Clubs*, 180.
8   Ibid., 181.
9   Ibid.
10   McElroy, *Age of Improvement*, 112.

ety the matter ended without incident. Five years later, however, another dispute erupted over party politics. Cautious-minded Tories threatened to "spy upon the conduct of the Society" in order to "take down the words of [the] night's debate if they interfered with questions of modern politics ... as such discussions being permitted were likely to produce within the wall of the [Edinburgh] University a political Society, perhaps a Jacobin Club."[11] The uproar caused by such an accusation created a storm of controversy; such a "high Insult to the honour of the Society" led to the resignation of many leading members and further magnified the fears of being associated with radical clubs.[12]

By 1802, Scottish Freemasonry was also "fragmenting and reforming into contesting structures," due largely to the politicization of the Grand Lodge.[13] Despite the leadership of distinguished loyalists such as Sir James Stirling[14] and George Gordon, Earl of Aboyne,[15] it is clear that the Grand Lodge was rapidly becoming a Whig body. Indeed, as Clark argues, associations without a clear political agenda—especially the freemasons—might easily "be drawn into political activity during periods of national upheaval."[16] With the election of the Hon. George Ramsay, 9th Earl of Dalhousie[17] as Grand Master in 1808, the Grand Lodge remained under Whig control until the election of James, 2nd Earl of Roslin, a Tory, in 1810. Notably, there were several Whig leaders affiliated with the Grand Lodge who were either directly responsible for or played a key role in the Masonic Secession of 1808. Francis Rawdon-Hastings, the Earl of Moira, joined the opposition in 1789 and became a close personal friend

---

11 Ibid, 113.

12 Ibid.

13 Steve Murdoch, *Network North: Scottish Kin, Commercial and Covert Associations in Northern Europe 1603-1746* (Leiden, 2006), 332.

14 See McFarland, *Ireland and Scotland*, 159. Stirling was Lord Provost of Edinburgh from 1790 to 1800 and Grand Master Mason of Scotland from 1798 to 1800.

15 See Thorne, *House of Commons Vol. 4*, 36. George Gordon, 5th Earl of Aboyne, whose mother "lionized Pitt," was "consequently on good terms with the statesman." Although he was "inconspicuous in both houses of Parliament," he was president of the Edinburgh Pitt Club, thus leaving "no doubt about his politics."

16 Clark, *British Clubs*, 461–462.

17 Ramsay, brother of Hon. William Maule (Grand Master 1808–1810 and devoted Foxite): was put up for Aberdeen Burghs in 1806. Thorne writes that the "Scottish Whigs worked strenuously for Ramsay, whose success was assured when the key burgh of Montrose declared for him," Thorne, *House of Commons Vol. 5*, 7.

of the Prince of Wales. By 1805, he was the Acting Grand Master of both Scotland and England. As will become clearer, Moira's interest in the Masonic Secession was directly related to his position in Freemasonry and his relationship with the Prince of Wales.[18]

The Whig Grand Lodge of Scotland was also supported by William Inglis of Middleton, Substitute Grand Master from 1805 to 1828. According to Lindsay, Inglis was a staunch Whig who attended the Bastille Dinner in 1789 and was "one of the most widely known Scottish Masons of all time ... who weathered one of the worst storms" in the history of Scottish Freemasonry.[19]

Indeed, the Whig element was intimately connected to another Edinburgh Lodge, No. 44 St. Luke's Lodge Holyrood House. According to Lindsay, the connection between No. 44 and the Grand Lodge cannot be understated. Between 1807 and 1860, "the Whigs of St. Luke exerted a preponderating influence there, for the reason that its senior members were the leaders of the Whig party in Scotland."[20] The presence of senior Whig leaders in each of these lodges suggests that although the "government of the country might be denied to the Whigs, there were many bodies ... where they could get a footing" and "rapidly acquire control."[21] Indeed, Whig bodies such as St. Luke's and the Grand Lodge of Scotland "gradually attracted to themselves the more talented and ambitious men of the rising generation, who could not see openings for ability without backing in the dominant party."[22]

---

18 See Lindsay, *Holyrood House*, 269–270.

19 Ibid., 269–270. Referring to William Inglis, Lindsay writes that "after he left [the Master's Chair of St. Luke's] in 1805, he dominated the Craft for the next twenty-three years as Substitute Grand Master in a manner unparalleled before or since. He could and did formulate the policy of Grand Lodge throughout his long tenure of office there; but he required for its successful issue a constitutional support on which he could rely. The way had to be prepared amongst the Lodges. Ears and eyes were essential in places where the Substitute Grand Master could only be received in his official capacity ... Inglis, then, needed a spy ... to see what things were on his side and what o' the other. Naturally he chose for the purpose his own Lodge of St. Luke, and so long as he governed the Craft he worked in closest co-operation with its Masters and Proxy representatives for other Lodges in Grand Lodge, and they reaped in his time, and after it, the fruits of Grand Office as the reward of their allegiance," 280.

20 Lindsay, *Holyrood House*, 299.

21 Ibid.

22 Ibid., 269–270.

Both the Grand Lodge of Scotland and No. 44 witnessed a marked intensification of Whig supporters following the Napoleonic Wars. Ultimately, their positions in the Masonic hierarchy would be determined by the strength and the "success or failure of that political party."[23] Lindsay maintains that

> from 1761 the number of Whigs admitted into [No. 44
> St. Luke's] ... had been steadily growing, and this fact, in
> the days when the demarcation between Whig and Tory
> extended even into Masonry, was enough to ensure that
> sooner or later St. Luke's Lodge would be almost entire-
> ly composed of Whigs ... In 1785 the day of the Whigs
> had not come ... The exhaustion of the country after the
> Napoleonic wars, and the economic conditions which
> followed them, broke the long Tory domination. The
> Whigs came in with Reform, and in Scottish Masonry,
> as in the other contemporary spheres of Scottish life, the
> Whigs carried it entirely after 1807.[24]

Political Exploitation and Masonic Compromise

After the dispute over precedence in 1737, Lodge Kilwinning refused to relinquish its power to grant charters, thus creating a rift between itself and the Grand Lodge. These differences, though not a central issue for almost fifty years, resurfaced in 1794. On 4 August of that same year, the Grand Lodge—perceiving Kilwinning to be in contempt of its authority and "pretending to have an equal right of Granting Charters"[25]—adopted a policy of "non-recognition and extrusion."[26] In no uncertain terms, it was resolved that "none of the Lodges holding of them ought either to visit or receive visits ... from any of the Lodges holding of the Kilwin-

---

23 Ibid., 250–251. See pages 251–253 for a list of notable Whig leaders, including Charles Hay, Lord Newton; John Wilde, "Advocate and Professor of Civil Law, 1792; author of *The Question Solved, or the Right of the Prince of Wales to be Sole Unlimited and Immediate Regent*, et., etc. (Edinburgh, 1788); *Address to the Society of the Friends of the People* (1793) and *Sequel to Said Address* (1797); The Rt. Hon. Sir James Mackintosh, "P. C., Whig Philosopher; Secretary of 'The Friends of the People,' and author of *Vindiciae Gallicae* in reply to Burke's *Reflections on the French Revolution* (1791)." See Cockburn, *Memorials*, 223–226 for a description of Charles Hay.

24 Ibid., 250–251.

25 Ibid., August 2, 1802.

26 Lindsay, *Holyrood House*, 294.

ning Lodge; although at the same time an individual member may visit a Lodge holding of the Grand Lodge [but] no compliment ought either to be paid to or received from such members."[27]

By 1802, the Grand Lodge renewed its effort to "compell the Kilwinning Lodge to return to her duty as a Constituent Member of the Grand Lodge and in future to desist from granting Charters and other acts and deeds which none but the Grand Lodge herself is intitled to exercise."[28] Appendix 8 reveals that—at least initially—the Grand Officers were quite adamant in their demands: forcing Kilwinning to relinquish any powers solely reserved for the Grand Lodge, namely the right to grant charters. Such claims were based on the argument that the resignation of William St Clair of Roslin in 1736 as the hereditary Grand Master effectively empowered the Grand Lodge of Scotland to assume complete and full control of all Masonic matters. As the patron and overseer of Scottish Freemasonry Roslin, upon resigning as Grand Master, gave all power and authority to the central governing body; therefore, no other lodge in Scotland could legally—according to the Grand Lodge—grant charters.

A committee was created for the special purpose of settling the issue. From August until November 1802, a Grand Committee searched the Register Office for "Grants or Charters by the King of Scotland [James VI] in favour of [the] St Clairs of Roslin appointing him Hereditary Grand Master."[29] However, a search of the Register House in Edinburgh for any documents providing incontrovertible proof that gave the Grand Lodge exclusive authority to warrant new lodges was unsuccessful. As a result, the Substitute Grand Master recommended that the "committee appointed upon that business to take what other steps might appear necessary for attaining the objects remitted to them by the Grand Lodge and at [the] same time renewing their powers to that effect which was agreed to."[30] Between the years November 1, 1802 and November 3, 1806, there were

---

27 Grand Lodge of Scotland Minutes, August 3, 1794.

28 Ibid. The minutes further stated that "it is evident that it would be a matter of the greatest importance to the Grand Lodge as well as honourable and advantageous to the Kilwinning Lodge were the Lodges holding of her received into and under the protection of the Grand Lodge of Scotland concurring as we must do that it would be for the honor, the dignity and the welfare of the Craft in general that Masonry in Scotland should be only practised in the Bosom of the Grand Lodge."

29 Ibid.

30 Ibid., November 1, 1802.

no Grand Lodge minutes regarding the dispute.[31] In 1805, William Inglis had been elected Substitute Grand Master, and his influence is clearly evident during the reconciliation between the Grand Lodge and Kilwinning over the lingering issue of Masonic precedence. Within 2 years of Inglis' election, the deadlock had been broken, and each lodge had appointed representatives to discuss the terms for a final settlement.[32] As Lindsay argues, it was "evident that secret pourparlers had been opened between Inglis and his Whig supporters in Grand Lodge, on the one side, and the Lodge of Kilwinning on the other."[33]

The Whig presence in the Grand Lodge and the problems with Kilwinning were not the only factors which contributed to the schism of 1808. Only 12 new lodges were chartered between the years 1795 to 1808. New charters had fallen over 50 percent during this period, compared to the previous 15 years when 27 new lodges were established. Significantly, there were no new charters between August 7, 1799 and December 3, 1806. This suspension of lodge expansion coincides not only with the Secret Societies of 1799, but also with the Maybole Trial and the beginning of the Masonic Secession. Thus it may be argued that this period of Masonic stagnancy, combined with the increased Whig presence and a polarization of party loyalties within the Grand Lodge, weakened the institution of Scottish Freemasonry and ultimately opened the door for a split.

On October 14, 1807, a conference was held in Glasgow to negotiate the terms of the agreement. In exchange for renouncing its charter-granting

---

31 On November 3, 1806, the Grand Lodge asserted that "it had long been the wish of the Grand Lodge that the differences subsisting between her and the Kilwinning Lodge should be settled and accommodated and in a very forcible manner pointed out the advantage that would result to both were the Kilwinning Lodge with the Lodges holding of her to return to their duty and allegiance and become subject to the controul of the Grand Lodge. Sir John mentioned that he had had several conversations with W. Blair the present Master of Kilwinning Lodge and others and from what he could learn Sir John had no doubts but a reconciliation might be brought about on terms not only honourable and advantageous to the Grand Lodge but to the cause of Masonry in general. Sir John therefore proposed that a Select Committee be named by the Grand Lodge with authority to open a Communication with the Kilwinning Lodge either by letter or by a meeting with the Master and a Committee of that Lodge in order to ascertain their views and demands. The Grand Lodge having taken this matter into consideration agrees to the propriety of opening a communication with the Kilwinning Lodge," Grand Lodge of Scotland Minutes.

32 Grand Lodge of Scotland Minutes, February 14, 1807.

33 Lindsay, Holryood House, 294.

privileges, Kilwinning would be placed at the head of the Grand Roll of Scotland. Furthermore, any lodges warranted under Kilwinning would be placed at the end of the roll pending authenticated proof of its charter, and the Master of the lodge was appointed as the Provincial Grand Master for the Ayrshire District.[34] Although the Grand Lodge granted several dispensations to Kilwinning, it had achieved what was arguably its prime objective since its creation: the consolidation of Masonic authority under one central body. The entire affair had been conducted without the participation of No. 1 Mary's Chapel. Despite the apparent settlement and willingness on both sides to affect an agreement, Kilwinning's ultimate capitulation and Grand Lodge's acceptance of its proposal were motivated by entirely different reasons. In 1750, after the election of Alexander, Tenth Earl of Eglinton, as the Grand Master of Scotland, the Grand Lodge "directed its daughters to hold no intercourse with any of the Kilwinning Lodges, and in all processions ... The Kilwinning Lodges were rigorously excluded."[35] Essentially, the exclusionary and marginalization practices of the Grand Lodge "had the effect of circumscribing its rival's influence ... as their position became seriously affected through it, and the prestige of these Lodges was gradually decaying."[36]

Although these tactics seemed to have the desired effect of forcing Kilwinning into negotiations, Lyon's assertion that the Grand Lodge of Scotland was more cordial and deferential during the entire ordeal is questionable. He writes that "out of respect for the susceptibilities of its less exalted contemporary, Grand Lodge was the first to propose a conference on the subject of the desired Union."[37] This claim of pity and understanding is contradicted later when Lyon maintains that

> while it must be admitted that it was highly desirable that Grand Lodge should secure the abdication of the only rival Institution in Scotland, it was surely no less important that it should preserve the inviolability of its own Charters. An amalgamation of the two bodies that would have preserved the integrity of Grand Lodge's prior obligations, and have satisfied Kilwinning for the sacrifice

---

34 Gould, *History of Freemasonry Vol. 2*, 395.

35 Lyon, *Mary's Chapel*, 265.

36 Ibid.

37 Ibid.

> of its independence ... But of all mundane institutions,
> a Chief Court of Freemasonry should have been the last
> to sacrifice principle to expediency in any of its transac-
> tions.[38]

Relegated to the second oldest lodge in Scotland, the members immedi-
ately expressed their disapproval over the handling of the situation. On
May 4, 1807, the Master of Mary's Chapel, John Brown, and one of his
Wardens, George Cunningham, complained to the Grand Lodge that

> the powers formerly granted to the committee on the
> business of Kilwinning were too Exclusive, that instead
> of granting to the committee full powers to arrange and
> finally settle all differences subsisting between the Grand
> Lodge and the Kilwinning Lodge, the Committee should
> only be directed to ascertain the claims of the Kilwinning
> Lodge and to Report leaving it to the Grand Lodge how
> far these demands were reasonable.[39]

Given its pronounced emphasis on achieving a settlement with Kilwinning, it is not surprising that the Grand Lodge responded to the objections by concluding that Cunningham's motion "was entirely irrelevant."[40]
After a formal written protest was duly ignored, Cunningham again
complained about the proceedings at a Grand Lodge meeting held on
November 2, 1807. Clearly governed by political priorities rather than
fairness, William Inglis at once orchestrated a counter-protest and Cunningham's motion to review the events was discarded. Realizing that the
displacement of Mary's Chapel as the senior lodge in Scotland was the
result of an elaborate scheme, Cunningham resorted to drastic measures
in an attempt to disrupt the remainder of the meeting. Blatantly reflecting the growing political divisions within the Grand Lodge, Cunningham
rose and objected to the nomination of the Hon. William Ramsay Maule
of Panmure—Whig M. P.—as the Grand Master Elect for the ensuing

---

38   Ibid., 274.

39   Grand Lodge of Scotland Minutes, May 4, 1807.

40   Ibid. The Grand Lodge justified its actions by asserting that "the Committee formerly
      named had acted upon the powers granted them, by opening a correspondence with
      the Kilwinning Lodge stating the powers given them. That the Kilwinning Lodge had
      named a Committee with equally ample powers and had agreed to meet the Grand
      Lodge Committee at Glasgow for the purpose of adjusting all matters," Ibid.

year, maintaining that "though he had been an Office-bearer of Grand Lodge for some years, he had never been within its walls."[41] Alternatively, Cunningham nominated the staunchly conservative Earl of Haddington, Thomas Hamilton.[42] Despite the dubious behavior of Maule, Cunningham's Tory nomination suffered a crushing defeat, confirming the overwhelming Whig presence in the Grand Lodge.[43]

This entire fiasco made it obvious that "politics were to be dragged into the matter and used to inflame the righteous indignation of the Lodge of Edinburgh over the manner in which it had been treated."[44] Regardless of a warning from Mary's Chapel that it was determined "neither to be sold nor compelled to resign [its] seniority, to attempt either of which will undoubtedly lead to a secession, in reality much to be dreaded, under the nose of the Grand Lodge, and which will ultimately lead to the fatal consequences which have taken place in England—namely, the formation of a new Grand Lodge,"[45] the threats were dismissed as meaningless at best.

The Unexpected Tory

The Whig presence within the Grand Lodge had forced through the union with Kilwinning[46] and had effectively guaranteed that any Tory

---

41 Lindsay, *Holyrood House*, 296. Maule, a Whig M. P., was known to be the "ringleader of a group of wild young men addicted to gambling, heavy drinking, destructive horseplay and sexual licence," Thorne, *House of Commons Vol. 4*, 571–572. He hardly seemed the ideal candidate for Grand Master. After coming into possession of his great-uncle's estates in 1792, Maule became one of the richest men in Scotland. According to Thorne, "he sustained this extravagant and dissipated lifestyle ... into which he probably fell the more readily in the absence of paternal discipline, to the end of his days, long after more decorous standards of behaviour had become the norm among his peers ... Maule, who joined the Whig Club in 1798, became an enthusiastic Foxite" and "supported his Whig friends in power," Ibid.

42 Lord Melville wrote of Thomas Hamilton, Lord Binning that "Mr. Pitt had a sincere attachment to him, and there never was a more enthusiastic worshipper of Mr. Pitt's memory than Lord Binning," Quoted in Thorne, *House of Commons Vol. 4*, 135.

43 Lindsay maintains that the "Master of St. Luke's and several other Whigs ... had seen him acting there as Grand Warden on several occasions, when his brother, The Earl of Dalhousie, was Grand Master. 'Notwithstanding these incontrovertible facts and even although he saw it to be almost the unanimous wish of the Grand Lodge that Mr. Maule be appointed,' Bro. Cunningham proposed in opposition The Earl of Haddington, and ... this nomination was defeated by 110 votes to 7," *Holyrood House*, 296–297.

44 Ibid.

45 Ibid., 271.

46 Ibid., 299.

candidate nominated for the office of Grand Master would be defeated. Leaving aside the problem of a disgruntled Mary's Chapel, the Grand Lodge of Scotland alone controlled the right to grant charters. Victory, however, was short-lived. During the negotiations, "a fresh trouble was developing" which became "commingled with the issues of the Kilwinning business."[47] As Lindsay argues, the key to this "fresh trouble is to be found in the particular manner in which politics entered into the daily life of the time."[48] In March 1807, 7 months before the settlement with Kilwinning, the government introduced the Catholic Emancipation Act. The new legislation was "highly obnoxious to the King, and, as the Whigs were obdurate on its retention, they were dismissed after one short year in office and without any assurance that they would not be similarly treated if ever they were returned to power again."[49]

Thus counterpoised, an overconfident Grand Lodge and embittered Tory minority, the impending explosion within Scottish Freemasonry was finally triggered by a request made to the Grand Lodge of Scotland to express the fraternity's appreciation for the King's support of the British people and constitution. Although a misrepresentation to describe Masonic political allegiances at this time as hostile to loyalism, it is likely that some masons—especially within the Grand Lodge—retained a suspicion of the uncritical, slavish adherence to every aspect of the constitution that marked the more purblind Tories. The Whig faction led by Inglis was "suddenly confronted by unexpected opposition from the Crown in a matter touching its politics, and the train was laid in Grand Lodge that required some exulting Tory to touch it off."[50] On May 4, 1807—the same day that Cunningham criticized the handling of the Kilwinning affair—Dr. John Mitchell, Master of the Caledonian Lodge in Edinburgh and a Tory, submitted to the Grand Lodge the following motion "That a humble address be presented to His Majesty expressive of their thanks, thankfulness and gratitude for the Paternal Solicitude he has been gra-

---

47 Ibid., 298.

48 Ibid.

49 Ibid., 299. King George, a Tory, decided to strike down a request from the government to allow Roman Catholics to join the army and he refused to grant Catholic relief. The King, "... implacable in his opposition ... demanded that a written assurance be furnished to him that the Catholic question in any form would never again be brought up," Wartski, "Secret Societies," 45. See also Dickinson, *Britain and the French Revolution*, 113.

50 Lindsay, *Holyrood House*, 299.

ciously pleased to evince for the happiness of his People in supporting the Established Religion of the Country and the principles of the British Constitution." Brother Brown [Master of Mary's Chapel] Seconded and supported the motion.

> Against the motion many arguments were urged particularly the impropriety of introducing and discussing Religious and Political questions in the Grand Lodge or any Masonic meeting. After a great deal of argument on both sides it was proposed that a vote should be taken. But before proceeding to the vote Brother Millar Proxy Master for the Lodge of St Thomas Arbroath moved that the Laws should be put in force and it was agreed to that Lodges Two years in arrear to the Grand Lodge should not be intitled to vote neither should Brethren be intitled to vote who were not in the Cloathing of their respective Lodges. The Vote was then put "Address" or "Not Address" when the Grand Clerk upon counting the numbers Declared there were 27 Voted "Address" and 28 "Not to Address." The Grand Lodge therefore negatived the motion for an address. Upon the state of the Voted being declared those Brethren who were in favour of the address in a Clamorous and unmasonic manner demanded a Scrutiny by again putting the vote but as several of the Brethren who voted and conceived the question decided, had [illegible] the meeting the request could not be complied with, besides the demand being irregular and contrary to all precedent was rejected. The Grand Clerk being a sworn officer and alone intitled to take down and Report the state of the votes which it appeared to the Chair had been done by him with every possible accuracy. The Senior Grand Master thought it his duty therefore to close the Grand Lodge.[51]

Cunningham's nomination and Mitchell's proposed address, although occurring on the same day and during a time of heightened political tension

---

51 Grand Lodge of Scotland Minutes, May 4, 1807. Interestingly, the *Petition and Complaint* contains more Grand Lodge minutes, including transcripts that are unavailable in the Grand Lodge archives.

in the Grand Lodge, do not necessarily suggest a Tory conspiracy to un-dermine Whig sentiments. According to Wartski, Mitchell was "attempt-ing to slap the Whig establishment of the Grand Lodge," and his motion was nothing more than a "flagrant piece of politics, which, if passed, would bring Grand Lodge into line with other bodies—Tory orientated, who had applauded the King's bigotry."[52] As we have seen, Masonic addresses to the King were not uncommon and often sent to congratulate the ruling monarch on a variety of issues. However, as Lindsay argues, "it was a very different matter for a Tory to repeat such a performance, as Dr. Mitchell did, in a Grand Lodge of Scotland under Whig control."[53]

Mitchell's address also signaled the first rumblings of discontent among the Tories. If the Whigs were to maintain control of the Grand Lodge, any challenges which threatened the balance of power had to be quickly suppressed. Given that the initial proposal was defeated by such a nar-row margin, a revote was demanded (Appendix 9). On June 19, 1807, the Grand Lodge of Scotland convened to address the issue, stating that it had received a letter from Dr. Mitchell of Caledonian Lodge in Edinburgh requesting a "Scrutiny of the votes given for and against the address moved to His Majesty in the Quarterly Communication of the 4th."[54] Despite strong objections from Inglis, the Grand Lodge approved Mitchell's request for a revote.[55] Led by James Gibson, one of the most "vehement of Scottish Whigs,"[56] the motion to address the King was soundly defeated by a margin of 95–47.[57] Gibson was also the origina-

---

52 Wartski, "Secret Societies," 46.

53 Lindsay, *Holyrood House*, 300.

54 Grand Lodge of Scotland Minutes, June 19, 1807.

55 In response to the letter from Dr. Mitchell, Inglis—on behalf of the Grand Lodge of Scotland—replied: "Though I have great doubts of my right to call such a meeting as you require which I rather think is vested in the Grand Master alone and though I continue decidedly of my former opinion that the demand of a Scrutiny is unconsti-tutional, conceiving that the Grand Clerk as the legal sworn officer of the Craft is the person who is regularly intitled to declare the state of any vote in the Grand Lodge being of course held from his official situation as beyond all suspicion of partiality. Yet notwithstanding the doubt I entertain and the opinion I have expressed the respect which I bear to the subscribers of the letter which I have had the honor of receiving ... induces me to comply with your request of convening the Grand Lodge," Grand Lodge of Scotland Minutes, June 19, 1807.

56 Lindsay, *Holyrood House*, 253.

57 Cockburn, *Memorials*, 84. Other key figures in the Whig party affiliated with St. Luke's were Adam Gillies, David Cathcart, and Malcolm Laing.

tor of the Bastille Dinner and, as Cockburn wrote, one of the "principal leaders of the true Whig party."[58] Under a strong showing of solidarity, the "Whigs had done their organizing well this time."[59] It seems as if most freemasons in attendance, upon "seeing the sense of the meeting so completely against the Scrutiny," confirmed their approval of the vote and maintained that they "would not agitate the question further."[60] The records of the initial vote and scrutiny reveal that the Grand Lodge felt it had handled the situation with much aplomb and dignity. The meeting eventually ended "with a vote of thanks from the victorious party to Inglis for the handsome manner in which he had conducted himself in the Chair throughout the business."[61]

Clearly, political maneuvering and manipulation had prevented the approval of Mitchell's address to the King. The Grand Lodge must have been aware of a minority Tory presence, but it chose to ignore it. As Wartski says, the "tendency of governments in power for very long periods is to become arrogant, and to disregard the opposition, which on the other hand veers towards resentment and desperation, so the schism between the parties [becomes] marked by tremendous bitterness and ill-feeling."[62] Indeed, the Masonic divide between Whig and Tory would increase during the ensuing political feud, ultimately culminating with a much-publicized court trial and accusations of a Tory conspiracy to destroy the Grand Lodge and defame Scottish Freemasonry.[63]

Discredit and Political Disenchantment

Having twice defeated the proposed address to the King, it is unclear why the Grand Lodge pursued the matter further. Apparently, it wanted to summarily vindicate itself of any misconduct and, at the same time, blame Mitchell for the entire political discord. Subsequently, he was suspended from all Masonic privileges. The Grand Lodge of Scotland had clearly changed its attitude regarding political affiliations. On August 1, 1791, it recorded that

---

58 Ibid.
59 Wartski, "Secret Societies," 46.
60 Ibid.
61 Lindsay, *Holyrood House*, 300.
62 Wartski, "Secret Societies," 45.
63 Grand Lodge of Scotland Minutes, May 25, 1808.

no Lodge shall have in it their power to intrude [upon] any Member of their Lodge merely on account of his differing in sentiments as to political affairs in the town or village where he resides, from the Majority of the Members of his Mother Lodge, or on any pretence of his becoming a Member or attending the meetings of their Lodges, and that the Brother thus aggrieved may immediately apply to the Grand Lodge for redress without petitioning his Mother Lodge for readmission.[64]

Under this statute, Gibson's actions were illegal. Unfortunately for Mitchell, the Grand Lodge and Gibson were of one mind regarding the situation. Even so, the Grand Lodge held a meeting on January 5, 1808 to consider the reasons for Mitchell's suspension. Significantly, the charges were made by Gibson, who alleged that Mitchell had proposed the secession of the Caledonian Lodge from the Grand Lodge of Scotland and had published a pamphlet which was insulting to the Grand Officers and all Scottish freemasons. Roman Eagle Lodge, claiming that the Caledonian Lodge held its monthly meeting on its stated night, chronicled the correspondence between the two lodges (Appendix 10). The members of Roman Eagle sought reconciliation: although disappointed with the actions of Lodge Caledonian, certainly Roman Eagle wanted to avoid further conflict. Brother Black, then the acting Master of Roman Eagle, personally visited Brother Mitchell and asked for an explanation of his actions. Despite such overtures, the lodges could not achieve a peaceful resolution.

Clearly, the Grand Lodge and Gibson wanted to pursue the matter further.[65] It appears that the Grand Lodge may have worked in conjunction

64 Ibid., August 1, 1791.
65 Lindsay writes that "unfortunately, Dr. Mitchell nor Gibson could leave well alone, and their differences were followed up outside Grand Lodge until 5th January, when Gibson laid before Grand Lodge a Petition against Dr. Mitchell, in which he alleged: (1) That Dr. Mitchell persisted in holding his Monthly Meetings on a date already expressly forbidden to him as belonging to Lodge Roman Eagle; (2) That at one of the Meetings he had suggested secession from Grand Lodge; (3) That when on the way to the annual Masonic Service in the Tron Church on St Andrew's Day, 1807, he had prevailed on his Lodge to leave the procession and to adjourn to Oman's Tavern, and further, though expected by the Acting Grand Master [Hon. William Ramsay Maule], he had sent neither apology nor Deputation to the Grand Festival, showing by these actions contempt for the religious Service in which his Brethren were engaged, dis-

with Gibson to bring forward the allegations against Mitchell, as this connection was established in Mitchell's response to the charges and suspension. First, Mitchell attacked Gibson's character, asserting that he was motivated by "private dislike, individual resentment" and "political hatred."[66] Possibly referring to other Whig leaders in the Grand Lodge, Mitchell mockingly declared that it "must be obvious to the members of the Grand Lodge, that there are many persons, who, not possessing so much of the 'milk of human kindness' as Brother Gibson, may bring forward accusations founded entirely on these motives."[67] Although there is a measure of sarcasm in his statements, Mitchell is careful not to offend the Grand Lodge. Instead, he made light of the political rivalries and directly implicated Gibson as the mastermind behind the controversy.

Next, Mitchell emphasized the dubious political aims of Gibson, claiming that "the undertrappers of the different parties, more zealous, more violent, and more unprincipled than those who are engaged in the higher departments of politics" and who "disturb the peace of society with their paltry intrigues. Gibson ... which he is known to be, is a tool of some party in the town of Edinburgh."[68] Mitchell's allegations, however, were quickly dismissed, largely due to their inflammatory nature. In the opinion of

---

respect to the Acting Grand Master, and, to the world, that there was a schism in the Fraternity; (4) That contrary to Masonic custom, he had, on December 28, 1807, refused to receive a Deputation from Lodge St David, Edinburgh, of which the Petitioner was Past Master," *Holyrood House*, 300–301. The actual petition was received by the Grand Lodge of Scotland on January 1, 1808. The petition and complaint asserted that "Brother Mitchell has done every thing in his power to disturb the peace of the Grand Lodge, and of the craft, by printing a libelous pamphlet, and by most disrespectful and improper conduct to the Grand Lodge, insomuch, that at the meeting of the quarterly communication of the Grand Lodge, held in the month of November last, a motion was made and seconded ... to expel him from the Grand Lodge," Grand Lodge of Scotland Minutes, January 1, 1808. Mitchell ignored Grand Lodge's edict to discontinue meetings on the same evening as Roman Eagle and challenged James Gibson to a duel, for which he was suspended from all Masonic privileges. See Seemungal, "The Edinburgh Rebellion," 322–325.

66   C. Stewart, printer. *An Exposition of the Causes Which Have Produced the Late Dissensions Among the Free Masons of Scotland, Addressed to the Brethren of the Order by the Edinburgh Lodges that Have Found it Necessary to Separate from the Grand Lodge of Scotland* (Edinburgh, 1808), 9–11.

67   Ibid. Furthermore, Mitchell maintained that the accusations were made "with the view of harassing and distressing the accused, and disturbing the harmony and tranquillity of the lodges before whom these accusations are brought," Ibid.

68   Ibid., 11.

the Grand Lodge, his answers were "scurrilous and malicious towards a Brother, and disrespectful to the Grand Lodge."[69] It is highly significant that although only Gibson is named as a member of a political party in Edinburgh, the Grand Lodge was visibly insulted by Mitchell's comments. Mitchell condescendingly insinuated that Gibson was not only a pawn of the Whig party, but also of the Grand Lodge.

Suggestions of political manipulation, however, were not enough to justify Mitchell's suspension. As such, the Grand Lodge of Scotland required tangible evidence of Mitchell's supposed campaign to undermine Scottish Freemasonry, which ultimately appeared in the form of invented lodge minutes and a stolen libelous pamphlet. Gibson claimed that the respondent "did, at one or another of the meetings of the Caledonian Lodge, propose that the lodge should make a secession from the Grand Lodge."[70] Mitchell argued that the charge was a "*fishing* accusation, made with the view of giving Brother Gibson the power of fishing for a charge out of every thing which the respondent ever said or did at any of the meetings of the Caledonian Lodge."[71] Interestingly, the accusation of secession was made at the Grand Lodge of Scotland on January 5, 1808; however, the minutes of Caledonian Lodge record no motion to secede until March 11, 1808. During the meeting, Lodge Caledonian recorded that "no proof is adduced to establish that the Right Worshipful Master [Dr. Mitchell] *did make a proposal to secede* from the Grand Lodge."[72] After the apparent fabrication of the secession charges, the members resolved that the "sentence of the Grand Lodge is particularly offensive to the Caledonian Lodge, as, in the whole of the persecution, originating, as they deem, in party spirit ... and, with a view to avoid further persecution, they discontinue their connection with the present Grand Lodge of Scotland."[73]

The decision to secede was not confined exclusively to the members of Lodge Caledonian. Other masons, such as the Senior Warden of Mary's Chapel and the Junior Warden of Edinburgh St. Andrew, also supported

---

69 Grand Lodge of Scotland Minutes June 13, 1808. Grand Lodge also stated that the pamphlet contained matter "highly injurious to the character and dignity of the Grand Lodge; and, upon the whole, that the conduct of Brother Mitchell had been in an eminent degree derogatory to the honour, and prejudicial to the interests of Masonry."

70 Stewart, *Exposition*, 17.

71 Ibid.

72 Caledonian Lodge Minutes, March 11, 1808.

73 Ibid.

the secession. The presence of an officer from Mary's Chapel is important, for it suggests that the lodge, still harboring resentment over the precedence controversy, was considering separation. Taking advantage of the dispute with Dr. Mitchell, Mary's Chapel now had the support of other lodges which were united in their common dislike of the Grand Lodge of Scotland.

Most damaging, however, was a pamphlet printed by Mitchell accusing Grand Lodge officers of fraudulent voting practices, intentional falsification of facts, and denying lodges equal representation in Masonic affairs. According to Mitchell, only "one imperfect proof copy of this circular letter [existed]," as "no other copy was in print or circulation ... [and] a worthy brother and member of the Grand Lodge, had been art and part in pilfering and abstracting copies of that letter from the printing-house."[74] In the pamphlet, Mitchell argued that "party-spirit ... on this occasion, carried the Chairman [Inglis] out of line of his duty. Everyone knows, that the Substitute Grand Master ... ought to take no side in a debate. It is only his duty to regulate the debate."[75] As a result—after the proposed address to the King had been debated—Inglis "entered widely into the field of politics:"[76]

> We had from him a long dissertation on, and explanation
> of the Test Act, of the analogy between Roman Catho-
> lics and Presbyterians in respect of Episcopalians. He,
> moreover, talked much of my Lord Howick, and of the
> views and measure of the late Minstiry, &c. In short, his
> speech was an echo of what 'all the talents' had advanced
> for themselves in both Houses of Parliament ... Mr. Ing-
> lis finally concluded, by conjuring the Meeting, as they
> regarded him, (forsooth!) as they respected their Acting
> Grand Master, the Earl of Moira, and as they wished to
> maintain the principles of Masonry, that they should dis-
> miss the motion.[77]

---

74   John Mitchell, "Pamphlet Referred to in the Substitute Grand Master's Deposition," cited in *Petition and Complaint at Brother Gibson's Instance Against Brother Mitchell* (Edinburgh, 1808), 83–84. The identity of the "worthy brother" is not revealed, though it is likely that Mitchell is referring to either Gibson or Inglis.

75   Ibid., 80.

76   Ibid.

77   Ibid.

Furthermore, Mitchell maintained that the initial tally of votes yielded 28 in favor of the address and 24 against. However, when the final decision was read from the chair, Inglis declared that the address was rejected by a vote of 28 to 27. As the Grand Lodge minutes note, a scrutiny was requested and subsequently denied, due to the finality of the vote and the impropriety of such a demand. Alternatively, Mitchell asserted that a revote was "peremptorily refused from the Chair, and all ... efforts to obtain it were drowned in the noisy shouts of triumph by the Chairman and his party. The Clerk made his escape *quamprimum* from the room, with all his books, paper, &c. and the Chairman would not hear another word on the subject."[78] Three months later, on March 7, 1808, the Grand Lodge upheld its initial ruling, asserting that "Brother Mitchell shall ... be suspended ... from all Masonic Privileges ... and the Lodges within Scotland are expressly prohibited from admitting or communicating with him ... with certification that if they act in the contrary, they shall be responsible to the Grand Lodge, for contempt of its authority."[79]

Despite the best attempts of the Grand Lodge to blame Mitchell for the turmoil, the charges against him were largely contrived in an effort to reassert Whig dominance and assure that any opposition would be "converted either into the partisan or a slave of the faction."[80] However, the Grand Lodge had overreacted to the Tory challenge; thus, political hatred, lingering resentment over issues of precedence, and outrage over the treatment of Mitchell had fueled the fires of rebellion. Subsequently, its Whig regime and tentative centralized control over Scottish lodges slowly began to crumble. Several Edinburgh lodges published a pamphlet to this effect, claiming that the Grand Lodge had attempted to

> confound the cause of masonic liberty which we are supporting, with the private quarrels of Messrs Gibson and Mitchell. This is the artifice which the rulers of the Grand Lodge have all along employed to mislead you, from the general questions not at issue. But it is needless to add, that with the private quarrels of these gentlemen, we have no concern whatever. Our object is, to point out the manner in which the projectors of this masonic con-

---

78   Ibid., 83–84.
79   Grand Lodge of Scotland Minutes, March 7, 1808.
80   Stewart, *An Exposition*, 31.

spiracy contrived to sap the laws of the institution, under the pretext of prosecuting crimes.[81]

In addition to negative propaganda emerging from discontented masons, the dispute received attention through the printing of satirical poems, Masonic polemics, newspaper articles, as well as the publication of Masonic minutes and the verbal and written exchanges among Mitchell, Gibson, and the Grand Lodge of Scotland. The *Petition and Complaint* published by Alexander Lawrie contains several anonymous works, including "The Scotch Diable Boiteaux or Asmodeous in Edinburgh: Edited By Zachariah Cleardoubt." "The Scotch Diable Boiteaux" is a satirical account of the feud between Gibson and Mitchell, supposedly narrated by a Scottish freemason. Cleardoubt ridicules not only the dispute among the various parties, but freemasons in general. Offering a ludicrous description of the narrator, the author claims that he is an

> old decrepid Highlander, with a hard weather-beaten and wrinkled countenance, cheek-bones so high, that they rendered it broader than long, *beautifully* shaded with *blood-red hair*, and farther adorned with immense whiskers of the same colour. On his head he wore a huge cocked hat, made of tartan, and his red locks were gathered behind into an enormous *queue*. On his body, he wore a dirty tartan waistcoat, and from it hung a *kilt* of the same chequered manufacture. On his distorted legs he displayed a pair of huzzars, without soles, and this elegant dress was covered by a thread-bare and tattered great-coat, which altogether formed a most ludicrous *tout ensemble.*[82]

---

81 Ibid., 34. The authors further assert that the Grand Lodge, "when spurred on by party–zeal ... imagine[d] that it would be better to sacrifice masonry altogether, if they could not get it converted into an engine to extend the principles of their party," Ibid., 40. Realizing that the Tories were not satisfied with the defeat of Mitchell's address, the Grand Lodge, "after exhausting every artifice to establish their power... [had] at length thrown off the mask, and [began] to deal forth in the way of *terror*... Not only are those who attempt[ed] to remonstrate, deprived of their *masonic* privileges; but as *citizens*, too, they [were] threatened with the vengeance of the *party*," Ibid., 51.

82 Cleardoubt, Zachariah, ed. *The Scotch Diable Boiteaux; Or Asmodeus in Edinburgh* (Edinburgh, 1808), 7.

The name "Cleardoubt" adds to the absurdity of the Mitchell affair, expressing a frivolous inability to grasp the reasons for such a feud. In "The Scotch Diable Boiteaux," the author explains that a "sketch of the following pages was picked up by me at the foot of the rock below Lord Nelson's Monument on the Calton Hill, where, I have reason to believe they had been dropt by the owner; and in order that neither the world may be deprived of them, I have thought proper to send them to the press."[83] Cleardoubt characterizes the freemasons as "desperadoes," and asserts that the entire dispute was "surely unwarrantable in a civilized country."[84]

This theme of derision was continued in "The Invocation, in an Inquiry Into the Feuds of Brothers M And G." In this satire, the author unashamedly ridicules Masonic rituals and emphasizes the ludicrous conduct of Mitchell and Gibson:

> Say, for the business I would fain discuss,
> Whence all thus uproar? whence this mighty fuss?
> What makes the Lodge of Scotland thus to shake,
> And to her very center trembling quake?
> What puts the craft in such a mighty pother,
> And sets one mason upon top of t'other?
> Say, has the secret, word, or sign, been told?
> And does th' unhallow'd world, withstep profane,
> Presumptuous dare the mystic rites to stain;
> With eye polluted, and with ear untaught,
> Imbibing knowledge at each copious draught,
> And learning secrets none but masons know,
> Without the ordeal masons undergo? —
> Such dire offences well might kindle ire,
> Might set the tamest lodge on earth on fire.[85]

---

83 Ibid.

84 Ibid., 27–28. Cleardoubt offers a final explanatory note, stating that "the world has been *favoured* with this production, chiefly for the purpose of preventing a mutilated copy, which, after having laid *fifteen thousand years* in the College Library, was intended to be published with such interpolations as might suit it to a more recent purpose, and it was the intention of the editor of that publication *even to have caricatured* the *dramatic personae*, which, after the *faithful* account here given of them, the world will perceive to be really *unnecessary*," 28.

85 "The Invocation, in an Inquiry Into the Feuds of Brothers M And G," printed in *Peti-*

After cynically analyzing the dispute, the author exhorts the Grand Lodge to stand as

> A striking proof to every future age,
> How much it deprecates unmanly rage,
> And teach the world for once this noble lesson,
> That every man who is a genuine Mason,
> Harbours an equal love to every brother,
> Nor passes one, where he condemns another,
> Remove the stigma men would now affix,
> And show 'tis love of justice prompts, not POLITICS.[86]

Crucially, the publications also reveal the influence of Whig politics on the Grand Lodge. For example, the author of the "Address to the Public on a Late Succession" argues that Mitchell's proposed letter to the King effectively "thanked him [the King] for having dismissed the ministry of Lord Grenville and Charles Fox, and turning out of their employments men who, in the opinion of the friends of Lord Melville, impeded their progress to the sweets of the place."[87] Moreover, the author asserts that it was "not the duty of the Grand Lodge of Scotland ... to approach the throne with an avowal that they are neither rebels nor papists."[88] Although the author stresses the Grand Lodge's unswerving loyalty to the Crown, his declarations smack strongly of Whig sympathies. Highlighting its moral superiority, the author further states that "fortunately, there were in the Grand Lodge of Scotland, individuals who, if they could not prevent the firebrand from being thrown, could at least stop the progress of the intended conflagration."[89]

---

tion and Complaint, 4.

86 Ibid., 11.

87 "An Address to the Public on a Late Secession of an Edinburgh Lodge of Free Masons and Some Events Therewith Connected," printed in *Petition and Complaint*, 15.

88 Ibid. The author declares that is was also not fitting "that they, through the same Grand Master ... should be graciously pleased to say, that he, in common with the greatest Ministers the country ever saw, the most accomplished orators the councils of state ever listened to; the most illustrious statesmen and most amiable of men that ever adorned humanity; that, in a word, the heir apparent to the Crown ... and Fox, were rebels, traitors, and atheists... Was it decorous to the head of the Scottish Masons ... to make him declare to the world, that the friends of his heart, and the companions of his councils, were traitors to royalty and enemies to God?" Ibid.

89 Ibid., 22.

The Secession

Notwithstanding such affirmations of Masonic loyalty, it became apparent that the situation had begun to spiral out of control. Similar to its response during the Maybole Trial, the Grand Lodge adopted a defensive strategy. Realizing that it was unable to successfully settle the dispute, Inglis and others ardently defended themselves against any misconduct and argued that their actions were warranted under the terms of the Secret Societies Act. On March 7, 1808, the Grand Lodge of Scotland forwarded transcripts of the case against Dr. Mitchell to the Modern Grand Lodge of England; Appendix 11 attests to the solidarity of the Masonic governing bodies, as the Moderns, Antients, and the ruling body in Ireland all expressed their approval of the actions of the Scottish Grand Lodge. Overall, the Modern Grand Lodge of England is much more vocal than the Antients in its support of the Grand Lodge of Scotland. Furthermore, language and tone are forthright and direct; in no uncertain terms, the Moderns stated that the Grand Lodge, "representing by regular delegation the Will of the whole Craft, is the proper and unquestionable depository of such Power."[90] Clearly, the Moderns viewed the Grand Lodge as the sole voice and authority of all Masonic matters. The implications of this communication parallel Bullock's assertion that the Grand Lodge attempted to impose a "centralist regime" on all constituent lodges.[91]

During the early stages of the trial, the Earl of Moira offered little or no assistance in the case. However, after receiving the transcripts of the case, Moira once again resumed his campaign to make the Grand Lodge the final authority on all Masonic matters. It is possible that Moira's sudden interest in the Masonic Secession arose from his failure to achieve any prominent position in the restructured Scottish government, which was mostly controlled by Whig hardliners such as Lauderdale and Erskine. Melville wrote to his son Robert, stating that "I suspect Lord Moira totally overrate[d] his influence in any quarter."[92] Sensing an opportunity to use the Grand Lodge of Scotland to revitalize his political career, Moira quickly assumed control of the dispute.

---

90 Modern Grand Lodge of England Minutes, April 6, 1808. Appendix 11 contains a full transcript of the minutes.

91 Bullock, *Revolutionary Brotherhood*, 15.

92 See Fry, *Despotism*, 280–281.

It is more likely, however, that Moira' actions were largely guided by his desire to "please his patron the Prince of Wales."[93] Both Moira and the Prince had taken a keen interest in the events in Scotland. Aware of the vulnerability of Scottish Freemasonry, they hatched a plan in England to "unite the two Grand Lodges under the Prince of Wales."[94] Although the Whigs in the Grand Lodge of Scotland initially viewed the Prince's endorsement as an advantage, it quickly became clear that Scotland was being used "as a lever to promote union in England."[95] Crucially, Moira's scheme failed. According to Dawson, his "complete misunderstanding of the Mitchell affair must have influenced the Grand Lodge of Scotland against a Union, especially as they would then have had to put up with Moira as the guiding influence on the Prince of Wales."[96]

Although temporarily avoiding the union, Moira's involvement proved to be an extreme error of judgment. Moira informed the Grand Lodge of Scotland that he had

> lately laid the subject before the Prince of Wales. His Royal Highness is of opinion, that the authority of the Grand Lodge should be strictly maintained, not only with the view of preserving Masonry from all those ir-regularities which would take place without the controul of that body, but because on no other terms will the Government now permit the existence of Lodges ... The Grand Lodge should consider ... a sentence of expulsion from masonry against Dr. Mitchell for his contumacy, to be followed by a similar sentence against every individ-ual attending what is called a Lodge under him, in case they persevere in maintaining that illegal meeting.[97]

At this stage, the Scottish Grand Lodge had abandoned all attempts to settle the dispute itself. Essentially, until Moira's participation, "the mat-ter was not *entirely* dictated by politics."[98] However, Moira's reference to

93 P. J. Dawson, commenting on Hamill's "The Earl of Moira," 45.
94 Ibid.
95 Hamill, "The Earl of Moira," 40.
96 Dawson, commenting on "The Earl of Moira," 45.
97 Grand Lodge of Scotland Minutes, April 25, 1808.
98 Lindsay, *Holyrood House*, 302, my italics.

the Secret Societies Act of 1799, stating that he and the Prince of Wales were of the opinion that the seceding lodges constituted an illegal society acting independently of the Grand Lodge of Scotland, made politics the central issue "to the exclusion of all else."[99] Moira completely misunderstood the situation, as he allegedly knew nothing of the extreme political implications of the case. Indeed, it is inexplicable that those advising the Grand Lodge "should not have considered that the interpretation sought to be placed on the Act, in view of its unambiguous terms in relation to Masonry, could not prevail."[100] By May 1808, Dr. Mitchell and his supporters were not adhering to the stipulations of the initial suspension.[101] Backed by the Grand Lodge of England and taking the advice of Moira, Mitchell was expelled from Scottish Freemasonry for openly seceding from the Grand Lodge of Scotland. Additionally, members of several Edinburgh lodges were suspended for communicating with Mitchell.[102]

Although it had no constitutional authority to hand down punishments of expulsion and could not legally bar freemasons from communicating with one another, the Grand Lodge was intent on forcing lodges to comply with its demands and imposing its authority on all Scottish freemasons. Certainly, Moira seized this opportunity to secure Grand Lodge dominance over all Masonic matters. Unfortunately, his involvement would ultimately result in the failure of the Grand Lodge to prevent The Masonic Secession of 1808.[103]

---

99 Ibid.

100 Wartski, "Secret Societies," 50.

101 Ibid.

102 Wartski writes that "on the 2nd May, 1808, Grand Lodge expelled Dr. Mitchell and all those in his Lodge who were party to the secession. Likewise, the Senior Warden and the Treasurer of Mary's Chapel, together with a member of Lodge Edinburgh St Andrew and one from Royal Arch Edinburgh, were suspended for attending one of Dr. Mitchell's meetings on the 11th March, 1808, and failing to apologise," Ibid. It is unclear as to the party affiliations of the other suspended masons. The main reason, however, for their suspension was communicating with Mitchell.

103 According to O'Gorman, "it was during these years that the party and the heir to the throne began to drift apart. The watershed was the 'Talents' ministry, when the Prince resented what he took to be the ministers' neglect of him. Grenville, in particular, disliked and distrusted him and was unwilling to fawn over him. After the death of Fox relations between the Whig party and the heir were never the same. Consequently, the Whigs were unable to take advantage of no fewer than four opportunities to enter governments between 1809 and 1812. The events of... 1806–07, and the mythology to which they had given rise, had taught the Whigs that they should never again be victims of the court that, therefore, they should only serve in a completely new ad-

The Downfall of the Grand Lodge

Scottish lodges reacted differently to the actions of the Grand Lodge. No. 25 St. Andrew, for example, recorded on June 27, 1808 that "from all Circumstances of the case taken together, this meeting cannot help regretting much that ever this Strife and Contention should have been meddled with or that it had been checked effectually in its Origin ... It would have saved the waste of a considerable sum of the public money ... and it would have tended to the peace and harmony of all the Lodges in Scotland."[104] Other lodges, however, such as No. 27 St. Mungo's, supported the Grand Lodge. In a minute dated July 27, 1808, No. 27 expressed its approval of the

> conduct of the Grand Lodge, in Suppressing every thing
> that may tend to prejudice the Brotherhood & most Cor-
> dially agree with them in all their late transactions and
> resolutions, as far as they have been communicated to us;
> and are determined to adhere to, and stand by our Mother
> Lodge, in support of her rights, which go hand and hand
> with our own. As On Our Admission we are all bound to
> Support the Grand Lodge & of course must do it.[105]

Not surprisingly, in a minute dated June 24, 1808, St. Luke recorded that its members

> had witnessed, with grief and indignation, the conduct
> of certain individuals belonging to several of the sister

---

ministration; that the old one must be declared at an end; and that they should have ultimate control over men and measures in the new one," *The Long Eighteenth Century: British Political & Social History 1688–1832* (London, 1997), 265.

104 No. 25 Lodge St. Andrew Minutes, June 27, 1808.

105 No. 27 St. Mungo's Lodge Minutes, July 27, 1808. The Master all stated, "Sir & Brother, The Communications from the Grand Lodge of the 10th of March, 10th May, 17th June & 16th July 1808, intimating their proceedings, I duly received and beg leave to return my grateful thanks for the honour done me. All these proceedings have been laid before the Brethren of the Lodge St Mungo No. 28 over which I have the honour to preside, and while we lament the Schism that has arisen among the Craft (viz. that when One Misunderstanding is as accommodated, a Wider One has broke out). We Most Sincerely approve of the Conduct of the Grand Lodge, in Suppressing every thing that may tend to prejudice the Brotherhood & most Cordially agree with them in all their late transactions and resolutions, as far as they have been communicated to us; and are determined to adhere to, and stand by our Mother Lodge, in support of her rights, which go hand and hand with our own. As On Our Admission we are all bound to Support the Grand Lodge & of course must do it."

Lodges of this city, who, finding it impossible to render the Grand Lodge of Scotland subservient to their political views, have, with a zeal worthy of better cause, exerted themselves to overturn the controuling power of the Grand Lodge, and subvert the Masonic constitution ... Under these circumstances, the Brethren of St. Luke's consider it their bounden duty, to declare their unshaken fidelity towards the Grand Lodge.[106]

Despite varying opinions, it is clear that such actions were consistently alienating masons. For example, on May 18, 1808, Lodge Edinburgh St. Andrew passed a series of resolutions stating that the suspensions were an "infringement upon their rights."[107] On June 13, 1808, the Grand Lodge of Scotland expelled all freemasons involved or associated in any manner with Dr. Mitchell. As a result, these masons—who were led by No. 1 Mary's Chapel—officially seceded from the Grand Lodge and formed the Associated Lodges Seceding from the Present Grand Lodge of Scotland. Historians have noted that the mishandling of the Mitchell Trial caused further friction among Scottish freemasons. Furthermore, the issue of precedence that had dogged the Grand Lodge from its inception in 1736 once again resurfaced, this time in a more rancorous and bitter form. Indeed, the establishment of the Associated Lodges effectively signaled the end of Grand Lodge's pursuit of complete constitutional and Masonic authority over all freemasons in Scotland. As Wartski maintains, it is obvious that

the situation in Grand Lodge had reached the point of near hysteria. Spite and rancour [were] rampant, where fact and discretion might have saved the day. The cavalier handling of the matter of precedence shows a lack of feeling towards the former premier Lodge, which naturally deeply resented its displacement after so many years. One would not have expected this sort of behaviour from Freemasons, let along those entrusted with the government of the Craft. The actions of the Grand

---

106 No. 44 St. Luke Lodge Minutes, June 24, 1808, cited in *Petition and Complaint*, Appendix No. II, 3.

107 Lodge Edinburgh St. Andrew Minutes, May 18, 1808, cited in *Petition and Complaint*, 6–7.

Lodge put the final touches to the revolt that followed, which, though it had been brewing, could have been prevented.[108]

Confronted with a Masonic rebellion, one final attempt was made to suppress the rising tide of revolt. In a gross misunderstanding of its powers, the Grand Lodge emphatically declared that

> the power of controuling the proceedings of every Lodge and Brother in Scotland, has always been vested in, and uniformly exercised by the Grand Lodge. The charters to all the Lodges in Scotland have been granted by it, under the express condition of obedience to the Grand Lodge; and every Brother becomes bound, at his admission, to obey its orders ... If the power is not to be vested in the Grand Lodge, where can it be placed? There is no other body which can hold it; and if there is no superintending power to administer the laws of the body, the Craft must be annihilated.[109]

The passage of the Secret Societies Act in 1799 resulted in the indefinite suspension of charter-granting privileges. During the Maybole Trial, the Grand Lodge of Scotland resumed its campaign to have this right restored. In a letter to Robert Dundas on March 2, 1803, it raised the questions of new warrants and, referring to Kilwinning, whether lodges were legally and constitutionally bound to obey the Grand Lodge.[110] Dundas' response is significant because in no uncertain terms, he asserted that not only was the Grand Lodge expressly prohibited from issuing charters, but also that it could not force Lodge Kilwinning to relinquish its authority of warranting new lodges. Crucially, Dundas declared that "nothing is said

---

108 Wartski, "Secret Societies, 51.

109 Ibid., June 13, 1808. The Grand Lodge further stated that "so very numerous a body of men as the Masons of Scotland, must be under laws and regulations, and there must be a power vested somewhere to enforce these laws and regulations. Where can this power be vested, but in the Grand Lodge, by which the Lodges are constituted, under the condition of obedience to its orders, and the Members of which are delegated by the whole Craft, where it has always been lodged, and whose decisions have always hitherto been cheerfully acquiesced in by the Brethren," Ibid.

110 The Grand Lodge wrote to Robert Dundas in an effort to determine if it was able to "resume [its] former powers of granting charters" and if it was "practicable for the Grand Lodge to compel the Kilwinning Lodge and the Lodges Erected to her to re-

in the above [Secret Societies] act with regard to the authority or control of the Grand Lodge of Scotland or indeed of any other Grand Lodge [and] that the Grand Lodge of Scotland has ever been recognised as a corporate Body so as to have a ... right of bringing an action before a court."[111]

It is unclear why the Grand Lodge assumed the rite to "superintend the conduct of all the Lodges in Scotland"[112] when such extraordinary claims of authority were emphatically denied by Dundas. The wording of the exclusion clause specifically referred to "any such Society or Lodge which shall, before the passing of this Act, have been usually holden under the said denomination and in conformity to the Rules prevailing among the said Societies of Freemasons."[113] The amendment to the original Secret Societies makes no mention of the authority of the Grand Lodges; essentially, the amendment asserts the authority of Masonic lodges as determined by their individual laws and regulations, not those enforced by the Grand Lodge of Scotland. Thus, the Grand Lodge assumed an unconstitutional measure of authority, as it was not definitively guaranteed in the Masonic exclusion clause.[114] Perhaps the Grand Lodge was genuinely unaware of these stipulations. However, it is more likely that its actions were ultimately influenced by the pervading sense of confusion among freemasons and Moira's misinterpretation of the Secret Societies Act.

The Grand Lodge of Scotland also attempted to justify its actions by stressing the charitable aims of the organization. In very similar terms used during the controversy over granting charters, it asserted that the Seceding Lodges were preventing the distribution of charitable funds. It appears as if the Grand Lodge sensed that political accusations could do nothing to bring about a satisfactory conclusion to the ordeal; thus, Mitchell was blamed (tacitly for the political upheaval) and overtly for the destruction of the Grand Lodge and Masonic charity.

> If the Grand Lodge is to be annihilated, how is the charity, hitherto so faithfully distributed by it among the indigent Brethren, their widows and children, to be con-

---

turn to the bosom and become Members of the Grand Lodge," Grand Lodge of Scotland Minutes, March 2, 1803.

111 Ibid.
112 Ibid.
113 Lambert, *House of Commons Sessional Papers*, 33–35.
114 Ibid.

tinued? It must fall; and the objects of the charity must
be left to lament in unavailing sorrow. The destruction
of the Craft, and consequent failure of the charity, must
have been the consequences, if the Grand Lodge had
permitted the proceedings of Dr. Mitchell and his adherents to pass unnoticed.[115]

Intent on upholding the sentences of expulsion and punishing the Seceders, the Grand Lodge of Scotland warned that Masonic meetings were
permitted only in legally constituted lodges, in accordance with the Secret Societies Act and the laws of the Grand Lodge of Scotland. Furthermore, it threatened to withdraw the charter of any lodge that "interfere[d]
with politics,"[116] and all meetings would then be "interdicted by the civil
magistrate."[117] Lulled into a false sense of confidence through the assur-
ances of Moira, the Grand Lodge concluded its resolution by stating that
"it is impossible to conceive, that the laws of any country could permit
meetings of persons, bound by an oath of secrecy, were even a suspicion
to be entertained, that politics were discussed at them."[118] The decision to
expel all members of the newly formed Associated Lodges and the subsequent referral of the case to the Civil Magistrate were the direct result of
Moira's involvement. Eventually the case went to court, although it ended
in an embarrassing defeat for Moira and the Grand Lodge of Scotland.[119]

The application for the interdict resulted in an interlocutory against the
officers of the Associated Lodges and the Grand Lodge of Scotland. Feeling that a minor victory had been achieved, Moira sent a letter to James
Clerk, Sheriff Depute of Edinburgh. Assuring Clerk of his intentions,
Moira stated that he had ordered the Substitute Grand Master of Scotland to present a complete list of all masons expelled in connection with
the Associated Lodges. Drawing authority from the Secret Societies Act,
Moira asserted that he "spoke ... with decisive confidence because the
exemption in favour of Masonic meetings was admitted into the Act in

115 Quoted in *Petition and Complaint*, Grand Lodge of Scotland Minutes, March 7, 1808.
116 Grand Lodge of Scotland Minutes, June 29, 1808.
117 Ibid.
118 Ibid.
119 Appendix 12 chronicles the National Archives of Scotland Papers CS/235/M39/2,
which details the case against the Grand Lodge of Scotland the sworn Certificate of
Mary's Chapel Lodge.

consequence of my assurance to Mr. Pitt that nothing could be deemed a Lodge which did not sit by precise authority from the Grand Lodge and under its direct superintendence."[120] On November 30, 1808, the Grand Lodge of Scotland submitted an application for an interdict against the meetings of the Associated Lodges and a Bill of Suspension. [121] Additionally, the Bill of Suspension stated the intentions of the Grand Lodge to establish itself as the "only legal, in its fullest meaning, body in Freemasonry in Scotland."[122]

In December 1808, the Courts granted the interdicts. However, the Associated Lodges appealed to the Second Division of the Court of Session on February 11, 1809. During the appeal, Lord Justice Clerk Hope stated his disapproval over the admission as evidence of a letter written by Moira which implicated the Prince of Wales. According to the Lord Justice, "a most serious improper attempt had been made by the complainers to influence the decision of the Court, by production of, and founding upon, the letter from the Earl of Moira, containing the opinion of the Prince of Wales."[123] Subsequently, Moira's letter was removed from the Court. On July 7, 1810, Hope handed down the following judgment:

> The Lords having resumed consideration of this process and advised the mutual memorials for the parties in respect the Suspenders insist in the Character of Office bearers of a Self-Constituted Society which is not enti-

---

120 Grand Lodge of Scotland Minutes, August 11, 1808.

121 Wartski, "Secret Societies," 54. The Grand Lodge submitted the application "on behalf of certain interested individuals." As Wartski writes, the Grand Lodge of Scotland "had no *locus standi in judicio* due to its status as a voluntary organization. Thus the Bill of Suspension had to be issued in the name of specific masons," Ibid.

122 Ibid., 55.

123 From the *Edinburgh Star*, quoted in *Petition and Complaint*, 6–7. The Lord Justice asserted that if the "letter alluded to had been authorized by the Prince, and written by the Noble Earl, with the view of inducing their Lordships to decide the cases before them in one way or another, he would certainly move ... that the letter should be burnt by the hands of the common executioner," Ibid. Lindsay notes that "as, however, it was a confidential letter to Mr. Inglis, the Agent responsible for its inclusion in the Process would appear at the Bar to give an explanation. Inglis ... offered to accept the whole responsibility, although he submitted that the letter formed part of the Record for the Grand Lodge party, and was, therefore, a proper production. On the top of this the three Whig Counselors for the minorities (John Clerk of Eldin, John Greenshields and The Hon. Harry Erskine) lodged a Minute in which they stated they had advised its production," *Holyrood House*, 308.

tled to the privileges of a Corporation Repel the Reasons
of Suspension Refuse interdict and Discern.[124]

The decision of the Courts hinged on the defense of the Associated Lodges. Asserting their rights as explained in the Secret Societies Act, the Seceders maintained that their meetings were not seditious and the Grand
Lodge had distorted the provision of the original Act. Characterizing this
interpretation as a "gross perversion," the Associated Lodges noted that
the Act, "from beginning to end, never once made any mention of the
Grand Lodge, or of any disputes that might exist between one Lodge and
another, [or] about their internal regulations or rules of management."[125]
Perhaps more importantly, a "certificate upon oath by two of the Members of the mason Lodge called Mary's Chapel Lodge ... in terms of an Act
of Parliament pass'd in the year seventeen hundred and ninety nine" was
submitted (Appendix 12).[126] Contained in this sworn declaration was the
assertion that politics were prohibited from lodge meetings, according to
stipulations set forth by Masonic and national law:

> It is a fundamental and fixed principle amongst all reg-
> ular Free Mason Lodges in this Country that they shall
> at no time enter upon or discuss any political subject re-
> garding either church or State and this restriction is now
> also made apart of the law of the Kingdom, by an act
> of Parliament passed the Twelfth day of July Seventeen
> hundred and ninety nine which specially Statutes and

---

124 National Archives of Scotland, West Register House CS/235/M39/2.

125 Printed in the *Petition and Complaint,* and quoted in the *Edinburgh Star,* 5–6. The Seceders argued that the act "was passed at an alarming period in the history of this
country ... [but] by a strange perversion, however ... the complainers supposed that
all Masonic meetings that did not conform to the rules of the Grand Lodge, that did
not recognise its supremacy, and act according to its orders, were *seditious meetings*
in the sense of the act," 5. See also *Exposition,* 63–70. The Seceders also stated that
the Grand Lodge is "neither more nor less than a masonic committee, appointed by
some of the Scottish lodges for the purpose of presiding over and representing them
in public processions, &c. and for managing the distribution of the funds collected for
charitable purposes. It has likewise been in the use of settling matters of precedency
and masonic etiquette among the several lodges holding under it but on no occasion
till now has it presumed to interfere with the radical rights of individual masons, much
less to abridge or curtail them," *Exposition,* 63.

126 National Archives of Scotland CS/235/M39/2, "Certificate of [Illegible] Mary's
Chapel Lodge 25 March 1809". The sworn declaration lists four members of Mary's
Chapel lodge, not two.

Declares That from and after that date no Mason Lodge
in Scotland shall be allowed to meet buy on the express
condition that two of the Members of each Lodge do annually make oath in presence of a Justice of Peace that
they continue to meet for the purposes of Free Masonry
only. Notwithstanding these wise and salutary laws, both
of the Legislature and the Grand Lodge of Scotland as
well as certain instructions given and obligations come
under at admission into the Craft (which cannot be explained).[127]

The success of the Associated Lodges was due, in large part, to their common resentment of the Grand Lodge.[128] In a politically charged address
on February 14, 1809, the Grand Secretary of the Associated Lodges addressed the lodges, stating that

It has fallen to our lot to live in eventful times—times
as eventful in the annals of Masonry, as they are in the
history of Modern Europe. We have lived to see a despotism newly akin to the system of a neighbouring Tyrant, attempted to be established among the British Masons. But we have resisted the odious usurpation with a
Spirit the Masons of future ages will commemorate ...
They sought to enslave us, by debarring individual Masons from the privilege of going where they pleased ...
We spurned the ignoble bondage ... [and] most just, my
friends, is the punishment which has overtaken the de-
stroyers of the order.[129]

It is clear that the Seceders felt that the Grand Lodge had overstepped
its authority. Although all expulsions were eventually revoked on March

---

127 Ibid. See Appendix 12 for a full transcript of the declaration.

128 Lyon writes that "there were ... common grounds upon which the Secessionists were
united, viz., First, a resistance of the aggression upon their rights that was involved in
Grand Lodge passing sentences of suspension and expulsion without affording to the
Brethren implicated the opportunity of defending themselves in the way provided
by its Constitution; second, the vindication of the right to meet as Freemasons, and
as such to be recognised by law, independent of Grand Lodge, and in defiance of its
alleged authority over them," Lyon, *Mary's Chapel*, 309.

129 Mary's Chapel Lodge Minutes, February 14, 1809.

31, 1813, with the exception of Dr. Mitchell's, the Associated Lodges achieved their goal of preventing the Grand Lodge of Scotland from gaining complete Masonic authority over Scottish lodges. Ultimately, the Grand Lodge had been "defeated on every point."[130]

Conclusion

The court finally ruled that the entire dispute was a "mere controversy in Masonry and, being the chief subject discussed by the complainers, was sufficient to satisfy the Court that the whole of this business, in its form and merits, was a mere Masonic dispute, which never should have been made the subject of a discussion at law."[131] Fortunately, the Seceders returned to the Grand Lodge and, according to Lyon, this decision avoided the "erection of a multiplicity of rival Grand Lodges."[132] The political address intended for the King was ultimately transmitted to the Secretary of State for the Home Department, but the King refused to accept it.[133] Had the Grand Lodge of Scotland sanctioned the address, it is likely that the Masonic Secession of 1808 would have never occurred. Alternatively, the Grand Lodge could have retained the right to withdraw its support from the motion, while still permitting Dr. Mitchell to send the address to the King without its approval. Yet it was precisely these pretended powers that were the focal points of the seceding lodges. Lyon succinctly emphasizes the mistakes made by the Grand Lodge of Scotland, stating that "the Secession, though precipitated by Grand Lodge's unconstitutional interference in a petty quarrel between the Lodges Caledonian and Roman Eagle, was doubtless the result of several combined motives, in which politics and personal antipathies had a share."[134]

Significantly, the prominent Whig members of both St. Luke's and the Grand Lodge of Scotland did little to positively influence the outcome of the trial. Party politics wavered, and the initial solidarity and strength of the Whig party disintegrated. Although Wartski questions whether or

---

130 Lindsay, *Holyrood House*, 310.

131 Printed in the *Petition and Complaint*, and quoted in the *Edinburgh Star*, 5–6.

132 Lyon, *Mary's Chapel*, 309.

133 As argued in Chapter 4, "all public bodies of any standing were urged to send in loyal addresses to George III. More than 400 immediately did so, and many continued to at every excuse: by 1796 the King was sick of the sight of them, and ordered that they should be sent straight to Dundas without bothering him," Fry, *Despotism*, 168.

134 Lyon, *Mary's Chapel*, 306.

not the Grand Lodge "hoped to bulldoze its way through in the hope of frightening the Seceders into submission,"[135] it is clear that such aggressive tactics and the use of the Secret Societies Act both failed. Inevitably, political ambition conflicted with the age-old pragmatism of Anderson's *Constitutions*, and not surprisingly, the Secession resulted in the public humiliation of Scottish freemasons and an embarrassing defeat for the Grand Lodge of Scotland.

---

135 Wartski, "Secret Societies," 61.

"A WILLINGNESS TO RETURN TO THE FOLD": THE LASTING IMPACT OF THE GRAND LODGE OF SCOTLAND

" To round off this sorry tale, it remains to say that moves began on both sides for reconciliation."[1] So concludes Wartski, who is unhindered in his criticism of the Grand Lodge of Scotland and its handling over the Masonic Secession. The immediate effective consequences of the schism are significant, illustrating the divisive rivalries present within an organization that traditionally prohibited political debate, as "such Discussions sharpening the Mind of Man against his Brother might offend and disunite."[2] Indeed, as Lindsay asserts, the disorder and confusion prevalent among Scottish freemasons during the late 1790s and early 1800s "nearly wrecked Scottish Freemasonry."[3]

Mitchell's proposed address to the King, the smouldering issue of precedence, and the formation of the Associated Lodges could be justified in political terms. Clearly, conflicting Whig and Tory ideologies sparked the bitter dispute, as "politics in the beginning of the [nineteenth century] ran high in all parts of the country, and nowhere more than in Edinburgh."[4] By 1812, even after the Associated Lodges had "professed a willingness to return to the fold," Whig opposition in the Grand Lodge prevented a settlement from being effected. Major William Miller of Dalswinton, Master of St Luke's Lodge, objected to the settlement as it was "beneath the dignity of the Grand Lodge."[5] Despite such lingering resentments, all suspensions and expulsions except Dr. Mitchell's were

---

1   Wartski, "Secret Societies," 61.

2   Modern Grand Lodge of England Minutes, February 6, 1793.

3   Lindsay, *Holyrood House*, 311.

4   Lyon, *Mary's Chapel*, 306.

5   Lindsay, *Holyrood House*, 310. Lindsay notes that Miller was an officer of the Royal Horse Guards and the second son of Patrick Miller, "the patron of Burns and pioneer of steam navigation. He figures in Burns' election ballad of 'The Five Carlins' as the 'Sodger Youth' who was returned as Whig M. P. for Dumfries in 1790," Ibid., 282. According to Thorne, Patrick Miller joined the Whig Club on June 7, 1795, *History of Parliament Vol. 4*, 589–590.

rescinded, and the Masonic Secession officially ended on March 31, 1813.[6]

The emerging importance of this trial, however, has been overlooked because historians have focused too narrowly on its political implications. As Wartski and others have suggested, parliamentary legislation and divisions within the Grand Lodge along party lines clearly inspired the frantic conduct and motivated the actions of the justifiably concerned Scottish freemasons. Furthermore, Lyon acknowledges that the secession "was precipitated by Grand Lodge's unconstitutional interference in a petty quarrel."[7] Nevertheless, in these assessments are frequently revisited the trademark conclusions of Masonic historians, namely that any conflicts were ultimately the result of "several combined motives,"[8] a vague assessment somewhat excusing the actions of the Grand Lodge.

Even so, in the final analysis, the impact of national politics and lodge rivalries is far less than that of the Grand Lodge of Scotland on eighteenth-century Scottish Freemasonry. This study has focused on the Grand Lodge's wider influence by tracing its complexities as it and Freemasonry evolved in several stages throughout the 1800s. Between the years 1700 and 1736, Scottish lodges were an important part of British society and were appreciated for their contributions to many aspects of public life. The creation of the Grand Lodge of Scotland, however, was the single most influential event in eighteenth-century Freemasonry, as it marked a crucial point in shaping the administrative framework and development of the organization.

Following its establishment in 1737, lodges were held accountable to a central ruling body. Immediately seizing upon its opportunity to assume complete control over all Masonic affairs, the Grand Lodge instituted a system of precedence among lodges and demanded that all freemasons recognize it as the putative head of Scottish Freemasonry. Unlike the English Grand Lodge, it symbolized the convergence of operative traditions with speculative innovations. Consequently, a sharp sense of anxiety gradually filtered through many operative lodges. From 1737 onward, a

---

6   Gould observes that "it is worthy of note that it was in this year [1808] that the union of the two rival Grand Lodges of England was effected," *History of Freemasonry Vol. 2*, 398.

7   Lyon, *Mary's Chapel*, 306.

8   Ibid.

viable concern was the unity of Scottish freemasons, who were at times engaged in disputes over precedence and the imposition of a central governing body. For much of the eighteenth century, however, there was little interaction between the Grand Lodge and lodges outside of Edinburgh. This lack of communication and the absence of a clearly definable ideological function likely caused most lodges to view the Grand Lodge with indifference.

Whether or not lodges embraced the newly created federal system, Scottish Freemasonry enjoyed a time of expansion and influence. Until the creation of the Grand Lodge, Freemasonry was primarily an improvement society. Although it continued to function in this capacity throughout the eighteenth century, from 1740 until 1785 the masons emphasized its role in the public as well as the private sphere. Lodges were chartered at a rate unmatched at any other time during the eighteenth century; members of other clubs and societies joined the Masonic fraternity, manifesting a keen interest in enlightenment sociability and the ability of lodges to compete with other associations; and Freemasonry confirmed itself as a leader among charitable organizations, with service to the community being the self-proclaimed mission of the Grand Lodge. Indeed, the Grand Lodge facilitated much of this expansion and progress, allowing lodges to retain some autonomy while gradually increasing its authority and legal hold over Scottish masons.

During the late 1790s, however, the Grand Lodge asserted itself as a real and powerful presence. National fears of a French-inspired revolution produced a wave of skepticism of all clubs and societies that met and deliberated in private. Certainly, the impact of government legislation passed to regulate such perceived threats was only a partial consequence of the recent criticism of Freemasonry. Perhaps more important, though, was the Grand Lodge's interpretation of parliamentary acts as extensions of its power to enforce national as well as Masonic legislation. Without the radical environment in which the Unlawful Oaths and Secret Societies Acts were passed, it is highly unlikely that the government and Masonic responses would have been so intense.

By 1799, the Grand Lodge of Scotland had come to view itself as the final voice in all Masonic affairs, also reserving the power to sue any lodge failing to adhere to the stipulations set forth by the Secret Societies Act.

The heavy-handed tactics displayed by the Grand Lodge—including threats of suspension, exclusion from the Grand Roll, and legal action—undoubtedly played a key part in forming the popular resentment which ultimately resulted in the Masonic Secession of 1808.

Conceivably disenchanted and frustrated by the rising tide of scrutiny, the Grand Lodge replaced moderation and reason with an overzealous need to assert itself in the volatile environment created by the French Revolution. Essentially, the futility of the government to regulate radical societies and the "failure of the state to respond to the problems and challenges" posed by seditious organizations mirrored the failure of the Grand Lodge of Scotland to mediate Masonic conflicts and command respect from its lodges.[9] Motivated by fears of government reprisal and at times a malicious enthusiasm to enforce the Acts of Parliament, the Grand Lodge used the backdrop of the French Revolution and the uncertainty surrounding the freemasons to augment its power. This is clearly evident during the Mitchell Trial and the dispute with Kilwinning Lodge. Yet even as the Grand Lodge pursued noncompliant lodges, its actions were largely superficial. Noncommittal in its decisions, ignoring the simmering tensions between the Kilwinning and Edinburgh lodges which had existed for the better part of a century, and attempting to arbitrate fraught judicial proceedings, the Grand Lodge of Scotland abjured compromise and pursued what Clark calls a "centralist regime."[10]

Besides emphasizing the significance of the Grand Lodge of Scotland on the development of Scottish Freemasonry, this thesis has demonstrated that its actions throughout the eighteenth century were partially, if not largely, responsible for the various conflicts during the 1790s and early 1800s. Whereas the English Grand Lodge was singularly successful in the circulation of Masonic publications and managing and monitoring all aspects of Freemasonry, Scotland's overall lack of promotion, poor attempts to protect the interests of operative masons, and the defiant nature of several Edinburgh lodges prevented it from effectively gaining and retaining absolute authority over Scottish Masonic affairs. The issue of precedence, the Maybole Trial, and the Masonic Secession are all connected by the creation of a main governing body and the period of crisis ushered in by

---

9   Clark, *British Clubs*, 468.

10   Ibid., 339. This was achieved through the return of membership lists, collection of annual dues, and the use of threats, suspensions, expulsions, and court proceedings.

the divided loyalties and political agenda of the Grand Lodge of Scotland. As such, those masons who opposed the unconstitutional seizure of power were not influenced by a radical consciousness. Rather, they were motivated by a desire to preserve certain hierarchical, authoritative, and political boundaries within Freemasonry.

The impact of the turmoil did not end in 1812. According to Lyon, "a feeling of dissatisfaction and lukewarmness continued to prevail in Mary's Chapel."[11] Several more unsuccessful attempts were made to regain its position at the head of the Grand Roll, and in 1824 the lodge was suspended from all Masonic privileges after several officers were charged with misconduct. The Grand Lodge should be noted for its success in establishing a Masonic community. Any accomplishments, however, are invariably overshadowed by its inability to firmly enforce the prohibition of political and religious discussions.

---

11 Lyon, *Mary's Chapel*, 309.

BIBLIOGRAPHY

Aberdeen Lodge No. 1(3) Minute Books. Aberdeen Masonic Lodge No. 1(3). Aberdeen, 1725–1810.

Ancient Grand Lodge of England Minute Books. Ancient Grand Lodge of England, 1786–1810.

Ancient Stirling No. 30 Minute Books. Ancient Stirling Masonic Lodge No. 30. Stirling, 1738–1810.

Anderson, James. *The Constitutions of the Freemasons, Facsimile Edition.* London, 1976.

Andrews, Corey. "Paradox and Improvement: Literary Nationalism and Eighteenth-Century Scottish Club Poetry." Unpublished PhD Thesis, Ohio University, 2000.

Andrews, Corey. *Literary Nationalism in Eighteenth-Century Club Poetry.* Lewiston, NY: Edwin Mellen, 2004.

Andrews, Corey. "Drinking and Thinking: Club Life and Convivial Sociability in Mid-eighteenth Century Edinburgh." *Social History of Alcohol and Drugs* 22 (2007): 65–82.

Ars Quatuor Coronatorum. Transactions of the Quatuor Coronati Lodge No. 2076. London, 1886–Present.

Barruel, Abbe. *Memoirs, Illustrating the History of Jacobinism.* London: printed for the translator, by T. Burton, No. 11, Gate-Street, Lincoln's-Inn Fields. Sold by E. Booker, No. 56, New Bond-Street, 1798.

Bathurst, W. "The Evolution of the English Provincial Grand Lodge." *AQC* 79 (1966): 216–232.

Beaurepaire, P. Y. "Researching Freemasonry in the Twenty–first Century: Opportunities and Challenges." *JRFF* 1 (2010): 249–257.

Belles Lettres Society. *Roll of the Members of the Belles Lettres Society (Edinburgh, Scotland).* Farmington Hills: Thomas Gale, 2005.

Berman, Ric. *The Foundations of Modern Freemasonry: The Grand Architects—Political Change and the Scientific Enlightenment, 1714–1740.* Brighton: Sussex Academic Press, 2012.

Berman, Ric. *Schism: The Battle that Forged Freemasonry.* Brighton: Sussex Academic Press, 2013.

Berman, Ric. "The London Irish and the Antients Grand Lodge." *Eighteenth–Century Life* 39 (2015): 103–130.

Burke, J. M. and Margaret Jacob. "French Freemasonry, Women, and Feminist Scholarship." *The Journal of Modern History* 68 (1996): 513–549.

Black, Jeremy. *Eighteenth-Century Europe.* Basingstoke: Macmillan, 1999.

Brims, John. "From Reformers to 'Jacobins': The Scottish Association of the Friends of the People." In *Conflict and Stability in Scottish Society 1700–1850.*, ed. T. M. Devine. Edinburgh, 1990.

Brims, John. "Scottish Radicalism and the United Irishmen." In *The United Irishmen: Republicanism, Radicalism and Rebellion,* ed. Kevin Whelan. Dublin: Lilliput, 1993:151–166.

Broadie, Alexander, ed. *The Cambridge Companion to the Scottish Enlightenment.* New York: Cambridge University, 2003.

Broadie, Alexander. *The Enlightenment in Scotland: The Historical Age of the Historical Nation.* Edinburgh: Birlinn, 2001.

Brown, Rhona. "Literary Communities and Commemorations in the Edinburgh Cape Club." *Journal for Eighteenth-Century Studies,* Special Issue on *Networks of Improvement* 38 (2015): 525–539.

Brown, Stephen. "Robert Burns, the Crochallan Fencibles, and the Original Printer of *The Merry Muses of Caledonia.*" *Studies in Scottish Literature* 38 (2012): 92–107.

Bullock, Steven. *Revolutionary Brotherhood: Freemasonry and the Transformation of the American Social Order.* Chapel Hill: University of North Carolina, 1996.

Cameron, C. A. "On the Origin and Progress of the Chivalric Freemasonry in the British Isles." *AQC* 13 (1900): 156–174.

Carr, Harry. "Grand Lodge and the Significance of 1717." *AQC* 79 (1966): 289–292.

Carr, Harry. *Lodge Mother Kilwinning No. 0: A Study of the Earliest Minute*

Books 1642 to 1842. London: Quatuor Coronati Lodge, No. 2076, 1961.

Carr, Harry. *The Mason and the Burgh. An Examination of the Edinburgh Register of Apprentices and the Burgess Rolls*. London: Quatuor Coronati Lodge, No. 2076, 1954.

Carr, Harry. "Three Phases of Masonic History." *AQC* 77 (1964): 256–262.

Castle, E. J. "Enquiry Into the Charge of Gnosticism Brought Against the Freemasons and Templars." *AQC* 19 (1906): 209–228.

Clark, Peter. *British Clubs and Societies 1580–1800: The Origins of an Associational World*. Oxford: Oxford University, 2000.

Clarke, J. R. "The Formation, 1751–1813," in *United Grand Lodge of England 1717–1967*. Oxford: Oxford University, 1967:92–128.

Clawson, Mary Ann. *Constructing Brotherhood: Class, Gender, and Fraternalism*. Princeton: Princeton University, 1989.

Cleardoubt, Zachariah, ed. *The Scotch Diable Boiteaux; Or Asmodeus in Edinburgh*. Edinburgh: printed by John Moir, 1808.

Clifford, Robert. *Application of Barruel's Memoirs of Jacobinism to the Secret Societies of Ireland and Great Britain*. Farmington Hills: Thomas Gale, 2005.

Cochin, Augustin. "The Theory of Jacobinism." In *Interpreting the French Revolution*, ed. François Furet. Cambridge: Cambridge University, 1981:164–204.

Cockburn, Henry. *Memorials of His Time*. Edinburgh: James Thin, Mercat, 1971.

Cowan, Brian. *The Social Life of Coffee: The Emergence of the British Coffee House*. New Haven, CT: Yale University, 2011.

Crawley, Chetwode. "The Rev. Dr. Anderson's Non-Masonic Writings, 1712–1739." *AQC* 18 (1905): 28–42.

Crawley, Chetwode. "The Templar Legends in Freemasonry." *AQC* 26 (1913): 45–70.

Curl, James Stevens. *The Art and Architecture of Freemasonry: An Introductory Study*. London: B. T. Batsford, 2002.

Dawson, P. J. commenting on "The Earl of Moira, Acting Grand Master 1790–1813," J. M. Hamill. AQC 93 (1980): 44–46.

Dickinson, H. T. ed. *Britain and the French Revolution, 1789–1815*. London: Basil Blackwell, 1988.

Dickinson, H. T. "Popular Loyalism in Britain in the 1790s." In *The Transformation of Political Culture: England and Germany in the Late Eighteenth Century*, ed. Eckhart Hellmuth. Oxford: Oxford University Press for the German Historical Institute, 1990:503–533.

Dilworth, Mark. "Two necrologies of Scottish Benedictine Abbey's in Germany." *IR* 9 (1958): 173–203.

Dinwiddy, John. "Conceptions of Revolution in the English Radicalism of the 1790s." In *The Transformation of Political Culture: England and Germany in the Late Eighteenth Century*, ed. Eckhart Hellmuth. Oxford: Oxford University Press for the German Historical Institute, 1990:535–560.

Draffen, George. "Scottish Masonic Periodicals." *AQC* 92 (1979):191–199.

Draffen, George. *Scottish Masonic Records 1736–1950: A List of All the Lodges at Home and Abroad*. Edinburgh, 1950.

Duffy, Michael. *The Younger Pitt*. Harlow, 2000.

Dundee Ancient Lodge No. 49 Minute Books. Dundee Ancient Masonic Lodge No. 49. Dundee, 1789–1810.

Dyck, Ian, ed. *Citizen of the World: Essays on Thomas Paine*. New York: St. Martin's, 1988.

Edinburgh Society for the Encouragement of Arts, Sciences, Manufactures, and Agriculture. *Rules and Orders of the Edinburgh Society, for the Encouragement of Arts, Sciences, Manufactures, and Agriculture*. Edinburgh, 1755.

Edwards, Lewis. "Anderson's Book of Constitutions of 1738." *AQC* 46 (1933): 357–430.

Elliot, Marianne. "Ireland and the French Revolution." In *Britain and the French Revolution*, ed. H. T. Dickinson. London: Basil Blackwell, 1985:202–219.

Elliot, Marianne. *Wolfe Tone: Prophet of Irish Independence*. New Haven, CT: Yale University, 1989.

Emerson, Roger. "The Contexts of the Scottish Enlightenment." In *The Cambridge Companion to the Scottish Enlightenment*, ed. Alexander Broadie. New York: Cambridge University, 2003:9–30.

Emerson, Roger. "The Enlightenment and Social Structures." In *City and Society in the 18th Century*, eds. Paul Fritz and David Williams. Toronto: Hakkert, 1973:99–124.

Emerson, Roger L. "The Social Composition of Enlightened Scotland: The Select Society of Edinburgh, 1754–1764." *SVEC* 114 (1973): 291–329.

Emsley, Clive. *Britain and the French Revolution*. Harlow: Longman, 2000.

Faivre, A. *Access to Western Esotericism*. Albany, NY: State University of New York, 1994.

Ferguson, William. *Scotland, 1689 to the Present: The Edinburgh History of Scotland Volume 4*. Edinburgh: Oliver and Boyd, 1965.

Ferrone, Vincenzo. *The Intellectual Roots of the Italian Enlightenment. Newtonian Science, Religion, and Politics in the Early Eighteenth Century*. Atlantic Highlands, NJ: Humanties, 1995.

Firminger, W. K. "The Romances of Robison and Barruel." *AQC* 50 (1937): 31–69.

Fitzpatrick, John C., ed. *The Writings of George Washington from the Original Manuscript Sources 1745–1799*. Washington: Government Printing Office, 1939.

Fritz, Paul and David Williams, eds. *City and Society in the 18th Century*. Toronto: Hakkert, 1973.

Ford, R. *Song Histories*. Glasgow: William Hodge, 1900. Fry, Michael. *The Dundas Despotism*. Edinburgh: Edinburgh University, 1992.

Furet, François, ed. *Interpreting the French Revolution*. Cambridge: Cambridge University, 1981.

Gaffney, Clare. *Index of Fellows of the Royal Society of Edinburgh Elected From 1783–1882*. Edinburgh: Manpower Services Commission (STEP) Project for the preservation of Scotland's Cultural Heritage, 1980.

Gallin, Richard G. "Scottish Radicalism, 1792–1794." Unpublished PhD Thesis, Columbia University, 1979.

Gilbert, R. A. "The Role of Bibliography in Masonic Research," *AQC* 103 (1990): 124–149.

Goodman, D. *The Republic of Letters: A Cultural History of the French Enlightenment*. Ithaca, NY: Cornell University, 1994.

Gould, Robert Freke. *A Concise History of Freemasonry*. London: Gale and Polden, 1903.

Gould, Robert Freke. *Gould's History of Freemasonry Throughout the World*. New York: C. Scribner's Sons, 1936.

Grand Lodge of Scotland. *Chartulary and List of Lodges and Members: 1736–1799*. Edinburgh, 1736–1799.

Grand Lodge of Scotland Minute Books Vol. I, 1736–1765. Grand Lodge of Scotland. Edinburgh, 1736–1765.

Grand Lodge of Scotland Minute Books Vol. II, 1765–1795. Grand Lodge of Scotland. Edinburgh, 1765–1795.

Grand Lodge of Scotland Minute Books Vol. III, 1795–1810. Grand Lodge of Scotland. Edinburgh, 1795–1810.

Grand Lodge of Scotland. *Jubilee Year Book of the Grand Lodge of Antient Free and Accepted Masons of Scotland*. Edinburgh: Grand Lodge of Scotland, 2001.

Grant, Sir Francis. *A Brief Account of the Nation, Rise, and Progress, of the Societies, for Reformation of Manners &c. in England and Ireland: With a Preface Exhorting to the Use of Such Societies in Scotland*. Edinburgh: printed by George Mosman, and are to be sold at his shop ... 1700.

Gray, James T. *Freemasonry in Maybole, Carrick's Captial: Fact, Fiction and Folks*. Ayr: Alloway, 1972.

Great Britain Parliament House. *House of Commons Report of Committee of Secrecy of the House of Commons*. London: printed for J. Wright, and J. Debrett, 1799.

Hamill, J. M. "The Earl of Moira, Acting Grand Master 1790–1813." *AQC* 93 (1980): 31–48.

Hamill, J. *The Craft: A History of English Freemasonry*. Wellingborough: Crucible, 1986.

Hamill, J. *The Craft: A History of English Freemasonry*. Addlestone: Lewis Masonic, 1994.

Harrison, J. F. C. "Thomas Paine and Millenarian Radicalism." In *Citizen of the World: Essays on Thomas Paine*, ed. Ian Dyck. New York: St. Martin's Press, 1988: 73–85.

Haunch, T. O. "Grand Lodge 1717–1751." *AQC* 79 (1966): 264–270.

Haunch, T. O. "The Formation," In *United Grand Lodge of England 1717–1967*. Oxford: Oxford University, 1967:47–91.

Hecht, Hans, ed. *Songs from David Herd's Manuscripts*. Edinburgh: W. J. Hay, 1904.

Heckthorn, Charles William. *The Secret Societies of All Ages and Countries*. New York: University Books, 1965.

Heidle A. and J. A. M. Snoek, eds. *Women's Agency and Rituals in Mixed and Female Masonic Orders*. Leiden: Brill, 2008.

Hellmuth, Eckhart, ed. *The Transformation of Political Culture: England and Germany in the Late Eighteenth Century*. Oxford: Oxford University Press for the German Historical Institute, 1990.

Hewitt, A. R. "The Grand Lodge of England: A History of the First Hundred Years, 1717–1817." *AQC* 80 (1970): 151–168.

Hof, Ulrich Im. "German Associations and Politics in the Second Half of the Eighteenth Century." In *The Transformation of Political Culture: England and Germany in the Late Eighteenth Century*, ed. Eckhart

Hellmuth. Oxford: Oxford University Press for the German Historical Institute, 1990:207–218.

Hughan, W. J. "Origin of Masonic Knight Templary in the United Kingdom." *AQC* 18 (1905): 91–93.

Hunter, William. *Incidents in the History of the Lodge Journeymen Masons,
Edinburgh, No. 8*. Edinburgh: Robert Dodds; Crawford and M'Cabe,
1884.

Hyland, Paul, ed. *The Enlightenment. A Sourcebook and Reader*. London:
Routledge, 2003.

Israel, J. I. *Enlightenment Contested: Philosophy, Modernity and the Emancipation of Man, 1670–1752*. Oxford: Oxford University, 2006.

Israel, J. I. *Democratic Enlightenment: Philosophy, Revolution and Human
Rights*. Oxford: Oxford University Press, 2013.

Jackson-Houlston, C. M. "You Heroes of the Day: Popular Song and
Ephemeral Publication, 1803." Conference Paper, Oxford-Brookes
University. Oxford, 2003.

Jacob, Margaret C. *Living the Enlightenment: Freemasonry and Politics in
Eighteenth-Century Europe*. New York: Oxford University, 1991.

Jacob, Margaret C. *The Newtonians and the English Revolution 1689–1720*.
Ithaca, NY: Cornell University, 1976.

Jacob, Margaret C. *The Radical Enlightenment: Pantheists, Freemasons, and
Republicans*. London: Allen and Unwin, 1981.

Jacob, Margaret C. "The Radical Enlightenment and Freemasonry: Where
We Are Now." *REHMLAC* 5 (2012): 11–24.

Jenkins, P. "Jacobites and Freemasons in Eighteenth-Century Wales,"
Welsh Historical Review 9 (1979): 391–406.

Jones, Bernard E. *Freemason's Guide and Compendium*. New York: Macoy
Publishing and Masonic Supply Company, 1950.

Journeymen Masonic Lodge No. 8 Minute Books. Journeymen Masonic
Lodge No. 8. Edinburgh, 1707–1810.

Kahler, Lisa. "Freemasonry in Edinburgh 1721–1746: Institution and Context." Unpublished PhD Thesis, University of St. Andrews, 1998.

Kahler, Lisa. "The Grand Lodge of Scotland and the Establishment of the Masonic Community." In *Freemasonry on Both Sides of the Atlantic*, eds. R. William Weisberger, Wallace McLeod, and S. Brent Morris. Boulder, CO: East European Monographs; New York: Distributed by Columbia University Press, 2002:87–122.

Kelly, W. R. "The Advent of Royal Arch Masonry." *AQC* 30 (1917): 7–55.

Kennedy, Michael L. *The Jacobin Clubs in the French Revolution: The First Years*. Princeton, NJ: Princeton University, 1982.

Killen, John, ed. *The Decade of the United Irishmen: Contemporary Accounts, 1791–1801*. Belfast: Blackstaff, 1997.

Kinghorn, Alexander M. and Alexander Law, ed. "The Journal of the Easy Club." *The Works of Allan Ramsay*. Vol. 6. Edinburgh, 1945–74.

Knoop, Douglas and G. Jones, "An Anti-Masonic Leaflet of 1698." *AQC* 55 (1942): 152–154.

Knoop and Jones. *The Genesis of Freemasonry*. Manchester: Manchester University, 1947.

Knoop and Jones. *The Scope and Method of Masonic History*. Oldham: printed for the Association by F. & G. Pollard (Oldham) Ltd., the Wellington Press, 1944.

Knoop and Jones. *The Scottish Mason and the Mason Word*. Manchester: Manchester University, 1939.

Knoop and Jones. *A Short History of Freemasonry to 1730*. Manchester: Manchester University, 1940.

Kosseleck, Reinhart. *Critique and Crisis: Enlightenment and the Pathogenesis of Modern Society*. Oxford: Berg, 1988.

Lambert, Shelia, ed. *House of Commons Sessional Papers of the Eighteenth-Century*. Wilmington, DE: Scholarly Resources, 1975.

Law, Alexander. "Allan Ramsay and the Easy Club." *Scottish Literary Journal* 16 (1989): 18–40.

Lawrie, Alexander, printer. *Petition and Complaint at Brother Gibson's Instance Against Brother Mitchell, and His Answers Thereto; With the Procedure of the Grand Lodge Thereon and Proof Adduced.* Edinburgh: printed by A. Lawrie, 1808.

Lindsay, Robert Strathern. *A History of the Mason Lodge of Holyrood House (St Luke's) No. 44.* Edinburgh: T. and A. Constable at the University Press, 1935.

Logue, Kenneth J. *Popular Disturbances in Scotland, 1780–1815.* Edinburgh: John Donald, 1979.

Lynch, Michael. *Scotland: A New History.* London: Pimlico, 2000.

Lyon, David Murray. *History of the Lodge of Edinburgh (Mary's Chapel), No. 1, Embracing An Account of the Rise and Progress of Freemasonry in Scotland.* London: Gresham, 1900.

McCracken, J. L. "The United Irishmen." In *Secret Societies in Ireland,* ed. T. Desmond Williams. Dublin: Gill and Macmillan, 1973:58–67.

McDowell, R. B. *Ireland in the Age of Imperialism and Revolution: 1760–1801.* Oxford: Clarendon, 1979.

McElroy, Davis Dunbar. "The Literary Clubs and Societies of Eighteenth-Century Scotland, and their Influence on the Literary Productions of the Period from 1700 to 1800." PhD Thesis, Edinburgh University, 1952.

McElroy, Davis D. *Scotland's Age of Improvement: A Survey of Eighteenth-Century Literary Clubs and Societies.* Pullman: Washington State University, 1969.

McFarland, E. W. *Ireland and Scotland in the Age of Revolution.* Edinburgh: Edinburgh University, 1994.

Macbean, E. "Formation of the Grand Lodge of Scotland." *AQC* 3 (1890): 172–182.

MacDermot, Frank. *Theobald Wolfe Tone: A Biographical Study.* London: n.p., 1939.

MacLeod, Emma Vincent, "Scottish Responses to the Irish Rebellion." In *These Fissured Isles: Ireland, Scotland and British History, 1798–1848,* ed. Terry Brotherstone. Edinburgh: John Donald, 2005:123–140.

Maitland, William. *The History of Edinburgh: From its Foundation to the Present Time*. Edinburgh: n.p., 1753.

Mary's Chapel Lodge No. 1 Microfilm and Minute Books. Mary's Chapel Lodge No. 1. Edinburgh, 1708–1767.

Mason, Roger A., ed. *Scots and Britons: Scottish Political Thought and the Union of 1603*. Cambridge: Cambridge University, 1994.

Matthew, H. G. C., and Brian Harrison, eds. *Oxford Dictionary of National Biography: From the Earliest Times to the Year 2000*. Oxford: Oxford University, 2004.

Medical Society of Edinburgh. *List of Members, Laws, and Library Catalogue of the Medical Society of Edinburgh*. Edinburgh: n.p., 1820.

Meikle, Henry W. *Scotland and the French Revolution*. London: Frank Cass, 1969.

Mellor, A. "Eighteenth-Century French Freemasonry and the French Revolution." *AQC* 97 (1984): 105–114.

Melton, James Van Horn. *The Rise of the Public in Enlightenment Europe*. Cambridge: Cambridge University, 2001.

Miller, A. L. "The Connection of Dr. James Anderson of the 'Constitutions' with Aberdeen and Aberdeen University." *AQC* 36 (1923): 86–103.

Mitchell, John. "Answers for John Mitchell, Right Worshipful Master of the Edinburgh Caledonian Lodges; To the Petition and Complaint of James Gibson, Proxy-Master of the Lodge of St Andrew's of Aberdeen, and a Member of the Lodge of St David, Edinburgh, cited in *Petition and Complaint at Brother Gibson's Instance Against Brother Mitchell*. Edinburgh: A. Lawrie, 1808:7–28.

Mitchell, John. "Pamphlet Referred to in the Substitute Grand Master's Deposition," cited in *Petition and Complaint at Brother Gibson's Instance Against Brother Mitchell*. Edinburgh: A. Lawrie, 1808:79–86.

Mitchell, Martin J. *The Irish in the West of Scotland: Trade Unions, Strikes and Political Movements*. Edinburgh: John Donald, 1998.

Modern Grand Lodge of England Minute Books. Modern Grand Lodge of England, 1777–1810.

Money, John. "Freemasonry and the Fabric of Loyalism in Hanoverian England." In *The Transformation of Political Culture: England and*

Germany in the Late Eighteenth Century, ed. Eckhart Hellmuth. Oxford: Oxford University Press for the German Historical Institute, 1990:235–271.

Money, John. "The Masonic Movement; Or, Ritual, Replica, and Credit: John Wilkes, the Macaroni Parson, and the Making of the Middle-Class Mind." *Journal of British Studies* 32 (1993): 358–395.

Mulvey-Roberts, Marie. "Hogarth on the Square: Framing the Freemasons." *British Journal for Eighteenth-Century Studies* 26 (2003): 251–270.

Munck, Thomas. *The Enlightenment: A Comparative Social History 1721–1794*. London: Arnold, 2000.

Murdoch, Steve. *Network North: Scottish Kin, Commercial and Covert Associations in Northern Europe 1603–1746*. Leiden: Brill, 2006.

Newman, Aubrey. "The Contribution of the Provinces to the Development of English Freemasonry." *AQC* 117 (2004): 68–82.

Newton, Edward. "Brethren Who Made Masonic History." *AQC* 78 (1965): 130–145.

Ó Ciosáin, Niall. *Print and Popular Culture in Ireland, 1750–1850*. London: Macmillan, 1997

O'Connor, James. *History of Ireland 1798–1924*. London: Arnold, 1925.

O'Gorman, Frank. *The Long Eighteenth Century: British Political & Social History 1688–1832*. London: Arnold, 1997.

O'Gorman, Frank. "Pitt and the 'Tory' Reaction to the French Revolution 1789–1815." In *Britain and the French Revolution 1789–1815*, ed. H. T. Dickinson. London: Basil Blackwell, 1989:21–37.

Old Inverness St. John's Kilwinning Lodge No. 6 Minute Books. Old Inverness St. John's Kilwinning Masonic Lodge No. 6. Inverness, 1737–1810.

Orphoot, John, printer. *The Invocation, in an Inquiry into the Feuds of Brothers M and G, A Poem*. Edinburgh: printed by himself, 1808.

Parkinson, R. E. "Ireland and the R.A. Degree." *AQC* 79 (1966): 181–193.

Péter, Robert, ed. *General Introduction*, "A Historiography of Freemasonry in the British Isles in Light of Recent Scholarship," in *British Freemasonry, 1717–1813. Volume I: General Introduction and Institutions*. London: Routledge, 2016.

Piatgorsky, A. *Who's Afraid of Freemasons? The Phenomenon of Freemasonry*. London: Harvill, 1997.

Pick, Fred L. and G. Norman Knight. *The Freemason's Pocket Reference Book*. London: Frederick Muller, 1983.

Prescott, Andrew. "The Unlawful Societies Act of 1799." Conference Paper, Canonbury Masonic Research Centre. London, 2000.

Prescott, Andrew. "The Study of Freemasonry as a New Academic Discipline." In *Vrijmetserarij in Nederland*, ed. A. Kroon. Leiden: OVN, 2003.

Radice, F. R. "Reflections on the antiquity of the Order of the Royal Arch." *AQC* 77 (1964): 201–210.

Ramsay, John of Ochtertyre. *Scotland and Scotsmen of the Eighteenth Century: In Two Volumes*. Edinburgh: Blackwood, 1888.

Robbins, Alfred. "Dr. Anderson of the *Constitutions*." *AQC* 23 (1910): 6–34.

Roberts, J. M. *The Mythology of Secret Societies*. London: Secker and Warburg, 1972.

Robertson, James. Personal Letter, Laing MSS II 1769–1770. Reprinted with the permission of the University of Edinburgh Library.

Robison, John. Personal Letter, Laing MSS II 500. Reprinted with the permission of the University of Edinburgh Library.

Robison, John. *Proofs of a Conspiracy Against All the Religions and Governments of Europe, Carried on in the Secret Meetings of the Freemasons,*

Illuminati, and Reading Societies, Collected from Good Authorities. London: Printed for William Creech, and T. Cadell, Junior, and W. Davies, 1797.

Roman Eagle Lodge No. 160 Minute Books. Roman Eagle Masonic Lodge No. 160. Edinburgh, 1785–1810.

Royal Arch Maybole No. 198 Lodge Minutes. Royal Arch Maybole Lodge No. 198. Maybole, 1796–1810.

Ruddiman, Walter, ed. *Caledonian Mercury.* 3 March 1760, No. 5956. Edinburgh, 1760.

Ruddiman, Walter, ed. *Caledonian Mercury.* 2 December 1769, No. 7390. Edinburgh, 1769.

Scanlan, M. D. J. "The Origins of Freemasonry: England." In *Handbook of Freemasonry*, eds. H. Bogdan and J. A. M. Snoek. Leiden: Brill, 2014.

Scoon & Perth Lodge No. 3 Minute Books. Scoon & Perth Masonic Lodge No. 3. Perth, 1725–1810.

Seemungal, Lionel. "The Edinburgh Rebellion 1808–1813." *AQC* 86 (1973): 322–325.

Seggie, J. Stewart. *Annals of the Lodge of Journeymen Masons No. 8.* Edinburgh: printed for the Lodge by Thomas Allan and Sons, 1930.

Select Society. *Resolutions of the Select Society for the Encouragement of Arts, Sciences, Manufactures, and Agriculture.* Edinburgh: n.p., 1755.

Select Society. *Roll of the Members of the Select Society.* Edinburgh: n.p., 1758.

Sher, Richard B. *Church and University in the Scottish Enlightenment.* Edinburgh: Edinburgh University, 1985.

Smellie, William. *Account of the Institution and Progress of the Society of the Antiquaries of Scotland.* Edinburgh: sold at the Museum of the Society and by William Creech, and Thomas Cadell, London, 1782.

Smout, T. C. *A History of the Scottish People, 1560–1830.* London: Fontana, 1998.

Smyth, Jim. "Freemasonry and the United Irishmen." In *The United Irishmen: Republicanism, Radicalism and Rebellion*, ed. Kevin Whelan. Dublin: Lilliput, 1993:168–175.

S. N. Smith, "The So-Called 'Exposures' of Freemasonry of the Mid-Eighteenth Century." *AQC* 56 (1943): 4–36.

Snoek, J. A. M. "Retracing the Lost Secret of a Master Mason." *Acta Macionica* 4 (1994): 5–53.

Snoek, J. A. M. "On the Creation of Masonic Degrees: a Method and its Fruits." In *Western Esotericism and the Science of Religions, Selected Papers Presented at the 17th Congress of the International Association for the History of Religions*, eds. A. Faivre and W. J. Hanegraaff. Leuven: Peeters, 1998:145–190.

Snoek, J. A. M. "The Earliest Development of Masonic Degrees and Rituals: Hamill versus Stevenson." In *The Social Impact of Freemasonry on the Modern Western World*, ed. M. D. J. Scanlan. London: Canonbury Masonic Research Centre, 2002:1–19.

Snoek, J. A. M. "The Evolution of the Hiramic Legend in England and France." *Heredom* 11 (2003): 11–53.

Snoek, J. A. M. *Initiating Women in Freemasonry. The Adoption Rite.* Leiden: Brill, 2012.

Snoek, J. A. M. "The Adoption Rite, its Origins, its Opening up for Women, and its 'Craft' Rituals.'" *JRFF* 4 (2013): 24–43.

Society in Scotland for Propagating Christian Knowledge. *A Short State of the Society in Scotland for Propagating Christian Knowledge.* Edinburgh: printed for William Brown, and sold by him, 1732.

Spater, George. "Introduction: Thomas Paine—Questions for the Historian." In *Citizen of the World: Essays on Thomas Paine*, ed. Ian Dyck. New York: St. Martin's Press, 1988:1–14.

Spencer, N. B. "Exposures and Their Effect on Freemasonry." *AQC* 74 (1961): 142–145.

Speth, G. W. "Scottish Freemasonry Before the Era of Grand Lodges." *AQC* 1 (1886–88): 136–149.

St. Andrew No. 25 Minute Books. St. Andrew Masonic Lodge No. 25. University of St. Andrews, 1725–1810.

St. Mungo's Lodge No. 27 Minute Books. St. Mungo's Masonic Lodge No. 27. Glasgow, 1767–1810.

Stauffer, Vernon. *New England and the Bavarian Illuminati*. New York: n.p., 1918.

Stevenson, David. *The Beggar's Benison: Sex Clubs of Enlightenment Scotland and their Rituals*. East Linton: Tuckwell, 2001.

Stevenson, David. *The First Freemasons: Scotland's Early Lodges and Their Members*. Aberdeen: Aberdeen University, 1988.

Stevenson, David. "James Anderson (1679–1739): Man and Mason." In *Freemasonry on Both Sides of the Atlantic*, eds. R. William Weisberger, Wallace McLeod, and S. Brent Morris. Boulder, CO: East European Monographs; New York: Distributed by Columbia University Press, 2002:199–242.

Stevenson, David. *The Origins of Freemasonry: Scotland's Century 1590–1710*. Cambridge: Cambridge University, 1988.

Stevenson, David. "Four Hundred Years of Freemasonry in Scotland." In *Scottish Historical Review* 9 (2011): 280–295.

Stevenson, John. "Popular Radicalism and Popular Protest." In *Britain and the French Revolution 1789–1815*, ed. Harry T. Dickinson. London: Basil Blackwell, 1989:61–82.

Stewart, C., printer. *An Exposition of the Causes Which Have Produced the Late Dissensions Among the Free Masons of Scotland, Addressed to the Brethren of the Order by the Edinburgh Lodges that Have Found it Necessary to Separate from the Grand Lodge of Scotland*. Edinburgh: printed by C. Stewart, and sold by John Anderson, 1808.

Stewart, A. T. Q. *A Deeper Silence: The Hidden Roots of the United Irish Movement*. London; Boston: Faber and Faber, 1993.

Stewart, T. "European Periodical Literature on Masonic Research: A Review of Two Decades of Achievement." In *Freemasonry on Both Sides of the Atlantic*, eds. R. William Weisberger, Wallace McLeod, and S.

Brent Morris. Boulder, CO: East European Monographs; New York: Distributed by Columbia University Press, 2002:805–936.

Stirling, Amelia H. *A Sketch of Scottish Industrial and Social History*. London: Blackie, 1906.

Szechi, Daniel. *The Jacobites: Britain and Europe 1688–1788*. Manchester: Manchester University, 1994.

Tait, William. "Early Records of the Royal Arch in Ireland." *AQC* 36 (1923): 193–194.

Thomis, Malcolm and Peter Holt. *Threats of Revolution in Britain 1789–1848*. London: Macmillan, 1977.

Thorne, R. G. *The History of Parliament: The House of Commons 1790–1820*. London: Secker and Warburg, 1986.

Torrington, William F, ed. *House of Lords Sessional Papers Session 1789–9*. New York: Oceana, 1974.

Turnbridge, Paul and C. N. Batham. "The Climate of European Freemasonry 1750–1810." *AQC* 83(1970):248–73.

United Grand Lodge of England. *United Grand Lodge of England 1717–1967*. Oxford: Oxford University, 1967.

Vibert, Lionel. "Anderson's Constitutions of 1723." *AQC* 36 (1923): 36–85. Vibert, Lionel. "The Early Freemasonry of England and Scotland." *AQC* 43 (1930): 195–226.

Vieler, Douglas. Commenting on "Politics and Freemasonry in the Eighteenth Century." *AQC* 104 (1991): 43–44.

Waite, Arthur Edward. *A New Encyclopedia of Freemasonry*. London: W. Rider, 1921.

Wallace, Mark C. "Music, Song and Spirits: The Lighter Side of Scottish Freemasonry." *History Scotland* 4 (2004): 38–44.

Wartski, L. D. "Freemasonry and the Early Secret Societies Act." Monograph Compiled and presented by the author for private circulation by the District Grand Lodge of Natal of Antient Free and Accepted Masons of Scotland.

Weinstein, Benjamin. "Popular Constitutionalism and the London Corresponding Society." *Albion* 34 (2002): 37–57.

Wells, Roger. *Insurrection: The British Experience 1795–1803*. Gloucester: Allan Sutton, 1983.

Weisberger, William R., Wallace McLeod, and S. Brent Morris, eds. *Freemasonry on Both Sides of the Atlantic*. Boulder, CO: East European Monographs; New York: Distributed by Columbia University Press, 2002.

Weisberger, William R. ed. "J. T. Desaguliers: Newtonian Experimental Scientist." In *Freemasonry on Both Sides of the Atlantic*, eds. R. William Weisberger, Wallace McLeod, and S. Brent Morris. Boulder, CO: East European Monographs; New York: Distributed by Columbia University Press, 2002:243–278.

Whelan, Kevin. *Fellowship of Freedom: The United Irishmen and 1798*. Cork: Cork University, 1998.

Williamson, Peter. *Williamson's Directory, for the city of Edinburgh, Canongate, Leith, and suburbs, from June 1775, to June 1776*. Edinburgh: printed by and for Peter Williamson, 1775.

White, Terence De Vere. "The Freemasons." In *Secret Societies in Ireland*, ed. Thomas Williams. Dublin: Gill and Macmillan, 1973:46–57.

Williams, T. Desmond, ed. *Secret Societies in Ireland*. Dublin: Gil and Macmillan, 1973.

Williamson, Arthur H. "Number and National Consciousness: The Edinburgh Mathematicians and Scottish Political Culture at the Union of the Crowns." In *Scots and Britons: Scottish Political Thought and the Union of 1603*, ed. Roger A. Mason. Cambridge: Cambridge University, 1994:187–212.

Worts, F. R. "The Development of the Content of Masonry During the Eighteenth Century." *AQC* 78 (1965): 1–15.

Yates. Francis. *The Art of Memory*. London: Routledge and Kegan Paul, 1966.

Yates, Francis. *The Rosicrucian Enlightenment*. London: Routledge and Kegan Paul, 1972.

APPENDICES[1]*

APPENDIX 1:

Occupational Returns for Scottish Lodges

The following occupational returns are taken directly from specified lodge's minutes and records. Each record provides the year in which professions were recorded and the members for that particular year. Occupations are listed in alphabetical order and are followed by the number of men representing the specific trade. For the purposes of classification, tradesmen refer to those occupations that are artisanal, such as wrights, ironmongers, clocksmiths, or merchants; victualler refers to any occupation characterized by food or drink, for example vintners, distillers, or baxters. Activities including writing, conducting, teachers, or government officers are classified as professionals, and gentlemen are defined as those men whom are either referred to as gentlemen or have no occupation associated with their name. Following each list is a summary of all entrants and occupations and a statistical analysis of each of the four major categories as listed above.

No. 1 Mary's Chapel 1736–1751[2]

March, June, September, and December of 1735
82 Members, and of those:

Masons (43)
Glazier (2)
Slater
Plumber
Wright (5)
Baillies (3)

---

1   *The appendices—including court records from the National Archives of Scotland—were transcribed from the original manuscripts and overall remain faithful to the text. In certain instances, however, I edited punctuation to clarify meaning and improve sentence structure. Due to water and fire damage, defacement, and general deterioration, various parts of the documents are illegible. Where appropriate, I have added conjectural emendations.

2   Occupational returns cease in 1751.

Clerk
Collector of the Customs
Baron of Exchequer
Architect
Vintner (3)
Merchant
Smith (2)
Sailor
Writer
Teacher of Math
Marble Cutter
Watchmaker
Gentlemen (14)

Totals
56 Tradesmen
9 Professionals
14 Gentlemen
3 Victualling

1736
Mason (2)
Baillie
Merchant

1737
Baillie
Wright (2)
Merchant
Mason

1738
Baxter
Glover
Surgeon

Merchant (2)
Tailor
Turner
Book Seller
Vintner
Mason

1740
Master of Music (2)
Upholsterer
Baxter(6)
Slater

1741
Writer
Saddler
Gentleman
Book Keeper
Deacon

1742
Wright
Slater
Mason
Writer
Poultry Man

1748
Mason (3)
Wright
Writer
Baxter

1751
Mason

Silk Dyer
Wright (6)
Poultryman (2)
Weaver
Writer
Gentleman
Bookbinder

1752
Wright
Weaver

1753
Wrights (3)
Writer
Gentleman
Bookbinder

1761
Sailor
Merchant (3)
Painter
Gardner
Butler
Flesher (2)
Mason
Drovers (2)
Jeweller
Wright
1762
Hatter
Flesher (4)
Merchant (3)
Gentleman
Student

Printer
Wright
Barber (2)
Glover
Brewer
Shoemaker
Candlemaker
Weaver

1763
Merchant (6)
Wright
Flesher (2)
Cooper
Former
Baxter (3)
Gardner
Mariner
Brewer

1764
Flesher (2)
Wright
Merchant (5)
Sailor (2)
Student
Mason
Writer

1765
Ironsmith
Overseer
Former
Merchant (5)
Shoemaker

Vintner
Officer of Law
Brewer
Founder

1766
Merchant (6)
Goldsmith
Gentleman
Writer (2)
Glazier
Farmer

1767
Writer (3)
Merchant (4)
Surgeon
Shoemaker
Baxter
Glazier
Military
Watchmaker (2)
Student
Printer

1768
Collector of the Customs
Merchant (6)
Writer
Gentleman

1769
Hosier (2)
Gentleman (2)
Merchant (6)

Baxter
Vintner
Grocer
Painter
Seal Cutter
Writer
Tailor
Dyer
Wright
Baxter

Architect (1)	Baillie (5)
Barber (2)	Baron of Exchequer (1)
Baxter (14)	Bookbinder (2)
Bookkeeper (1)	Bookseller (1)
Brewer (3)	Butler (1)
Candlemaker (1)	Clerk (1)
Collector of the Customs (2)	
Cooper (1)	Deacon (1)
Drover (2)	Dyer (1)
Farmer (1)	Flesher (10)
Former (2)	Gardner (2)
Gentleman (22)	Glazier (4)
Glover (2)	Goldsmith (1)
Grocer (1)	Hatter (1)
Hosier (2)	Ironsmith (1)
Jeweller (1)	Marble Cutter (1)
Mariner (1)	Mason (54)
Master of Music (2)	Merchant (48)
Military (1)	Officer of Law (1)
Overseer (1)	Painter (2)
Plumber (1)	Poultryman (2)
Printer (2)	Saddler (1)
Sailor (4)	Seal Cutter (1)

Shoemaker (3)   Silk Dyer (1)
Slater (3)   Smith (2)
Student (3)   Surgeon (2)
Tailor (2)   Teacher (1)
Turner (1)   Upholsterer (1)
Vintner (6)   Watchmaker (3)
Weaver (3)   Wright (24)
Writer (14)

Totals:
Occupations: 60
Entrants: 282

54 Masons
145 Tradesmen
22 Gentlemen
1 Military
36 Professional
24 Victualling

199 Tradesmen (71%)
36 Professional (13%)
24 Victualling (8%)
22 Gentlemen (8%)

No. 1(3) Aberdeen (1736–1751)

1736
Masons (47)
Merchant (3)
Goldsmith
Squarewright (2)
Wright

Surgeon
Shipmaster (3)
Gentleman (46)
Advocates (2)

Totals:
Tradesmen (54%)
Professional (3%)
Gentleman (43%)

25 July 1748
Merchant(3)
Doctor of Grammar
Mason (2)

21 November 1750
Clerk
Writer
Mason (5)

30 November 1751
Wright

Complete Totals:
120 Members
54 Masons
6 Merchants
1 Goldsmith
2 Square Wrights
2 Wrights
1 Surgeon
3 Shipmasters
46 Gentleman
2 Advocates
1 Teacher

1 Writer
1 Clerk

12 Occupations Represented

65 Major Tradesmen
46 Gentlemen
6 Professionals
3 Seafaring

Totals
Tradesmen (54%)
Gentleman (38%)
Professional (5%)
Seafaring (3%)

No. 2 Canongate Kilwinning: 1737–1757

Pre–July 1737
Gentlemen (40)
Merchant (9)
Engraver
Surgeon
Architect
Writer (2)
Military
Writer to the Signet (3)
Bookseller
Painter
Jeweller

13 July 1737
Gentleman (3)

Musician (3)
Surgeon (2)
Merchant

1738
Gentlemen (3)
Merchant (4)
Baillie
Musician
Writer to the Signet
Minister
Baxter
Servant
Vintner
Sword Maker
Dancing Master
Town Treasurer
Writer

1739
Gentleman
Students of Physics (2)
Merchant

1740
Merchant
Gentleman

1741
Gentlemen (4)
Writer (3)
Merchant
Schoolmaster

1742
Gentleman (2)

1744
Students of Physics (2)

1745
Student
Merchant

1747
Advocate (2)
Gentleman

1748
Doctor
Writer

1751
Writer (3)
Surgeon
Merchant (5)
Advocate
Minister

1752
Distiller (3)
Clerk (2)
Military (5)
Writer (12)
Gentleman (15)
Accountant (2)
Merchant (17)
Druggist
Student (4)

Printer
Goldsmith (3)
Teacher (2)
Writing Master
Brewer
Linen Draper
Doctor
Surgeon (4)
Advocate (2)
Minister
Bookseller
Clothier
Wright (2)
Architect (2)
Servant (3)

1753
Minister
Gentleman (6)
Surgeon (3)
Brewer (3)
Merchant (5)
Doctor
Writer
Military (2)
Engineer
Seal Cutter
Accountant
Wright

1754
Servant
Merchant (5)
Writer (3)
Student (10)

Military (3)
Surgeon
Brewer
Carpenter
Advocate
Butler
Gentleman (2)
Coppersmith

1755
Student (5)
Comedian
Wright
Tailor
Gentleman (3)
Merchant (2)
Banker
Writer
Stabler
Jeweller

1756
Student (6)
Writer (2)
Gentleman (3)
Brewer
Musick Master
Merchant
Farmer
Writer to the Signet

1757
Gentleman (7)
Writer
Architect

Military (4)
Student (2)
Advocate (3)
Merchant (2)
Cabinet Maker
Musician
Physician

1758
Gentleman (12)
Builder
Servant
Military (5)
Student (8)
Advocate (2)
Writer (2)
Merchant (2)
Physician
Vintner
Minister
Bookseller
Cooper (2)
Printer

1759
Gentleman (7)
Musician
Servant (2)
Student (5)
Writer (2)
Merchant (2)
Surgeon
Military (8)
Merchant
Linen Draper

1760
Gentleman (5)
Merchant (2)
Student (14)
Deputy
Wright
Organist
Sailor
Brewer
Military

1761
Merchant (4)
Gentleman (6)
Writer (2)
Student (3)
Architect
Goldsmith

1762
Military
Student (11)
Merchant (4)
Writer (5)
Gentleman (6)
Jeweller
Goldsmith

1763
Student (5)
Gentleman (5)
Cabinet Maker
Merchant (5)
Writer (6)
Military

Architect
Postal Worker
Servant

1764
Gentleman (3)
Student (4)
Merchant (4)
Writer (4)
Military

1765
Gentleman (10)
Writer (4)
Merchant (2)
Student (8)
Military

1766
Writer (3)
Merchant (3)
Gentleman (6)
Student (4)

1767
Advocate
Gentleman (2)
Student (6)
Merchant (2)

1768
Student (8)
Merchant (3)
Writer
Gentleman (2)

1769
Merchant (11)
Gentleman (7)
Coach Wright
Student (14)
Military
Writer

1770
Gentleman (5)
Merchant (4)
Writer (2)
Student (12)

Totals
632 Entrants
55 Occupations

273 Professionals (43%)
167 Gentlemen (26%)
145 Tradesmen (23%)
34 Military (6%)
13 Victualling (2%)

Accountant (3)	Advocates (12)
Architect (6)	Baillie (1)
Banker (1)	Baxter (1)
Bookseller (3)	Brewer (7)
Butler (1)	Builder (1)
Cabinet Maker (2)	Carpenter (1)
Clerk (2)	Clothier (1)
Coach Wright (1)	Comedian (1)
Cooper (2)	Coppersmith (1)
Dancing Master (1)	Deputy (1)
Distiller (3)	Doctor (3)

Druggist (1)

Engineer (1)

Engraver (1)

Farmer (1)

Gentlemen (167)

Goldsmith (5)

Jeweller (3)

Linen Draper (2)

Mason (0)

Merchants (103)

Military (34)

Minister (5)

Musician (6)

Music Master (1)

Organist (1)

Painter (1)

Physician (2)

Postal Worker (1)

Printer (2)

Sailor (1)

Schoolmaster (1)

Seal Cutter (1)

Servants (9)

Stabler (1)

Students (134)

Surgeons (13)

Sword Maker (1)

Tailor (1)

Teacher (2)

Town Treasurer (1)

Vintner (2)

Wright (5)

Writers (62)

Writing Master (1)

Writer to the Signet (5)

No. 6 Inverness Occupations: 1736

1736 (31)

Masons: 22

Writers: 3

Sheriff Clerk: 1

Merchants: 1

Masters of Music: 1

Writers to the Signet: 1

Officers of the Excise: 1

Military: 1

23 Major Tradesmen

7 Professionals

1 Military

Totals:
31 Members
8 Occupations
Major Tradesmen (74%)
Professionals (23%)
Military (3%)

No. 8 Journeymen Lodge: 1737–1758[3]

12 October 1737
Merchant (1)

1738
Wright
Masons (12)
Maltman

1739
Merchant
Mason (4)

1740
Mason (2)
Surveyor

5 August 1741
Mason (3)

17 November 1742
Mason (2)

---

3   Where no occupation is listed, it is assumed that the new members are Gentlemen.

18 May 1743
Mason (3)

14 November 1744
Mason

6 February 1745
Mason (2)
Wright
Slater

1747
Mason (7)
Glazier

1748
Mason (8)

1750
Mason (6)

1751
Mason (10)

1753
Mason (13)
Wheelwright (1)
Writer (1)

19 November 1754
Gentleman (3)
Tailor
Painter
Mason (9)

12 November 1755
Mason (19)
Slater

2 February 1756
Gentlemen (6)

6 February 1758
Mason (6)

Totals
129 Entrants
11 Occupations
107 Masons
2 Merchants
1 Painter
1 Tailor
2 Slaters
1 Wheelwright
1 Writer
1 Glazier
2 Wright
1 Surveyor
1 Maltman
9 Gentlemen

117 Major Tradesmen (91%)
9 Gentlemen (7%)
1 Professional (1%)
1 Victualling (1%)

No. 30 Stirling: 1739–1776

1739 (5)
Surgeon
Writer
Merchant
Wigmaker
Shoemaker

1740 (32 Listed; occupations are given,
some are illegible or have no occupation)

Wrights: 2
Copper/Goldsmiths: 2
Writers: 3
Merchants: 9
Wigmakers: 1
Gentlemen: 5
Gardeners: 1
Masons: 3
Tailors: 1
Doctors: 1
Shoemakers: 1

1745: (16)
Gentlemen: 3
Painters: 1
Military: 5
Falconer: 1
Surgeon: 1
Merchant: 1
Writer: 1
Baker: 1
Watchmaker: 1
Servant: 1

1749: (15)
Writers: 3
Fleecemaker: 2
Gentleman: 2
Mason: 3
Plasterer: 1
Merchant: 3
Wright:1

1750 (6)
Merchants: 3
Dyer: 1
Glazier: 1
Mason: 1

1751 (7)
Military: 1
Merchant: 2
Dyer: 1
Masons: 3

1755 (2)
Masons: 1
Wrights: 1

1756 (1)
Writer: 1
Drawer: 1

1757 (7)
Merchants: 2
Mason: 1
Coallyrieve: 2
Brewer: 1
Vintner: 1

1758 (4):
Masons: 2
Gunsmith: 1
Shoemaker: 1

1770 (9)
Ship Carpenter
Mason
Ironsmith
Barber
Merchant
Gunman
Brewer: 2
Dancing Master

1771 (4)
Surgeons: 2
Maltman: 1
Minister: 1
1774 (8) Occupations not listed

1776 (19)
Maltman
Wright
Stockingmaker
Baker
Brewer
Armourer
Mason: 2
Shoemaker
Potioner
Weaver
Slater
Officer of Excise
Cabinetmaker

Armourer: 1
Bakers: 2
Barbers: 1
Brewers: 4
Cabinet Makers: 1
Coallyrieves: 2
Coppersmiths: 1
Dancing Masters: 1
Doctors: 1
Drawers: 1
Dyers: 1
Falconers: 2
Fleece Makers: 1
Gardeners: 1
Gentlemen: 10
Glaziers: 1
Goldsmiths: 1
Gunsmiths: 2
Ironsmiths: 1
Maltmen: 2
Masons: 17
Merchants: 22
Military: 8
Minister: 1
Officers of Excise: 1
Painter: 1
Plasterers: 1
Potioners: 1
Servant: 1
Ship Carpenters: 1
Shoemakers: 4
Slaters: 1
Stocking Makers: 1
Surgeons: 4
Tailors: 1

Vintner: 1
Watchmakers: 1
Weavers: 1
Wigmakers: 2
Wrights: 5
Writers: 9

Entrants: 121
41 Occupations Represented
17 Masons
56 Major Tradesmen
10 Gentlemen
8 Military
9 Victualling
21 Professionals

Major Tradesmen (60%)
Professionals (17%)
Gentlemen (9%)
Victualling (7%)
Military (7%)

No. 47 Ancient Dundee

1745 (16)
Bleachers: 1
Clocksmiths: 1
Founders: 1
Joiners: 1
Masons: 1
Merchants: 6
Officers of Excise: 1
Surgeons: 1

Wigmakers: 1
Wrights: 1
Writers: 1

Totals for 1745:
13 Tradesmen
2 Professional
1 Gentleman

81% Tradesmen
13% Professional
6 % Gentlemen

March 1770 (38)
Accountants: 1
Cordiners: 1
Curriers: 1
Gardeners: 1
Joiners: 3
Mariners: 10
Merchants: 5
Shipmasters: 5
Shoemakers: 3
Smiths: 2
Tailors: 1
Vintners: 1
Wigmakers: 1
Wrights: 2
Writers: 1

Totals for 1770:
20 Tradesmen
15 Seafaring
2 Professional
1 Victualler

53% Tradesman
39% Seafaring
5% Professional
3% Victualling

Complete Totals:
54 Members
22 Occupations
33 Tradesmen (61%)
15 Seafaring (28%)
4 Professional (7%)
1 Victualler (2%)
1 Gentleman (2%)

No. 160 Roman Eagle

1789 (22)
Medical: 17 (77%)
Tradesmen: 2 (9%)
Gentlemen: 2 (9%)
Non-artisan: 1 (5%)

Professional: 82%
Tradesmen: 9%
Gentlemen: 9%

APPENDIX 2:

List of Suspended Lodges

The following list of suspended and expelled lodges is taken from the Grand Lodge of Scotland Minutes, 6 November 1771. All penalties resulted from the failure of lodges to pay dues, annual monies, subscription fees, charitable donations, or any other arrears owed to the Scottish Grand Lodge.

Lodge Extrusion

The Grand Lodge considered those lodges which were still in arrears. The following lodges were Struck from the Roll of the Grand Lodge:

Edinburgh Kilwinning Scots Arms
Perth & Scoon
Dunblane
Bathgate
Forres
Drummond Kilwinning from Greenock
Edinburgh from Dunfermline
Thurso

The following lodges were Suspended:

Montrose Kilwinning

Linlithgow Kilwinning
Leshmahagow
Old Lodge Lanark
Old Lodge Kilmarnock
Dunse
Old Lodge of Peebles
St. Andrew
Bervie
Coltness
Aberdeen Kilwinning
Fort William
Auchterarder
Dysart
Cumberland Kilwinning At Peebles
Inveraray

Cumberland Kilwinning at Inverness
Banff
Dumfries Kilwinning
Hamilton Kilwinning
Campbelltoun
Haddington
Inverkeithing
St. Michaels Dumfries
Stonehaven
Saint Ebbe
Moncur
Kirkcaldy
Castle of Dunbar
St. Regulus Coupar of Fife
Lanark Kilwinning
Annan St. Andrews
Fort George
Irvine Navigation
New Monkland Montrose
Elgin Lodge at Leven
Fort George at Ardersier
St. Leonard Lodge Kinghorn
St. Ayles Lodge Anstruther
Operative Lodge Banff
Wigtoun Kilwinning
Glammis
Eskdale Kilwinning
Nithsdale St Paul's
Hawick
Cambuslang Royal Arch
Rutherglen Royal Arch

The following Lodges Under the Charge of the Provincial Grand Master for the Western District in Scotland were also Suspended and the Grand Secretary is directed to Acquaint him of the same:

Greenock Kilwinning
Royal Arch Glasgow
Thistle Lodge Glasgow
St. Mark's Glasgow

APPENDIX 3:

Grand Lodge of Scotland Officers

The list of Grand Lodge Officers is taken from Grand Lodge of Scotland Minutes, 1736–1800, and the *Jubilee Year Book of the Grand Lodge of Antient Free and Accepted Masons of Scotland*, printed by the Grand Lodge of Scotland (Edinburgh, 2001). Also included are other Grand Offices held, and biographical information as recorded in the *Oxford Dictionary of National Biography: From the Earliest Times to the Year 2000* (2004) and *Williamson's Directory, for the city of Edinburgh, Canongate, Leith, and suburbs, from June 1775, to June 1776* (1775).

Grand Masters

1736: William St Clair of Roslin[4]

1737: George, 3rd Earl of Cromarty[5]

1738: John, 3rd Earl of Kintore

1739: James, 14th Earl of Morton[6]

1740: Thomas, 8th Earl of Strathmore and Kinghorn[7]

1741: Alexander, 5th Earl of Leven and 4th Earl of Melville

1742: William Boyd, 4th Earl of Kilmarnock[8]

1743: James, 5th Earl of Wemyss[9]

1744: James, 8th Earl of Moray

1745: Henry David Erskine , 10th Earl of Buchan[10]

1746: William Nisbet of Dirleton[11]

1747: The Hon. Francis Charteris of Amisfield, afterwards 7th Earl of Wemyss[12]

1748: Hugh Seton of Touch

---

4   (1700–1778) Archer and Golfer, Member of Canongate Kilwinning Lodge

5   (c. 1703–1766) George Mackenzie, Jacobite Army Officer

6   (1702–1768) Natural Philosopher; Grand Master of England, 1740; President of the Royal Society; Foreign member of the Academie Royale des Sciences in Paris

7   (*bap.* 1704, *d.* 1753)

8   (1705–1746) Jacobite army Officer

9   (1699–1756)

10   (1710–1767)

11   Shire Commissioner; Senior Grand Warden, 1743

12   Senior Grand Warden, 1746

1749: Thomas Alexander Erskine, 6th Earl of Kellie[13]

1750: Alexander Montgomerie, 10th Earl of Eglinton[14]

1751: James, Lord Boyd, afterwards 15th Earl of Erroll

1752: George, Lord Drummond, Lord Provost of Edinburgh[15]

1753: Charles Hamilton-Gordon, Advocate[16]

1754: James, Master of Forbes, afterwards 16th Baron Forbes

1755–1756: Sholto Charles, Lord Aberdour afterwards 15th Earl of Morton

1757–1758: Alexander, 6th Earl of Galloway[17]

1759–1760: David, 6th Earl of Leven and 3rd Earl of Melville

1761–1762: Charles, 5th Earl of Elgin and 9th Earl of Kincardine[18]

1763–1764: Thomas, 6th Earl of Kellie

1765–1766: James Stewart, Lord Provost of Edinburgh[19]

1767–1768: George, 8th Earl of Dalhousie[20]

1769–1770: Lieutenant-General James Adolphus Oughton

1771–1772: Patrick, 6th Earl of Dumfries

1773: John, 3rd Duke of Atholl[21]

1774–1775: David Dalrymple, afterwards Lord Hailes[22]

1776–1777: Sir William Forbes of Pitsligo, 6th Baronet

1778–1779: John, 4th Duke of Atholl[23]

1780–1781: Alexander Lindsay, 6th Earl of Balcarres and 23rd Earl of Crawford[24]

1782–1783: David, 11th Earl of Buchan[25]

---

13 (1731–1781) Composer; Grand Master 1763–1764

14 (1723–1769) Politician and Agricultural Improver

15 Junior Grand Warden, 1738

16 Deputy Grand Master, 1752; 1788–1789

17 Grand Master of England, 1757–1761

18 (1766–1841)

19 Deputy Grand Master 1761–62; Senior Grand Warden, 1751

20 (d. 1787)

21 (1729–1774) Politician; Grand Master of England, 1771–1774

22 Deputy Grand Master, 1754; Junior Grand Warden, 1752

23 Grand Master of England, 1775–1781; 1791–1813

24 (1752–1825) Army Officer and Colonial Governor

25 (1743–1829) Antiquary and Political Reformer

1784–1785: George Gordon, Lord Haddo[26]

1786–1787: Francis Charteris, Lord Elcho, afterwards 8th Earl of
Wemyss

1788–1789: Francis, 8th Lord Napier of Merchistoun[27]

1790–1791: George, 16th Earl of Morton

1792–1793: George, 9th Marquis of Huntly, afterwards 5th Duke of
Gordon[28]

1794–1795: William John, 5th Earl of Ancrum, afterwards 6th Marquis of
Lothian[29]

1796–1797: Francis, Lord Doune, afterwards 10th Earl of Moray[30]

1798–1799: Sir James Stirling, 1st Baronet, Lord Provost of Edinburgh[31]

1800–1801: Charles William, Earl of Dalkeith, afterwards 4th Duke of
Buccleuch

Deputy Grand Masters

1736–1745: Captain John Young

1745–1750: Major John Young

1751: Colonel John Young

1752: Charles Hamilton–Gordon

1753: Joseph Williamson[32]

1754: David Dalrymple

1755–1760: George Fraser[33]

1761–1762: James Stewart[34]

1763–1764: Joseph Williamson

1765–1766: Hon. Alexander Gordon

1767–1768: Lord Robert Kerr

---

26 (1764–1791); Deputy Grand Master, 1780
27 (1758–1823) Army Officer
28 (1761–1853)
29 Deputy Grand Master, 1793–1794
30 Deputy Grand Master, 1795
31 (1740–1805) Banker; Lord Provost: 1790–1792, 1794–1796, 1798–1800
32 Deputy Grand Master, 1763–1764
33 Substitute Grand Master, 1752–1754
34 Senior Grand Warden, 1751

1769–1770: Sir William Erskine[35]

1771–1772: Hon. Colonel William Napier

1773–1775: William Barclay[36]

1776–1777: James Boswell

1778–1779: James Murray

1780: Lord Haddo

1781: Francis Charteris, Jr.

1782–1785: Dr. Nathaniel Spens

1786–1787: James, 9th Lord Torpichen

1788–1789: Lord Binning

1790–1792: George, Earl of Erroll

1793–1794: William, Earl of Ancrum

1795: Francis, Lord Viscount Doune

1796–1798: George Ramsay, 9th Earl of Dalhousie[37]

1800: Robert Dundas Saunders

Substitute Grand Masters

1737–1751: John Douglas

1752–1754: George Fraser

1755–1766: Richard Tod[38]

1767–1770: Andrew Allison

1771–1772: Dr. John Cairnie

1773: Richard Tod

1774–1775: James Rannie

1776–1781: Nathaniel Spenser

1782–1783: William Charles Little

1784–1797: Thomas Hay[39]

1798: John Clark

1799–1804: John Clark[40]

---

35 (d.1795) Lieutenant–General of Torrie, Fife; First Baronet

36 Junior Grand Warden, 1771–1772

37 (1770–1838)

38 Substitute Grand Master, 1773

39 Junior Grand Warden, 1782–1783

40 Senior Grand Warden, 1796–1798

Senior Grand Wardens

1736: Sir William Baillie of Lamington[41]

1737: William Congalton

1738: Patrick Lindsay[42]

1739: Henry David, Lord Cardross

1740: Captain Arthur Forbes of Pittencrieff

1741: Sir Andrew Mitchell of Westshore[43]

1742: Sir Robert Dickson of Carberry

1743: William Nisbet of Dirleton

1744: Major John Robertson of Arnock

1745: Alexander Tait[44]

1746: Francis Charteris of Amisfield

1747: Samuel Neilson[45]

1748: John Sinclair[46]

1749: Andrew Hay[47]

1750: Charles Mack[48]

1751: James Stewart[49]

1752: Joseph Williamson

1753: Dr. John Boswell

1754: James Lumsden

1755–1756: Dr. Henry Cunningham

1757–1758: David Ross

1759–1760: Walter Stewart

1761: Captain John Wemyss

1762: Governour John Wemyss

1763–1764: Andrew Alison

---

41 Junior Grand Warden, 1769–1770

42 Junior Grand Warden, 1753

43 Advocate

44 Merchant

45 Deacon of the Masons in Edinburgh

46 Writer in Edinburgh; Junior Grand Warden, 1747

47 Junior Grand Warden, 1746

48 Mason and Deacon of Edinburgh Masons; Junior Grand Warden, 1749

49 Edinburgh Attorney

1765–1766: Sir John Whitford

1767–1768: Alexander Elphinstone

1769–1770: Dr. James Lind

1771–1772: Andrew Balfour

1773: James Boswell

1774–1775: James Geddes

1776–1777: Simon Fraser

1778–1779: George Stewart

1789–1781: Robert Dalzell

1782–1783: Alexander Fergusson

1784–1785: George Gordon

1786–1787: Sir John Sinclair, Bart. Of Stevenson

1788–1791: J. Younger Stewart of Allanbank

1792–1794: Colonel William Douglas Clephan[50]

1795: Sir James Foulis

1796–1798: John Clark

1799–1801: John Trotter

1802–1803: Sir George McKenzie, Bart.

Junior Grand Wardens

1736: Sir Alexander Hope of Kerse[51]

1737: Dr. Charles Alson

1738: George Drummond

1739: Archibald McAulay[52]

1740: David Kennedy[53]

1741: James Colquhoun[54]

1742: Sir John Scott of Ancrum

1743: John Murray of Broughton[55]

---

50 Junior Grand Warden, 1791

51 (1769–1837) Army Officer

52 Lord Provost of Edinburgh

53 Advocate

54 Lord Provost of Edinburgh

55 (1714–1715) Baronet; Also called Secretary Murray, Mr. Evidence Murray; Jacobite Agent and alleged Traitor; Member of Canongate Kilwinning

1744: Thomas Allan[56]

1745: John Brown

1746: Andrew Hay

1747: John Sinclair[57]

1748: James Morie[58]

1749: Charles Mack

1750: Captain James Ogilvie[59]

1751: John Henderson of Leison

1752: David Dalrymple

1753: Patrick Lindsay

1754: Alexander Cunygham[60]

1755–1756: William Budge

1757–1758: William McGhie

1759–1760: Major James Seton

1761–1762: Honourable Alexander Gordon

1763–1764: Alexander Wight[61]

1765–1766: Sir William Forbes

1767–1768: Harry Bethune

1769–1770: William Baillie

1771–1772: William Barclay

1773: Harry Erskine

1774–1775: William Smith

1776–1777: David Maxwell

1778–1779: John Ramsay

1780–1781: William Farquharson

1782–1783: Thomas Hay

1784–1785: William MacKillop

1786–1787: James Home

1788–1789: James Wolfe Murray[62]

56　Dean of Guild

57　Deputy Master of the Lodge Drummond Kilwinning from Greenock

58　Painter in Edinburgh

59　Shipmaster in Leith

60　(1703–1785) Third Baronet; Physician

61　Advocate

62　General James Wolfe

1790: Captain John Sett

1791: Col. William Douglas Clephan

1792–1794: Viscount Francis Doune

1795: Andrew Houston

1796–1798: Robert Moir

1799: A.E. Maitland Gibson

1800–1801: Sir Charles Douglas, Bart. of Kilhead

1737–1800

1736–1752: John MacDougal

1753–1773: Alexander MacDougal

1774–1794: William Mason

1795–1798: Robert Meikle[63]

1799–1811: William Guthrie (joint Secretary with Alexander Laurie, 1810–11)

Grand Treasurers
1737–1800

1736: Dr. John Moncrieff

1737–1754: Thomas Milne

1755–1756: James Ewart

1757–1764: James Hunter

1765–1779: Baillie James Hunter

1780–1783: James Hunter Blair[64]

1784–1800: John Hay

Grand Chaplain
1759–1800

1759–1785: John McClure

1786–1794: James Wright

1795–1805: John Tough, D.D.

---

63   Grand Clerk, 1779–1794
64   Lord Provost of Edinburgh

Grand Clerk
1736–1800

1736–1751: Robert Alison (Archibald Kennedy, Assistant)
1752–1757: James Alison
1758–1765: George Beam[65]
1766–1768: Archibald Megget[66]
1769–1778: David Holt
1779–1794: Robert Meikle
1795–1798: Thomas Sommers (Suspended 5 August 1799)
1799–1836: James Bartram (1821–1836, John Maitland, Assistant)

Grand Officer
1737–1800

1737–1740: Alexander Sinclair
1741–1759: Robert Miller (1757–1759, Thomas Cochran, Assistant)
1760–1767: Thomas Cochran
1768: David Malcolm
    Grand Officer renamed: Grand Tyler, 1769

Grand Tyler[67]
1769–1800

1769–1778: John Bradford
1779–1787: William Henry
1788–1794: Robert Hamilton
1795–1807: William Reid

---

65 Writer in Edinburgh
66 Master of Edinburgh St. Andrews
67 Grand Officer renamed Grand Tyler in 1769

APPENDIX 4:

Grand Lodge of Scotland Minutes Regarding Charter-Granting Privileges

The following minutes are extracted from the Grand Lodge of Scotland records from November 1799 to March 1803. They reveal not only the sense of urgency present among the Grand Officers during the conflict over charter-granting privileges, but also the extent to which the Scottish Grand Lodge relied on the English Grand Officers to assist them in the matter.

25 November 1799

Right Worshipful Brother Inglis Master of St. Luke's Lodge Stated that he had considerable doubts whether under the Act passed in the present Session of Parliament entitled "An Act for the more effective suppression of Societies Established for Seditious and Treasonable purposes," the Grand Lodge had powers to Grant New Charters. He Therefore Moved that a case be made out and laid before The Lord Advocate of Scotland for his opinion and advice upon the Subject. And should His Lordship be of Opinion that the Grand Lodge under the above Act had not Powers to Grant such Charters he moved that the Grand Lodge should Solicit his Lordships assistance in an application to Parliament (should this appear necessary) for remedying this defect as well as for vesting certain Powers in the Grand Lodge which would naturally benefit their poor.

3 February 1800

It was then stated that the committee appointed by the Meeting of 25th November last in compliance with the order of that meeting had directed the Grand Clerk to draw up a Memorial and case which they had laid before the Lord Advocate of Scotland for his opinion respecting the Question whether the Grand Lodge had powers under the late Act of Parliament to Grant Charters of Constitution and Erection and that the Lord Advocate had given a clear opinion that the Grand Lodge had no powers under that Act to Grant New Charters and that it would be necessary to apply to parliament for such alterations of the Law as might appear necessary. And after reading the memorial and case with the opinion of the Lord Advocate there on it was stated by the Right Worshipful Bro. Inglis Master of St. Luke that he as one of the committee appointed for that purpose had waited on the Lord Advocate at the Consultation, that tho his Lordship had not so Expressed in his opinion yet his Lordship had appeared to him and the other Brethren of the Committee that should the Grand Lodge deem an application to Parliament necessary he would most cordially give them every assistance in his power towards obtaining such alterations as might tend to the advantage of the Grand Lodge and the Good of the country.

Brother Inglis therefore moved that full and ample powers should be given to the same Committee to take such steps as they think proper by application to Parliament or otherways for obtaining the great object in view as stated in the case and opinion.

28 February 1800

The Committee having taken into consideration the powers more exclusively vested in them by last Quarterly Communication and concurring that the two great objects anxiously wished to be attained by the Grand Lodge of Scotland are—

1. That the Legislature should recognise their former powers of Grand Charters of Constitution and Erection to new Lodges and

2. That Parliament would be pleased to grant them a *persona standi in judicio* a right regarding which doubts at least are entertained

Resolved:

1, That the only possible mode of accomplishing the ends in view is by endeavouring to obtain the interference of the Legislature in their favor

2, That as the Grand Lodge of England according to the information of the Committee stand in the same predicament as that of Scotland, an application should be made to her thro the present Most Noble Grand Master for their joint and hearty cooperation

3, That the Committee are humbly of opinion that Enactments of the following import attached to any Bill of a public nature which may be passing thro Parliament would completely answer the purposes required

1, And Whereas by An Act passed in the present Session of Parliament being the 39th of his Majesty Intitled "An Act for the more effectual suppression of Societies established for Seditious and Treasonable Purposes" certain exemptions were introduced by that Statute in favor of Societies holden in this kingdom under the denomination of Lodges of Free Masons which should before the passing of the said Act have been usually holden under the said denomination and in conformity to the Rules prevailing among the said Societies of the Free Masons. And Whereas it had been the immemorial usage of the Grand Lodge of England and of Scotland to Grant Charters or Warrants for the Erection of New Lodges, an Ancient Practice which by the enactment in the said Statue before recited they are virtually tho not expressly prohibited from continuing which is the cause of considerable loss to the Charitable Masonic funds thro'out the United Kingdom. Be it enacted by the Kings most Excellent Majesty, by and with the advice and consent of the Lords Spiritual and Temporal and Commons in this Parliament assembled an by the authority of the same, that the said Grand Lodges of England and Scotland respectively shall from and after the passing of this Act be entitled to grant such Charters or Warrants of Erection in favor of new Lodges as they have formerly been in use to do by Ancient usage anything to the contrary in the said Act before referred to notwithstanding Charters or Warrants shall be obliged to comply literally with the Provisions and regulations contained in the foresaid Act under the pains and penalties therein expressed.

2, And Whereas doubts have been entertained of the right of the said Grand Lodges of suing in Courts of Law the Subordinate Lodges holding of them respectively for their accustomed fees, Be it Enacted by authority foresaid in and of an Establishment whose funds are entirely directed to charitable purposes that from and after the passing of this Act the said Grand Lodges of England and Scotland shall be entitled in name of their Treasurer, Secretary, or Clerk for the time or in the name of all or other of the said office bearers to sue the said subordinate Lodges holding of the Grand Lodges respectively for the accustomed and ordinary fees payable by them to procure verdicts and decreets for the same in any of His Majesty's Courts of Law in Great Britain.

3, That the Right Honourable and Most Worshipful Sir James Stirling Baronet Grand Master Mason of Scotland be requested to transmit copies of this Minute and of the Memorial and Case laid before the Lord Advocate and of his Lordship's opinion thereon to the Right Honourable Henry Dundas, His Grace the Duke of Athole Grand Master of the Ancient Fraternity of Free Masons of England, and the Right Honourable The Earl of Dalkeith Grand Master Elect of Scotland, with a copy of this Minute to the Right Honourable The Lord Advocate, in treating their powerful Interest and Support in favour of the proposed measure.

[Signed] James Stirling

8 August 1800

The Grand Clerk having produced the following Letter and the same having been read and considered by the Committee they approved thereof and ordered it to be printed and dispatched to the Lodges in arrear by the Grand Secretary *quam primum* which is as follows—viz.:

"In consequence of the late Act of Parliament respecting Mason Lodges and the Enactments therein contained the Grand Lodge of Scotland considered it their duty to pass several Resolutions regarding the due and proper observance of that Law a copy of these Resolutions they directed to be sent to every Lodge in Scotland holding under the Grand Lodge with a circular letter dated the _____5 day of August 1799 recommending to these lodges instantly to comply with the whole requisites of the Act of Parliament and also with the Resolutions of the Grand Lodge.

The Grand Lodge was happy to see the promptitude with which many of the Lodges have complied not only with the Enactments of the Act of Parliament but also with the Resolutions of the Grand Lodge thereby Evincing their Loyalty and attachment to the laws of the Land and likewise their ready obedience to the Rules and Regulations of the Grand Lodge.

As Several of the Lodges in the Country however, have not yet complied with the resolutions of the Grand Lodge (notwithstanding a second letter has been sent to them) by paying up their arrears and taking out their certificates, and being led to believe that this neglect may have proceeded from a motive of delicacy or inability to discharge those Arrears, The Grand Lodge hereby intimate to such Lodges as are still in arrear that upon proper cause shown they will accept of a reasonable composition for such arrears—Those Lodges therefore that have not yet come foreward are hereby directed to send up a Statement of their situation and circumstances with a list of members entered into their Lodge since last Settlement with the Grand Lodge, and at the same time an offer of what composition the Lodge can afford to give, and should such composition appear reasonable they may depend upon the same being accepted of.

Should this opportunity be neglected and no offer of composition made betwixt and the 10th day of January 1801 the Grand Lodge is determined to send a proper officer thro every Lodge of Scotland that may be in Arrear in order to ascertain not only the circumstances and situation of every Lodge but likewise to know what Lodges are still in Existance in order that a proper Roll may be made up, and none permitted to stand thereon but such as are deserving of the Countenance and protection of the Grand Lodge."

23 January 1801

It was stated to the committee that in terms of the Minute of 28th February last copies of that Minute with copies of the Memorial and Case and the Lord Advocates opinion thereon had been by Sir James Stirling Baronet transmitted to the Right Honorable Henry Dundas, His Grace the Duke of Atholl, The Earl of Dalkeith, and the Lord Advocate with letters from Sir James to each of these Gentlemen, but nothing had been done in consequence thereof—That of late several applications had been made for Charters for new Lodges but situated as the Grand Lodge presently is with regard to the Act of Parliament she has thought it advisable not to grant any—That as Parliament is now met it would be desirable could some steps be taken to attain the objects in view.

The Committee are therefore of opinion that a General Committee of the Grand Lodge should be called to consider of the steps necessary to be adopted for carrying the Minute and Resolutions of the 28th February last into effect, and they therefore appoint said Committee to meet on Wednesday first at one o'clock in Hunters Tavern and that Letters shall be sent to the Earl of Dalkeith Grand Master, Major Dundas Depute Grand Master, and all the other Members of the Committee and that previous thereto, they appoint the Grand Clerk to send Extracts of the whole papers and Minutes relative to the above business to the Depute Grand Master.

11 February 1801

In Consequence of the Appointment of the General Committee of the Grand Lodge of 28 January last the Select Committee waited upon the

Grand Master and Explained to him the purpose of their visit, and after reading to his Lordship the Minutes of the Grand Lodge relative to an application to Parliament for an alteration of the late Act regarding Mason Lodges—The Right Honorable and Most Worshipful The Grand Master approved of the Steps that had already been taken on points so interesting to the Craft, and informed the Committee that he intended to be in London by the first of next month, when he would ... take the earliest opportunity of Communicating with the Duke of Athole Grand Master of the Ancient Fraternity of Free Masons in England, with whom it was his Lordships opinion the Grand Lodge here should by all means endeavour to cooperate in the application to Parliament and that he should likewise make it his business to lay the matter before His Majesties Ministers. In the mean time His Lordship requested to be put in possession of extracts of the whole proceedings of the Grand Lodge relative to the above business which the Committee appointed to the Grand Clerk to transmit to the Grand Master with all convenient dispatch.

3 April 1801

Thereafter the Grand Clerk stated that he had taken it upon him to write to the Grand Master reminding him of his promise to Communicate with his Majesties Ministers regarding the Application to Parliament for an Extension of the Powers of the Grand Lodge with regard to granting Charters and that His Lordship had been pleased to return the following answer:

"Great George Street April 9th 1801—Sir I have never lost sight of the business relative to the application to Parliament to grant more extensive powers to the Grand Lodge of Scotland. But I beg to observe to you that for some time after my arrival in Town it was not very clear who were and who were not his Majesties Ministers and I did not know to whom with propriety to apply. After that period a stop was put to all public business in consequence of the Kings Illness. Until I heard that his Majesty had considerably regained his strength I did not Judge it proper to add any thing to the business that was of necessity to come before him, and I do not think any Minister at liberty to give any Answer to an application of the importance of mine without taking his commands on the subject. I shall now lose no time in bringing the business foreward
I am your obedient servant
[Signed] Dalkeith

3 August 1801

Thereafter a letter was read from the Right Honourable and Most Worshipful The Earl of Dalkeith Grand Master Mason of Scotland which is of the following Tenor Viz.

Dear Sir,

I have received an Answer from Government relative to the Granting further powers to the Grand Lodge of Scotland to this effect "that it is not expedient to allow more Lodges to be established at the present moment." Have the goodness to communicate this information to the person so that it may be laid before the Grand Lodge.

Yours Sincerely,

[Signed] Dalkeith, addressed to Sir James Stirling Baronet, Edinburgh

And a letter likewise read from the Earl of Aboyne renewing his application for a Charter in favour of his Lordship and other officers of the Aberdeen 6th Regiment of North British Militia, together with the Petition from Mr. Fraser of Stricken formerly before the Grand Lodge also Craving a Charter for a lodge to be Erected at Mormond in Aberdeen Shire, which Petition and letter together with that from the Earl of Dalkeith having been considered by the Grand Lodge, they are of opinion that as it is not thought Expedient by the Legislature to allow more Lodges to be established at the present time, and in these circumstances as it would be imprudent to adopt measures that might give offence to the Government by assigning Charters of Dormant lodges to the present applicants, as had been proposed. It was therefore moved by Br. Laurie and Seconded by Right Worshipful Brother Laidlaw that the further consideration of this business should be referred to the Standing Committee with power to them to take such steps as may appear Expedient and to Report.

16 May 1803

It was reported that the Grand Clerk had in consequence of the Recommendation of the Grand Lodge at the Quarterly Communication in February last wrote to the Grand Secretary of England and the following is his letter and Answers thereto:

To Robert Leslie Esq. Secretary to the Grand Lodge of England 10 February 1803.

"Since the passing of the late Act of Parliament respecting Mason Lodges the Grand Lodge of Scotland has uniformly declined to grant any warrants or Charters for holding new Lodges, but now that Peace is restored and those reasons which induced the Legislature to inforce the enactments of that Statute no longer exist hopes have again arisen that the power of granting charters may again be exercised. But as the Grand Lodge of Scotland has always been scrupulously anxious to adhere to the wishes of the Legislation and determined to do nothing inimical to the Interest of the Ancient Grand Lodge of England with whom for so many years she has lived on the happiest terms I am therefore directed to inform you that the Grand Lodge of Scotland proposes to take the opinion of the Kings Counsel hire, whether or not they are at liberty now to resume their former powers of granting warrants for Erecting and Establishing new lodges. Before taking this step they are extremely solicitous to be informed if the most Worshipful the Grand Lodge of England have since the passing of the above Act of Parliament granted any new warrants and whether in consequence of the Peace (and the cause of Alarm now happily done away) they either have resumed or consider themselves entitled to resume their former powers of granting new warrants to Lodges. As every thing is ready for consulting counsel and a great many applications for warrants lying in the Table I hope to be favoured with your answer in course."

[Signed] The Grand Clerk, James Bartram

1st Answer: London 16 February 1803

"We have not granted any Warrant or Charter for holding new Lodges in England but we have found it expedient to transfer old warrants and Nos. granted before the passing of the Act of Parliament, taking care that such old Warrants be first registered with the Clerk of the Peace in the district where the Lodge is to be held pursuant to the terms of the Statutes. I shall communicate your letter to the Grand Lodge at our next meeting and if any thing occurs upon mature consideration I am confident our Right Worshipful Grand Lodge will do everything consistent with their duty and in concert with you Right Worshipful Grand Lodge. I am signed Robert Leslie, GS" addressed to James Bartram Grand Clerk

2nd Answer from Grand Secretary of England addressed to James Bartram Esq. Grand Lodge of Scotland

Grand Lodge of England, 2nd March 1803

I did not fail to lay your valued letter of the 19th February last before the Grand Lodge of England and I am directed to express to you their sincere thanks for the kind and reasonable communication of the steps which you think it advisable to take for the revival of the powers which have been so unhappily suspended. The Grand Lodge of England under the Ancient Constitutions takes a most lively Interest in the measure which has occupied your attention and they have resolved to cooperate with you in the steps that may be thought the most advisable to obtain the end. We who have seen more nearly the unfortunate deviations from the Ancient and pure system of Masonry which led to the Traitorous abuse of its sanctions that compelled the Legislature at length to interfere and regulate the powers under which the Established institutions were to act have been most rigid in the observance of the Rules laid down for our Government. In no instance have we granted a new warrant in England tho we do not conceive ourselves restricted from yielding to any application from abroad. The utmost power that we have exercised in this Kingdom has been that of reviving or transferring warrants that had lately become dormant and this after the ... perusal of the Statute we found ourselves intitled to do.

In consequence of your letter and animated by the same spirit we resolved to make an immediate application to the Right Honourable The Attorney and Solicitor General of the Crown by Memorial to ascertain the point of Law or to pave the way for its repeal if found to be against us. Our most Worshipful Master His Grace the Duke of Athole declares his readiness to take an active part in cooperation with any of your Grand Officers and those of Ireland who may be in London in laying the case before his Majesties Ministers and Soliciting an amendment of the Act as the only legitimate means by which the Ancient Powers can be restored to the Grand Lodges of England, Scotland and Ireland so long happily and inseperately united together. It has however occurred that since this matter first engaged your attention public affairs have become too critical for the agitation of this question at this moment. It has been thought advisable to defer the application to a season of profound Tranquility when every objection on the score of external alarm may be removed. In the propriety of this delay we have no doubt but your will concur with us. We shall hail the return of general repose with anxiety as a season favourable to the aim of our rights and in conjunction with your powerful Grand Lodge and that of Ireland shall exert all our influence to obtain them. By order of the Grand Lodge I am most respectfully Right Wosrhipful Secretary and Brother and yours truly Robert Leslie, Grand Secretary

It was further Reported that the Committee appointed for that purpose had prepared a Memorial and Queries relative to the power of the Grand Lodge to the Grant Charters and likewise with regard to the question respecting the Kilwinning Lodge and the following are Queries put to the Lord Advocate upon both questions viz.

1st Is the above recited Act of Parliament still in force, and if so is it competent and would it be advisable (now that peace is restored and the cause which induced the Legislature to pass said Act no longer exists) for the Grand Lodge of Scotland to resume her former powers of granting charters?"

Should both these questions be answered in the negative

2nd Is the Grand Lodge intitled to assign Charters granted to lodges now dormant as seems to be the practice in England?

3rd Had the Kilwinning Lodge a right to assume to herself the power of granting Charters Knowing as she did that these powers were by St Clair of Roslin vested in the Grand Lodge of Scotland?

4 If the Grand Lodge is found to have the only rights to grant Charters what are the proper steps to be followed for compelling the Kilwinning Lodge to discontinue her assumed power?

Lastly Is it practicable for the Grand Lodge to compell the Kilwinning Lodge and the Lodges Erected to her to return to the bosom and become Members of the Grand Lodge (she being the Head of the Masonic body in Scotland) subject to her laws and regulations and if so what means ought to be adopted to inforce their compliance?

Answer by the Lord Advocate of Scotland to the above Questions—

1st "The Act of Parliament quoted of the 39th of the King ch. 79 is not limited either in its principal or in its enactments to the continuance of the War; and not being in any other shape made temporary nor having been since repealed it of course remains still in force and therefore it is not lawful or competent for the Grand Lodge to grant Charters to new Lodges.

2nd   I am of opinion that it is not competent for the Grand Lodge to transfer the Charters of dormant Lodges to new ones.

3rd   It appears to me that the Kilwinning Lodge had no power to assume to herself the power of granting charters, but as nothing is said in the above act with regard to the authority on control of the Grand Lodge of Scotland or indeed of any other Grand Lodge I am of opinion that Lodges which had met under the authority of the Kilwinning Lodge previous to the passing of the above act must be considered as Lodges of Freemasons and intitled to the privileges of the Act of Parliament.

I do not know that the Grand Lodge of Scotland has ever been recognised as a corporate Body so as to have a persona standi or right of bringing an action before a court of law and therefore I do not know that the Grand Lodge can take any competent steps in its own name, indeed it was determined that a mason lodge had no persona standi ... But if the Grand Lodge will be so good as to furnish me with a list of the Lodges which have been Erected in Scotland either by the Kilwinning Lodge or by any other authority than there own since the passing of the above Act I will direct the proper Magistrates to make inquiry with regard to them and if necessary suppress them.

4   This query is already answered and I am afraid that the Grand Lodge has no means of bringing back the Kilwinning Lodge to obedience but by her own Censures which probably the Kilwinning Lodge will not regard. The opinion of [Signed] C. Hope

St Andrews Square
March 1803

APPENDIX 5:

Grand Lodge Minutes Regarding the Maybole Trial of Sedition

The following minutes are taken from the Grand Lodge of Scotland records.

10 April 1800

The Meeting having been called in consequence of a complaint brought at the instance of The Right Worshipful Quintin McAdam present Master of the Maybole Lodge No. 14 against the office bearers and members of the Royal Arch Lodge Maybole No. 264 complaining of certain irregularities practiced by them—The meeting having taken the matter under their serious consideration Order the Grand Clerk to Serve the said complaint upon the Office Bearers of the said Royal Arch Lodge Maybole No. 264 and appoint them to give in Answers thereto within Ten days from this date and also appoint Two of their Members to attend a Meeting of the Grand Lodge to be held for the purpose on the 24 day of April current in order to answer such questions as many be found necessary to be put to them. The Meeting likewise appoint M. McAdam to attend said Meeting in order to Substantiate the charges set forth by him against the said Lodge, Recommending to both parties on that day to bring foreward such proof as they may judge necessary of the Charge and Exculpation. The committee conceiving that the Grand Lodge in a case of this importance will come to an instant decision.

19 May 1800

Thereafter it was Stated from the Chair that it was usual to read the Minutes of the last Quarterly Communication and take up with business as had been remitted to Committees but at this time the Most Worshipful The Grand Master Moved that the Grand Lodge would dispense with the other business before them and proceed to the Consideration of the Complaint brought at the instance of Quintin McAdam Master of St Johns Lodge Maybole No. 14 against the Royal Arch Lodge Maybole No. 264 as he understood both parties had come to Town in compliance with the order from the Grand Lodge dated 10th April last and he therefore Moved that the Minutes of the Grand Lodge regarding that business should be read which was done accordingly.

The complaint itself was then read and Answers thereto by the Royal Arch Lodge Maybole, and also the complaint formerly exhibited against the said Lodge with the proceedings held thereon before the Grand Lodge. When a debate took place as to the Relevancy of the Charges now brought and after a considerable discussion the Grand Lodge Found that none of the Charges brought against the Members of the Royal Arch Lodge Maybole no. 264 prior to the 6th day of February 1797 the date of the Letter form the Grand Lodge authorising them to hold Mason Meetings were competent to be the subject of Investigation before the Grand Lodge because till that date they were in no shape under their Jurisdiction. But the Grand Lodge Find it Competent for Brother McAdam to prove by witnesses or otherways the charges subsequent to the date of the Letter form the Grand Lodge authorising them to hold meetings under their authority.

Right Worshipful Brother McAdam was thereupon asked if he had any Evidence to adduce in support of the Charges brought when he answered that he had two witnesses to Examine. And William Hamilton Mason in Maybole was accordingly brought foreward but before giving Evidence in the matters in dispute he requested the Grand Lodge to put him upon his oath. The witness was ordered to withdraw when a debate took place upon the propriety of examining him regarding Royal Arch Masonry or Knights Templars, seeing that these degrees of Masonry were not sanctioned or authorised by the Grand Lodge of Scotland and consequently all of the members of the Grand Lodge totally strangers to these orders of Masonry. The Grand Lodge therefore Found that no questions should be put to the witness regarding Royal Arch Masonry or Knights Templars. That the Grand Master should put such questions to him as appeared pertinent to the Matters in dispute, that if any of the members of the Grand Lodge had questions to propose to the witness they should be submitted to the Grand Master and thereafter to be put to the witness if thought competent. And the witness again being brought forth to the Bar and being Solemnly Sworn and Interrogated Depones "That he was a Member of No. 14 – was not expelled form that Lodge. That he was two or three months a member of No. 264, That when he was a member of that Lodge it was opened as No. Blank. That an application was made to the Grand Lodge for a Charter, and that the Lodge had a letter from Brother Sommers then Grand Clerk authorising them to hold Meetings at the time he was a Member. Depones, that he never saw Apprentice,

Fellow Craft, or Master mason entered in the Royal Arch Lodge Maybole that he never saw anything in this Lodge practised in the above three orders different from other Lodges, That he never saw Paines Age of Reason in this Lodge, That he never saw anything Profane or Immoral, or any thing inimical to the Church or State in the Lodge, That he never was in any other Royal Arch or Knights Templar Lodge but the Royal Arch Lodge Maybole no. 264 and all this is truth."

Quintin Stewart Taylor in Maybole being next called on the part of the Complainer but previous to his being Examined he likewise requested to be put upon oath and being Solemnly Sworn and Examined Depones "That he is a Member of the Lodge No. 14 Maybole that he was a Member of the Royal Arch Lodge No. 264 a very short time after they got their Letter from the Grand Lodge but was only present at one meeting after that Letter was obtained. That there was nothing inimical to the Church or State practised in that Lodge so far as he saw while he was a member. That he never say Paines Age of Reason in that Lodge and all this is truth.

Brother McAdam was then asked if he had any further Evidence to be adduced when he answered that he had not.

The Brethren of the Royal Arch Lodge Maybole No. 264 were then asked if they had any Evidence to adduce in Exculpation when they produced certificates from Royal Arch Lodge Ayr and from St Davids Lodge Tarbolton Certifying their good conduct as Masons and also Certificates from the Minister and Elders of the parish Certifying their good conduct as Men and Christians. They also produced a Certificate from Captain Shaw Commander of the Maybole Volunteers testifying that Eighteen of the Members of that Lodge were in his Corps, all of which being read to the Grand Lodge Brother James Gibson Moved that the Charges brought forth against the Royal Arch Lodge Maybole No. 264 had not been proved, that therefore the Grand Lodge should honourlably acquit them thereof, and that the Complainer should be censured for bringing so groundless and vexatious a Charge.

Right Worshipful Brother Inglis Moved an Amendment to the effect that the Grand Lodge should simply find that the Charges against the Royal Arch Lodge had not been proved.

Brother Gibson agreed to withdraw his motion leaving it to the Grand Master to do as he thought proper. The Grand Lodge accordingly adjourned this Meeting till Monday next at 7 o'clock in the evening then to take the business again under consideration and to give their opinion upon the above complaint.

Before Closing the Lodge Right Worshipful Brother Laurie of Cannongate and Leith, Leith and Cannongate said he had a Motion to make which from what had passed tonight, he hoped would meet with the approbation of the Grand Lodge. He therefore Stated "That the Grand Lodge of Scotland Sanctioned the three great orders of Masonry and these alone of Apprentice, Fellow Craft and Master Mason being the Ancient order of St John But understanding that other descriptions of Masons under various Titles had crept into the Country borrowed from other Nations which he conceived to be inconsistent with the purity and true principles of the order. He therefore Moved that the Grand Lodge of Scotland should Expressly prohibit and discharge all Lodges from holding any other Meetings than that of the three orders above described under this Certification that their Charters shall be forfeited *ipso facto* in case of transgression.

26 May 1800

In the Course of calling the Roll a proxy Commission was presented from St Johns Lodge Maybole No. 14 in favor of Brother Thomas Chapman Writer in Edinburgh and Sustained.

The Minutes of the Quarterly Communication of 3 February Minutes of an Open Committee 11 February, Minutes of a Committee of 24 February and Minutes of 28 February all last being read were unanimously approven of.

Thereafter the Grand Lodge of Scotland having taken into their most serious consideration the complaint brought before them at the instance of the Right Worshipful Quintin McAdam Master of St Johns Lodge Maybole No. 14 against the Member of the Royal Arch Lodge No. 264, with the oaths of the witnesses and writings produced; Find that no proof has been adduced tending to Establish improper or unmasonic conduct on the part of the Members of the said Lodge No. 264 posterior to the day on which the Grand Lodge authorised their Meetings under their Sanction, to which period the Complainers proof was limited and therefore acquit the Members of said Lodge therefrom accordingly. Hereby at the same time, testifying their approbation of the said Masonic zeal of the said Brother McAdam, whose information the Grand Lodge are sensible warranted him to make his complaint the subject of discussion and recommend to the Members of the Lodge no. 264 to practise only that simple Masonic conduct alone sanctioned by the Grand Lodge. And further recommending to both Lodge to bury their differences in oblivion and in future to Communicate together in Harmony and Brotherly Love.

The Grand Lodge appoint their Clerk to transmit to each of the above Lodge an Extract of the whole procedure that has taken place upon the above complaint with a copy of the judgement of the Grand Lodge thereon Ordaining the two respective Lodges to Engross in their Minute Books the Judgement of the Grand Lodge upon the said complaint.

Right Wosrhipful Br. Lawrie's motion respecting Royal Arch Masonry and Knights Templars was then taken under consideration when Brother David Wilkie moved that in place of the words "that their charters shall be forfeited ipso faction case of transgression" the following words should be inserted viz. "that the Grand Lodge will most positively proceed on information of an infringement of this express prohibition to censure or to the forfeiture of their charters of the offending Lodge according to the circumstances of any particular case which may be brought before them" And this amendment being agreed to.

The Grand Lodge appoint the above Resolution to be printed and a copy of it sent to every Lodge in Scotland holding under her, and the Substitute Grand Master Committee are appointed to meet for the purpose of drawing up a circular letter to be transmitted along with the above Resolution any five of the said Committee to be a quorum.

2 June 1800

Right Worshipful Brother Laurie moved and it was seconded that an Extraordinary Meeting of the Grand Lodge should be called for the purpose of preparing and drawing up an address to His Majesty Congratulating him on his providential escape from the daring and atrocious attempt on his Sacred Life. The Grand Lodge accordingly request Brother Laurie to wait upon the Grand Master and to State to him that it is the unanimous wish of this meeting that he would call an Extraordinary meeting of the Grand Lodge for the above purpose.

The Substitute Grand Masters Committee are approved to meet of Friday Evening at 7 o'clock in order to frame a circular letter to be sent with the Resolution respecting Royal Arch Masonry.

APPENDIX 6:

Lodge Royal Arch Maybole No. 264
Regarding the Maybole Trial of Sedition

No. 264 Lodge Royal Arch recorded the initial events of the Maybole. Trial of Sedition; the following passages are excerpted from the minute books of No. 198 from 7 August 1799 until 14 July 1800.

7 August 1799

... The Master in the Chair he Informed the Meeting that he had Received A letter from the Substitute Grand Master of Scotland demanding in the name by the Authority of the Most Worshipful the Grand Master us to Send in to Edinburgh the Lodges Charter under Cover to the Grand Secretary. The Above demanded was made in Consequence of a representation given in By Maybole No. 14 Setting forth that we had obtained our Charter by unconstitutional and Illicit means to which are Sent in a Representation only A Copy whereof is lodged in the Chest.

5 September 1799

... in Kilwinning Lodge Room when he and the Depute Master Qualifyed themselves in terms of the Late Act of parliament Intitled an Act for the Suppression of Seditious Societys before Mr. James Hume Esq. Justice of the peace for the Sher. Of Air he then stated to the ... Lodge the Communication from the Substitute Grand Master respecting the Charter they all were of opinion that it was Imprudent to demand the Charter untill we were served with the charges and in every Respect undergone A Registar Tryal but in order to Serve us the Air Killwinning in Conjunction with the Rest agree to grant Certificates in our favour and Send them to the Grand Lodge.

24 October 1799

... the Master in the Chair he Informed the meeting that they were Called together in order to Consider of A Letter which he had received from the Right Worshipful John Clark Substitute Grand Master of the Grand Lodge of Scotland. The Letter being Read and the Contents Investigated the whole of the Brethren Expressed their Surprise at the demand without any Reason being Assigned that might Occasion it at the Same time are all of opinion that when the Charter is sent if they that Instant Cease from being a Lodge and Can neither meet nor Act as Such during its Absence and in Consideration of the great Trouble and Expences that Attended the obtaining it are unwilling to give it up untill Some proper Cause is assigned Whereby the demand Can be made with propriety And also an Equal Valid Authority in its place. After much Consideration on the Subject the whole of the Brethren Came to the following Resolution that our Charter we would not part with upon any pretence whatsoever but in order to Answer the demand of the Most Worshipful the Grand Master as far as Lays in our power do hereby order our Secretary to Make out a True and faithfull Copy of the Charter and Send it to the Grand Master directed to the Grand Secretary but if the Copy of the Charter do not Serve the Grand Lodge we farther Resolve that if the Grand Lodge is pleased to Cause the Grand Clerk to make out a new Charter of the Same date Tenor and Signature of the Copy and Send it to us fuly Compleate we will pay the Expences Attending the making it out and the moment that it comes to hand we will send off to the Grand Lodge the one which we hold. At the Same time order the Secretary to make out a Copy of this Minute and send it along with the Charter.

5 March 1800

... It was stated to the Meeting that the Depute Master had been in Edinburgh and had Conversed with our Proxy Master and understood that our Business would be brought on before the Grand Lodges first Quarterly Communication being the first Monday of May the Lodge being well Aware that desperate attempts would be made Against us in Consideration of which they Considered on the propriety of Sending one of the Brethren to Edinburgh first meeting to attest the Representatives there anent the Statement of facts And answering of Questions that might be put in order to Clear what ever dubious doubts might Remain. The Lodge was of opinion that it would be highly proper that A General Meeting Should be summoned against next Monthly Meeting for that purpose.

April 1800

... the Master in the Chair he Informed the Meeting that it would be highly proper that A petition Should be Sent to the Most Worshipful the Grand Lodge of Scotland praying that they would put a Stop to the present Dispute which still Continues to Rage in Maybole Lodge No. 14 and at the

Same time it would be proper for the Information of the Most Worshipful the Grand Lodge that A Brother Should be Sent there first Quarterly Communication So that Every Information in our power Shall be given to the End that this disagreeable matter might be brought to A Conclusion which was agreed to.

16 April 1800

... the Depute Master in the Chair he Informed the Meeting that he had it in Command from the Right Worshipful Master to Inform them that he had Got A Letter from the Right Worshipful the Grand Clerk of the Grand Lodge of Scotland Inclosing Information to the Lord Lewtenant of Air Shire by Quintin McAdam in Turnberry Also A Copy of the Minute of the Standing Committee of the Grand Lodge in Consequence of Said Information which Minute ordained us to Lodge Answers thereunto with in Ten days from the date thereof which the Right Worshipful had sent of Inclosed to the Grand Lodge. And also to send two of the Members of the Lodge to Attend the Grand Lodge upon the 24th of April Currant in order to Answer what Ever Questions the Grand Lodge might think proper to put the whole of the Papers from the Grand Clerk was produced and read. Accordingly it was moved that Two Brothers should be Appointed to Go to Edinburgh Agreeable to the orders of the Most Worshipful the Grand Lodge of Scotland therefor we do hereby appoint Brother John Andrew our Late Right Worshipful Master and Gilbert Wilson of Eden our Treasurer to attend said Meeting at the time prefixed and then and there to answer such Questions as the Grand Lodge Shall think proper to put. We do hereby grant full power and free Liberty to the before Mentioned brethren in Conjunction with our proxy Master to present any Petition Remonstrance note or Memorial to the Grand Lodge in our behalf as they may See Cause so to do which petition Remonstrance note or Memorial Shall have as full force as if we ourselves were personally present this being Considered as their Lawfull Authority without any Contradiction whatsoever.

26 May 1800

... Brother John Andrew and Gilbert Wilson Stated to the meeting that they had Attended the Grand Lodge of Scotland on the 19th Instant Agreeable to the orders given them Last Quarterly meeting Reports that the Grand Lodge was opened in the Inner Parliament house Sir James

Stirling Grand Master in the Chair the Information to the Lord. Lewt. Of Airshire was read and our answer thereto the Charge being found Irelivant Br. McAdam deserted them but produced other – these Last were Members Allowed to be Sustained And the Tryal proceeded accordingly. Brother McAdam produced as Evidence his Past Worshipful Master Hamilton and Quintin Stewart Both Members of No. 14 they being Solemnly Sworn did Declare that they knew of nothing in our Conduct that was Irregular.

The Evidence being Closed on Br. McAdams part there was produced on our part Certificates from the Provincial Masters of the four Lodges in Air held on the 25th October 1798 Signed by the whole Masters who preceeded Also A Certificate from St Davids Tarbolton No. 174 and from Air Royal Arch No. 220 with Ten Certificates of our officebearers Moral Character and Certificates for Eighteen of our Members who are Volunteers. These were all Read and Consigned into the hands of the Grand officers it was then moved that Br. McAdam and his Lodge Should be past under the highest Censure but the Grand Master not having made up his mind he wished that the motion should be withdrawn untill this night which was Accordingly done.

9 June 1800

... the Master in the Chair he Informed the Meeting that they were Called together In Consequence of him having Received the official Information from the Grand Clerk of the Grand Lodge of Scotland Respecting the Tryal as Narratted in the Last Minute the proceedings being read to the lodge the Master gave orders that they should be Ingrossed in the Book.

14 July 1800

... the Master in the Chair he Informed the Meeting that they were Called together in Consequence of A Circular Letter which he had Received from the Grand Lodge of Scotland Respecting the practising of Any order of Masonry but St Johns viz. Apprentice fellow Craft and Master Mason the letter being Read to the Lodge the Brethren unanimously Expressed their approbation of the Measure and hereby order their Secretary to Transmit Information to the Grand Secretary to Assure the Grand Lodge that we would punctually observe the order.

APPENDIX 7:

National Archives of Scotland: JC26/305
Regarding the Maybole Trial of Sedition

The National Archives of Scotland contain detailed records of the Maybole Trial of Sedition, including the Charges against John Andrew and Robert Ramsay, Declarations and Exculpations of the Accused, and Witness Testimonies. The entire proceedings occur from 30 June 1800 until 17 September 1800.

Criminal Letters/His Majesty's Advocate/Against John Andrew September 1800 Ayr

At Maybole the Thirtieth day of June Eighteen Hundred Years. In consequence of a warrant Granted by John Murdoch Esq. Sheriff Substitute of Ayrshire of date the twenty Eighth of June Current on a petition at the instance of Robert Aiken and James Hume Procurator fiscals of the County of Ayr. John Andrew Shoemaker in Maybole being brought before the said Sheriff and examined Declares that he was born in the Town of Maybole and has resided there the most of his life time. That besides his employment he Kept a private School for about Eighteen Months which he gave up about six weeks ago, That in the year May and seventeen ninety three or May and ninety four to the best of his remembrance he entered as a Mason with the Royal Arch Lodge at Ayr and was raised there to the degree of Master Mason, That he afterwards joined the Maybole Lodge No. 14 and continued therein until when he and some others of the lodge understood that they could be further Instructed in Masonry by some of the Members in St. James's lodge in Newton upon Ayr. That the declarent along with Robert Ramsay right in new yards near Maybole accordingly went and waited upon the Office bearers and some of the members of said St. James's Lodge of Newton, and were instructed by them in some higher points of Masonry than what they Knew before, particularly by Rodger McClellan then Master and present Master of that lodge, which parts were Chair, Arch, Royal Arch and Knight Templar.

That when they returned home several others of the Maybole lodge applied to them to be instructed in the degree above mentioned but they declined to do so until they should have the sanction of William

Hugh Logan Surgeon in Maybole the then Master of the Lodge. That the declarent upon this applied privately to Wm. Logan who told him that if there was nothing wrong in it, and for the Good of Masonry he had no objections to it upon which the declarent gave it as his opinion answering what good it might do he could not say, but he was certain it could do no harm.

Thereupon after this the Declarent had private Meetings with others of the Members of the Loge No. 14. And he and the said Robert Ramsay with the assistance of Wm. Moor an Irishman then weaver in Maybole, John Kelly labourer at New Mills as he thinks, Several Members to be Arch, Royal Arch, and Knights Templars, among whom were William Hamilton Mason and Quintin Stewart Taylor both in Maybole and this was before they got either a letter or a Charter from the Grand Lodge of Scotland. And being shown a Book Titled "Regulations of the Grand Assembly of Knights Templars held at Maybole he Declares That it contains the Rules and regulations of that assembly and all the Minutes of their procedure.

That after they had obtained their letter from Thomas Sommers then Clerk to the Grand Lodge and afterwards a Charter they did raise several of the Members to the Degrees of Arch, Royal Arch, and Knights Templar, but this they did not consider as having been done under their Charter or as having any connection with their Lodge No. 264, And that there are many Members of that Lodge who are not higher then Master Masons and being Interrogated what are the particular Ceremonys or forms that are followed out in making Masons, Arch, Royal Arch and Knights Templars, Declares That they never used any other ceremonys than those by which the declarent and Robert Ramsay were initiated with these degrees by the Master of St. James's Lodge of Newton, but that he considers himself bound by the terms of his own initiation not to reveal any of these Ceremonys, to any person but those who inclined to be initiated therein as he was because he understood himself bound in that manner by an oath he had taken When he was himself initiated which he never saw committed to writing, and which he administered afterwards in the same form and tenor from his memory to those he initiated afterwards, and being interrogated if he could now repeat that oath or the Substance of it, Declares that he thinks he could but would wish to have some time to consult with some of his other Brethren of St. James's Lodge where it was administered to him, whether he is at liberty to divulge it or not, and he would rather on that account wish to decline it at present. And being farther Interrogated whether in these higher orders of Masonry there may be signs, Symbols or materials used of any kind in the Compleating of their Instruction the Same objection to Exhibite and divulge, that he has Stated to the Condescending upon the words of his obligation Declares that he has the very same objections to this one as to the other. Declares that sometime after they had obtained their Charter from the Grand lodge the Declarent and said Robert Ramsay, John McClure Junior Mason in Maybole and some others went to Tarbolton at desire of some of the Members of St Davids Lodge there and initiated a number of the Members the Members into these higher orders of Masonry which he thinks might be the number of eight or Ten, and being Shown a Book Titled "Paine's age of reason" and being asked if he wrote for it to London Declares that he did write to London for it To a Brother he had chose who accordingly sent it to him, and that the cause of his writing for it was His having got a perusal of the Bishop of Landoff's answer to Paine's Age of Reason and having read that Book, he could not understand the Bishop's reasoning till he had seen the book to which it was in answer. That after having said book for sometime in his possession he remembers to have given it to the said Robert Ramsay with instructions to him to read it by himself as he considered it a production of dangerous Consequence to [Illegible] and to return it to him so soon as he had read it, but which he never saw afterwards until he saw it produced in the Grand Lodge of Scotland as he understood by Wm. McAdam at Turnberry.

All which he declares to be truth ...

[Signed] John Andrew

[Signed] William Gordon, witness and John Murdoch

[Signed] William Eaton, witness

Declaration of Robert Ramsay 1800

George by the Grace of God King of Great Britain, France, and Ireland Defender of the faith

To ... our Court of Justiciary, Messengers at Arms our Sheriffs in that part of Conjunctly, and Severally, specially Constitute, Greeting, Whereas it is humbly meant and complained to us by our Right Trust Robert Dundas Esq. of Arniston our Advocate for our Interest upon John Andrew Shoemaker in Maybole And some time Schoolmaster there And

Robert Ramsay Cartwright there That Albeit by the laws of this and of every other well governed Realm, Sedition, As Also, the wickedly and & feloniously administering or causing to be administered unlawful oaths, more especially when such oaths import an obligation not to reveal or discover crimes which it is the duty of every good Citizen and Loyal subject to divulge and bring to light; are crimes of an heinous nature and Severely punishable Yet true it is and of Verity that the said John Andrew and Robert Ramsay above complained on are both or one or other of them guilty actors or art and part of the aforesaid Crime or Crimes In so far as the said John Andrew and Robert Ramsay did under the Shew and pretence of a Meeting for Masonry, Some time in the course of the year One thousand seven hundred and Ninety Six, at Maybole parish of Maybole and County of Ayr; along with others their associates, most of them from Ireland, form themselves into an illegal club or association Styling itself "The Grand Assembly of Knights Templars" or bearing some such name; which club or Association under pretence of initiating into the Ceremonies of Masonry, did admit various persons as Members, and did at said admission perform various ceremonies partly with a view to vilify and undermine the established Religion, and partly to represent the Constitution and Government of the Country As oppressive and Tyrannical; and did with this view oblige those who were admitted Members to take, and did Administer to them an oath binding them among other things "to conceal the Secrets of the Order of Knights Templars, Murder and Treason Not excepted" or an oath of some such import and tendency; more particularly the said John Andrew and Robert Ramsay above complained on or one or other of them being Members of the said Association did at Maybole Aforesaid On the Twenty Second day of August, One thousand Seven hundred and Ninety Six, at a Meeting held by the said illegal Association, and at which The said John Andrew Acted as Master or Preses wickedly and feloniously administer or cause to be administered to Quintin Stewart Taylor [and William Hamilton] an oath or engagement binding him "to conceal and not to reveal or discover the Secrets of the Order of Knights Templars, Murder and Treason Not excepted," Or an oath or engagement of a Similar impart.

Further, the said John Andrews, and Robert Ramsay above complained on, or one or other of them did at Maybole Aforesaid On the seventeenth day of December One thousand seven hundred and Ninety Six or upon one or other of the days of that Month or of the Month of

November immediately preceding or of January in the year one thousand Seven hundred & Ninety Seven immediately following at a Meeting held by the said illegal Association at which the said John Andrew above complained on, Acted as Master, Or Preses, wickedly and feloniously administer Or cause to be administered to William Hamilton Mason in Maybole aforesaid an oath or engagement binding him "to conceal and not to reveal or discover the Secrets of the Order of Knights Templars, Murder and Treason not excepted," Or an Oath Or engagement of similar import.

And the said John Andrews and Robert Ramsay having on the Thirtieth day of June one thousand eight hundred, been brought before John Murdoch Esquire sheriff Substitute of the County of Ayr, did in his presence emit and Sign a Declaration each; Which two Declarations, together with the following writings or papers Viz. A paper or writing entitled "Regulations of the Grand Assembly of Knights Templars held at Maybole," and bearing among the others the subscription of John Andrew on the back thereof. Copy of a letter dated Maybole Ninth January One thousand Seven hundred and Ninety eight, bearing to be addressed to the Grand Secretary of the Grand Lodge of Scotland, and Signed William McFannet. As also, a paper entitled "Charges Against John Andrew and others late Members of Maybole St John's Lodge of Free Masons No. 14 now belonging to the Royal Arch Lodge Maybole No. 264." Together with a printed Copy of a book or pamphlet entitled "The Age of reason, being an investigation of True and fabulous Theology by Thomas Paine" And having the words John Andrews 1796 Maybole in printed letters on the first page of the said Pamphlet; will also be used in evidence Against the said John Andrew and Robert Ramsay ... and will for that purpose in due time be lodged in the hands of the Clerk of the Circuit Court of Justiciary before which they are to be tried that they may have an opportunity of Seeing the same: At least, times and place libelled the aforesaid Crime of Sedition was committed, and the said unlawful Oaths administered or caused to be administered, And the said John Andrew and Robert Ramsay above complained on Respectively, and will for that purpose in due time be lodged in the hands of the Clerk of the Circuit Court of Justiciary before which they are to be tried that they may have an opportunity of Seeing the Same.

At least, times and places libelled the aforesaid crime of Sedition was committed, and the said unlawful Oaths administered, And the said John Andrew and Robert Ramsay are both of them guilty actors or art and part of the aforesaid Crime or Crimes.

All which or part thereof being found proven by the Verdict of an Assize before The Lord Justice General, Lord Justice Clerk, and Lords Commissioners of Justiciary in a Circuit Court of Justiciary to be holden by them or any one or more of their number within the Tolbooth or Criminal Court house of Ayr upon the Seventeenth day of September Next, the said John Andrew and Robert Ramsay above complained upon ought to be punished with the pains of law to deter others from committing the like crimes in all time coming.

Our will is Herefore and we charge you Strictly and Command that incontinent these our letters Seen ye pass and in our Name an Authority lawfully Command and Charge the said John Andrew and Robert Ramsay above complained upon To compear and to come and find Sufficient Caution and Surety acted in the Books of Adjournal That they shall compear before our said Lords in a Circuit of Justiciary to be holden by them or any one or more of their Number within the Tolbooth or Criminal Court House of Ayr upon the said seventeenth day of September Next to come in the hour of cause there to under by the law for the Crimes above mentioned and that under the pain contained in the Acts of Parliament And that ye charge them personally if they can be apprehended and failing thereof at their dwellings and by Open Proclamation at the Market Cross of the head Burgh of the Shire, [Illegible] or other Jurisdiction where they dwell to come and find the said caution and Surety acted in manner foresaid within Six says Next after they are Charged by you thereto under the pain of Rebellion & putting of them to the horn wherein if they faill the said six days Being by gone and the said Caution and Surety not found nor no Intimation made by them to you of the finding thereof That incontinent thereafter ye denounce them our Rebels put them to our horn and escheat and [illegible] bring all their moveable goods and gear to our use for their contempt and disobedience and That ye within fifteen days thereafter cause Registrate these our letters with the Executions thereof in our books of Adjournal conform to the Act of Parliament and if they come and find the said Caution and Surety acted in Manner foresaid and Intimation being always made by them to you of the finding thereof That ye Summon [Document ends here].

Exculpation for John Andrew and Robert Ramsay

At Maybole the thirtieth day of June Eighteen Hundred Years In consequence of a Warrant Granted by John Murdoch Esq. Sheriff Subst. of the

County of Ayr, of date the twenty Eighth of June Current on a petition at the instance of Robert Aiken and James Hume Procurators fiscal of the Country of Ayr, ... Robert Ramsay cart wright in Maybole being brought before the Lord Sheriff Substitute and Examined Declares That he has resided in Maybole for these three years and upwards and lived in Cul-lyzean [Culzean] or the near neighbourhood of it since his Infancy, That about four or five Years past at new year's day last he was admitted a Member of the Maybole Lodge No. 14, to the degree of a Master Mason, That the declarent and John Andrew Shoemaker in Maybole hearing that there was higher degrees of Masonry to be obtained at Ayr they went down and made application to St. James's Newton. That Rodger McClellan Master of that lodge with the assistance of some other of the Brethren raised them to the degree of Arch Royal Arch and Knight Templars, That when they came home some of the Members of the Maybole Lodge No. 14 were de-sireous also to be admitted ... they applied to Dr. Logan in Maybole who was Master of the Maybole Lodge for his authority and particularly for the loan of the cloathing of the lodge as they could not make them with it, That Dr. Logan acquainted them if it was for the Good of Masonry he had no objections that any of the Members of the lodge No. 14 should satisfy themselves and agreed to give or lend them part of the cloathing of the lodge for that purpose. Declares that he was present when William Hamilton Mason and Quintin Stewart Taylor Hugh Niven Mason John McClure Junior Mason all in Maybole & all Members of the Lodge No. 14 of Maybole were admitted to the degrees of Masonry of Arch, Royal Arch, and Knight Templar as aforesaid. That sometime afterwards Dr. Logan discharged them from having any further Meetings and the declarent never was present at any afterwards.

Declares that soon after this the declarent and some others applied to the Grand Lodge of Scotland for a Charter That they first obtained in a letter from Thomas Sommers, Grand Clerk and afterwards a Charter from the Grand Lodge in consequence of which they were instated & Erected into a regular lodge No. 264. Declares That after they obtained said Charter some of the Members of the lodge No. 264 were raised to the higher degrees of Masonry above Mentioned, Declares that some Members belonging to saint Davids Lodge Tarbolton entered with the Maybole Lodge No. 264 and requested the assistance of some of their Members to go to Tarbolton and assist them in going and obtaining the higher degrees of Masonry above mentioned. That the declarent the said

John Andrew and John McClure Junior went to Tarbolton and assisted in initiating several of their Members to these higher Mysteries of Masonry under the authority of their own lodge, the Master, Wardens and whole of the office bearers so far as the declarent recollects were admitted to these higher degrees of Masonry and being Interrogated what are the particular ceremonys in initiating persons to the higher degrees of Masonry above mentioned.

Declares that he does not think himself at liberty to divulge these to any except Brethren of the same degree, and looks upon himself bound to Keep every thing given him as a Mason Secret from an entered apprentice to a Knight Templar, and being Interrogated if there was an oath or obligation administer'd to him & others initiated into the higher degrees or Masonry above mentioned Declared there were.

And being further interrogated if he can recollect and repeat that Oath & obligation or the substance of it Declares that although he can repeat part of it he does not think himself at liberty to do so, or any other part of Masonry for the reason above given, Interrogated if in these higher orders of masonry there are Signs, Symbols or materials used in compleating their instruction, different from the other degrees of Masonry and if so has he any objection to Exhibit or divulge the same, Declares that there are Symbols & signs used in the higher orders of masonry other than that in the lower and that every degree of Masonry has its own distinguishing Signs & Symbols. All of these he chuses to keep secret for the Reason before Assigned, Declares that four or five years ago he got the loan of Paine's Age of reason from John Andrew above mentioned, That he kept it some time in his possession and he thinks he gave it to John McClure in New Daily to take back to Said John Andrew and he never saw it since until it was Shown him this day, all which he declares to be truth.

[Signed] Robert Ramsay John Murdoch
[Signed] William Gordon, witness
William Eaton, Witness

Declaration Against John Andrew 1800

Summon as Assize hereto not exceeding the number of forty five persons Together with such witnesses as best know the verity of the premises whose Names shall be given to you in a list Subscribed the said Complainers All to compear before our said Lords, day and place foresaid. The said persons of Inquest to pass upon the Assize of the said John Andrew and Robert Ramsay to bear, leal and soothfast. Witnessing in so far as they know or shall be asked at them anent the said John Andrew & Robert Ramsay their guiltiness of the Crimes libelled, Ilk Witness and Assizes under the pain of one hundred merks Scots—According to Justice—As ye will answer to us thereupon. The which to do we commit to you full power by these our letters delivering them by you duly executed and indorsed Again to the bearer Given under our signet at Edinburgh the twenty sixth day of August in the fortieth year of our Reign 1800.

[Signed] Ex Deliberatione Dominorum Commissionariorum Justiciaria
Ja: Anderson Dept.

Exculpation for John Andrew and Robert Ramsay
By His Majesty's Advocate

That they are Criminally pursued at the Instance of our Advocate for our Interest for the Crime of Sedition and others in Manner Mentioned in the Criminal libel raised Against them there anent. The diet whereof is fixed before our Lord Justice General, Lord Justice Clerk, and Lord Commissioners of Justiciary in a Circuit Court of Justiciary to be holden by them or any one or more of their Number within the Criminal Courthouse of Ayr to the Seventeenth day of September Instant And that the Complainers have Sundry relevant defences to propose against the said libel for eliding thereof; And also Sundry relevant exceptions and Objections to propose Against the Witnesses and Assizers whereof they will be heavily prejudged by the peremptory diets of the Circuit Court unless remeid be provided thereto As is alledged.

Our will is herefore and we Charge you That on Sight hereof ye pass And in our Name and Authority lawfully summons, warn and Charge such witnesses As best know the verity of the premises whose names shall be given to you in a list Subscribed by the said Complainers, Or either of them, personally, or at their dwelling places, All to compear before our said Lords in a Circuit Court of Juiticiary to be holden by them or any One or More of their Number within the Criminal Court house of Ayr upon the said Seventeenth day of September Instant, in the hour of cause, there to bear, leal and soothfast witnessing in so far as they know or shall be asked at them current the said John _____ Andrew and Robert Ramsay their Innocence and exculpation of the Crimes libelled, Ilk Witness under the pain of One Hundred Merks Scots—According to Justice—As ye will answer to us thereupon. The which to do we commit to you full power by these our letters delivering them by you duly executed and indorsed Again to the bearer Given under our signet at Edinburgh the fifth day of September in the fortieth year of our Reign 1800.

[Signed] Ex Deliberatione Dominorum Commissionariorum Justiciaria

Ja: Anderson Dept.

8. Execution of Witnesses in Criminal Witnesses/The Majesties Advocate Against Andrew & Ramsay

Upon the first day of September Eighteen Hundred years John Blacklock Messenger at Arms passed at Command of Criminal Letters raised at the instance of Robert Dundas Esquire of Arniston His Majesties advocate for his Majesties Interest against John Andrew Shoemaker in Maybole and sometime Schoolmaster there and Robert Ramsay Cartwright there And by Virtue thereof in his majesties name and authority Command-ed and Charged the said John Andrew and Robert Ramsay To Compear and Come and find sufficient Caution and Surety acted in the Books of adjournal that they shall Compear before the Lord Justice General, Lord Justice Clerk and Lords Commissioners of Justiciary in a circuit Court of Justiciary to be holden by them or any one or more of their Number with-in the Tollbooth or Criminal Courthouse of Ayr upon the Seventeenth day of September Current in the hour of Cause thereto underlie the law for the Crimes mentioned in the said Criminal Letters and that within the space under the pains and made Certification as is therein expressed. This I did after the form and tenor of the said Criminal letters in all points which are dated and Signeted at Edinburgh the twenty Sixth day of August last By delivering to the said John Andrew & Robert Ramsay and each of them a full double of the said Letters to the Will with a List of Assizers names & designations that are to pass upon their assize and a list of the Witnesses names and designations that are to be adduced against them with a short Copy by way of charge Subjoined thereto Subserved by me both personally apprehended upon the said first day of September and year foresaid which copies did bear the day and date hereof witnesses name & designations therein insert present thereat & hereto Subscribing

Viz. James Gordon Messenger in Ayr & Wm Hogg Sheriff officer there.
[Signed] James Gordon, Witness   [Signed] John Blacklock
[Signed] William Hog, Witness

Charges read against Andrew & Ramsay

Intran John Andrew Shoemaker in Maybole and Sometime Schoolmaster there and Robert Ramsay Cartwright there. Pannels Indicted and Accused at the instance of His Majesties Advocate for his Majesties Interests of the Crimes of Sedition and administration of unlawful oaths in manner mentioned in the Criminal Lybell raised and prosecuted against them there anent bearing (here record the Criminal Letters).

The libel being read over the panels pled not guilty.

The Lord Justice Clerk having considered the Lybell against the Pannells Finds the same Relevant to infer the pain of Law; but allows the pannells a proof of all facts and circumstances that may tend to exculpate them or alleviate their Guilt, and Remits the Pannells with their lybell as found relelvant to the knowledge of an Assize.

John Clerk Advocate procurator for the Pannels Admitts that the Declarations of the Pannels lybelled on were omitted by them voluntarily and freely, and that they were in their sound mind, and Sober senses at the time.

[Signed] John Clerk

The Procurator for the Pannels concluded his Evidence in Exculpation.

The Advocate Depute Summ'd up the Evidence on the part of the Crown. Wm. Clark Summ'd up the Evidence on the part of the Pannels. The Lord Justice Clerk, charged the Jury:

The Lord Justice Clerk, Ordains the assize instantly to enclose, in this place, and to return their verdict in the same place tomorrow at Eleven O'Clock forenoon, the whole fifteen assizers then to attend, continues the Diet against the panels, and the whole other diets of Court till the same time. And ordains the Pannels in the meantime to be committed to Prison.

Intran John Andrew & Robert Ramsay Pannels Indicted and accused et supra

The persons who past on the Assize of the panels returned the following verdict

At Ayr the seventeenth day of September one thousand eight hundred years—

The above assize having inclosed made choice of the said William Cunningham to be their chancellor an the said Alexander Smith to be their clerk and having considered the Libel raised and pursued at the instance of his Majesty's Advocate for His Majesty against John Andrew & Robert Ramsay Pannels the interlocutor of relevancy thereon pronounced by the Lord Justice Clerk the evidence adduced in proof of the libel and the evidence in exculpation they all in one voice find the facts Lybelled not proven. In witness whereof Their said Chancellor and Clerk have Subscribed these presents in their names and by their appointment place and date aforesaid [Signed] Wm. Cunningham Chancellor, Alex. Smith Clerk

The Lord Justice Clerk In respect of the foregoing verdict Apologizes the Pannels and dismisses them from the Bar.

APPENDIX 8:

Grand Lodge Minutes Regarding Lodge Kilwinning and the Issue of Precedence

The following minutes are excerpted from the Grand Lodge of Scotland records, 2 August 1802 until 4 May 1807.

2 August 1802

The Substitute Grand Master also stated that the Grand Clerk had obtained from Hays Manuscript in the Advocates Library Two Charters or Grants by the Masons of Scotland the first in favor of William St Clair of Roslin appointing him and his heirs to be their Patrons and Judges and Subscribed by William Shaw Master of Work and Several other Masons in Scotland without a date. And the 2nd Charter or Grant dated in 1630 by the Masons of Scotland in favor of Sir William St Clair of Roslin Ratifying and Confirming the former deed and of new Constitution and ordaining the said William St Clair and his heirs to be their Patron Protector and Overseer in all time coming. He further stated that from the above deeds and other information the Grand Clerk had every reason to believe that King James the 2nd vested the sole and compleat right of Hereditary Grand Master in St Clair of Roslin and that it was probable that a deed to that effect might be found were a search made in the Register Office where Grants and deeds of that nature are deposited. That it was well known to the Brethren that the late William St Clair of Roslin had in the 1736 resigned his Hereditary Grand Mastership into the hands of the masons of Scotland regularly Constituted with power to them to elect their own Master in short that he had vested in the Grand Lodge the sole and only right to Grant Charters and regulate in the Craft as he and his predecessors had been in the practice of doing for many centuries—That altho the Kilwinning Lodge attended at Roslins Resignation in 1736 and was one of those lodges who accepted and received the above Resignation, assisted at the Election of the Grand Master and continued to act and vote as Constituent Members of the Grand Lodge as then Established for several years after its constitution yet for some reason or other that Lodge many years ago thought proper to withdraw herself from the protection of the Grand Lodge and has ever since pretended to Consider herself as not bound to pay any respect to the mandate of the Grand Lodge, but in dispute thereof and in contempt of her authority has for many years been in the practice of Granting Charters of Constitution and Erection to new Lodges and in short ... pretending to have an equal right of Granting Charters with the Grand Lodge of Scotland.

Now it must be evident from the above Grants or Charters by the Masons of Scotland as well as by the Grants from the King the St Clairs of Roslin had the Exclusive right of regulating in the Craft and Granting Charters of Constitution and Erection. It cannot be disputed therefore that when St Clair in 1736 Resigned all these powers and privileges in favour of the Grand Lodge the Grand Lodge alone had and now have the only and Exclusive Title to Grant Charters, the more especially as the Kilwinning Lodge (if ever it had a right to Grant Charters which is very much doubted) completely relinquished that right by attending at and actually receiving that resignation acquiescing therein and Continuing to act and vote as a Constituent member of the Grand Lodge for several years after its institution. In these circumstances it is evident that it would be a matter of the greatest importance to the Grand Lodge as well as honourable and advantageous to the Kilwinning Lodge were the Lodges holding of her received into and under the protection of the Grand Lodge of Scotland concurring as we must to do that it would be for the honor, the dignity and the welfare of the Craft in general that Masonry in Scotland should be only practised in the Bosom of the Grand Lodge.

The Substitute Grand Master therefore moved and it was agreed to that upon enquiry it should be found that the Grand Lodge can compel the Kilwinning Lodge to return to her duty as a Constituent Member of the Grand Lodge and in future to desist from granting Charters and other acts and deeds which none but the Grand Lodge herself is intitled to exercise ... with full power and authority to them to make every search and investigation necessary for obtaining such deeds or grants as may tend to ascertain the powers and privileges of the Grand Lodge. To obtain legal advice with regard to these powers and to take such steps in consequence of that advice whereby correspondence or otherways as may appear to them necessary for obtaining the object in view and to report.

1 November 1802

The Substitute Grand Master then stated that in consequence of the Grand Lodge the Grand Clerk had caused a search to be made in the Register Office for Grants or Charters by the King of Scotland in favor of St Clairs of Roslin appointing him Hereditary Grand Master, but nothing of the kind could be found there. The Substitute Grand Master therefore recommended to the Committee appointed upon that business to take what other steps might appear necessary for attaining the objects remitted to them by the Grand Lodge and at same time renewing their powers to that effect which was agreed to.

2 February 1807

The Substitute Grand Master stated that the Grand Lodge had at the Quarterly Communication on the 3rd of November last appointed a committee to open a Communication with the Kilwinning Lodge with powers to ascertain the views of that Lodge and the Demands she might make and to Report the Grounds on which a Reconciliation could be ordained. He submitted to the Grand Lodge that the powers thereby given were too limited and would therefore recommend to the Grand Lodge to invest the Committee formerly named with full and ample powers to meet with a Committee of the Kilwinning Lodge at Edinburgh or any other place to be agreed upon mutually, when every point in dispute between the Grand Lodge and the Kilwinning Lodge might be fully and finally adjusted on the terms that might appear to the respective Committees most for the Honor and advantage of both Lodges, and also to vest powers of the Subcommittee to a smaller number of that Committee who should have the same powers.

The Grand Lodge having considered this matter are of opinion that it will be for the advantage of the Grand Lodge that a reconciliation be brought about between her and the Kilwinning Lodge, and therefore Grant full power and authority to the Committee formerly named to meet with a Committee from the Kilwinning Lodge in Edinburgh or any other place to be mutually agreed upon and finally to arrange and Settle all disputes presently subsisting between the Grand Lodge and the Kilwinning Lodge in the way and manner said Committee may judge most for the Honor, Interest and advantage of the Grand Lodge, with power to said Committee if they deem it necessary to name a Subcommittee of their own number and to invest said Subcommittee with all the powers hereby granted to the Select Committee.

14 February 1807

The Committee having taken into their particular consideration the powers originally vested in them by the Grand Lodge with the additional powers committed to them at last Quarterly Communication and being convinced of the necessity of appointing a small Sub Committee agreeable to these powers for the final settlement of the Existing differences between the Grand Lodge and the Lodge of Kilwinning if such shall be found practicable ... The Select Committee authorised the Grand Secretary and Grand Clerk to take such steps as they may think proper for communicating to the Presiding officers of the Kilwinning Lodge their present proceedings for affording them an opportunity of appointing a small committee for meeting with this Subcommittee and the view of the final arrangement proposed and the Subcommittee is directed to meet from time to time as they may think necessary and to Report their proceedings to this Committee.

4 May 1807

Br. David Wilkies motion regarding Grand Lodge Certificates was taken up and discussed at some length when a motion was made and agreed to that the same be referred to the Standing Committee to investigate the matter and likewise with power to suggest the most proper method to be adopted for compelling the Lodges in arrear to Settle these arrears and to Report against next Quarterly Communication.

Right Worshipful Brown Master of Marys Chapel moved and it was seconded by B. Cunningham one of his Wardens that the powers formerly granted to the committee on the business of Kilwinning were too Exclusive that instead of granting to the committee full powers to arrange and finally settle all differences subsisting between the Grand Lodge and the Kilwinning Lodge, the Committee should only be directed to ascertain the claims of the Kilwinning Lodge and to Report leaving it to the Grand Lodge how far these demands were reasonable.

On the other hand it was contended that the Committee formerly named had acted upon the powers granted them, by opening a correspondence with the Kilwinning Lodge stating the powers given them. That the Kilwinning Lodge had named a Committee with equally ample powers and had agreed to meet the Grand Lodge Committee at Glasgow for the purpose of adjusting all matters. That the respective Committees would have met before this time had it not been for the circumstances that several members of the Kilwinning Committee were obliged to attend the Country Meeting on the 30th ... and the Circuit Court at Ayr on the 2nd. The present motion was considered as intirely irrelevant and the Grand Lodge therefore negatived the same without a division.

APPENDIX 9:

Grand Lodge Minutes Regarding the Masonic Secession

19 June 1807

The Substitute Grand Master stated that the reason of calling the Extraordinary Meeting would be best Explained by the following letter addressed to him as Substitute Grand Master.

Edinburgh 3rd

June 1807

"Right Worshipful Sir

We request you will be pleased to call a meeting of the Grand Lodge any day within twelve or fourteen days from this date in order to make a Scrutiny of the votes given for and against the address moved to His Majesty in the Quarterly Communication of the 4th.

An Answer to this address to Dr. Mitchell ... as requested with your earliest conveniency; and failing such answer in three days from this date we must consider it as a denial to the above request.

We are respectfully
Right Worshipful Sir
Your most humble Servants"

The following is the answer returned by the Substitute Grand Master to the above requisition

Edin. 6 June 1807

"R. Worshipful Sirs,

Though I have great doubts of my right to call such a meeting as you require which I rather think is vested in the Grand Master alone and though I continue decidedly of my former opinion that the demand of a Scrutiny is unconstitutional, conceiving that the Grand Clerk as the legal sworn officer of the Craft is the person who is regularly intitled to declare the state of any vote in the Grand Lodge being of course held from his official siYet notwithstanding the doubt I entertain and the opinion I have expressed the respect which I bear to the subscribers of the letter which

I have had the honor of receiving of 3rd induces me to comply with your request of convening the Grand Lodge for submitting the requisition ... To their consideration and in this view I have fixed Friday the 19th for this special purpose.

The absence of the Grand Clerk from Town and circumstances personal to myself have prevented my appointing an earlier day.

I have the honor to be respectfully
R. Worshipful Sirs
Your obedient and very humble Servant
[Signed] William Inglis
Substitute Grand Master

The above letters having been read the Substitute Grand Master stated that in consequence thereof he had called this meeting and having in his letter above quoted stated his opinion on the subject he left it to the Brethren to determine whether a Scrutiny should or should not be granted.

Br. Mitchell and others insisted that they were intitled to have a Scrutiny. On the other hand it was contended that a Scrutiny could not now be demanded as they had not at the time taken the proper and regular method to intitle them to such scrutiny. But in order to save time and much altercation Br. James Gibson proposed and it was agreed to that the Sense of the meeting should be taken whether there should be a Scrutiny or not leaving all objections to the legality of the votes to be discussed afterwards. It was then proposed that two Brethren should be named to take down the votes when Br. Cunningham of Mays Chapel [was] appointed for that purpose. The names of the Brethren called over and the question put "Scrutiny" or "No Scrutiny." Br. Cunningham and Br. Thomson declared that there were "95 voted no Scrutiny" and "47 voted Scrutiny" making a majority of 48 against the Scrutiny. Whereupon Br. Brown sated that seeing the sense of the meeting so completely against the Scrutiny he for himself would not agitate the question further.

Br. James Gibson then moved the thanks of the Grand Lodge to William Inglis Esq. Substitute Grand Master for his so readily agreeing to call this meeting and likewise for the handsome manner in which he had conducted himself in the Chair throughout this business. This motion having been seconded was unanimously agreed to and the Substitute Grand Master closed the Lodge in proper form.

APPENDIX 10:

Roman Eagle Lodge Minutes Regarding the Masonic Secession

January 1807

The Lodge being regularly constituted agreeable to the rules of the Craft. The Right Worshipful Master Brother Black was sorry to observe to the Lodge, that the Right Worshipful Master Brother Mitchell of the Caledonian Lodge for reasons but Known to himself had usurped our night of meeting he had not only done so by Letting to the individual members of his Lodge, but also by Public advertisement in the Edinburgh Newspapers, the Right Worshipful Master therefore proposed, that the standing Committee of this Lodge which meets the first Friday after every meeting, should draw up a Letter forthwith, send it to the Right Worshipful Master of the Caledonian complaining of the unjustifiable and unbrotherly conduct of their proceedings in holding their public monthly meeting upon the fourth Friday of the month which was well known to be our night for that purpose for the last Seven years and the Right Worshipful Master had no right to, but the Master of the Caledonian and the Lodge under his Charge upon this representation would see the folly and impropriety of their Unmasonic Conduct ... Altho the meeting of this Evening was not very numerous not more than fifty being present owing as before stated to the Caledonians meeting in the same Night, the Brethren were remarkably Genteel and spent the Evening with that harmony and Conviviality which has always Characterised the Roman Eagle Lodge when the R.W. Black was at their head.

February 1807

The Lodge being regularly constituted agreeable to the rules of the Craft the Right Worshipful Brother Black rose to inform the Lodge that a Letter had been sent to the Right Worshipful Brother Mitchell of the Caledonians complaining of the conduct of that Lodge in usurping the night of meeting used by this night of Roman Eagle, and that the Secretary Brother Drummond had received for answer "That the Committee of the Caledonian Lodge having fixed upon that Night for their meeting for certain obvious reasons Known to themselves, and public notice of same having been given in the Edinburgh Newspapers they could not now retract from it." The Right Worshipful Brother Black therefore proposed that a Memorial and Petition be drawn up by the Monthly Committee of this Lodge and presented to the Grand Lodge of Scotland setting forth the unmasonic conduct of the Caledonians and praying the Grand Lodge of Scotland may give orders that the Caledonians shall alter their night of meeting. This met with the hearty concurrence of all present and the Committee was desired to prepair the Memorial and Petition accordingly.

March 1807

The Lodge being Regularly constituted according to the rules of the Craft Right Worshipful Brother Black rose to inform the Brethren that he had personally spoken to Right Worshipful Brother Mitchell of the Caledonians anent their usurpation of the fourth Friday but Right Worshipful Brother Mitchell declin'd giving up that right, he had also to inform the Brethren that the Memorial and Petition in terms of last monthly meeting was now made out by the Committee and would be presented to the Grand Lodge of Scotland without delay. The Lodge express'd their satisfaction to see that the Office Bearers had not been remiss in their duty and requests that the Right Worshipful Brother Black as well as the other office Bearers would use their utmost endeavours with the Grand Lodge to compel the Caledonians to give up the fourth Friday and adopt another night for their meeting, for the honour and dignity of this Lodge Roman Eagle.

February 1808

The Lodge being regularly constituted agreeable to the rules of the craft, Right Worshipful Brother Black informed the Brethren that in obedience to their instructions he had Petitioned and attested to the different Meetings of the Grand Lodge against Dr. John Mitchell of the Caledonians for his usurpation of the Fourth Friday, and he was happy that his Petition was Sustained and the fourth Friday confirmed as the Night of Meeting of the Roman Eagle.

APPENDIX 11:

Grand Lodge of England Minutes Regarding the Masonic Secession

Modern Grand Lodge of England:

6 April 1808

A Communication from the Grand Lodge of Scotland relative to Dr. John Mitchell and the Caledonian Lodge at Edinburgh was read, and the proceedings of certain Individuals who seceded with Dr. Mitchell from the Lodge were stated by the Grand master in the Chair whereupon it was Resolved

That the Thanks of this Grand Lodge be transmitted with all cordiality to the Grand Lodge of Scotland for the above Communication.

That it is absolutely necessary for the welfare of Masonry and for the preservation of the Ancient Landmarks that there be a superintending Power competent to control the proceedings of every acknowledged Lodge. And that the Grand Lodge representing by regular delegation the Will of the whole Craft is the proper and unquestionable depository of such Power.

That it is contrary to the principles of Masonry for any Lodge to publish its Sentiments upon Political Subjects inasmuch as the agitation of any sort of political Question or the discussion of any public affair is strictly forbidden amongst Masons. The Grand Lodge itself though acting for the Interest of the whole Craft not being certifiable for departing from this Rule unless in some case of obvious and extreme necessity.

That this Grand Lodge concurs entirely in the Justice of the opinions which the Grand Lodge of Scotland thought itself bound to enforce, and trusts that no Lodge under the Constitution of England will in any shape countenance resistance to an authority exerted upon Principles universally recognised by all true and faithful Brethren.

23 November 1808

The Acting Grand Master informed the Brethren that he had received a communication from the Grand Lodge of Ireland applauding the Principles professed by this Grand Lodge in its declaration to the Grand Lodge of Scotland and desiring to co-operate with this Grand Lodge in every particular which may support the Authority necessary to be maintained of the representative body of the whole Craft over any individual Lodge. The Grand Lodge of Ireland pledges itself not to countenance or receive as a Brother any person standing under the interdict of the Grand Lodge of England for Masonic transgressions. Thereupon it was

Resolved that the Acting Grand Master be requested to express to the Grand Lodge of Ireland the due sense which this Grand Lodge entertains of so cordial a communication.

Antient Grand Lodge of England:

1 June 1808

Upon reading the proceedings of the Right Worshipful. Grand Lodge of Scotland In the Matter of Complaint and Petition of Bro. Jas. Gibson agst. Bro. John Mitchell late Master of the Caledonian Lodge Edinburgh It was resolved that the Grand Lodge of England relies with Confidence upon the Justice of the Grand Lodge of Scotland in the Statement of their proceeding and Expulsion of Bro. John Mitchell late Master of the Caledonian Lodge Edinburgh and in the exertion of their Authority as founded on the true principles of Masonry universally acknowledged and that the Grand Lodge of England will at all times strenuously exert itself in the Union to long and happily Subsisting between the Grand Lodges of England Scotland and Ireland.

APPENDIX 12:
<hr>

National Archives of Scotland: CS/235/M39/2
Regarding the Masonic Secession

The National Archives of Scotland contains records of the Masonic Secession, including the complaint by Mary's Chapel Lodge against those supporting Dr. Mitchell.

Certificate of [Illegible] Mary's Chapel Lodge 25 March 1809

I Robert [Illegible] Depute Clark of the Peace for the Shire of Edinburgh do hereby certify That there have been lodged with me a certificate upon oath by two of the Members of the mason Lodge called Mary's Chapel Lodge attested by John Ballantyne and Thomas Sommers in terms of an Act of Parliament pass'd in the year seventeen hundred and ninety nine entitl'd "an Act for the more effectual suppression of Societies established for seditious and treasonable purposes; and for better preventing treasonable and seditious practices" Together with their [illegible] of said Lodge its usual times and places of meeting and a list of the attending Members to be recorded in terms of the said Act as witness my [illegible] at Edinburgh this twenty fifth day of March eighteen hundred and nine years.

George by the Grace of God of the United Kingdom of Great Britain and Ireland King and defender of the Faith

Messenger at arms our Sheriffs in that part [illegible] specially constituted Greetings whereas It is humbly meant and shown to us by [Illegible] William Wilkie Master, David Pitcairn Depute Master, and James Thomason and Joseph Deas Wardens of the Free Mason Lodge called Edinburgh Mary's Chapel holding of the Grand Lodge of Scotland, for ourselves and the whole other Members of said Lodge, That it is a fundamental and fixed principle amongst all regular Free Mason Lodges in this Country that they shall at no time enter upon or discuss any political subject regarding either church or State and this restriction is now also made apart of the law of the Kingdom, by an act of Parliament passed the Twelfth day of July Seventeen hundred and ninety nine which specially Statutes and Declares That from and after that date no Mason Lodge in Scotland shall be allowed to meet buy on the express condition that two of the Members of each Lodge do annually make oath in presence of a Justice of Peace that they continue to meet for the purposes of Free Masonry only. Notwithstanding these wise and salutary laws, both of the Legislature and the Grand Lodge of Scotland as well as certain instructions given and obligations come under at admission into the Craft (which cannot be explained). Doctor John Mitchell Physician in Edinburgh took upon him at the quarterly communication of the Grand Lodge in May Eighteen hundred and seven to make a motion to address us for our recent attention to the interests of our Religion, which however both poor its spirit and sentiments was neither more nor less than a complementary address to us for our late dismissing our late ministers and chusing our present ones in their stead. This address was opposed on the simple but solid ground that it was completely political and therefore, as such totally unconstitutional in a freemason lodges. After a great deal of altercation by Dr. Mitchell and his associates, the matter was put to a vote, as the easiest way of getting quit of so improper a discussion when the motion for the proposed address was negatived. It might then have reasonably been expected of a person of Dr. Mitchell's Education and experience, that, as he was Master of the Caledonian Lodge and had a good example to shew, he would have endeavoured to make amends for his fault and by wise and constitutional means endeavoured to heal the breach which his own imprudence had nearly made, and shewn by his future conduct that he was a good mason and wished to cultivate that harmony and brotherly love which has for many ages adorned the fraternity. Instead of this however Dr. Mitchell and a few associates contrived by every artifice and every scheme in their power to stir up mischief through the whole craft in Scotland in general and to create commotions and divisions amongst the Edinburgh Lodges in particular.

And having even proceeded the length to promote rebellion in the Caledonian Lodge (of which he was then Master) against all Masonic authority in this country and entirely to secede from the Grand Lodge from which he had obtained a charter making him bound to abide by all laws made or to be made by the Grand Lodge, and under which his Lodges was solemnly consecrated, a complaint was at length presented to the Grand Lodge against him for various improper acts but particularly for advising and instigating a rebellion in the Caledonian Lodge against the power and authority of the Grand Lodge, a good deal of procedure was had therein and a proof adduced on both sides, on advising all which (on printed statements) the Grand Lodge in one of the fullest meetings ever held within its walls, pronounced (Seventh March Eighteen hundred and eight) a decision finding Dr. Mitchell was guilty of endeavouring to Seduce the Caledonian Lodge from their allegiance to the Grand Lodge of Scotland, and hold masonic meetings independent of its authority, and in defence of its express orders "that he was likewise guilty of printing and publishing a pamphlet or letter containing matter highly injurious to the character and dignity of the Grand Lodge and upon the whole that the conduct of Brother Mitchell has been in an eminent degree derogatory to the honor and prejudicial to the interests of masonry."

The Grand Lodge by the same occasion therefore <u>Suspended</u> Dr. Mitchell <u>sine die</u> from all Masonic priviledges and declared he should not be reponed till he made a regular application at a Quarterly communication previous to the communication at which the same was to be taken up. This sentence which only Suspended Dr. Mitchell till he made a regular application expressive of his regret for what he had done, and wishing to be reponed, was assuredly very lenient. But in place of having the effect which it ought to have had on Dr. Mitchell and his adherents they immediately grew worse and worse—instantly met and openly declared that they threw off all allegiance to the Grand Lodge—published their resolutions and actually held a public meeting in defiance of the Grand Lodge's authority. It is much satisfaction however to know that the proceedings of the Grand Lodge in the whole of this business which were sent to the Grand Lodges of England and Ireland, have been (as they have communicated) approved of in every particular in the most unqualified manner by these high authorities. Of this date (Second day of May Eighteen hundred and eight) Doctor Mitchell and certain of his adherents were accordingly expelled from all masonic privileges. This much for the information of our Lords of Council and Session and in explanation of the nature of this contest and its consequences. The complainers now complain of certain other masons calling themselves members of their Lodge of Mary's Chapel and prayed for an Interdict against their holding any Masonic meetings either now or afterwards.

Dr. Mitchell having carried his seditious and rebellious principles against the authority of the Grand Lodge into the complainers said Lodge, he there got certain devotees, who like himself resolved to Secede from the Grand Lodge, and hold separate and Schismatical meetings in defiance of its powers and authority.

Part of these persons are John Brown, Samuel Cunningham, John Weir, and John Murray, the first calling himself Master, the second Depute

Master and the third and fourth Wardens of Marys Chapel Lodge and who tho' all of them were expelled by the Grand Lodge on the fourth day of July last from all Masonic privileges have taken it upon them publicly to advertise a meeting this Evening. The Complainers therefore applied to our said Lords for an Interdict against the said John Brown, Samuel Cunningham, John Weir and John Murray and all their other pretended office Bearers and Members of thief pretended Lodge from meeting or holding pretended Masonic meetings either now or in the future, and that for the following among other reasons.

Primo (vide Resolutions of the Grand Lodge of England page fifth of minutes Second day of May Eighteen hundred and eight) "It is absolutely necessary for the welfare of Masonry and for the preservation of the Ancient Landmarks that there be a superintending Power competent to control the proceedings of every acknowledged Lodge. And that the Grand Lodge representing by regular delegation the Will of the whole Craft is the proper and unquestionable depository of such Power."

Secundo. Both the law of the Country, and the special laws of the Grand Lodge, as well as the Charters issued by it, Expressly prohibit all separate and Schismatical mason meetings by any persons whatever, except such as are authorised by and conform to the regulations of the Grand Lodge.

Tertio. The said John Brown, Samuel Cunningham, John Weir and John Murray are expelled by the Grand Lodge (vide Page Eighth of minute dated fourth day of July Eighteen hundred and eight) from all masonic privileges within Scotland.

And Quarto. It was therefore submitted as manifest that all such meetings as are here attempted are a direct violation of the Statute law of the Nation, as well as a gross Infringement of the laws and regulations of the Grand Lodge, and are further highly injurious to the Regular Lodge of Mary's Chapel of which the Complainers are the only legal office bearers holding of, and acknowledged by the Grand Lodge. Therefore and for other reasons to be proposed at discussing the complainers beseeched our said Lords for Letters of Suspension and Interdict against the said John Brown, Samuel Cunningham, John Weir and John Murray and all other office Bearers of their pretended Lodge and others their adherents from holding any masonic meetings whatever within Scotland so long as they are expelled from Masonic priviledges and do not adhere to and hold of the Grand Lodge. Nevertheless the complainers have instantly found sufficient caution acted in the Books of our council and session for fulfilling and obtempering whatever judgement shall be given by our said Lords of Council and Session against them. In case any such be upon discussing the reasons hereof and also for payment of whatever sum our said Lords shall please modify in case of wrongous Suspending. Our Will is therefore and we charge ye lawfully summon, warn and charge the said John Brown, Samuel Cunningham, John Weir and John Murray personally or at their respective dwelling places To compear before the Lords of our Council and Session At Edinburgh or where it shall happen them to be for the time the Twenty fourth day of February next in the hour of cause with continuation of days to answer at the instance of the said complainers in the forsaid matter and to hear and see the same haill effect and execution thereof simpliciter suspended upon the said complainers for the reasons and causes forsaid.

[Illegible] We and the said Lords have expressed the same haill effect and execution thereof with all that has followed or may follow thereupon for the reasons and causes forsaid in the meantime while the Third day of March next that the verity may be known Because Alexander Laurie Bookseller in Edinburgh has become Cautioner for the Complainers as ye will answer to us thereupon. The which to [Illegible] ommitt to you our full power by these our Letters delivering them by you duly assented and indorsed again to the Bearer Given under our Signet At Edinburgh the Eighth day of November In the Forty ninth year of our Reign 1808.

TABLES

Table 2.1. Total Number of Occupations for No. 47, 1745 and 1770

	1745	1770
Tradesmen[1]	9	11
Professional[2]	2	2
Seafaring[3]	0	2
Victualling[4]	0	1
Gentlemen[5]	1	0

Table 3.1. Number of Scottish Lodges 1736–1800[6]

	1736	1750	1765	1785	1800
Edinburgh	6	11	15	19	20
Provincial	43	76	127	204	254
Colonial/Abroad	0	1	13	22	31
Military	0	3	12	21	25
TOTAL	49	91	168	267	330

1   Tradesmen refer to all major distributive trades, for example shoemakers, smiths, and slaters.
2   Professionals are defined as those men working in completely non-operative trades such as writers and clerks.
3   Seafarers include shipmasters and sailors.
4   For example, baxters, vintners, and brewers.
5   Gentlemen are propertied or landed gentry.
6   The figures are taken from George Draffen, *Scottish Masonic Records 1736–1950: A List of All the Lodges at Home and Abroad* (Edinburgh, 1950). The Edinburgh category includes only those lodges in the city of Edinburgh.

Table 3.2. Scottish Masonic Districts and Lodges, 1747

District–Edinburgh City and Midlothian: Mary's Chapel, Edinburgh Kilwinning, Canongate Kilwinning, Leith Kilwinning, Canongate & Leith, Leith & Canongate, Journeymen, Dalkeith Kilwinning, Drummond Kilwinning from Greenock, Edinburgh from Dunfermline, Vernon Kilwinning, Lodge of Holyrood House, Scots Lodge in Canongate
Overseers: Grand Master, Deputy Grand Master, Substitute Grand Master

District 2–Glasgow City, North Ayrshire, North & South Lanarkshire, East & West Dunbartonshire, Inverclyde, Argylle and Bute, East Renfrewshire, Renfrewshire: Kilwinning, Lodge of Glasgow St. John, Glasgow Kilwinning, Old St. John, St. John Kilwinning, Lodge of Glasgow St. Mungo, Hamilton, Greenock Kilwinning, Dumbarton Kilwinning, Coltness, Kilbride
Overseer: Doctor Mullison

District 3–Perth and Kinross: Perth & Scoon, Dunkirk, Crieff, Auchterarder
Overseer: Gideon Shaw

District 4–South Ayrshire, Dumfries, Galloway: Maybole, Kirkcudbright
Overseer: Collector Malison

District 5–Stirling, Falkirk, West Lothian: Torpichen Kilwinning, Falkirk, Stirling, Bathgate, Linlithgow, Dunblane
Overseer: [Illegible] Hope of Carse

District 6–Fife: Coupar of Fife, St Andrews, Dunfermline, Falkland, Dysart
Overseer: Mr. Melville of Balyartie

District 7–Aberdeen City, Aberdeenshire, Dundee City, Angus: Montrose, Bervie, Operative Lodge Dundee, Ancient Lodge Dundee, Aberdeen
Overseer: Ross Thomson or John Cumming

District 8–Scottish Borders: Dunse, Old & New Peebles, Selkirk
Overseer: John Murray

District 9–Inverness, Moray and The Highlands: Old Inverness, St. Andrews Inverness, Forres, Fort William, Kilmolymock, Cumberland Kilwinning, Duke of Norfolk Lodge
Overseer: John Bailly, Writer to the Signet

District 10–Orkney: Kirkwall, Orkney, Thurso
Overseer: William Budge, Writer to the Signet

Table 3.3. Scottish Masonic Districts and Lodges, 1756

District 1–Inverness, Moray, and The Highlands: Old Inverness, St. Andrews Inverness, Cumberland Kilwinning, Inverness, Kilmolymock, Dyke, Forbes, Huntly, Banff
Provincial Grand Master: Sir William Dunbar

District 2–Aberdeen City, Dundee City, and Angus: Peterhead, Aberdeen, St. Machar, Bervie, Montrose, Ancient Dundee, Operative Dundee
Provincial Grand Master: David Dalrymple, Advocate

District 3–Fife: St. Andrew, Cupar of Fife, Falkland, Dysart, Inverkeithing, Dunfermline
Provincial Grand Master: John Cunningham the Younger

District 4–Scottish Borders: Haddington, Selkirk, Old Lodge of Peebles, Cumberland Kilwinning, Peebles, Kelso
Provincial Grand Master: James Gidderdale, Esq., Collector of Excise at Kelso

District 5–Glasgow City, East and West Dunbartonshire, North and South Lanarkshire: Kirkintilloch, Glasgow Kilwinning, Glasgow St. Mungo, Argyle Lodge Glasgow, Royal Arch Glasgow, Greenock Hamilton, Lanark
Provincial Grand Master: Archibald Hamilton

District 6–Dumfries and Galloway: Dumfries Kilwinning, Journeymen Lodge of Dumfries, St. Michael Dumfries, Kirkcudbright
Provincial Grand Master: Andrew Crosbie, Esq.

Table 3. 4. Districts According to George Draffen's *Scottish Masonic Records*

District	Date
Metropolitan	1736
Glasgow City	7 February 1739[7]
Stirlingshire	6 February 1745
Fifeshire and Kinross	7 August 1747
Invernesshire	13 August 1747
Caithness	11 November 1747[8]
Peebles and Selkirk	1747
Wigtoun and Kircudbright	1747
Orkney and Zetland	1747
Dumfriesshire	2 February 1756
West India Islands	1769
Jamaica	1771
Ayrshire	1792
Lanarkshire Upper Ward	4 May 1801
Argyll and the Isles	1801
Banffshire	1801

---

7   Glasgow City is never specifically mentioned; Draffen likely is referring to the Western District.

8   Caithness District is never specifically mentioned in the Grand Lodge minutes.

Table 3.5. New Lodges per District, 1736–1800

	1736–50	1751–65	1766–85	1786–1800
Edinburgh[9]	16	6	5	2
Western Lodges	22	12	24	17
Perth & Kinross	5	2	4	3
Dumfries & Galloway	8	6	21	9
Stirling	6	4	3	5
Fife	5	8	4	2
Aberdeen & Angus	6	9	11	5
Scottish Borders	5	3	3	1
Highlands	11	5	5	5
Orkney & Shetland	2	1	0	1
Western Isles	0	0	1	0
Un–located	1	0	0	0
TOTAL	87	56	81	50

---

9   For the analysis of the Districts, Edinburgh includes those lodges in Midlothian.

Table 3.6. Occupations of Provincial Masons

	Major Trades	Professional	Gentlemen
Aberdeen	57	5	38
Inverness	77	23	0
Stirling	74	17	9
Dundee	91	7	2

Table 3.7. Occupations of Edinburgh Masons

	Major Trades	Professional	Gentlemen
Mary's Chapel	79	13	8
Canongate Kilwinning	31	43	26
Journeymen	92	1	7
Roman Eagle	9	82	9

FIGURES

Figure 2.1. Dundee Recruitment Patterns, 1745

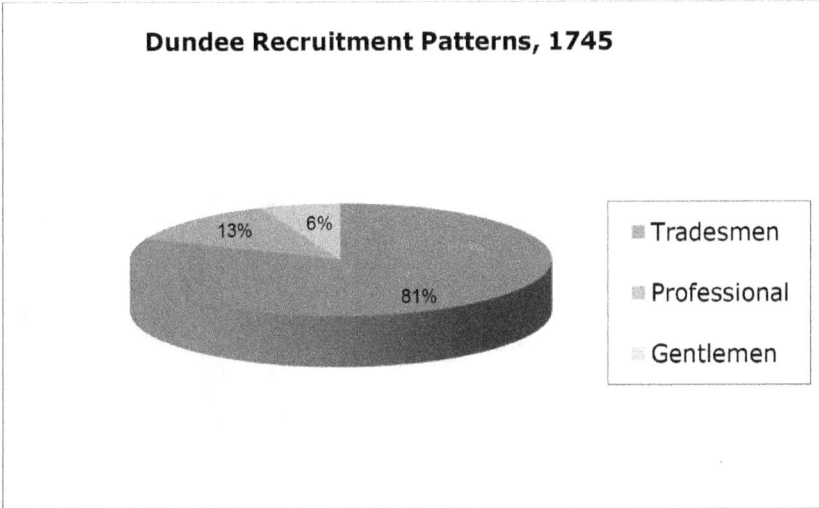

Dundee Recruitment Patterns, 1745

13% 6%
81%

Tradesmen
Professional
Gentlemen

Figure 2.2. Dundee Recruitment Patterns, 1770

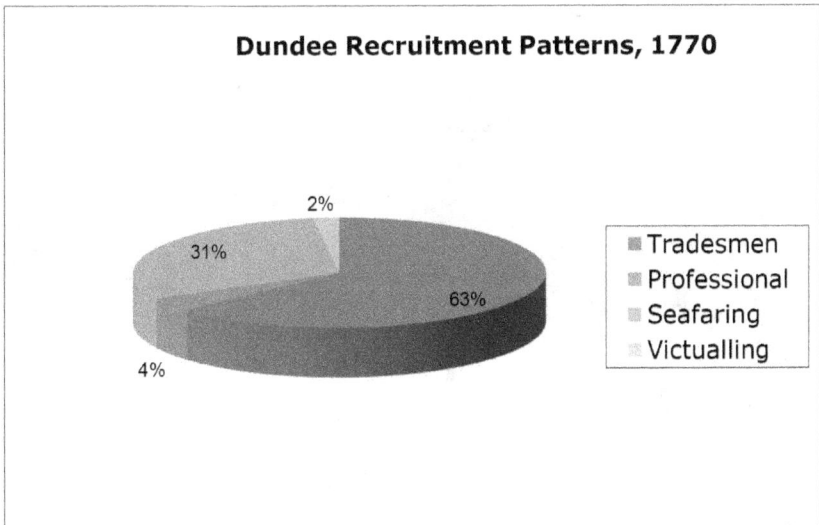

Dundee Recruitment Patterns, 1770

2%
31%
63%
4%

Tradesmen
Professional
Seafaring
Victualling

Figure 3.1. Regional Comparison of Scottish Lodges, 1736–1800[1]

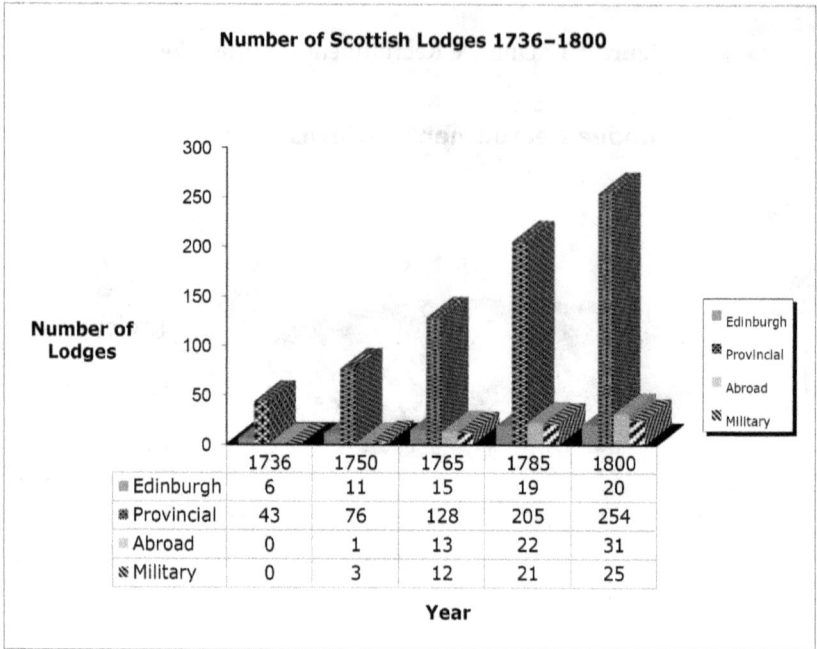

Number of Scottish Lodges 1736–1800

	1736	1750	1765	1785	1800
Edinburgh	6	11	15	19	20
Provincial	43	76	128	205	254
Abroad	0	1	13	22	31
Military	0	3	12	21	25

Figure 3.2. New Lodges per District, 1736–1750

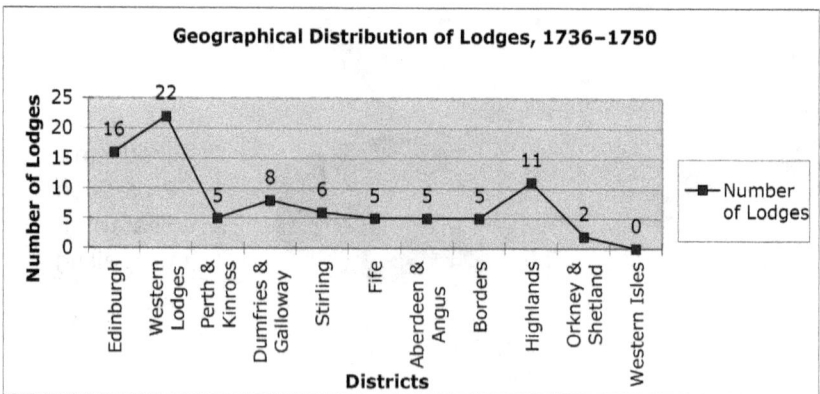

Geographical Distribution of Lodges, 1736–1750

---

1   The Edinburgh category only includes lodges located in the city.

Figure 3.3. New Lodges per District, 1751–1765

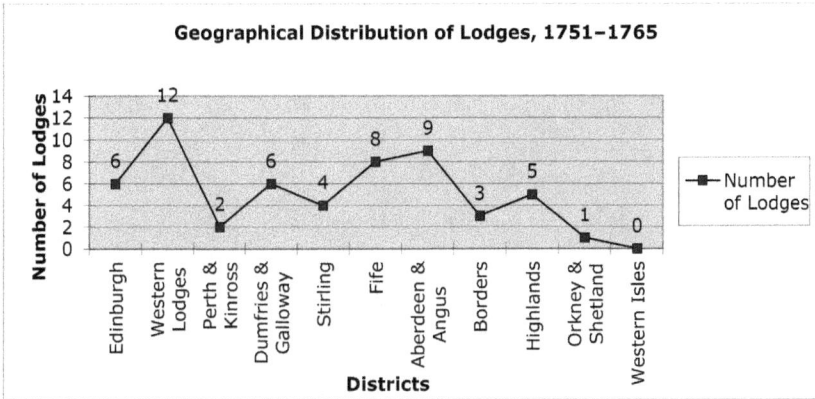

Geographical Distribution of Lodges, 1751–1765

Figure 3.4. New Lodges per District, 1766–1785

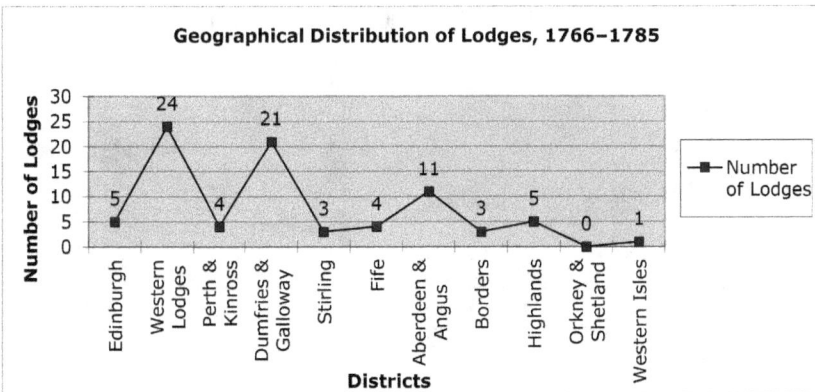

Geographical Distribution of Lodges, 1766–1785

Figure 3.5. New Lodge per District, 1786–1800

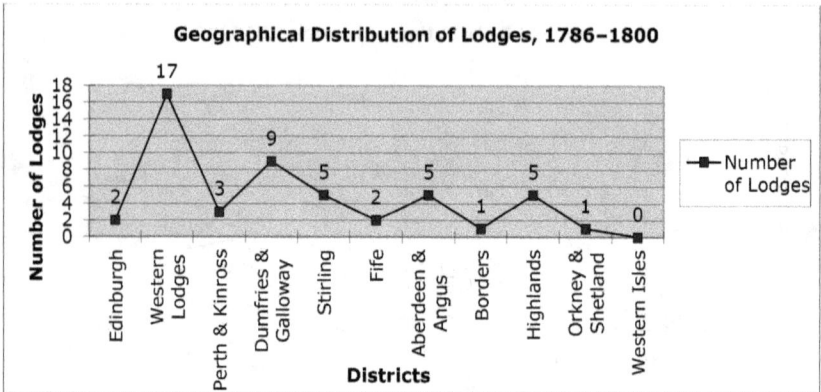

Geographical Distribution of Lodges, 1786–1800

Figure 3.6. Overall Trends of the Five Largest Districts, 1736–1800

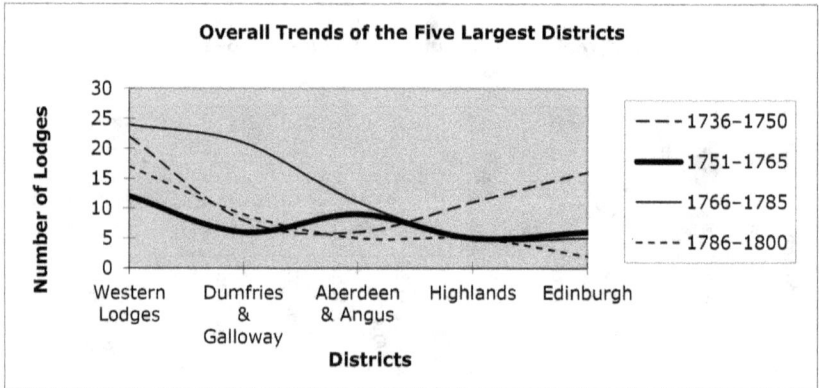

Overall Trends of the Five Largest Districts

Figure 3.7. Overall Trends of the Six Smallest Districts 1736–1800

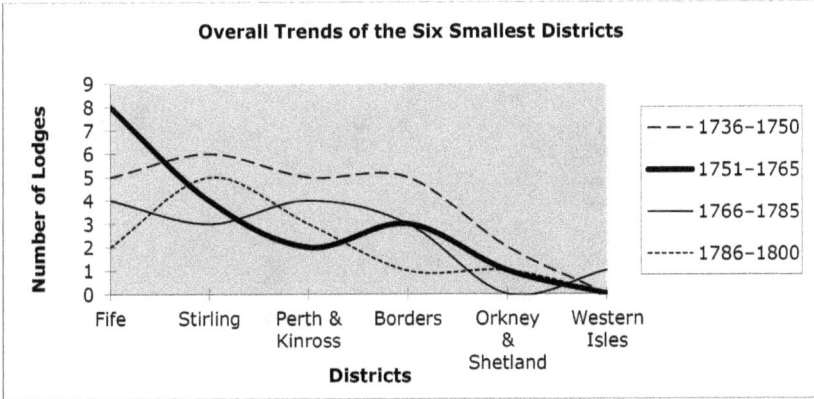

Figure 3.8. Total Number of Lodges per District, 1736–1800[2]

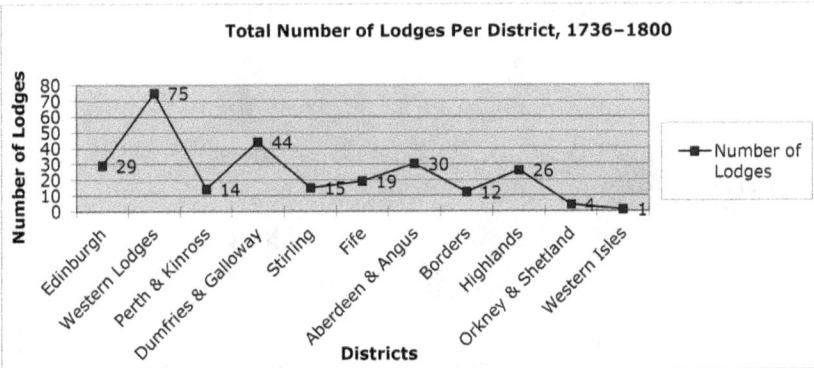

---

2   The totals do not reflect military and colonial lodges or the one un-located lodge, New Tarbet (1738).

Figure 3.9. Occupational Returns, 1736–1776

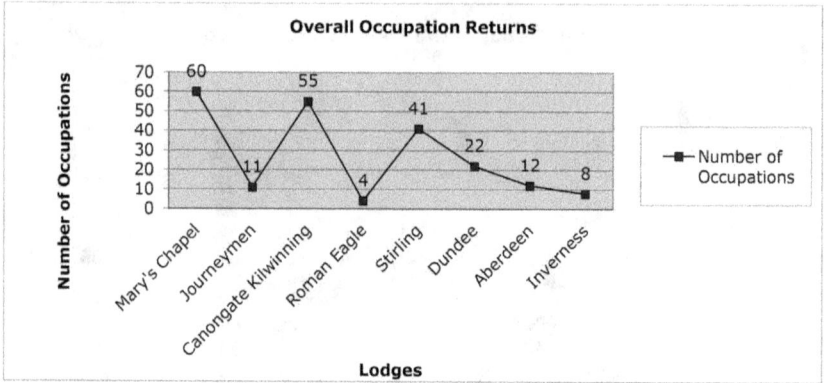

Figure 3.10. Edinburgh Lodge Occupational Comparison

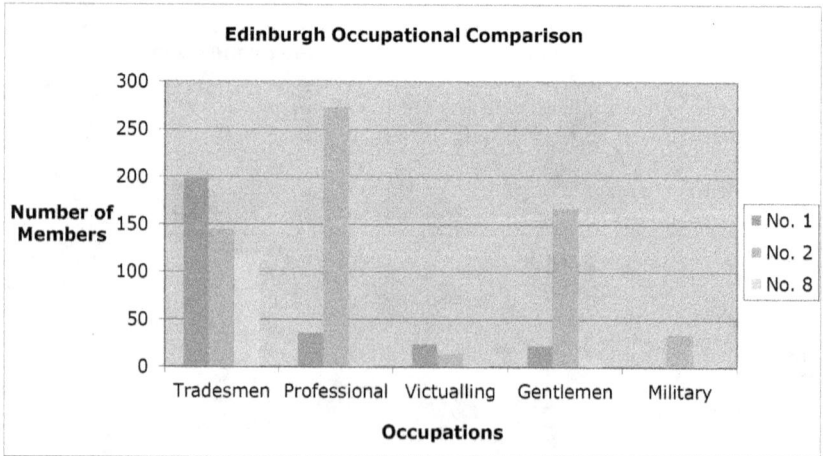

Figure 3.11. Provincial Lodge Occupational Comparison

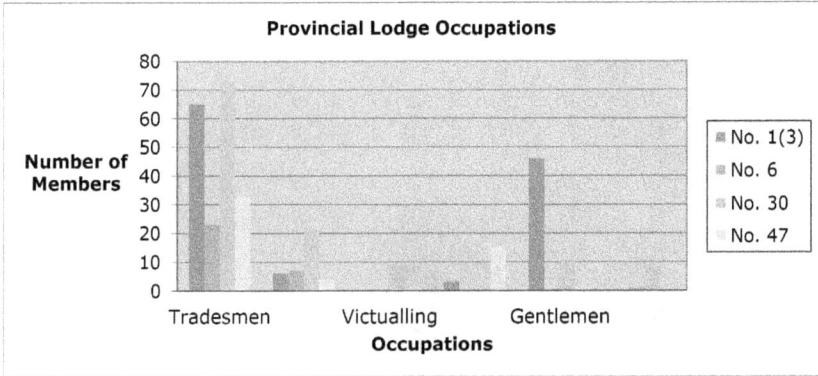

www.ingramcontent.com/pod-product-compliance
Lightning Source LLC
Chambersburg PA
CBHW052119270326
41930CB00012B/2690